D0583460

The Postwar Development of the Republic of Vietnam

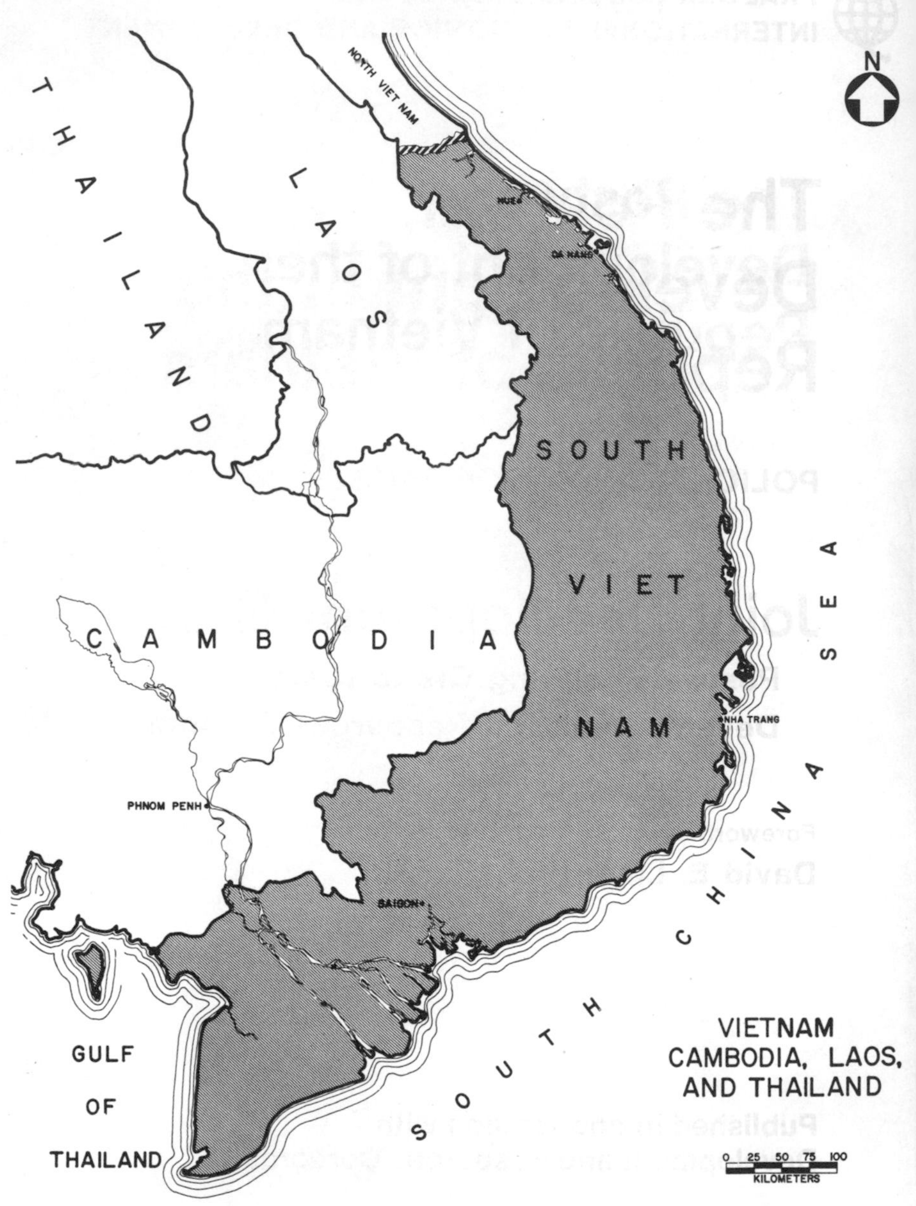
N
THAILAND
LAOS
NORTH VIET NAM
HUE
DA NANG
SOUTH VIET NAM
CAMBODIA
NHA TRANG
PHNOM PENH
SAIGON
SOUTH CHINA SEA
GULF OF THAILAND
VIETNAM
CAMBODIA, LAOS,
AND THAILAND
0 25 50 75 100
KILOMETERS

PRAEGER SPECIAL STUDIES IN
INTERNATIONAL ECONOMICS AND DEVELOPMENT

The Postwar Development of the Republic of Vietnam

POLICIES AND PROGRAMS

Joint Development Group

Postwar Planning Group (Saigon)

Development and Resources Corporation (New York)

Foreword by
David E. Lilienthal

Published in cooperation with
Development and Resources Corporation

PRAEGER PUBLISHERS
New York • Washington • London

The purpose of Praeger Special Studies is to make specialized research in U.S. and international economics and politics available to the academic, business, and government communities. For further information, write to the Special Projects Division, Praeger Publishers, Inc., 111 Fourth Avenue, New York, N.Y. 10003.

The views and recommendations expressed in this study are those of the Joint Development Group and not necessarily those of the Government of Vietnam or of the U.S. Government.

PRAEGER PUBLISHERS
111 Fourth Avenue, New York, N.Y. 10003, U.S.A.
5, Cromwell Place, London S.W.7, England

Published in the United States of America in 1970
by Praeger Publishers, Inc.

Library of Congress Catalog Card Number: 79-114437

Printed in the United States of America

FOREWORD

The twentieth century has witnessed more of war's destruction and cruelty and killing than all the wars since the beginning of recorded history. This is hardly a distinction of which to be proud. But this must also be said: that following each major war of this century the victors have held out to the vanquished a measure of compassion and generosity quite new in human history. For these historic acts of reconciliation and humanitarianism--whether in France or Germany or Japan or South Korea or battered England--the major credit--and most of the burden--of such restoration and reconstruction was accepted by the American people.

The Vietnam postwar report embodied in this volume is therefore more than an exhaustive and careful appraisal of the prospects for reconstruction and development in Vietnam, when the fighting ceases: indeed, in some cases, while the fighting still continues. This report is in a sense a recognition of the profound moral sensibilities of the American people. For the basic assumption that caused the U.S. to initiate these studies, and carry them on jointly with the Vietnamese, is as important as the facts adduced and the sanguine conclusions. That assumption is that there exists in the American people today, as in the past, a deep reservoir of compassion and generosity to the victims of a war.

Will the American people respond to this historic impulse to heal and rebuild after the end of the Vietnam war about which there has been such profound division of opinion, a war so costly in men and treasure? No one at this point can say.

What one can say, however, is that perhaps for the first time the factual and technical groundwork for postwar reconstruction and development was prepared, prudently, in advance of the end of the war in order that such preparation--the essence of this report--may diminish chaos and confusion when the time for reconstruction has arrived.

The report itself describes the origins of these unusual postwar development studies and the composition of the two private groups who worked together to produce the report and appraisal. The reader's attention is particularly called to these matters, so that he will understand that this is not an "official government" document, though financed by public funds.

In an article in Foreign Affairs for January, 1969, entitled "Postwar Development in Viet Nam" the present writer concluded with these words:

> Writing of Viet Nam in a recent issue of Foreign Affairs, the editor of this journal concluded with these words: "In the final accounting, the United States will be judged by its behavior when the fighting is over." Much the same accounting should be applied as well to the behavior of others "when the fighting is over": South Viet Nam; North Viet Nam; members of the international community which have been supporting one or the other of the combatants, or have been critical of them; and Japan, which is so deeply concerned in Southeast Asia's future.

As co-Chairman of the Joint Development Group, I am impelled to add this further personal word: although the report looks only to the opportunities for development of South Vietnam, its spirit extends to the comparable potentials for postwar reconstruction of North Vietnam as well.

David E. Lilienthal

Development and Resources Corporation
One Whitehall Street
New York City
January 9, 1970

PREFACE

Seldom have the postwar development prospects of a country at war received the attention that they are now receiving in Vietnam, so that the transition to a peacetime economy and the taking hold of policies for growth can be sensibly directed to the central issues. Without this attention to the postwar problems and the adjustments needed, the economy would likely flounder before it found its way. No study, however exhaustive, can hope to delineate in detail all of the problems nor how they will appear in the postwar period. Yet the specification of types of policies to meet major contingencies will go far to meet the needs for planning.

We discussed the classical problems of a economy war in a November, 1967, report and in several working papers: inflationary pressures, distortion of spending patterns reflecting the concentration on military affairs, a large number of refugees who have fled to the cities for security, and the disruption of agricultural production. Unlike many other nations at war, however, Vietnam has some structural economic strength in improved port facilities, roads, and other infrastructure that have been built during the war, a newly trained labor force, and an absence of large external war debts that must be carried into the postwar period.

The legacies of the war are not all negative; in some cases the strengthening of the economy during the war will ease the postwar problems. These elements are reflected in the recommendations and priorities that are described in this book.

The postwar objectives are dictated in large part by the wartime conditions: the control of inflation and the avoidance of serious deflation after the war; a humane and economically effective program to resettle refugees where they can survive and thrive; the re-establishment of conditions of security of persons and movement; and the reconstruction of agriculture. But in addition, there are positive objectives to stimulate private and public investment in development projects, to prepare specific project plans in each of the various sectors so as to achieve a balanced and vigorous development effort, and to encourage the economy to attain a position in exports and imports so that it can continue its development programs without large amounts of external concessionary aid. Programs designed to meet these objectives are described in this book.

The objectives that are set forth for Vietnam are not overly ambitious. They define a position that includes both effective means to achieve growth and development and equity in the dispersion of the benefits and burdens of the future. Above all, both the ends and the means are related directly to the capabilities of the country as they exist now and should exist after the war. In our opinion, the programs outlined here, if followed in their essential respects, provide assurance of the economic future of Vietnam.

Economic reconstruction and development will require determination and dedication to national purpose. But there are good grounds for believing that the characteristically hard-working people of Vietnam will appreciate why a crescendo of effort is necessary. Indeed, when it is demonstrated to them by appropriate decisions and actions that richer and more rewarding lives are realistic possibilities for them as well as their children, we believe that they will enthusiastically subscribe to this effort and participate in it. Assistance in the reconstruction and development effort will be needed, but the policies and programs which will shape the future are ones which the Vietnamese nation will wish to achieve primarily by their own efforts.

This study was prepared by the Joint Development Group. At a meeting in Manila in October, 1966, the then Chief Executive of Vietnam's Central Executive Committee and the President of the United States agreed it was timely, even in a period of increasingly bitter and destructive warfare, to prepare for the progress and prosperity of Vietnam in peace. It was decided that an effort should be made, by Vietnamese and Americans working together, to examine the probable problems and opportunities of the postwar period, and to establish policies and programs for the rapid restoration and development of the Vietnamese economy once peace should arrive--whenever that might be and however it should come about.

The Joint Development Group is the result of these decisions. It has no official, recognized status in either Government, and consisted, at the start, of private Vietnamese citizens and a private American company, communicating freely with governmental and non-governmental agencies, but developing judgments and opinions which were their own and independent.

On the Vietnamese side the joint Vietnamese-American effort was assured by a Letter of Service, dated February 2, 1967, appointing Professor Vu Quoc Thuc, of the University of Saigon, to organize and preside over a Postwar Planning Group, and directing that Group "to undertake, in cooperation with American specialists, the studies necessary for the design of measures, programs and projects for the development of the economy of Vietnam in the postwar period, and to make recommendations concerning them to the Government."

On the American side, the effort was assured by an Agreement between the Government of the United States, the contracting agency being the Agency for International Development, and Development and Resources Corporation, a private company of which Mr. David E. Lilienthal is Chairman. The Agreement between AID and the Corporation stipulated, among other things, that the Corporation's work is to be "part of a joint planning effort with a group selected by the Government of Vietnam." No attempt was made by either Government to define or regulate the relationship between the Vietnamese and American components of this enterprise; the relationship has been allowed to develop naturally: Vietnamese and American specialists have collaborated closely on virtually every aspect of the work, office premises are shared, and in practice a single joint group has emerged. Although there are, fortunately, numerous examples--outside the major sphere of military operations--of Americans and Vietnamese working well together for the common purpose, the close-knit partnership of the Joint Development Group may be unique.

The Chairman of Development and Resources Corporation, with two members of his staff, paid a first visit to Vietnam in February, 1967, held preliminary discussions with Professor Vu Quoc Thuc, the Government of Vietnam and United States officials, and established a resident representative for the Corporation in Saigon. In the following months, the Chief of the Postwar Planning Group enlisted the support of a number of qualified professional men and research assistants (mostly, at the start, from the Universities), while a mission of five staff members from Development and Resources Corporation carried out a reconnaissance of Vietnam intended to reveal the principal areas of interest on which the Joint Development Group should thereafter concentrate its attention. This brief survey responded to a specific undertaking given by the Corporation in its Agreement with USAID, and the results were embodied in a Report submitted to the Agency on May 22, 1967. Problems were identified in the broad field of economic policy, and also in Agriculture, Industry, Manpower, Infrastructure and Institutional Development, and it is within these principal areas that the activities of the Joint Development Group have since been concentrated.

The size of the Vietnamese Postwar Planning Group has varied from time to time according to needs and availability, but generally it has consisted of 15 or 16 men of professional qualifications, and about 30 research assistants--graduate students from the University of Saigon. The majority of its members have found it impossible to provide more than part-time services to the development planning effort and from time to time members of the Postwar Planning Group have been lost, permanently or temporarily, to the military draft; and others have been called away to assume official appointments, including Professor Vu Quoc Thuc himself, who became Minister of State (though continuing to supervise the activities of the Group) in June, 1968. On the other hand, fruitful cooperative arrangements have been established between the Group and the technical services of the Ministries, especially Agriculture and Public Works, so there has been no dearth of professional assistance and counsel. It has not been difficult to recruit additional research assistants to answer particular needs: thus, in August and September, 1967, 120 young men came forward from the Universities of Saigon and Dalat to assist in a socio-economic survey of some 600 villages throughout the Republic.

These surveys, based on a questionnaire designed by senior members of the Postwar Planning Group, constituted probably its most significant activity in the early months of its existence. It was intended to serve two purposes - to create popular interest and participation in a national development planning effort, and to reveal the primary topics of public concern. The results of the survey left no doubt where the public interest lies--in economic progress and the higher standards of living it will enable ordinary men and women to achieve, rather than in the rapid development of the Central Government's social services, though the latter are obviously not absent from the catalogue of popular desires.

On the American side, the Development and Resources staff of the Joint Development Group has averaged over the period some ten specialists a month with further contributions being supplied by Development and Resources consultants visiting Vietnam for periods of one or two months at a time.

It was not intended - and with these limitations on staff it would not have been possible - that the Joint Development Group should undertake original studies of its own of all the multitudinous aspects of postwar economic development. On the contrary, it has been enjoined to make the fullest use of work done by others, since not to have taken such work into account would have resulted in duplication and waste. (A number of original studies have, of course, been undertaken, but these have relied upon information and data provided by the regular agencies of the Government.) Where it has seemed to us that subjects were adequately covered already by the Ministries or other agencies of the Government or by USAID, our function has been to take cognizance of what is being done or what is proposed and to adapt it to the overriding need for a realistic, balanced strategy for total national development. Consequently, the programs initiated or designed by both Governments have been used freely in the course of the work and are apparent in several chapters of this book. Where changes in emphasis and in priorities are suggested, it is because of the need to place specific sectoral programs in the context of the total national interest, for the Joint Development Group's judgment of priorities is based not on what is desirable in a particular sector of activity, but on what we believe it is practicable to expect the entire national economy to achieve in the first ten years after the war with the resources at its disposal. The resources, inevitably, will be more tightly circumscribed than the expectations.

This, in a sense, is the reason for the Joint Development Group's existence. The plan now presented is not a final, definitive one that can be used for national reconstruction immediately and without modification. In important particulars, it still needs much elaboration and refinement, and changes in substance may also be indicated as events unfold. It does represent what we believe to be the first attempt for many years, perhaps the first attempt ever, to bring all the elements of economic development into context and to present to the Government of Vietnam a comprehensive view of the prospects as a whole. We believe it to be suitable for endorsement as the basis for a ten-year development program upon which Ministries and other Governmental agencies, with whatever assistance may be required from the Joint Development Group, can establish their detailed sectoral plans.

The method of work has been to identify particular subjects for study by the members of the Group, both senior and junior, and to encourage the latter to describe problems and suggest solutions in individual, published discussion papers. Over forty of these papers have been published or are in the final stages of production. A wide, at first almost a random, variety of topics has been covered. In a good many cases the published papers concern discrete and specialized subjects, possibly not of general importance to postwar economic development, but representing a deliberate effort to persuade the younger members of the Group what political economy is about - analyzing the facts of a situation and seeking ways to improve it. In other papers - those, for instance, concerned with the Mekong Delta, Forestry, and Fiscal Policy, among others - the effort has been more pointed, and is concerned with the exploitation of available resources in particular areas of the country or with specific and significant issues of economic policy. Frequent reference has been made to these discussion papers in the body of this volume, for they contain much of the detailed argument on which our conclusions and recommendations are founded. In addition to these papers in the regular series, a special series of twelve other papers deals with various aspects of the development of the Mekong Delta.

The Group has not pursued its task in isolation from other planning and policy-making agencies. That would have been a sterile exercise. Partly through the Chairman of the Postwar Planning Group, and partly by direct contact with department heads in the various Ministries, mutually helpful relationships have been established, and the recommendations now presented represent the ideas of other people as well as our own. The proposals for the Mekong Delta, for instance, are, in part, the result of the conclusions reached at a Seminar organized by the Ministry of Public Works and the Joint Development Group in November, 1967, which was attended by representatives from the Ministry, from the Joint Development Group, and from the National Institute of Statistics, the Directorates of Navigation, Highways, Fisheries, Water Supply, Agricultural Research, Rice Production, and many other government services, as well as from such interested agencies as the National Mekong Committee and Electricity of Vietnam. Relations with the Ministries of Public Works and Agriculture have been particularly close; much of the technical material used in the Report comes from those sources. The help of some of the extra-governmental agencies - the Agricultural Development Bank, the Industrial Development Center, the Development Bank of Vietnam, the National Bank, the Planning Division of Electricity of Vietnam and many others has been enlisted, and so has that of the Universities of Saigon, Hue and Dalat.

There have also been frequent discussions with agencies external to Vietnam, some of which are potential sources of financial and technical assistance to Vietnam after the war, including the United Nations (through its Resident Representative in Saigon), the Food and Agricultural Organization and the Asian Development Bank. The International Committee for the Lower Mekong has been consulted on frequent occasions and has been kept informed; a flood control study of the river carried out in May, 1968, was made possible by the documents and technical services with which the Committee supplied us. The Chairman of the Postwar Planning Group attended the meeting of the Committee in Bangkok in January, 1968, and an American member of the Group attended a subsequent meeting at Canberra. Several embassies of foreign government - including those of Australia, Japan, Canada and West Germany - have taken an interest in the progress of the work, and have been supplied with copies of particularly appropriate discussion papers.

The closest relationships have, of course, been maintained with the US Agency for International Development, especially with the Divisions of Economic Policy (which administers the contract between the Agency and Development and Resources Corporation) Public Administration, Engineering, Domestic Production, Labor and Industry. Much original data collected by the Agency and the findings of many of its wide researches have been used in the work of the Group. At all times the advice and encouragement of AID staff with their extensive knowledge of the country have been of the greatest assistance.

In November, 1967, a preliminary report was submitted to the President in which the Joint Development Group described the state of the economy in general terms, provided some tentative predictions concerning its growth after the war, and indicated certain programs - in water control, agriculture, industry and refugee resettlement, which it believed could be initiated even while the war was still being fought. The subsequent activities of the Group have not been limited to planning but have had something of a promotional character, especially in industry and water control programs. The events of Tet, 1968, destroyed our early hopes that something more constructive could be done immediately to alleviate the lot of the refugees.

To the extent that the recommendations of the Report are accepted by the Government of Vietnam, the Joint Development Group proposes that these promotional activities be emphasized through 1970. Though the end of the war is not clearly in sight, it is at any rate closer than it was when we last reported. It is a matter of some urgency now that programs which exist on paper and in varying degrees of detail should be made ready for implementation. This requires not merely the elaboration, in association with the Ministries concerned, of the general ideas expressed in some of the chapters of this book, but appropriate allocations of technical skills, the establishment of suitable institutions to manage particular programs, and, above all, the assuring of infusions of external financial and technical assistance and of private investment necessary for a decade of growth. In each chapter, an account is given of the particular tasks to be undertaken: the general objective also needs expressing, it is to convert plans into action and aspirations into realities.

The study divides naturally into two main parts: Part I is concerned largely with economic and political policies for the furtherance of economic growth; Part II deals in the main with the development programs advocated for the main sectors and for the regions of Vietnam.

Throughout the Report the rate of exchange used, unless otherwise specified, is VN $118 = US $1.00. In certain chapters the order of costs of programs have been divided into Vietnamese piasters and foreign exchange requirements. In other chapters costs have been quoted in US dollars and where no breakdown is given it may be assumed that there will be some local currency requirement which has not as yet been identified.

Two versions of the study were originally prepared: one in Vietnamese and the other in English. Neither version, however, with some exceptions, was a direct and literal translation of the other, and the topics included were sometimes given different treatment and varying degrees of emphasis depending on our relative interests in certain topics. This liberty of approach is inherent in the nature of the Joint Development Group; the study is the result of a free exchange of opinions between Vietnamese and American members over a period of two years, during which time neither attempted to impress particular viewpoints or dogmas on the other. In these circumstances it is worth emphasizing that as regards the general development policies and strategies to be adopted we have regularly found ourselves in substantial agreement. There are no differences regarding the essentials of economic policy and the development program; and there are no differences in our definition and concept of the objective to which Vietnam should aspire.

CONTENTS

Chapter | Page

LIST OF TABLES

Table		Page

LIST OF FIGURES

PART I

POLICIES FOR ECONOMIC DEVELOPMENT

CHAPTER 1 FRAMEWORK AND GROWTH PATTERN OF THE POSTWAR ECONOMY

The task of postwar economic development will be the exploitation of the natural and human resources of the country with the objective of achieving a prosperous economy and a stable society. Within a decade, systematic exploitation of the nation's economic potentials can at least increase per capita income by one-third and Gross National Product (GNP) by 50 percent. GNP will grow faster than per capita income but per capita consumption will also increase. For some time the nation will have to allocate an important portion of economic resources to national security and defense and an important portion of economic products to exports in order to finance imports. With an appropriate set of policies, it is believed that the termination of dependence on foreign aid can be achieved within ten years.

A short period of reconstruction, which may last from two to three years, will be necessary for the attainment of these long-run economic objectives.

RECONSTRUCTION AND DEVELOPMENT PROBLEMS

The projects and programs proposed in this study have been prepared under the assumption that peace will be achieved with territorial integrity. In other words, that part of Vietnam south of the 17th parallel will be the geographical framework for the implementation of development policies.

However, they would prove no obstacle to a decision to establish economic and commercial ties between North and South Vietnam should this become a possibility. On the contrary, the strategy for reconstruction and development of the infrastructure, of the economy, of industry, agriculture, and foreign trade would need but minor modification to obtain the benefits which could stem from such an inter-regional economic relationship.

Programs require to be developed to correspond initially to a reconstruction phase to be completed within two to three years, and then to a development phase to be undertaken in the following seven years. There will, however, be no sharp line of division between reconstruction and development. The two phases are distinguished by the kinds of programs to be undertaken.

THE RECONSTRUCTION PHASE

The basic aim of reconstruction is to lay a solid foundation for long-term development. The economy cannot begin to grow rapidly until many of the distortions caused by the war have been corrected or ameliorated. The resettlement of refugees in particular will be a dominant problem at least in the initial phase of two or three years.

There are additional problems which will be caused by developments in the labor market. Before the war Vietnam had a serious unemployment rate. The war has brought about a state of full employment and, in many branches of activity, a situation of labor scarcity. An important portion of human resources has been absorbed by the armed forces and by war-related branches of civil activities. Between six months and a year after the termination of the war, it will be necessary to guard against a tendency toward a general decline in employment resulting from a reduction in or termination of war-related economic activities.

The postwar economy, therefore, will present many special and difficult problems: on the one hand, there is the need to accelerate reconstruction, both to achieve economic recovery and to maintain employment at a high level (even though this level many not be as high as in wartime). An excessively high employment level is often the origin of the increase of inflationary pressure. On the other hand, both deflationary and inflationary pressures should be avoided. The difficulty lies in the fact that the effort to maintain a high employment level to avoid social instability will be constrained by the need to minimize inflationary pressures or, at least, to avoid adding to existing pressures.

A human resource recovery strategy will aim at two objectives in the reconstruction phase: first, resettlement programs must consolidate and strengthen rural society and bring back into production land that has been abandoned during the war. The whole refugee problem will clearly be a costly and complex affair. Second, educational programs to encourage and support a higher rate of school attendance are needed to improve the quality and productive capability of the young labor force.

In infrastructure, reconstruction must start with projects aimed at restoring the transportation and telecommunications networks to normalize economic transactions between production and consumption regions.

The key to agricultural recovery is the rapid achievement of self-sufficiency in rice to be followed by resumption of exports of agricultural products. In 1968, the value of exports was insignificant compared with the prewar level of US$80 million. In 1968, 90 percent of imports were financed by American aid and by the sale of Vietnamese piasters to the allied armed forces and to foreign contractors for expenditure in Vietnam.

In order to achieve self-sufficiency in agricultural products and to resume the exportation of these products within two to three years, an agricultural restoration fund in foreign exchange as well as in Vietnamese piasters will be needed amounting to nearly VN$4 billion, or eight times the budget of the Ministry of Agriculture and Agrarian Reform in 1967.

During the reconstruction phase, three major tasks in the industrial sector must be accomplished. The first is the reconstruction of damaged production facilities; the second is the restoration of the production rate of industries which have declined because of warfare; the third is the inauguration of a number of new industries, including industries approved for establishment during 1965-67, to lay the foundation of long-term development.

Industrial reconstruction, the repair of the infrastructure, and the restoration of agriculture have to be planned regionally as far as is feasible in order that the nation may have firm regional foundations on which to base economic development. In other words, war wounds sustained by all the regions will have to be healed and production facilities in both rural and urban areas will have to be renewed before the commencement of the development phase. Within the framework of regional development during the immediate postwar reconstruction, the five northern provinces deserve priority in the planned allocation of funds because they have been damaged the most by the war.

An early start is also envisioned for the agricultural development of the Mekong Delta, for which detailed plans for water control are now in preparation. Other regional development plans are being considered for the Central Highlands, for the coastal lowlands of the II Corps Tactical Zone, and for the provinces surrounding Saigon.

The accomplishment of the planned objectives of the reconstruction phase depends on two major economic factors: the ability of the economy to mobilize domestic and foreign capital to finance the plan, and the extent to which inflationary pressures can be modulated.

OBJECTIVES AND PROBLEMS OF LONG-TERM ECONOMIC DEVELOPMENT

Within the framework of the over-all goals, long-term development must aim at the following economic targets:

1. The mobilization of all of the people into a production force which is development-oriented and recognizes the need for effective economic action;

2. An increase in per capita income and consumption; with the proviso that per capita consumption will not be able to keep up with increases in production since savings must be marshaled to support the rate of growth of the economy;

3. The maintenance of a high rate of employment in an atmosphere of relative price stability;

4. A reduction in the gap between the standards of living and the wealth of the different social classes and of the different regions by a redistribution of income through taxation and expenditure policies;

5. Raising the rural standard of living by increasing agricultural productivity and purchasing power in this sector, by land reform, by programs for rural electrification, and by the establishment of regional centers to achieve gradual integration of rural and urban life;

6. The provision of enhanced educational facilities for the future generation. It is hoped that compulsory primary education can be attained within ten years and technical education improved to extend the population's capacity to participate in the general economic growth process;

7. Ending the dependence on concessionary foreign aid.

It is unlikely that all of these objectives can be attained simultaneously. In the ordinary course of development there may be conflicts among two or more of the objectives, and compromises will have to be made, with achievements in one direction partly offset by sacrifices in another direction. While we recognize that such compromises may be inevitable, it is nonetheless valuable to set forth the full range of the objectives. Growth may be limited by a restricted natural resource endowment (though this is uncertain), by an inability to stimulate the motivation for development strongly enough, or by extraneous elements, but we assume that such elements will not be dominant.

DEVELOPMENT PATHS OF THE POSTWAR ECONOMY

Rates of Economic Growth

It is precarious to try to predict the exact path that the economy will follow in the postwar period. Much depends on the way the war ends and the speed with which resources can be transferred from military activities to development programs. But some guidelines are required now and should be refined in 1970.

We have assumed a minimum and a maximum expansion path for the economy. These are not extreme values in the usual sense of that term; the minimum path assumes that growth occurs, though admittedly the economy might actually decline if no steps are taken to initiate development. Similarly, the maximum figure might be exceeded with a determined effort to increase investment and exports.

The minimum figure is one that permits about a 1 percent increase in per capita income in this period. In a rough pragmatic way this sets the floor for economic performance consistent with political stability, and it is also consistent with average past economic performance. The maximum figure is essentially set by limitations on the rate of investment (both public and private) and on the rate of growth of exports. Some further aspects of these limitations are discussed in Chapters 3 and 4.

An adjustment in national income expenditure patterns to shift resources in a major way will be required and can be illustrated in the following figures:

Expenditure	Recent Experience (% of GNP)	More "Normal" Pattern (% of GNP)
Consumption (public plus private)	100-105	80-90
Investment	5-10	10-15
Exports	0-5	10-20
Imports (negative item)	20-25	15-20

The percentage figures shown as "recent experience" are typical of the last few years of the 1960's. The sum of all four (with imports as a negative) adds to approximately 100% of the Gross National Product.

The changes in the economy necessary for a postwar adjustment to a development path are of two major kinds: (1) a relative decrease in consumption and an increase in public and private investment (i. e., an increase in savings); and (2) an increase in exports, probably combined with some relative decrease in imports through import-substitution investment. The first adjustment is needed in order to get the investment in production that will lead to a growth in income and employment and absorb resources released from military uses. The second is needed to provide a growing volume of foreign exchange so that in ten years or so the economy can continue to expand and dispense with concessionary aid.

If the lowest growth path is the target, GNP will increase at the rate of 4 percent in the reconstruction period and 5 percent in the development period. This is the growth path that has to be achieved to meet the needs of a growing population and to improve somewhat the standard of living of each person; the minimum growth path is also feasible given present resources.

In the minimum path, GNP will increase by half (52 percent) over ten years. The estimated sectoral composition of GNP for the two assumptions is shown in Table 1.1. The origin of this growth lies in the increase of agricultural production and industrial production and in the early but limited expansion of exports. Though the rate of growth of the industrial sector will be higher, agricultural production will remain the most important component of GNP. Agriculture in the long run will be diversified and industries will use agriculture and forestry products as bases for expanded output. The production pattern of the nation after ten years will be a shift of the structure of output and an increase of the ratio of commodity output to the GNP.

The path of maximum growth has been estimated at 6 percent in the first three years of the plan and 7 percent in the subsequent seven years. These are growth rates which would not cause serious inflation because the industrial sector should experience a sudden upsurge and agricultural production would double. It is also assumed that the world market for agricultural commodities would be favorable, with high and stable prices.

Income and Consumption

When the war ends, development plans will have to cope with an annual rate of population growth of at least 2.6 percent.

At this rate of population growth, if the minimum growth path is achieved, average per capita income will increase in

TABLE 1.1

Estimated Value of GNP in Productive Sectors, 1969 and 1978 (US$ millions)

Productive Sector	GNP 1969 Minimum	GNP 1969 Maximum	GNP 1978 Minimum	GNP 1978 Maximum
Agriculture	834	866	1,251	1,299
Industry	313	326	627	652
Infrastructure	203	211	491	604
Service	178	185	294	362
Government	671	697	736	907
Other sectors	1,024	1,064	1,509	1,373
Total	3,226	3,321	4,910	6,047

the first three years at an annual rate of over 1 percent and in the next seven years at the annual rate of over 2 percent. In total, after ten years, average per capita income will increase 20 percent.

In ten years, the over-all standard of living will improve but the nation will require the sacrifice of the consumption of a portion of the fruits of economic progress and development. The sacrifice required consists of the relative reduction of consumption, and an increase of savings and capital investment, to facilitate the self-financing of the national budget and to meet the need for expansion of export trade to replace foreign aid. Although the 2.6 percent population growth rate is assumed to apply initially, measures to restrict the birth rate may have to be considered to lower the population growth from 2.6 percent to 2 percent. Many countries have not been able to improve the standard of living of their people despite refined plans because population increases at a rate faster than the rate of expansion of the economy or the rate of productivity improvement.

The Balance of Payments

In the growth process, the expansion of exports plays a very important role and is a key to ending dependence on concessionary foreign aid.

In the years 1958-68 Vietnam's dependence on foreign aid has manifested itself in two ways: on the one hand, the revenues in piasters are used as a partial offset to the budget deficit; on the other hand, imports are required in large volume to sop up excess purchasing power and thus to offset inflationary pressures. Both conditions should change in the postwar period.

To attain independence from foreign aid, an increase in exports and a gradual relative decrease in imports is called for. In 1968, imports were valued at about US$750 million, composed mainly of consumption goods, while exports were insignificant (US$20-$30 million). Nearly half of the imports were financed by foreign exchange through the sale of Vietnamese piasters to allied armed forces and foreign embassies. The remainder has been financed by U. S. aid. Clearly, when the war ends, the allied armed forces are gradually withdrawn, and the foreign contractors reduce their level of operation, the main source of foreign exchange used to finance imports will dwindle. For that reason and because of the necessity of reducing consumption, the value of imports should decline relatively in the ten-year period, and the greatest effort to expand exports will be needed.

However, it is neither feasible nor desirable to reduce imports below a certain level relative to the GNP because a high and sustained growth rate requires imports of capital goods, raw materials, and certain consumer goods that cannot be produced locally. The two major estimates of import level that have been suggested are as follows:

1. The value of imports should decline from the present level of US$750 million (1968) to US$450 to $550 million beginning in 1972, when the reconstruction period has terminated and the sale of piasters can no longer be relied on as a source of foreign exchange. In the reconstruction phase to 1972, imports have to be maintained at the relatively high levels indicated until exports can expand and domestic production of import substitutions can take place. In ten years, imports as a

percentage of GNP will decline from 20-25 percent to about 15 percent;

2. The value of capital goods as a percentage of total imports should increase from 20-30 percent to 50-60 percent after ten years.

For exports, several phases of expansion are foreseen. The export of rice, rubber, and other subsidiary agricultural products will be restored to at least the prewar level within two to three years of the end of the war. Their value will be increased gradually by the increase of agricultural exports (both traditional and new products) and by the increase of exports of industrial goods based on forest and other products. The potential for exports is discussed further in Chapter 2.

The value of exports should reach at least US$250-$300 million and, with a determined effort, could climb to over $400 million.

In the tenth year, it is quite possible that the deficit in the balance of payments will not be eliminated completely; however, the deficit should be at a level of about US$100 million and can be financed by capital inflows caused by foreign investors, supplier loans, and other revenues. Economic independence in the area of foreign trade must be understood as the ability to finance a deficit by long-term loans rather than by grants or other concessionary aid. Economic independence does not imply the exclusion of all capital movements.

Public Expenditure and Taxation

It is estimated that public expenditures (excluding defense expenditures) as a proportion of GNP must be reduced from over 20 percent in 1968 to 15 percent in 1978, and that there must be a shift from consumption expenditures toward public investment. At present, because of the war, the national economy has a large defense budget as well as a sizeable fund to support war-related activities, and an administrative system which has been growing in recent years to meet security and defense needs.

The maintenance of a large budget in peacetime, even when financed by taxes, is still a source of inflationary pressure because taxation beyond a certain point becomes itself a source of inflationary pressures. However, because of the uncertainties of the postwar situation in Vietnam, the maintenance of a defense and security budget is postulated equal to no less than 15 percent of GNP, a level experienced by other countries in the same predicament.

Tax revenues as a percentage of GNP will have to increase from 9 percent in 1968 to 15 percent in ten years (from VN$40 billion to more than VN$80 billion). This increase will require the application or modification of many tax sources.

There must be provision for a shift in the structure of tax revenues in the ten years. Internal revenues, particularly income tax revenues, as a percentage of total revenues will increase.

Investment and Its Financing

To achieve a rate of growth that would increase GNP by half in ten years, as suggested previously, it is estimated that over-all investment in the ten years has to reach at least VN-$600 billion. The investment output ratio in the first three years is expected to be slightly higher than the ratio applicable to the later years because of important reconstruction expenditures in the early years.

The government will probably have to bear more than 50 percent of the total investment required, although the stimulation of private investment is a key objective. Government investment will be made in areas of social overhead and, consequently, in areas where private enterprises cannot be interested. Much of the investment made by the government will go to three main infrastructure areas: irrigation, agricultural extension, and education.

Because heavy emphasis must be laid on the role of private enterprise in long-term economic development, it is envisaged that the private sector will undertake all industrial investment and the major share of housing investment.

The amount of foreign aid needed in the ten years prior to economic independence will be on the order of US$2.5 billion (Table 1.2). As development proceeds, foreign aid will finance more investment requirements than consumption and will make an important contribution to public investment.

In the long run, the encouragement of saving and mobilization of capital within the country are essential to the achievement of economic growth within the framework of economic

TABLE 1.2

Minimum Ten-Year Investment and Financing Sources

Source	Investment US$ billions
Total investment	$5.5
Internal saving	$3.7
Foreign aid to finance investment	1.8
Total needs of foreign aid, including import consumption financing	$2.5

independence. Three types of measures should be implemented to increase savings, and to stimulate investment:

1. Revision of laws governing investment to make it easier to undertake new ventures, and the establishment of a security market;

2. Revision of the interest rate structure to stimulate private savings, and the establishment of an organized money market;

3. Taxation changes to raise government revenues available for public investment.

The participation of foreign capital coming from nations of the free world will be necessary. At present it is difficult to estimate the volume of such foreign capital but contacts with financial, economic, and development interests abroad in the course of the preparation of this study reveal an interest on the part of foreign investors in the postwar development of Vietnam.

Additional details of the means for achieving a successful expansion path through appropriate economic policies are provided in the succeeding five chapters.

CHAPTER 2 ECONOMIC POLICIES FOR GROWTH

The economic development of Vietnam will require not only careful planning but the application of economic policies that directly stimulate growth through public action or establish an environment in which private initiative can operate effectively. There is no single best set of policies to accomplish the objectives, for these policies must also change to meet changing conditions. These pose difficult problems even for the experts, and there may be disagreements from time to time as to the best actions to take to meet a specific situation. We are not primarily concerned with this range of policy problems because we are not trying to predict the exact course of events in the postwar period, though it is inevitable in this chapter, and the succeeding ones on monetary and fiscal policies, that some of the alternative situations and the actions required to meet them are discussed. Such economic discussions of the issues are meant to illuminate the range of choices that are likely to be open.

There is another sense in which policy choices and alternatives are important; that is, the way such choices reflect the kind of political environment in which development occurs, whether, for example, through central government control the majority of resources are channeled to productive use or, alternatively, whether the private sector will have a significant role in such decisions. The choices finally made in these and similar matters together make up a large part of the strategy of development that will be followed in the postwar period.*

---

*See Economic Policies in the Transition to Peace and After, Working Paper No. 23 (Joint Development Group (JDG), June, 1968).

INVESTMENT PRIORITIES IN AGRICULTURE AND INDUSTRY

Vietnam is now and will continue for some time to be primarily an agricultural country. Agricultural pursuits contribute the largest single share of the gross national product and involve a large majority of the population. This will not change appreciably in the decade after the war, for although relative rates of growth are likely to be somewhat different, with an industrial growth rate of 7 percent possible in contrast to 5 percent or less in agriculture, the shares of the two sectors will change very slowly.

It is often said that for development to occur, the agricultural sector must supply the labor for industry to expand, and since traditionally there is underemployment in agriculture, this transfer of labor should not adversely affect production of agricultural products or cause food prices to rise. This way of looking at the problem causes no concern to Vietnam. Although there is every reason to believe that a vigorous development effort in industry will be forthcoming (as described in Chapter 9), the additional amounts of labor and agricultural raw materials required for the industrial expansion will be readily available. Demands within agriculture create no constraints on industrial development in Vietnam. Quite the contrary, the developments in the two sectors are complementary, and if they are not necessarily to be kept at the same pace, they should not, at least, become widely disparate in their rates of growth.

As a practical matter most countries have ignored agricultural development at their peril, and have later found it most difficult to make up lost ground and to attain a satisfactory rate of agricultural growth. Total growth of an economy is far more likely to be held back by lagging agriculture than by lagging industry. That is most certainly the case for Vietnam, since the level of agricultural output achieved will in part determine the amount of imports required, and, most importantly, the amount of exports and foreign exchange that are available.

Sometimes the matter is stated in terms of competition between the two sectors for limited investment (or agriculture versus industry), and typically the analysis shows that investment in industry should be preferred and brings greater benefits to the economy. The argument is sometimes based on a generally lower capital-output ratio in investment, so that one unit of investment in industry contributes a larger amount directly to the national product than a similar unit in agriculture. Sometimes the argument is based on a desire to cut down on industrial imports through import substitution (a topic that is examined later in this chapter), and sometimes there is simply an unreasoned preference for development of industry because that creates the image of a modern economy.

We believe that these are not useful ways to pose the problem of priorities in development between industry and agriculture. Choices of projects always have to be made, of course, after an evaluation of their costs and benefits, but an argument that attempts to show that investment in industry is, as a general matter, superior to investment in agriculture is clearly faulty and is arrived at only by focusing on some facts and ignoring others. But one thing is clear: Vietnam, for reasons that are amply described in various places in this study, must undertake a deliberate program to strengthen and stimulate the growth of agriculture. Complementary investment in industry, both to supply products that are needed in agricultural production and to supply those desired for consumption by farmers with rising incomes, will most surely grow and, as we have observed above, at a rate of growth above that for agriculture. A determination of the best pace for investment in both sectors will emerge from later detailed project analyses, but an economic policy of growth for Vietnam that gives first place to industry is surely in error.

PUBLIC AND PRIVATE SECTOR ROLES

If Vietnam is to develop at a satisfactory pace, the energies of both the public sector and the private sector are needed to complement and strengthen each other in undertaking productive investment, in marketing products, and in carrying on the many commercial activities of a growing economy. The roles of the two probably will not be equal, even assuming that equality is somehow measurable, but the complete dominance of the public sector that is found in centrally directed economies is not appropriate for Vietnam in the future and, indeed, it would represent a change from current conditions.

The majority of fixed investment in the country in recent years has originated in the private sector. The public sector has contributed less than 20 percent of new fixed investment, but this is an unnaturally low figure due to the high level of current operating costs of the war. In many other developing countries, under normal conditions, public investment typically ranges between 40 percent and 60 percent of the total. The exact figure at any one time depends on the vitality of the private sector and its evaluation of risks and rewards, and on the ability of the government to obtain savings from the budget. In the postwar period the share of total investment attributable to the public sector will almost surely rise, and must do so if the many needs of social infrastructure are to be met.

The responsibilities for development assumed by the public sector and those retained by the private sector divide roughly along traditional lines. Investment responsibility for roads, schools, health and sanitation, and possibly areas in housing, is clearly in the hands of the government. In Vietnam the provision of electric power, and particularly rural electrification, is unlikely to be sufficient without direct government investment, though private technical assistance in operations during an interim period will improve efficiency. The sectors of manufacturing, commerce, trade, and finance are in general the ones that should be left to the private sector. Investment in these sectors has in the past primarily originated in the private sector, with perhaps a few specific exceptions such as textiles. There are, however, three important points to note about future private investment in these sectors, which should be among the fastest-growing ones in the economy. First, in some specific cases mixed public and private ventures are very likely to be more successful than either public or private alone. One such case is fertilizer production, which is discussed in Chapter 9 (on industrial development). There may well be other cases where mixed ventures are preferable, possibly in instances of very large scale investment. Such ventures have worked well in other countries. Second, the public sector in Vietnam has made substantial investment in manufacturing industry and is taking steps to divest itself of such investments and return these activities back to the private sector. It is entirely appropriate that this be done, since these investments have in the past shown consistent losses. It is hoped that the process of divestment can be achieved soon. The valuation of assets of these companies may, however, pose some difficulties. Unfortunately the depreciated historical cost of the assets is not the proper base for market valuation. These companies only have a value to a private investor based on their present and future projected profitability, that is, their value as going concerns, and it may be necessary simply to write off as a loss part of the asset costs in order to dispose of them. The United States has had exactly this experience with plants built with public funds during World War II, and ultimately sold them at a fraction of historical cost.

Third, and most importantly, the private sector will fulfill its role of generating growth in productive investment providing it has freedom from unnecessary controls and regulations in starting a risky venture and carrying it through. On this point the present situation must be reformed to create the correct kind of competitive environment, particularly in allowing freedom of action to meet market demands as an entrepreneur sees them. The competitive market is one of the most efficient instruments for achieving the best use of men and money in the interests of all of the people. Yet at present, perhaps as a result of war demands and the need to control inflation, new private investment is subject to many controls, starting with application of approval of the project in principle, and extending to an evaluation of the use of equipment and materials, approval of construction and imports, and later regulation of management of the plant. In a wartime environment strict controls to conserve foreign exchange and prevent speculative short-run profits are justified, but if development is to occur, many of these controls and regulations on private business must be removed, They were originally imposed because of the war and their raison d'être will cease with the end of the war. It is easy to fall into the habit of piling control upon control, often ill-designed to promote either economic efficiency or social equity, and with near-disastrous effects on the economy. There are more examples of such controls than can be listed in this study, but a major requirement after the war is for a commercial and incorporation code that establishes the right of the investor in a business to manage and conduct his affairs as he will, subject to general regulations ensuring that this does not lead to monopoly or economic power that is used against the public interest.

The public sector has the primary responsibility for guiding the economy along paths of development and for guaranteeing that the benefits are spread to the people. It has an impressive arsenal of policy instruments to accomplish these objectives. Through tax policy and public welfare programs it meets the requirement for equity in sharing burdens and benefits of development. Through monetary and fiscal policy it controls the availability of credit, guides investment, and provides the capital needed in infrastructure. It has additional controls over trade and other activities. With these instruments at its command, the public sector should require only minimal direct controls and restrictions on private business.

In speaking of the private sector it should be noted that a significant part of that sector is made up of Vietnamese of Chinese descent. The business activities of this group are extensive and in some instances possibly even dominant. They account for a large part of the conduct and financing of import trade and the marketing and processing of agricultural products, and are active in many lines of trade and commerce. These activities contribute a great deal to the successful functioning of the economy now, and they are essential to development in the future; therefore, the participation of this group in development and their contribution to the growth of Vietnam should be as welcome as the contribution of all other citizens. In fact, they should be expected to perform in this way. Special controls on or discrimination against this group are not only unnecessary but actually are against the best interests of the country. On the other hand, if there are activities of the group that lead to the formation of monopoly power in lines of business or that result in the exercise of economic power contrary to the development goals of the country (for example the export of capital), such activities should be penalized and controlled to the same extent as for all other groups in the society. If this course of action is followed, the greatest benefit to the country will occur, and economic activities from whatever source will be judged by how well they contribute to economic growth.

We cannot in this book consider in detail every case where the public sector and the private sector meet and divide responsibility. What has been done is to outline the basis for an open economy--one that can take advantage of individual initiative as well as group action for the benefit of the whole country. This general policy will lead to the most rapid and efficient development of resources and the equitable distribution of the benefits of growth. Additional aspects of this economic policy are discussed in this chapter and in succeeding chapters.

EXPORT PROMOTION AND IMPORT SUBSTITUTION

Vietnam cannot increase its per capita income above the rate of population growth by concentrating solely on the development of industries and agriculture to serve the domestic market from its own resources. This is true for several reasons, one being that the resources of Vietnam are not diversified enough to supply the variety of goods that are wanted. There is a technical or natural resource limitation. But also, to develop local industry and agriculture at all normally requires capital goods that are not produced locally and must be imported. Moreover, as incomes rise, there is an increased demand for consumer goods of wide variety, and the growth of more complex local industries again raises the demand for imported capital goods. The spiral does not continue indefinitely since some balance is reached between local production and imports, but for a country in the early stages of development, such as Vietnam, the process described is quite typical. As local industry and agriculture grow, imports will also grow, and to earn the foreign exchange necessary to pay for the imports of consumer goods and capital goods, exports of products, supplemented by inflows of capital funds, are needed.

The range of problems suggested by this simple description is great, and the problems themselves are complex. What is the relationship between the potential growth of gross national product and the level of imports and exports? Can a country grow as satisfactorily with imports and exports at 5-10 percent of GNP as at 15-20 percent? What are the opportunities and the limits on substituting local production for imports as a strategy of development? What are the potentials for the growth of exports in Vietnam in the future? If imports and exports grow at different rates, how will internal growth be affected and what are the needs for external assistance to meet a balance of payments deficit? Can Vietnam achieve self-sustaining growth without the injection of large inflows of capital? These are just a few of the perplexing problems that must be somehow solved in preparing a development plan. Only a complete model of the economy will permit consistent answers to the questions, for the growth of output and income, the level of investment, exports, imports, and other variables are interrelated. We do not yet have such a model, but for some key issues a rough but practical guide to future needs can be outlined.

A policy of import substitution has appealed to many countries, often to their later regret. As a general rule the domestic market should be large enough to support at least one plant of efficient size, that is, one that can produce at costs competitive with import prices. If such a rule is not adopted, the economy is likely to end up with many small units producing inferior products at high costs. Such units invariably need permanent protection from competition from imported goods; tariffs and other taxes must be maintained at high rates, and the consumers must continue to pay relatively high prices for goods. Such high prices dampen demand while fostering continuing production for a smaller market. Resources are not used as efficiently as they could be and ultimately this seriously impairs the ability of the country to grow.

An emphasis on import substitution as a means to growth is usually linked to the desire to industrialize the economy. Many countries fear that they will simply become exporters of raw materials and agricultural products and will have to import industrial products and capital goods. Industrial development is somehow regarded as more favorable than agricultural development, and is considered the mark of a developing country. Moreover, reliance on agricultural and raw material exports as a source of foreign exchange to finance development is regarded as risky in the extreme. The alternative is to stress industrialization and import substitution rather than the development of exports, and thus to try to grow with a lower level of foreign trade. The several elements of this argument, which may sound attractive as a course of action for Vietnam, are worth examining closely.

The lack of confidence in agricultural exports as a source of foreign exchange is based on several notions: (1) the terms of trade inevitably move against agriculture; (2) the demand for such products is apt to be weak or uncertain because of competition from other sources; (3) a country that relies on exports of a few major products to a few markets is highly vulnerable because prices of the products may suddenly drop and reduce foreign exchange earnings drastically. Each of these notions may be true at times, but not necessarily for Vietnam or not necessarily to a significant degree, if certain steps are taken in the postwar period.

It has not been demonstrated that the terms of trade (that is, the ratio of export prices to import prices) inevitably move against exporters of agricultural and raw material products. The historical evidence is ambiguous; the results depend on the period of time chosen and the composition of the indexes used. For some raw materials and agricultural products, prices have held up well and may increase as industrial demands and output grow. The import price index for Vietnam from 1962 to 1968 rose only about the same amount as the implicit GNP deflator, although the composition of imports was in general weighted with goods that have more volatile prices than the kinds of capital goods that normally account for a large fraction of imports in developing countries.

Many of the arguments presented on the inability of agricultural and raw material exports to support development have been based on Latin American experience with coffee and sugar, whose markets and prices have deteriorated rapidly in the past and are relatively weak today. It is true that in more normal times Vietnam has secured almost 90 percent of its export earnings from rubber and rice. Rubber has suffered competitively from synthetic rubber, but it has been estimated that the world market demand for natural rubber will continue to grow, though at a lower rate than for synthetics. Nevertheless, if Vietnam had to rely in the future on these two exports alone, the outlook would be bleak. Specialization on a few export crops does have risks; many underdeveloped countries do in fact have a high concentration of exports in a few products, such as coffee, sugar, bananas, tea, rubber, and cocoa. The prices of these products have often fluctuated widely and in some cases overproduction has depressed prices badly. This might happen with rubber, and in a longer period with rice, but as is discussed below, Vietnam can diversify exports to avoid the risks of overdependence on a few crops. The opportunities for diversification include both a larger number of agricultural products and raw materials and a sharp increase in exports of processed goods and manufactured products. This degree of diversification should greatly reduce the vulnerability of Vietnam to sudden fluctuations of prices of a few products or to the deterioration of conditions in a few markets.

Because Vietnam is, relatively, a small country, it will not have a large share of the total export market in any major product, but it may in fact have a share in a regional market for some products large enough for changes in the volume of Vietnam's exports to have an effect on prices and market conditions. In those cases it is important to manage the marketing of the product so as to obtain the best possible terms of sale; in most cases, however, Vietnam will simply meet a world market price, and must adjust costs to be competitive.

The substitution of domestic production for imports is applicable in Vietnam, and may gain strength as development occurs, but it is not a course of action to be pursued in haste, since more often than not it leads to overprotection of domestic industry. There is already evidence of investment taking place in uneconomic facilities in metals and synthetic fibers; such investment would not occur without tariff and customs protection which permits the local producers to operate successfully at high production costs. There is no real reason now to search frantically for real opportunities for efficient import substitution. Chapter 9 discusses in some detail a list of industrial plants and products that should be profitable investments primarily to serve the domestic market. Most of these would produce goods that are imported now or that would probably be imported in increased volumes after the war. The unfolding of these investment opportunities will reveal many instances of import substitution. We are not yet ready to provide quantitative measurements of the extent and pace at which this could occur within ten years after the war, but some rough idea may be obtained by considering the major categories of imports in 1966. In that year seven commodity groups accounted for just under half of total import licenses. These were rice, motorcycles (two-wheeled and three-wheeled, including parts), textile fabrics, iron and steel products, petroleum products, chemicals (fertilizers and other), and trucks and buses (including parts). The import volumes of at least three of these groups were significantly inflated by war-related needs and might decrease (relatively) in a peacetime development period. These are iron and steel; petroleum products; and trucks and buses. Plans are in existence for a petroleum refinery in Vietnam to operate on imported crude oil. That would have the effect of retaining the value added in refining in the country.

Several other commodity groups of imports might easily be replaced, at least in part, by domestic production. It is expected that in no more than two years after the end of the war, rice production could provide all domestic requirements and yield an exportable surplus. Vietnam can move rapidly into the assembly of motorcycles, with successively increasing domestic production of parts of the vehicle. This type of program has been successful in the automobile industry in several Latin American countries. It should be far simpler to implement efficiently with motorcycles than with automobiles. Chemical fertilizers are also included in the short-run development plan for local production.

Although the full details of import substitution cannot as yet be described, it is evident that there are opportunities in a range of commodities and products. Probably only in three major industry groups is it likely that substitution of domestic production for imports would be unwise and inefficient, at least in the short-run: basic metals processing and finishing; many chemical groups; heavy machinery and capital goods. These, however, contain many items required for investment in development. For these there is no substitute for imports; but in other areas, import substitution should move forward as rapidly as cost comparisons will permit, because, for a given level of exports, a decrease in imports is equivalent to a decrease in the amount of capital that must be borrowed abroad.

The development of exports and export markets should have the highest priority in the postwar period. Chapter 9 discusses several important projects whose primary objective is to earn foreign exchange. The prospects are bright, not only for these projects, but also for the expansion of exports as a whole. Nevertheless, to translate prospects into realities will take a concentrated effort.

It is unrealistic to try to project detailed export potentials, because so many uncertainties exist that affect such figures. Studies of specific world markets and the technical and economic feasibility of producing various products are required in order to have confidence in details. But it is important to have some notion of the possible range of exports. The analytical work we have undertaken so far provides a basis for the order-of-magnitude estimates shown in Table 2.1. These are estimates that might be achieved in ten years. The totals indicate a wide range in the possibilities, with the high figure almost three times the low one. What can be said about these figures? Rubber and rice together in the past accounted for about 90 percent of total exports but are projected at a much lower percentage in the future because of diversification, particularly in industrial products. It is said that the rubber industry can be brought back to its former peak production and

TABLE 2.1

Annual Export Potential
(US$ millions; 1967 prices)

Commodity Group	Export Potential Low Estimate	High Estimate
Rubber	40	60
Rice	40	90
Fish products	10	40
Other agricultural products (cinnamon, vegetables, animal feeds, tea)	20	80
Industrial	50	170
	160	440

that good planting stock is available. In Chapter 7 it is estimated that within ten years 1.5 million tons of rice can be available for export, and the figures on industrial products include pulp, plywood and wood products, and a variety of other products. Fresh and, more importantly, processed fish products could be the real surprise in exports, but it will take substantial investment in processing facilities and a great deal of technical assistance and training to achieve the result. Indeed, the levels of investment, market development, and training needed to reach the high estimate of almost half a billion dollars annually in exports may be beyond the capabilities of the economy even in ten years; yet, without the most intense effort to expand exports, economic growth may falter or become unduly dependent on external aid, thus delaying the time when the economy can sustain its own growth.

The low and the high estimates can be related to past peak export performance in order to show what is involved. The peak was about US$80 million in the early 1960's, so that the low estimate is twice as high and the high estimate almost six times as high as the previous peak. But there was no real effort made to expand exports in those days. The experience of a few entrepreneurs in developing exports in the last few years and in the midst of war is evidence of what might be accomplished.

In any case Vietnam cannot grow steadily if it neglects foreign trade. A policy that turns toward autarchy and internal development alone will surely fail. The issues of growth and eventual economic independence hang in the balance.

EXTERNAL AID AND ECONOMIC INDEPENDENCE

The effort necessary to expand exports to earn foreign exchange and to substitute local production for imports to conserve foreign exchange raises the question of the size of the foreign trade sector in Vietnam's future, and also raises the question of external aid requirements to ease the transition to self-sustained growth.

Obviously no country can let a deficit in its balance of payments continue to grow without serious consequences. There is less strain if a country can grow with imports and exports at, say, 10 percent of the gross national product annually, than if the figure is 20 percent or higher. Is it possible to grow with low exports and imports, since a figure of 10 percent of GNP in exports probably could be readily managed by Vietnam in the next decade? The answer is that large, developed countries with many resources can have ratios of foreign trade to GNP as low as 10 percent or less and grow successfully. While there is no rigid relationship between the ratio of foreign trade to GNP and the growth of GNP, the probability of an underdeveloped country, such as Vietnam, growing at a satisfactory rate with both imports and exports around 10 percent of GNP is highly unlikely. Table 2.2 shows the average ratio of imports or exports to GNP and the growth rate of GNP in the early 1960's. Malaysia has a significantly higher ratio than the Philippines, Taiwan, and Thailand, and Burma a lower one. Although there are variations in the growth rate, the first four countries are doing reasonably well. Burma is not, and, although its troubles are not solely due to a rather low foreign trade involvement, limitations on imports needed for local development have dampened the growth rate rather markedly.

Vietnam should not take either Malaysia or Burma as a model in this respect, for the former has unattainably high ratios (and may be more than normally vulnerable to market shifts), and the latter has not succeeded in financing the foreign

TABLE 2.2

Ratio of Foreign Trade to GNP and Rate of GNP Growth

Country	Average Ratio of Exports or Imports to GNP	Average Rate of Growth of GNP
Malaysia	35 - 40	5 - 6
Philippines	15 - 18	4 - 5
Taiwan	17 - 20	8 - 9
Thailand	16 - 22	7 - 8
Burma	10 - 13	0 - 2

exchange needed for a development effort. In both cases, of course, there are additional elements in the situation that go beyond the simple characterization presented here. It seems likely that Vietnam will compare more closely in its postwar programs to the experience of the middle three countries, which have foreign trade ratios roughly in the range of 15-20 percent of a growing GNP.

There will be differences between the early years of the period (the transition) and the later years. Exports cannot be expected to increase immediately and, in instances of large new plants, may be delayed from three to five years; meanwhile, imports will continue at a relatively high rate, because of reconstruction needs and as a counterinflationary measure. With all of the uncertainties of the future it is perilous to make year-by-year estimates, but in aggregate figures it seems likely that the imports needed to sustain at least a 5 percent growth of the GNP will be about US$550-$650 million annually. In the year or so prior to 1968, import levels were in this same range. Normally we would expect that these levels, which have been swollen by the war, would decrease rather substantially and still be sufficient for sustained growth, but as income rises in the postwar decade, import demands will also rise, and by the end of the decade may be above the levels projected here. We cannot now assess the relative strength of this tendency to increase in comparison to the potential results of import substitution activities in terms of the net impact on import levels.

On a comparable basis exports are projected at about US$200 million in five years' time, rising, it is hoped, to US$400-$500 million by the end of the decade. As has been indicated previously, the performance of the export sector depends on the extent of the effort to develop such industries and products. The estimates made here are in the upper part of the range, and for that reason they indicate indirectly the consequences of lesser performance.

On this basis the trade gap would be about US$3 billion over the decade, but the greater part of it is likely to occur in the first five years, perhaps two-thirds of the total, and the remaining third in the second five years. The trade gap should decrease over the decade if the programs to expand exports and to limit imports are successful. In fact, if economic independence is to be achieved by the end of ten years, the balance of payments must not then be in a high deficit position requiring continued injections of foreign aid on concessionary terms. If the balance of trade shows a deficit, as it is projected to do even at the end of the period, the balance on services plus private capital inflows and a reasonable limit of suppliers' credits must be sufficient to bring the balance of payments into equilibrium.

It is believed that Vietnam might acquire foreign exchange through some services, particularly in tourism after the war. There will be curiosity on the part of people who have had sons, relatives, and friends serving in Vietnam, and if the natural attractions of places such as Dalat, Vung Tau, Nha Trang, and many others can be advertised and good facilities provided, a vigorous tourist industry can be created.

Chapter 9, on industrial development, identifies many profitable investments for private capital; some of them, such as the pulp plant, will require foreign investment and expertise. A rough tally of investments that might be attractive to foreign investors indicates that in the ten postwar years up to US$500 million in funds might be invested in the country. Some guarantees will have to be given to attract these funds, including guarantees against expropriation, against undue interference in managing the enterprise, and of permission to repatriate a major part of profits. Some limitations on repatriation are imposed by some countries and would be appropriate for Vietnam as well.

In spite of the best efforts to attract private foreign investment, or to build tourism or other services, about US$2.5 billion in concessionary foreign aid will be needed in the postwar decade. This is a large amount certainly, but less annually than the average amounts supplied in recent years. It is hoped that this aid will be supplied at low interest rates and with maturities of at least fifteen to twenty years. It is most essential that favorable terms exist, for if they do not, the debt service in interest charges and repayments will rise very rapidly. In fact Vietnam must be prepared for a rise in debt service burdens in any case. It has virtually no external debt now, which is fortunate, but that condition will not continue. We cannot now guess at the size or rate of increase of such burdens without knowing the terms of loans, but the experience of many other countries is extremely sobering. These burdens have often eaten up much of export earnings, have created or strengthened inflationary conditions in the country, and have led to a constant application to creditors to refinance existing debt. Vietnam should learn from this experience and do its utmost to avoid it, even at the cost of accepting a somewhat lower rate of growth.

Some countries have recently expressed a concern or an interest in the future financial needs of Vietnam for reconstruction and development. The United States has borne by far the largest burden in supplying aid, and a number of countries have benefited greatly through supplying goods and services; for example, both Japan and Taiwan have exported substantial amounts in the last few years to Vietnam. With the end of the war and the start of a period of development, to expect a reverse flow, in some cases, is not unreasonable. In fact it might now be appropriate to open the topic of external assistance to wider discussion.

We suggest to the Government of Vietnam that steps be taken informally to determine the desirability of having a conference of countries to discuss all aspects of postwar development needs and aid requirements in the coming years. There are some indications that several countries might favor such a conference, and if one is arranged, the United States, Japan, Taiwan, the Philippines, Korea, Australia, and Western European countries should be invited to participate. Private banks and financial institutions in these countries might also have a definite interest in attending. Perhaps the Asian Development Bank, whose interests in development extend throughout this part of the world, might be willing to undertake the task of convening such an informal conference. We suggest that it be asked to do so. This could be one step in helping Vietnam to plot its course toward eventual economic independence in ten years.

DEVELOPMENT AND PRICE STABILITY

The inflationary problems that are of such great concern now will not disappear with the end of the war. While direct war expenditures will drop, many war-connected expenditures cannot be so readily decreased. Demobilization of troops will take time, and expenditures on the logistics base will have to continue. The transition is a critical period, but it now appears unlikely that a serious deflation will occur, particularly if development programs are initiated and phased in during this same period. Consequently inflationary pressures may well continue for a number of years.

Development with price stability is unlikely to be possible. In Chapter 4, on fiscal policy, it is shown that the demands made on the public investment budget will be great, and though government revenues from taxes and other sources can rise, they will probably do so somewhat slowly. Also operating costs in the budget will be difficult to reduce without a thorough housecleaning and revision of the civil service system. For these reasons hopes for obtaining public savings in the budget are dim, at least for some years. With revenue lags, high public investment demand, and structural inertia in the public service, the pressure to resort to some deficit financing to undertake priority public programs probably cannot be resisted. The commercial import program, which has been used as a major counterinflationary instrument, cannot be continued indefinitely in that role and must be replaced by more normal monetary and fiscal measures. External aid should be turning toward development program support.

In these circumstances development will almost surely be accompanied by some price increases. The problem is to keep such increases within bounds or to have a guideline for monetary and fiscal policy to follow. Certainly the price increases of the past few years are unacceptably high as a guide to the future. Annual price increases of 30 percent or more are destructive. There are few standards of what a country can stand in price increases and still develop without severe strain, but we venture to suggest a twofold criterion. Average annual price increases over the years should be kept within the range of 5-10 percent, and no price increase in a single year should exceed 15 percent. Obviously this is a crude criterion which must be examined carefully before acceptance. It may prove too rigid and inappropriate, but it is a place to start and is offered in that sense.

REGIONAL COOPERATION IN SOUTHEAST ASIA

The internal development problems of Vietnam rightly command the attention of the country as a program is planned for the decade after the war. The resources of the country belong to its people and the opportunities for development are measured in terms of those resources. Foreign trade must be cultivated to provide the foreign exchange to buy imports, but this trade is subject to rules different from those that apply to internal trade.

In the ten postwar years, although the emphasis is on national development, there almost surely will be opportunities for expanding development regionally throughout southeast Asia, including all of Vietnam, Cambodia, Laos, and Thailand. Regional economic integration as a means to improve development possibilities for groups of nations has made remarkable progress in recent years, sometimes with quite remarkable benefits to the members, and sometimes not. But in principle, regional integration can accelerate the rate of growth and provide a wider and more stable basis for development. The opportunities among the countries of southeast Asia can be explored much more thoroughly but some of the potential benefits, as well as the latent constraints, are discernible now and deserve mention in a study on development policies for Vietnam. In the long run the richest development of the country lies in cooperative development with its neighbors, and that is equally true for every other nation in the region.

There are many attractions in regional economic integration; it broadens markets for goods, widens the range of investment opportunities that are profitable because of the market effects, permits greater specialization in economic activities, which usually leads to cost savings, provides a way to channel financial and real resources to the best uses, and increases the economic power of the group in dealing with world markets. These are the potential benefits, and they are substantial. As a practical matter, there are political and economic difficulties in fully realizing these benefits.

Integration in this sense does not simply include a prescribed set of economic activities or functions. The European Economic Community has a full customs union plus cooperation and agreement in many other matters, whereas the Latin American Free Trade Association has made only a few tentative steps to reduce customs barriers and to cooperate on certain multinational projects. Ultimate success in achieving benefits is more certain if the initial steps are simple ones that create some benefits to all without asking a sacrifice from any. With some small successes, it is easier to move to those ventures that require compromise and close cooperation. Such opportunities are often found in expanding trade among the countries via liberalized customs and regulations.

Trade expansion among the countries of southeast Asia is a definite possibility, including the resumption of trade between North Vietnam and South Vietnam. In the past this latter trade was not insubstantial, agricultural produce moving north and raw materials and some finished goods moving south. The composition of that trade would not be the same as before, because South Vietnam in particular has a wider range of products and costs and prices have changed, but some of the commodities previously exchanged might again be traded with mutual benefit. After the war the resumption of trade might well be a first step in a move toward normalization of relations. As a specific small step, the re-establishment of postal communications has been suggested as one that would have particular appeal.

Beyond trade between north and south there are possibilities for trade among all countries in the region. It is sometimes said that trade among countries with very similar economies is apt to be very low and to contribute little to further cooperation, since each country seeks to market the same products. Although this is logically true, the actual situation is often quite different. This was the argument used against the small countries that formed the Central American Common Market, which is now probably the most successful of the regional associations. Upon examination, it is typical for similar product groupings in different countries to comprise a variety of different specific products, and for existing specialization or processing habits to create opportunities for trade. Differences in raw materials or natural resources similarly create trade possibilities. The economies of the countries of southeast Asia are prima facie sufficiently different to support a greatly increased volume of trade among them. Moreover, industrial ventures among the countries, for instance for the exploitation of their joint forest resources to produce pulp and wood products on a large scale, extend the range of possible cooperative agreements.

Finally, the development of the Mekong River Basin is a multinational project that can only succeed if the riparian countries cooperate. No single country in the region can derive benefits from the development of the part of the basin within its boundaries equal to the benefits that can be achieved through joint action. Hydroelectric power for industry and home consumption, flood control, and the provision of water to irrigate millions of hectares of agricultural land are the prizes to be won, but only if the countries can agree and obtain external assistance to finance the projects.

Regional economic integration may not initially rank high in priority in comparison to internal development measures, but plans for the future need to be made in advance and Vietnam should show its support for regional cooperation and for the activities of the Asian Development Bank, which is seeking every means to foster such economic cooperation.

CHAPTER 3 MONETARY POLICIES

An appropriate set of monetary policies is essential for growth in Vietnam in the postwar period. Such policies are of equal or even surpassing importance at the present time and in periods of rapid economic adjustment because they include controls over the money supply and the conditions under which credit is available. These controls operate through the commercial banking system and through other financial institutions. During a war period, when normal fiscal policies are dominated by the need to support defense and total expenditure programs are swollen, major reliance for control of inflationary pressures in the economy fall on monetary policy and on direct governmental regulations of economic activity. In a peacetime economy, direct regulations can, and should, be largely replaced by normal fiscal and monetary measures that together will effectively stimulate the growth of investment, output, and income without severe inflationary or deflationary pressures. The combination of measures that are employed during wartime, often including credit restrictions on the private sector, exceedingly high levels of government expenditure programs (but almost none on developmental activities), large increases in currency, and varied direct restrictions, is generally quite different from the combination of measures required to stimulate growth. Changing such policies in the transition to a peacetime economy occurs during a time when many physical changes are going on in the economy. Monetary and fiscal policies are the key to successful conversion of the economy. A later chapter discusses fiscal policies, centered on tax and revenue policies and government expenditure programs. This chapter discusses monetary policies for growth.

The actual content of monetary policy at each point in time in the future cannot be stated with precision, since it depends on the conditions existing in the economy. Nor is it necessary to be this precise. Monetary policy is a flexible instrument. It is possible to appraise the usefulness of specific kinds of policies, to indicate their likely effectiveness, and to state some rules for their application, including some things that should be considered in the near future.

Monetary policy is defined here to include the performance of three functions: (1) the building of a financial sector in the economy that will adequately provide financial services for the economy and the establishment of conditions so that these institutions (commercial banks and financial intermediaries) will respond to changes instituted in credit policies or the money supply; (2) the establishment of policies to stimulate savings and investment in the economy, and through credit policies, help to maintain external equilibrium in the balance of payments; (3) the creation of conditions for a successful money or capital market in the future. These functions are not completely separable, but each has some distinctive features of importance for the future growth of the economy.

THE FUTURE IMPORTANCE OF CURRENT MONETARY FACTORS

It is difficult to write of postwar monetary problems without a complete description of the economy as it is transformed from war to peace. The problems of the day-to-day control of credit and money to keep the economy in reasonable balance are not the primary concern of a study aimed at postwar problems. Yet the problems of today do leave a legacy for tomorrow and we must try to take account of the elements that will persist into the future.

At the present time the major problem is the continuing inflationary pressure generated by war finance, where injections into the monetary system via issue of currency and advances from the National Bank of Vietnam (NBVN) exceed the absorption of funds via taxes and other revenue measures. This inflationary gap has been widening and probably will continue to do so as long as the war continues. The pressing problem is to find a way out of the dangers of this inflationary situation for the next few months or a year. Each time a budget is prepared, the same problem recurs, and additional monetary and fiscal measures must be found to offset increased levels of expenditure. This problem, which is so central to immediate short-term monetary policy, may carry over into a postwar period. It does not seem likely that total expenditure programs (including those associated with the U. S. military) will suddenly decrease, regardless of how negotiations go or what solutions are reached. There may well be sharp decreases in certain U. S. military expenditures (such as troop payments) but these will not have an impact within the country. A serious deflationary process does not seem at all likely in the transition; vestiges of inflationary pressures will probably persist for some time. This is an evaluation and a judgment that could prove false of course, if, in particular, peace brought a rapid demobilization accompanied by a sudden fall in U. S. external aid, but that combination of elements appears to be improbable.

The expansion of the money supply seems not to have induced an equal increase in prices, though it may be simply that the impacts are delayed. A calculation of the effects of changes in the money supply on price changes indicates an elasticity of almost one; that is, a 1 percent increase in the money supply leads to a 1 percent increase in prices, but with a delay of about six months. The full impact of the changes in the money supply will not be felt for some time.*

Yet it does appear that some part of the increased money supply is going into hoards. The usual methods for the flight of capital--gold sales, retention of export proceeds overseas, direct bank transfers, overinvoicing and underinvoicing of imports and exports--have not been in any great evidence, and prices have not risen dramatically although the money supply has. This hoarding has been attributed to feelings of uncertainty by the people as to what will happen in the future, particularly after the experience of Tet, 1968. They are assumed to be withholding decisions to spend for durables or similar

---

*Derived from a regression of percent changes in the money supply to percent changes in the consumer price index for working class families, with the change in the money supply lagged six months. This was for the period 1960-6/1968. The regression equation is

$$P = -.76 + .94\ M$$

where P is the change in prices and M is the change in the money supply.

goods because of this uncertainty. The fear is that these hoards of currency may be dishoarded in a short space of time and create inflationary chaos. Paradoxically this change in attitude could occur either through a return of confidence in the future, leading to a decision to spend the funds, or through a worsening of confidence in the value of the currency. The latter situation is by far the more serious. If an inflationary gap grows and currency is printed, it is conceivable that a hyperinflation might develop that could not be checked by an increase in imports. The present inflationary pressures generated by excess demand are very likely to continue into the future and complicate monetary problems of the transition to peace.

The inflationary situation is not helped by the policies that have been followed on interest rates. One reason people hold cash is because, with a low interest rate on deposits, it does not cost much to hold currency. They are not losing much of a return and they prefer the higher liquidity that currency has over bank deposits. A higher level of interest rates might induce people to hold deposits and other assets rather than cash and through this reduction in liquidity reduce inflationary pressures. For this and other reasons related to incentives to save, the present structure of interest rates is an unreasonable one and clearly needs revision. The appropriate kinds of policies and levels for interest rates both now and in the future are discussed later in this chapter. The suggestions made there are among the most important in the area of monetary policy.

Finally, the current imbalances in imports and exports have created strains on the exchange rate that only a specially designed import program and external aid have kept within bounds. The free market rate has fluctuated rather widely. The determination of the appropriate exchange rate for the future--one that will be reasonably stable, not impair growth or feed inflation, and one that will permit a reasonable balance of payments to be maintained--is one of the prime problems that must be faced. This issue is also discussed later in this chapter.

THE FINANCIAL STRUCTURE FOR THE FUTURE

As Vietnam develops, growth will occur in all sectors of the economy, though some will grow faster than others or receive a higher priority of treatment. The financial sector is one that is sometimes overlooked in terms of the growth of essential economic functions. It includes the commercial banks, the special investment institutions (the Agricultural Development Bank, ADB; the Vietnam Development Bank, VDB, formerly SOFIDIV; and the Industrial Development Center, IDC), plus institutions that may be created (mortgage banks, savings-and-loan-like associations, insurance companies). These provide the means for moving away from quasi-barter arrangements and bringing more of economic activity into the monetary economy. Through them it becomes easier to pay bills, to carry on business, to obtain credit for productive investment or for consumption needs, and to stimulate the increase of savings and capital. These are functions that need strengthening if agriculture, industry, and trade are to grow and prosper. In short, they are instruments for mobilizing savings and capital, and for helping to make monetary policies effective.

By most standards the financial sector in Vietnam is weak and underdeveloped, and this condition is not solely traceable to the war. It apparently has existed for a number of years. There has been a growth in financial assets and financial activity, sometimes at rather high rates, but virtually all of this only began in 1966, and much of it is due to the rapid growth of import trade that began then. Since in the postwar years the level of imports will almost certainly shrink from the peaks realized during the war, this recent growth may not be firm enough to sustain continuous future development in this sector.

One comparative measure of the characteristics of the financial system is briefly shown in Table 3.1, which compares the number of banks and number of persons per banking office for Vietnam and five other countries. The contrast between Vietnam and neighboring countries is readily evident from the numbers; in 1967 the Philippines had more than twice as many banking offices per unit of population as Vietnam, and all other countries in the selection were better off. Japan has one banking office per 15,000, and the United States one per 6000. But a few years ago the contrast was even greater; seven of the twenty banks in Vietnam were established in 1965 or later, and in 1967 only fourteen of the thirty-seven offices were in the provinces; twenty-three were located in the Saigon-Cholon area. Some market towns have no banking offices at all.

TABLE 3.1

Commercial Banking Structure in Selected Countries, 1967

Country	No. of Domestic and Foreign Banks	Total Number of Branches	No. Persons per Banking Office thousands
Vietnam	20	37	440
Taiwan	17	306	43
Korea	17	236	122
Pakistan	25	1747	62
Thailand	27	324	96
Philippines	37	188	175

The absence of commercial banking facilities has surely had an adverse effect on the conduct and growth of business and trade in the country. Because of a lack of such bank credit sources and financial services, other more informal arrangements have been made to supply minimal needs. Credit is supplied by merchants, relatives, and moneylenders. In the case of the first two, funds are apparently often lent at zero interest but the coverage of such a system is sharply limited to family or close business associates. For example, major fish merchants in Saigon will lend money to their provincial suppliers. Borrowing from moneylenders is done at very high interest rates and often short maturities. It is not a stimulus to normally profitable ventures. The local institution of the <u>hui</u> is widely used in Vietnam but it has been shown that it frequently leads to implicity irrational economic choices in the use and commitment of funds.

These informal credit arrangements cannot be expanded to meet the needs of growing commerce and industry during a development period. They will probably not be completely supplanted by banking operations for a rather long time, longer than the ten-year horizon for development planning that is taken in this study, but a movement should be made to provide incentives to expand commercial banking throughout the country in the postwar period.

The government of Vietnam has taken some steps via tax concessions to make it more attractive to establish branch banks in the provinces. In the present circumstances these probably will be only partially successful, but may be increasingly effective in the postwar period. In any case the expansion of commercial banking facilities should be in the hands of the private sector, though the Credit Commercial (CCVN), a government bank, has more provincial branches than any other, and should be encouraged to supply competitive market pressures on private banks to expand their operations.

To some extent the expansion of facilities after the war may occur naturally. The business of the banks has been concentrated primarily in the financing of imports, which has accounted for over 50 percent of total business. The ease and profitability of import financing are also the reasons for the establishment of the new banks after 1965. Funds can be turned over three or four times a year and the risks are small, a classical example of the older commercial banking theory that loans be self-liquidating. The banks have not been aggressive in searching for loan opportunities in industry and agriculture, nor in developing savings departments. The former opportunities have been largely left to the special banks ADB, VDB, and IDC, and the development of further loanable funds via savings departments has been impaired by the interest rate policies of the central bank, NBVN.

The commercial banks have naturally concentrated on the most lucrative lending in imports, but after the war, the volume of imports will probably drop, as has been mentioned earlier; therefore, the banks will have to pursue a more aggressive policy in developing business with industry, agriculture, and commerce, and, in fact, it is necessary that they do so if the credit needs of these sectors are to be met. This should not require any special incentives by the government, though it may require some education in aggressive and effective banking practices by the banking community.

There are four special financial institutions that provide credit and financial services: the ADB, VDB, IDC, and Caisse de Refinancement pour le Développement de l'Industrie (the refinancing fund). In general they make short-term and medium-term loans. At the present time they do not make loans for longer than about seven years at interest rates that range up to about 8 percent. We are not concerned here with the rules and regulations governing the operation of these institutions. They are dictated in large part by the present conditions of the war. But there are two important questions concerning their postwar functions and operations. The first is a question of their future relationships with the commercial banks, the division of responsibility for supplying credit, and the amount of competition or cooperation among them. The second question concerns the amount of loanable funds that these institutions will have available in the future and the appropriate source of such funds.

Many of the funds available to industry and agriculture now originate with these institutions. As has been mentioned above, in the future the commercial banks should also be sources of credit for these sectors. There may be competition for loans between these institutions and the commercial banks but this is not a very likely event. In all probability the demand for loanable funds will be greater than can be supplied by all of the banking community unless vigorous efforts are made to stimulate savings. This problem is discussed below under the heading "Interest Rate Reforms." These four special institutions should provide a lead in meeting credit needs but they will not be able to supply the major part. Their funds now come through the government and while an increase in such funds can be obtained and may be virtually the only source in the short run, over a longer period of time these institutions should explore the possibilities for obtaining funds through the sale of their own securities. This would permit them to tap a wider money market.

Just as the refinancing fund now is the means for banks to obtain additional funds for industrial development, at some time in the future it might be appropriate for the ADB to assume this additional responsibility in the case of agricultural loans. This would place these institutions in a position to exercise some additional degree of restraint on or stimulation to the commercial banks.

The more important question is what level of loanable funds or bank credit will be required in the future to finance investment and rising economic activity. There can be no very precise answer to this question. Much depends on the composition of investment, the rate of growth of markets, the extent of government participation in programs, and many other factors. In Chapter 7, a special estimate is made of agricultural credit needs over the ten postwar years. The estimate of VN$30 billion is about ten times the amount in use in 1968. Chapter 9 outlines a large list of industrial projects that may be undertaken in the ten years, with explicit estimates of fixed capital financing requirements but without estimates of actual credit needs. These are only two of the sectors. Housing mortgage needs is surely another large one.

Some rough ideas of credit needs in the future can be obtained by reference to other countries. For a sample of countries the average ratio of bank credit to the gross national product is about 30 percent. Normally credit needs rise somewhat more rapidly than the rate of increase of the GNP, so that for a rate of increase of 5-6 percent in GNP, credit requirements might rise by 7-8 percent annually. This assumes that the basic relationship between credit needs and GNP from which growth takes place is at least 10-15 percent; otherwise the rates of increase may be higher. Table 3.2, shows how low this ratio is for Vietnam. In 1966 and 1967 credit expansions were unnaturally swollen by import financing, but except for 1966 the ratio is deliberately held down as a war measure to curb inflation; however, the experience of the early 1960's does not show much tendency to grow.

Crude estimates can be misleading, but it appears that postwar credit needs in Vietnam for a growing economy will be five to fifteen times the amounts now available, assuming a vigorous private sector. For that reason it is important to encourage strongly the growth of savings through appropriate policies, discussed below, and to consider how public sector revenues may be raised and made available for investment (discussed in Chapter 4).

Finally, the composition of the money supply and its relationship to the GNP also suggest some structural problems for the future, as well as indicating some of the monetary policy problems in the short run in control of inflation. For a country with Vietnam's per capita income the total money supply is typically about 13-15 percent of GNP and currency

TABLE 3.2

Financial Ratios in Recent Times
(VN$ billions)

Year	Bank Credit[a]	Time Deposits[b]	GNP	B/GNP	T/GNP
1960	4.3	.9	81.8	5.3	1.1
1961	5.7	.9	84.5	6.7	1.1
1962	6.9	.9	93.8	7.4	1.0
1963	7.5	2.0	100.3	7.4	2.0
1964	7.6	2.2	114.3	6.6	1.9
1965	7.4	2.8	144.8	5.1	1.9
1966	29.2	8.3	240.9[c]	12.1	3.4
1967	27.3	8.3	352.0[c]	7.8	2.4

[a]Loans and investments to private sector.
[b]At commercial banks.
[c]Preliminary estimates.

is about 65 percent of the total.* As Table 3.3 shows, the money supply is 20-25 percent of GNP and very likely will rise in the next few years. Structurally this is the level appropriate to a country with a per capita income of over $300,

---

*Derived from equations fitted to data for about 70 countries:

$$M/GNP = -6.57 + 4.74 \ln GNP/P$$
$$C/M = 114.31 - 11.38 \ln GNP/P$$

where M is the money supply, C is currency, P is population, and ln is the natural logarithm; J. Curley, "Financial Structures in Developing Countries," in Fiscal and Monetary Problems in Developing States, Proceedings of the Third Rehovoth Conference (New York, 1967).

TABLE 3.3

Relationships of Money Supply and Components to GNP
(VN$ billions)

Year	GNP	Currency	Demand Deposits	Money Supply	C/M	M/GNP
1960	81.8	11.2	5.5	16.7	67.0	20.4
1961	84.5	12.2	5.0	17.2	70.9	20.4
1962	93.8	13.2	6.3	19.5	67.8	20.8
1963	100.3	15.5	6.8	22.3	69.5	22.2
1964	114.3	19.0	8.4	27.4	69.3	24.0
1965	144.8	32.8	14.8	47.6	68.9	32.9
1966	240.9	46.0	17.4	63.4	72.6	26.3
1967	352.0	62.2	20.4	82.6	75.3	23.5

at which level more activities are monetized. This level of per capita income is three or four times that for Vietnam. The ratio is high because of the inflationary kind of finance that has had to be used during the war. Moreover, the ratio of currency to the money supply is exceedingly high, 75 percent in the most recent year tabulated, indicating how relatively little demand deposits (and time deposits) have grown. Currency is the most liquid of monetary or near-money assets, and the large amount of currency in circulation raises the possibility of a big increase in velocity in a short time, one that might be difficult to control. In the postwar period a redress of these monetary relationships will have to be made, but there is also the possibility that a different interest rate policy even now might operate to decrease the liquidity of the system.

INTEREST RATE REFORMS

The short-run requirements for policies to help control inflation and the longer-run development requirements for savings to finance productive investment are both dependent in part on an appropriate structure and level of interest rates. It is quite evident that neither set of requirements is met by the present structure of rates and that interest rate reform is perhaps the major problem for monetary policy.

The immediate problem of inflation control is not strictly our concern. It is the responsibility of officials of the government who must prepare policies to meet current needs. Moreover, the controls on inflation lie more in the area of tax and other fiscal measures than in the area of monetary and credit policies directly, though both kinds of measures are needed. Credit to the private sector has been limited to prevent undue inflation from that source.

It would also be desirable to raise interest rates now, to encourage the transfer of holdings of cash to deposits and other quasi-money. The purpose is to decrease the liquidity of the monetary system, which, as has been indicated above, is extremely liquid and, because of that fact, poses an inflationary threat. The interest rate structure is unrealistic and should be revised upwards.

It is possible that a sharp rise in interest rates would not be immediately effective. If confidence in future developments in the war and in the economy is shaken, the incentive provided by higher interest rates at any reasonable level of increase, may not be sufficient to cause people to part with the liquidity offered by holding currency. This may, of course, be the case now, but this condition probably will not continue at its present intensity and there is likely to be favorable effects on those individuals who do not feel so uncertain, who are willing to take somewhat greater risks, and who are attracted by the higher rates. Such groups exist particularly among commercial classes who hold substantial amounts of currency.

Since the interest rate is one of the prices in the economy, some may argue that an increase in this price will cause a rise in other prices, particularly of imported goods. But generally the interest cost is a small proportion of total cost and the effects of a rise in interest rates would be minimal. The rise in interest rates need not be equal across all kinds of loans and deposits. Through differential treatment the rates on deposits with varying maturities can be increased and the rates on loans of different kinds can be adjusted to a small increase. More is said on this point later in this section. Such adjustments would not have a serious effect on bank profits which now apparently run between 25 percent and 60 percent annually.

The stimulation of domestic savings to finance investment is necessary to prevent the gap between the two from hampering development programs or from throwing the burden increasingly on inflationary methods of finance. There are several ways that resources can be diverted from current use to capital use. One of these is through the inflationary process which tends to put funds into the hands of those who are likely to invest it. But inflationary methods of finance distort the economy and in general are self-defeating. The history of experience in a number of countries is evidence on this point and need not be reviewed here. Inflationary methods should not be relied upon for providing the funds needed for the development of Vietnam. This is not the same thing as saying that development can take place with strict price stability, since that normally is accomplished only with the most careful balancing of policies, but it does mean that no long-run consistent policies of deficit financing of investment and issue of new currency should be followed.

Through the raising of taxes and other revenue measures, the government may acquire resources (savings) for use in development projects, providing that current operating costs of the government are prevented from rising as fast (or faster) than revenues. The possibilities for raising revenues and government savings in the postwar period are discussed in Chapter 4. During the war condition, government savings are negative and are almost certain to remain so.

The level of interest rates on deposits and loans in Vietnam is summarized briefly in Table 3.4. Time deposit rates are graduated according to the period held but the differential is only 1 percent; the maximum allowable rate on time deposits is only 6 percent, and on savings deposits 4 percent. Since in the years 1966-68 the rate of increase of prices was 30 percent to 60 percent, the real rate of interest in Vietnam is highly negative. It is remarkable that time deposits have even held

TABLE 3.4

Structure of Interest Rates

Source of Interest	Rates Actually Applied	Maximum Rates Permitted
Deposits: commercial banks		
Demand deposits		
Under VN$300,000		2
Over VN$300,000	0.5 - 1.5	2
Time deposits		
1 to 3 months	3]	4
3 to 6 months	3.5]	
Over 6 months	4	6
Savings deposits		
Maximum VN$50,000	3	4
Over	2	4
Loans: commercial banks		
Secured loans	7 - 8	8
Unsecured loans	9 - 10	10
Agricultural Development Bank		
Short term (under 18 months)		
Marketing, mfg.	8 - 10	
Production	12	
Medium term (18 mos. -5 yrs.)	8	
Long term (over 5 years).	suspended	
Industrial Development Center	6.5	
Vietnam Development Bank	6.5	

at a steady level during this period and certainly they could not in such circumstances have been expected to rise.

Both Taiwan and Korea have, in the recent past, deliberately pursued a policy of raising interest rates on deposits and loans, as an anti-inflationary measure and to increase savings that could be channeled into productive investment. The experience of these two countries and the conditions that gave rise to the adoption of such policies are very relevant to the situation in Vietnam now, and are equally important to the establishment of interest rate policies for the development period.*

In 1949 and early 1950 Taiwan had a rapid increase in the money supply and prices, the former increasing almost tenfold between mid-1949 and mid-1950. Prices increased less rapidly but had almost tripled by mid-1951. The government in early 1950 attacked the inflation through a policy of paying high interest rates on time deposits. Certificates of deposit were issued for bank deposits with varying maturities. The first offering was for certificates of one-month maturity with an interest rate of 7 percent; at an annual rate this is 125 percent. The response of savers was rapid; time deposits rose eighteenfold in five months, and the price increases stopped at least for a time.

Over the next several years a number of refinements in the system were made. Certificates of deposit for three and six months, and one and two years were introduced. At first only one-month certificates were issued but as confidence was restored and the economy stabilized, certificates with longer maturities were issued and quickly accepted.

Initially the interest rates per month were quite high, for example, 4.0 percent on three-month certificates, 4.2 percent on six-month; but these gradually declined, and within a few

---

*Cf. R. J. Irvine and R. F. Emery, "Interest Rates as an Anti-Inflationary Instrument in Taiwan" (May 20, 1966), and R. F. Emery, "The Korean Interest Rate Reform of September, 1965" (October 3, 1966), mimeographed papers issued through the Division of International Finance, Board of Governors of the Federal Reserve System.

years the rates were .85 percent on three-month and 1.35 percent on six-month certificates, with somewhat higher rates for one and two years. The structure of rates was adjusted to the set of maturities, the lowest rates on the short-term certificates and higher rates on those with longer maturity. At one point bonds were issued with interest rates up to 18 percent. These bonds matured in two and a half years; no long-term securities (over five years) were issued because the objectives were achieved with the short maturities, but it is evident that the market was prepared to absorb long-term bonds if they were issued.

Korea followed the lead of Taiwan in pursuing a high interest rate policy to stimulate savings. In 1965 Korea dramatically raised the rate on time deposits from 15 percent to 34.5 percent; savings deposit rates were raised from 3.6 percent to 12 percent and the rates on all other types of deposits (except demand deposit rates) were similarly adjusted. Loan rates were also raised but not all types of loans were treated the same. Loan rates for export trade and on rice liens were left at lower levels; the discount rates on commercial bills was raised from 10-15 percent to 28 percent. These policies were successful in stimulating savings and did not have noticeable unfavorable effects on investment.

The lessons of the Taiwan and Korea experience are important ones for Vietnam to learn. They did not accept the standard doctrine on interest rates, that low rates are a necessity or that 6 percent is sacred, and they broke through to levels that caused substantial increases in savings. The interest rates used were high by usual rates in less-developed countries, but these rates were steadily decreased as time went on. At first short-term certificates of deposit were issued but gradually people learned to have confidence in longer maturities, and they were actively subscribed. Commercial bank profits were protected, in part by the central banks which paid interest on reserves or otherwise paid a subsidy to offset the potential losses from the high deposit rates. But loan rates were raised, though not uniformly. Loan rates for productive investment in agriculture and industry were not increased very much.

As an anti-inflationary measure now and as a prelude to a postwar program to raise savings significantly, it is suggested that the government undertake an interest rate reform.

The actual details and operating procedures are matters for the National Bank and the appropriate ministries to decide, in conjunction with the commercial banking system, but the general features of such a reform cover the following steps:

1. The issuance of three-month or six-month certificates of deposit carrying an attractive interest rate. (Specific suggestions on the rate are contained in a Joint Development Council study). It might be prudent to test the market by first trying a short-maturity certificate. The exact terms to be offered are best left to the National Bank in consultation with others. The situation in Vietnam is different from the situations in Korea and Taiwan, and a longer-term certificate may be successful. The terms should be such that the probability of achieving a significant volume of certificates by individuals and business is high.

2. Plans should be made for additional issues, assuming the first test is successful. Later issues can probably be longer maturing and with lower interest rates, if the Taiwan and Korea experience is any guide. Ultimately a range of short-term and long-term certificates can be employed as a tool of monetary policy.

3. Loan rates on most classes of loans by the commercial banking system should be approximately doubled, but possibly with discount rates on commercial paper increased more. Preferential treatment might be given to loan rates of the ADB. They might be retained at present levels or raised a nominal amount. The loan rates of the VDB and IDC should be raised to roughly preserve their present relationship to commercial bank rates. The appropriate mix of rates among classes of loans and institutions is one requiring very careful study.

4. The effects of such changes in both deposit and loan rates on commercial bank profits and incentives should be watched. Care is needed not to create windfall profits for banks that are turning over their money rapidly in the finance of imports. For that reason some narrowing of the margins between loan rates and deposit rates is probably justified. Bank profits have been very satisfactory, to say the least.

5. Consideration is needed of the appropriate rate on Treasury bonds and the 20 percent requirement on commercial

banks for purchase of such bonds. Initially it may be unnecessary to adjust these, but an analysis is needed of the interaction of the suggested interest rate reforms and these elements.

The suggested program of action outlined above is intended to move in the direction of a monetary policy more effective both in controlling inflation through reduction of liquidity and in establishing the basis for more intensive cultivation of savings.

CREATION OF A MONEY AND CAPITAL MARKET

In the postwar period there will be a need to establish expanded facilities for a money and capital market. By doing so the National Bank can have an additional means through which to exercise monetary policies, and such a market can help to get wider distribution of government securities and, later on, securities of quasi-public and private companies. The creation of such a market probably cannot be instituted now. As has been indicated previously, the commercial banking system and the set of other financial institutions are relatively underdeveloped, and it will take some time to strengthen them. However, in the Saigon-Cholon area there is a fairly heavy concentration of banks which presumably would form the nucleus for such an undertaking.

In the past there was a very informal money and capital market known as the Lefebvre market, and some say it still operates. The dealers and brokers met informally in the coffee houses around Ham Nghi and Vo Di Nguy. Apparently this informal market has served the limited purposes needed, and possibly the participants would be included in a more formal market built around the commercial banking system. The initial purpose of a money market should be to sell and distribute government short-term securities and to broaden the base for them. For example at the present time about 95 percent of treasury bills are sold to commercial banks and only 5 percent to other kinds of purchasers. It will be desirable as part of monetary policy to have a wider range of short-term government securities with differing maturities and interest rates. It must be emphasized that the creation of such a market will not be successful without the interest rate reforms that have been recommended above. At the present low interest rates, it is unlikely that there would be much of a market for government securities. Treasury bonds must be purchased by the commercial banks up to a fixed percentage of their deposits. Later on, with the expansion of financial institutions and credit instruments--and with interest rate reform--it should be possible to remove the requirement on the commercial banks for fixed purchase of treasury bonds and to permit them wider latitude in arranging their portfolios.

Ultimately the money market should be a means through which the National Bank could market a wide variety of treasury bills and bonds, which will strengthen the hand of the National Bank in monetary policy. Moreover at some time in the future it undoubtedly will be desirable for the ADB and the VDB to float bonds for the purpose of adding to their reserves to be used for loans to agriculture and industry. It may be noted, for example, that the Philippines Development Bank has issued bonds which are convertible into the preferred and common stock of private corporations in which the Philippines Development Bank has acquired an equity. This is one means to obtain wider distribution of the ownership of private securities, and it is recommended for Vietnam as well.

Normally the establishment of a primary money market built around the commercial banks and selected other financial institutions results in the creation of a secondary market involving other kinds of purchasers, including private individuals. The same should be expected in Vietnam, with a consequent strengthening of the whole money market.

Stock issues by private companies in Vietnam typically take two forms. For small private companies, the stock is sold to relations and friends. Larger companies have issued their stock in Paris and their shares are traded on the Paris Bourse. Some changes will be required in stock issuing practices in order to broaden the sale of such securities; for example, nominal stock will have to be denominated in a way to make it marketable. Initially the sale of stock of private companies would be through the commercial banking system, but as demand and supply conditions warrant, a more formal securities market might be established. There was in the past a draft decree for such a market, but it was not implemented. The necessary condition for the successful establishment of a securities market is that there be sufficient bid and asked prices so that price ranges do not fluctuate widely; otherwise there is a lack of confidence in the effectiveness of the market.

It is expected that a strong and persistent element of investment in the postwar period will be in housing and home construction. At present there is no efficient home mortgage market, and no institution to mobilize funds and make loans for these purposes. This is a lack that should be corrected. The creation of a special home mortgage bank, patterned roughly on the ADB, is the appropriate way to meet the problem. It could have features both of a mortgage bank and a savings and loan association, and should have the latitude and flexibility to set mortgage terms to stimulate home building. Care should be taken to prevent the bank from being used simply to finance the speculative building of apartment houses in Saigon. This is relatively simple to do through direct regulation or loan policy. The bank should also make every effort to stimulate savings deposits so as to acquire funds for loans. Initially funds from the government are needed to give it a start. Plans can be made now for the creation of a home mortgage bank.

It should also be pointed out that the growth of insurance and similar types of financial business will create funds that will seek investment in government or private securities. They should be expected to help stabilize such money and capital markets.

These suggestions do not have a high priority by comparison to other development programs, particularly in the early postwar phases when the economy is making a transition to peace, but some preliminary plans can be made by the National Bank in cooperation with the commercial banks so that the steps to create such markets are thoroughly understood and are ready for implementation.

EXCHANGE RATE POLICY IN THE FUTURE

It is the responsibility of the monetary authorities of a country to maintain a reasonable equilibrium in the balance of payments through exchange rate policies and appropriate credit and fiscal measures. Equilibrium is not synonymous with a neat balance of receipts and expenditures, but is defined as a condition without severe pressure on the exchange rate and reserves, without concurrent internal inflationary effects, and without rapidly mounting debt service charges. The definition is necessarily somewhat inexact, since an equilibrium in the balance of payments can be maintained with varying levels of these elements.

The war has, of course, badly unbalanced the accounts. Exports have dropped to very low levels and imports have risen drastically, till now imports are roughly 25 to 30 times the amount of exports. The large deficit in the balance of trade is met through favorable services payments (that is, spending of troops and contractors) and external aid. In fact, imports have been used as a primary anti-inflationary measure, designed to sop up purchasing power and hold down prices. They have been allowed to rise virtually without limit. Obviously this set of conditions cannot continue in the indefinite future. The level of imports will drop and the level of exports must rise, but external aid will still be required for some years. These issues are discussed elsewhere in this study. We are concerned here with the question of whether the current exchange rate of VN$118 to US$1 is likely to be viable in the future.

The free market rate (as represented by the Hong Kong rate) has in recent times been 50 to 70 percent above the official rate, and although it has fluctuated somewhat in response to favorable and unfavorable market conditions in Vietnam, it has shown no signs of eliminating the discount from the official rate, particularly if inflationary finance continues.

The "real" exchange rate has of course deteriorated a great deal since 1966. The "real" rate is the official rate of 118 deflated by an appropriate price index, normally the wholesale price index. In this sense the real rate (as of December, 1968, with a wholesale price index of 405) is only about 30, which has the effect of further stimulating imports and, in normal circumstances, depressing exports. Thus the effect of an overvalued rate is to unbalance foreign trade to an appreciable extent. This is further evidence that an appropriate adjustment of exchange rate policy is required.

At present levels of national income and output and current price ratios of domestic and imported goods, the piaster is almost surely an overvalued currency at an exchange rate of VN$118. At these levels, the demand for foreign exchange exceeds the supply even if the distortions brought on by the war are eliminated. Only if there were a drastic scaling down of the whole structure of prices and wages, and of incomes, is it likely that demand and supply would be equated somewhere near the price of VN$118, and such a structural deflation would almost surely be disastrous for the country. Some readjustments in the wage-price structure are needed, but not to the extent implied by the present exchange rate.

Devaluation is a painful action to contemplate at any time. As a practical matter the action must be safeguarded with controls over capital and credit to prevent capital flight and bank withdrawals in anticipation of the action. In retrospect the devaluation of 1966 appears both necessary and successful for its time, and in the postwar period a further devaluation is required. Since it is more damaging to confidence in the economy to have numerous adjustments, either formal devaluations or de facto ones, the objective of exchange rate policy in the future should be to make a once-and-for-all adjustment that can be maintained and that will contribute effectively to equilibrium in the foreign exchange market at a level consistent with development needs.

A policy of allowing the rate to fluctuate freely and find its own level through market forces would increase speculative activities and decrease confidence in the conduct of monetary management. Vietnam cannot afford this kind of policy. An alternative, of successive adjustments at intervals -- the so-called "creeping peg" requires a degree of monetary management and a delicacy that are difficult to achieve in normal circumstances, much less the present ones. In the future this alternative should be explored but for now, a policy of fixing a rate which can be maintained (even if this later needs to be changed) is preferable. At least in the short run it does not give rise to expectations of further rate changes as a regular matter.

It is precarious to try to estimate the extent of the devaluation that is needed without knowing how and when peace will come and the levels of incomes and finance at that time. An adjustment in the official rate of VN$118 is needed to bring about reasonable equality in demands and supplies of foreign exchange, after making allowances for some natural shrinkage in imports, an expansion of export through direct investment in specific export industries, and no serious postwar deflation in incomes.

The perequation tax, which was introduced to equate import prices of U.S. goods and those from other markets, is equivalent to multiple exchange rates in practice. Chapter 4 argues the needs for customs duties reform to simplify the system and to provide appropriate incentives and revenues. The perequation tax is a cumbersome, complex addition to the system of import duties and probably should be abandoned. If that is done, the exchange rate should be adjusted to take account of the average effect of the tax.

In short, an exchange rate adjustment will be required in Vietnam. The effects of such an adjustment in stimulating exports should be highly beneficial to future development, and the dampening effect on imports is equally welcome. The problem is one of timing, of choosing the appropriate rate, and, most importantly, of mobilizing all other policies--monetary, fiscal, and direct incentives to production--to prevent an internal inflation or at least to minimize it. This calls for careful planning and a firm hand in applying the measures.

The alternative to devaluation is reliance on complicated regulations, licenses, and controls on imports, special subsidies to exports, and a whole range of measures to control internal prices. And the likelihood of success is very small indeed. At best it would simply postpone the inevitable at a cost of introducing further distortions in the economy. Vietnam is now a high cost economy, in contrast to other Asian countries. A devaluation is virtually the only means to redress the balance, since wholesale deflation is ruled out. We believe the adjustment of exchange rate policy is of the greatest importance to the future health of the country.

It is far more injurious to have an overvalued currency than a somewhat undervalued one. The latter provides incentives for export-driven growth and can hardly be viewed by other countries as unfair competitive devaluation. What is needed in Vietnam is a stable rate that will contribute to confidence and to incentives for development investment. Preliminary plans need to be made now to determine the likely level that will be established under some alternative sets of circumstances.

CHAPTER 4 FISCAL POLICY

It is sometimes said that a primary problem of a developing economy that is starting from a low level of income and output is to adopt policies to transfer resources from private consumption to the public sector to create infrastructure in roads, ports, power, and those social goods that are necessary for other productive investment to be effective. This characterization emphasizes the importance of public sector investment programs in supplying basic capital needs and in providing guidance to the private sector. Second, it indicates the necessity of acquiring resources from the private sector through an efficient tax system. Raising government revenues through taxes and determining the level and direction of government spending are the two sides of fiscal policy. They are the specific subject of discussion in this chapter, and are of central importance in forming a development strategy for the postwar period.

Guidelines for future expenditure programs by the government are considered, both for the first few years after the end of the war and for a longer development period. As will be seen, there are some rather severe limitations on what may be accomplished, limitations primarily deriving from the war itself. In the following two sections we consider the sources of government revenues, first the internal tax system and second, the special problems involved in taxes on foreign trade (customs and similar duties). Suggestions are made for reform to improve the capability of the system to provide needed revenues both now and in the future. The final section discusses the budget as a management tool for evaluating government expenditure programs; suggestions are made for ways to improve expenditure decisions through a better use of the budget.

GUIDELINES FOR GOVERNMENT EXPENDITURES

When a development program is definitely undertaken by Vietnam, the direction and purpose of fiscal policy, both in the generation of tax revenues and in the type of expenditures, will change greatly. The war has blunted and to some extent simplified the role of fiscal policy. It is not now concerned with directing resources to a multitude of competitive uses with the objective of securing a rapid growth of output and income, nor is it primarily concerned with obtaining revenues in a way that will not disturb incentives to invest in productive enterprise. The expenditures are simply directed to supporting the war; funds are too short to think of economic development at this time. Normal peacetime expenditures of government are postponed and fixed capital is allowed to depreciate without repair. In Vietnam there has been a ban on expenditures that do not contribute directly to support of the war and most of the decrease has fallen on public investment in the civilian sector. The sacrifice has often been more apparent than real, for in a number of cases expenditures by the military have picked up responsibility for civilian programs. Military spending for the improvement of highways, harbors, wharves, airports, and the railroad have substituted for expenditures from the civilian budget on these items. The reason is, of course, that the development and maintenance of facilities are essential to military needs. The prime example is the improvement of the highway system which is being carried out in a program of complete renovation that will be completed by 1972. Military spending now reduces the need for civilian spending in the postwar period, and much of it is being done with U.S. military funds. The results of such programs are of genuine benefit to the economy, and in terms of the civilian budget the burden of investment in fixed capital is greatly reduced but at the same time some additional problems are created.

Military priorities and requirements are not the same as civilian requirements in the postwar period. Some excess capacity has been built, particularly in airports, seaports, and the railroad. In some cases this is not serious, but maintenance and operating expenses on the fixed investment are often heavy and the decision to let some of the capacity deliberately deteriorate or to write it off entirely is difficult to make. The marginal expense of keeping the capacity in working order often seems small and there is a strong temptation to keep it in operation, even though projections of future demand do not seem to justify it. This is one of the special expenditure problems of adjusting from a wartime to a peacetime economy and it is particularly relevant to Vietnam. Budget limitations will not permit all of the capacity in infrastructure in the transportation sector to be maintained in the future. It is fortunate, however, that through foreign aid and U.S. military expenditures, these facilities were constructed, for the country will enter the postwar period in a much more favorable position in infrastructure even though there is imbalance in the system. Military expenditures have resulted in overbuilding for postwar civilian needs in some areas, while in other areas of lesser interest to the military future investment by public authorities must be heavier. The picture of future investment needs in infrastructure is thus not one of uniformity across all areas.

The dominance of government expenditures that support the war effort is amply illustrated in Table 4.1, which employs a classification emphasizing the differences in four functions of government: general administration, such as the conduct of foreign affairs and finance; support of the war; economic development; social development. This does not imply that all activities of government do not support the war effort, however indirectly, but the classification in the table is meant to illustrate the varying objectives of government. In the postwar period, activities in economic and social development are expected to increase.

In 1967 war and war-related expenditures accounted for over three-quarters of total government expenditures. The proportion has been rising steadily for a number of years and may continue to inch up, but there is almost surely a limit to how far this can go. There are minimal levels of performance in the other groups necessary to prevent a breakdown in functions. It is unnecessary to try to estimate what these various limits may be. It is sufficient to point out that the present percentage of government expenditures devoted to support the war is at the upper end of the experience of any country in any other war.

Of course the absolute amounts of expenditures in all categories may continue to rise and at a rate faster than the increase in the gross national product. In 1960 government

TABLE 4.1

Government Expenditures[a] Program Patterns, 1960 and 1967

Government Function	Expenditures Percent 1967	1960
General administration[b]	6.2	14.5
National defense[c]	77.0	59.2
Economic development[d]	5.6	15.5
Social development[e]	11.1	10.8

[a]Excludes common expenditures and U.S. aid construction and development which did not exist in 1960.

[b]Includes General Government and Ministries of Foreign Affairs, Justice, Special Commissariat for Administration, Finance.

[c]Includes Defense, Information and Open Arms, Revolutionary Development, War Veterans, National Security.

[d]Includes Public Works, Communication and Transportation, Commerce and Industry, Agriculture, Planning and Development.

[e]Includes Youth, Education, Health, Labor, Social Welfare.

expenditures were about 19 percent of the GNP and then rose steadily to over 35 percent in 1965. After the devaluation of 1966 the percentage fell to about 27 percent but in 1968 showed signs of rising again to about 30 percent. By comparison, total government expenditures as a percent of GNP in Korea, the Philippines, and Thailand are between 12 percent and 20 percent. The distinction must be made between this ratio and the ratio of internally generated revenues to GNP. Only about 40 percent of total expenditures are met by revenues collected through the tax system. The rest comes from foreign aid and deficit finance (that is, advances from the central bank). In a later section of this chapter, on tax reform, it is pointed out that Vietnam should have done better than this in financing the war.

In Table 4.1 expenditures for the year 1960 are shown to provide a contrast with a time when relative expenditures on economic and social development were higher. There is no year in the recent past that has not been dominated by defense expenditures, but the year 1960 represents something of a change, indicating the directions that can be taken in the postwar period. Although relative expenditures for 1960 on economic development are much higher than for 1967, those on social development are virtually identical, a fact that is somewhat surprising.

The division of government expenditures by the economic character of those expenditures reveals some additional information on which to project expenditures in the postwar period. This material is shown in Table 4.2. Two out of every three piasters that the government spends from the budget goes to pay the wages and salaries of civil servants and the military. And half of all expenditures are for the military alone. This percentage has also been rising in the last few years. Public investment, on the other hand, is only 5 percent of total expenditures, or about 1-2 percent of the gross national product. Almost all of this is for the repair of public buildings. Expenditures on other areas of infrastructure are virtually nil, and this suggests that even the maintenance of facilities has been neglected. This is an abysmally low figure and indicates that public investment is indeed a casualty of the war. In fact, net fixed investment (that is, gross investment minus capital consumption allowances and increases in stocks) as a percentage of the net national product is now only 5 percent. It is not only public investment that is depressed; private investment is not in much better shape. No country can grow satisfactorily with a net investment rate of 5 percent. The figure must be raised to two to three times that amount. Clearly the rejuvenation of public investment expenditures and the stimulation of private investment expenditures are major economic tasks for the postwar period.

TABLE 4.2

Budget Expenditures by Economic Character[a]

Economic Category		Expenditure (Percent)
Wages and salaries		68.5
Civil	17.1	
Military	51.4	
Supplies and services		10.8
Transfers		14.5
Investment		5.0
Other		1.2
	Total	100.0

[a]Based on 1969 budget estimates.

The materials in Tables 4.1 and 4.2 indicate some of the conditions for the increase of public investment. Quite obviously an increase in investment expenditures on economic and social development is directly dependent on the level of expenditures on the military. If these fall because of partial demobilization of forces, the funds that are freed can be channeled to development projects, but care is needed to insure that they do not get absorbed in increased expenditures on government administration. If military spending does not decrease, there is little immediate hope of expanding public investment. The ways that are open to do this, in these circumstances, are not very attractive. The government could attempt, for instance, to commandeer private resources and direct their use through such devices as forced savings or a capital levy. While increases in revenues through the tax system are desirable, such drastic measures as these are probably politically infeasible. Direct intervention and central control of private resources is not the path to take. Second, the government could attempt to acquire additional resources through deliberate inflationary finance. At several places in this study we have indicated the defects of this process; ultimately it is self-defeating and leads to chaotic economic conditions. Third, the government could rely purely on foreign aid for infrastructure investment. This is a path that will be followed in any case, but it is a short-term solution that cannot be indefinitely continued. Moreover, this simply provides the foreign exchange component; it does not solve the problem of local currency needs for the project.

The large-scale restoration of public investment for development, consistent with the objective of achieving independence from concessionary foreign aid, is achievable only when the budget can be turned around and funds transferred from military expenditures to development programs. This will not occur in the transition years immediately following the end of the war, but it is entirely practical after that. The political risks of nondevelopment of the economy are considerable.

If we turn to the period when such transfers can be made, there is a question of the relationship between the fixed investment cost of public projects and the operating cost associated with them. When a school is built, operating costs of teachers' salaries, supplies, and so on, also rise, and the pattern of government expenditure is altered. Table 4.3 compares investment and operating (current) expenditures for Vietnam and four other Asian countries. The patterns are rather different in at least several cases, and the dominance of defense expenditures in Vietnam is again apparent. Public investment expenditures are relatively high in Korea, Malaysia, and Thailand, less so in the Philippines, but all are much higher than in Vietnam. The size of the percentages under social services indicate how rapidly these can grow in a developing country that is spending on education, health, and social welfare. A large part of the expenditures is for such personnel as teachers, public health nurses and doctors, and social workers, but there are also government officials in the ministries and administrators who manage the programs. The distinction is between operating personnel and overhead personnel. Current expenditures sometimes grow at the expense of investment expenditures because of a tendency to load the system with overhead personnel and the efficiency of the system

TABLE 4.3

Comparison of Current Investment and Expenditures in Five Asian Countries

(Percent of Total Expenditures[a])

Country	Current Expenditures			
	Defense	Economic Services	Social Services	Investment[b]
Vietnam (1966)	61.6	7.5	12.0	7.4
Korea (1967)	24.9	3.6	17.7	33.9
Malaysia (1967)	14.3	3.2	20.0	34.4
Philippines (1967-68)	13.2	15.3	32.0	16.8
Thailand (1967-68)	15.4	8.2	17.8	30.6

[a]Percentages do not add to 100 because the table does not show the percent for other current expenditures (general administration) and contributions to provincial and local governments, which are not always identified.

[b]Includes direct capital outlay plus net loans and advances.

Source: UN, Economic Commission for Asia and the Far East, Economic Survey of Asia and the Far East 1967, Table 36, pp. 200-201.

decreases. That seems to have happened in the Philippines, and Vietnam should learn from it.

It is a basic principle of public investment that current expenditures should not be allowed to rise more rapidly than total expenditures; otherwise the ability to finance investment is impaired. In Vietnam public savings are negative and will continue that way until the internal revenue system is strengthened and revenues from domestic sources rise. But difficulties with public investment programs are increased if current budgetary expenditures move upward at a high rate. This is a problem for responsible fiscal policy in the development years ahead.

In the chapters in Part II, which are concerned with separate economic sectors and geographic regions, specific investment programs of both a public and a private kind are described and cost estimates are attached to most of them. In general these are order-of-magnitude estimates, though in some cases they are more precise than this. These programs do not add up to a complete and comprehensive list of projects for public investment, for in many cases the analysis of the alternatives and of what is feasible is subject to many uncertainties. There is surely no shelf of blueprints of projects, though a beginning is being made and in 1970 the Joint Development Group will emphasize project identification and evaluation so that better guidelines for decision can be provided. It would be misleading to set forth annual levels for public investment with priorities and time schedules. In the first years after the war, the ability of the government to undertake public investment will be sharply limited, but should improve within five years and improve rapidly in the second five years. Indeed, a main limitation lies in the capacity to absorb projects, to do project planning and actually start implementation. There are physical limitations on manpower, management, and equipment, and these take time to overcome.

With these qualifications in mind, a brief recapitulation of investment programs may be useful. Costs are expressed in U.S. dollars but cover both foreign exchange and local currency. For many of the programs considered the split of currencies required is roughly equal, but for many industrial projects the foreign exchange component is higher than this and for typical construction projects it is lower.

1. Refugee resettlement: In the first two years after the war, refugee resettlement and bringing back into production abandoned lands will be a major undertaking. Of the estimated 1.4 million refugees, about half are in the five northern provinces. Program costs initially of about $80 million for family resettlement are foreseen and, in later years, up to $250 million additional for movement of people to new lands to improve their economic prospects may be needed.

2. Rural rehabilitation: The costs of rehabilitating of hamlets, helping to revive agricultural production, final pacification, and provision of credit are roughly estimated to add up to $200 million, some of it in the form of loans rather than investment.

3. Infrastructure: Estimates of infrastructure needs (exclusive of education, public health, and social welfare) are shown in Table 4.4. The amounts that can be absorbed are limited by several factors. To complete many of the programs (for example, electric power to the provinces) will take many times the funds shown.

4. Agriculture, forestry, fishing: Irrigation programs in the five northern provinces could come to $190 million (see Chapter 12) and to lesser amounts in the Central Highlands. The inventory of timber and replanting up to 10,000 hectares would come to $1 - $2 million within five years and expand thereafter. Public expenditures on fish land facilities, produce markets, research, and service functions would add $5 - $7 million in five years and might be much greater than this depending on the extent of public assistance in major agricultural projects (see Chapter 7). It is likely that public assistance, both direct outlay and provision of credit, will be needed to renovate agriculture.

5. Industrial development: Chapter 9 describes certain major industrial projects in chemical fertilizers, petroleum refining, wood pulp, and veneer mills and other wood-based products where public participation in investment would probably be desirable.

6. The Mekong Delta: The Mekong Delta is the largest integrated project in the country. It is expected that the foreign exchange costs will be financed externally but local currency costs could ultimately be in the hundreds of billions

TABLE 4.4

Estimates of Infrastructure Funding Needs[a]

	Foreign Exchange US$ Mill.	Local Currency VN$ Mill.	Total US$ Mill.
Highways	90.0	9,440	170.0
Ports	9.8	1,735	24.5
Waterways	2.5	295	5.0
Airports	3.0	236	5.0
Sanitation	34.5	5,070	77.5
Telecomm.	21.0	1,062	30.0
Power	122.5	6,195	175.0
Housing	51.0	14,200	170.0
Total	334.3	38,133	657.0

[a]Exclusive of railroad (funding completed), and of education, public health, and social welfare.

of piasters, though in the first few phases it will be only several hundred million. The projected costs could accelerate quickly.

7. Education, public health: Specific program costs in education are not available at this time but a target for expenditure is at least 4 percent of gross national product with 40 percent of that in fixed investment. The programs for other social services are still being formulated.

The details now available are discussed in succeeding chapters but the indications are that the demands for public investment during development will mount rapidly.

GOVERNMENT REVENUES AND TAX REFORM

Strengthening the base of government revenues from taxes and increasing the yields to provide the funds needed for public investment projects are two broad objectives of public policy.* Tax reform is a major instrument for attaining these objectives; therefore, it is desirable to consider the specific goals of tax reform before giving attention to the tax system itself.

The first, and undoubtedly most important, tax policy goal for postwar Vietnam is for the tax system to facilitate economic growth. This is so incontrovertible that it need not be demonstrated or debated. Also evident is that Vietnam will attempt to induce growth through national economic planning, which will involve both macro-planning and the identification of specific public investment projects.

There is some room for disagreement concerning the relative emphasis which should be given to public as compared with private investment in a development plan, but no one would dispute that the government in Vietnam will have to play an important role in the process of capital formation.

---

*This discussion of revenues and tax reform is based on Tax Policies for the Post-War Development of Vietnam, Working Paper No. 28 (JDG, August, 1968).

Besides the need to provide economic infrastructure in such forms as transportation, power, and flood control, there are extensive social demands in education, health, and housing. If economic growth is established as the paramount economic goal, the most important tax policy goal is to provide the domestic revenue resources necessary to finance target levels of public investment. This means, in effect, that taxation must be used to allocate resources from private consumption to public investment.

A second goal of taxation is efficiency: the tax system should contribute to an efficient use and allocation of resources within the private sphere for maximum output and growth. As a broad generalization, efficiency in the use of private resources means that the tax system should maximize private savings and investment and curtail conspicuous consumption and speculative activities. To be more specific: monopoly should be restricted and capital markets should be encouraged, savings should be channeled into high priority and socially desirable uses, both internal and external trade should be facilitated, foreign investment should be encouraged, and spending on luxury goods (whether manufactured internally or imported) should be discouraged. In view of Vietnam's past predilections, emphasis should be given to the development of an open economy and to the encouragement of foreign investment.

A third goal of taxation is its function in contributing to a better distribution of income. Although experience demonstrates that government expenditure policy is a more effective instrument for redistributive purposes than taxation, the effect of a progressive tax structure in making the market-determined distribution of income more equal is of such importance that few developed countries are without a strong progressive system of direct taxes on income and wealth. Furthermore, it could be argued that the tax system should play this role, in any case, if only to make an adjustment for the imbalances in the distribution of income and wealth which have occurred during conditions of wartime inflation and market distortions.

The last goal of taxation is virtually self-evident: The tax system should be easy to comply with and to enforce. A tax system in a developing country in general should be more simple than in a developed country, yet the kind of tax system now used in Vietnam is so complicated that it could be administered only with the most highly trained personnel. A complicated tax system is also difficult for honest taxpayers to comply with, and easy for the dishonest to evade and corrupt.

There is no doubt that the war, in general, has been debilitating on both compliance and enforcement. Civil service staffs have been stripped of manpower, and some of the men remaining in the service have been tempted into corruption by the reduction of their real incomes by inflation. Even after the war, progress in tax administration will be slow and gradual, principally because tax administration is a service, and there are limits to the productivity increases which can be introduced in a service sector in the short run. Actually, the most hopeful approach to improving both compliance and enforcement is through the indirect one of simplifying the tax laws so that they are more amenable to administration.

There is one major conflict that arises in the achievement of these several goals. Direct taxes--those on income and wealth--may be used for the dual purpose of fulfilling the allocative goal of providing additional revenues for public investment purposes as well as for promoting a more equal distribution of income. On the other hand, these are the very taxes, at lease if given too strong an emphasis, which can well blunt incentives to work, save, and invest.

Actually, much can be done to reconcile these issues at the level of tax policy implementation by emphasizing areas of direct taxation where the impact of taxes on incentives is more remote and more likely to restrict socially less desirable uses of income and wealth. For example, it would be possible in Vietnam to give greater emphasis to death and gift taxes, real property taxation (especially on residences), and the taxation of capital gains as realized at death under the income tax. On the other hand, the need for incentives can be acknowledged by a moderate approach to the taxation of corporations, especially those newly formed and in risky endeavors, and by restricting the highest marginal rate of the personal income tax to 50 percent. In any case, in a developing country a rate higher than this is seldom collectible anyway.

Tax Revenues: Past and Future

The revenues of the central government of Vietnam include both budgetary and extrabudgetary receipts. Budgetary receipts may be grouped into five main categories: (1) internal or domestic taxes; (2) other miscellaneous revenues (principally receipts from government agencies); (3) customs duties; (4) foreign aid; and (5) advances (deficit financing) from the National Bank. Extrabudgetary receipts were particularly high in 1966, approximately VN$20 billion, but after successive transfers of these receipts to the budget in 1967 and 1968, there remained a total of only about VN$2 billion for 1968 as compared to budgetary receipts of about VN$95 billion.

Relative orders of magnitude for the several categories of budgetary revenues in the 1967 national budget may be obtained from the following percentage breakdown: internal taxes, 25.9 percent; other revenues, 20.0 percent; customs duties, 21.0 percent; and foreign aid, 33.0 percent (see Table 4.5). Nevertheless, while these percentages have prevailed, it is quite clear that both customs and foreign aid will be reduced in the postwar period, and internal taxes will become a more important source of revenues. It is precisely for that reason that tax policy for the postwar period is so vitally important.

Typically, the Vietnamese budget operates at a deficit even after foreign aid financing. The deficit was relatively low, about VN$2.0 billion, in 1962, but was about VN$21.5 billion in 1965 and VN$20 billion in 1966. With an upsurge in foreign aid in 1967, the deficit fell in that year to VN$2.2 billion. Deficits are financed through a combination of drawing down Treasury balances, the issuance of Treasury bonds, and direct National Bank advances.

The corollary of a relatively low contribution of internal taxes to the budget is, of course, a predominant reliance on foreign trade taxes. And since American aid is the predominant source of funding for Vietnamese imports, this aid not only gives rise to most taxes on imports, but it also provides direct support of the budget through the generation of counterpart funds. These two sources, together with other aid-related revenues, amounted to about two-thirds of budgetary revenues in 1967. Thus, Vietnam under wartime conditions represents an extreme and very atypical case of the exposed economy, with the foreign trade sector disproportionately large, and taxes based on this sector (whatever may be their form or variety) actually representing the dominant element in the fiscal system.

Tables 4.5 and 4.6 provide a quantitative insight into the performance of the Vietnamese revenue system during the seven years, 1960-67. Referring to Table 4.5, first, it may be observed that budget revenues, exclusive of advances by the National Bank, increased only from 16.8 percent to 18.5 percent of the GNP from 1960 to 1967, and this increase is attributable only to the last three years of the period.* Considering that Vietnam was engaged in a large-scale war during the whole of the seven years under review, public revenues expanded much less than might have been expected, and certainly much less than would have been desirable as an anti-inflationary measure. Without question, Vietnam had the technical capacity to increase revenues considerably, especially those on imports, but it would be cavalier to take the position that a fully responsible and enlightened fiscal policy would have been possible under conditions in which governmental institutions were often fragile and insecure.

Table 4.5 also shows a process of slow erosion on the part of the internal tax system. From 1960 to 1967, internal taxes fell from 44.7 percent to 25.9 percent of budgetary revenues, and from 7.5 percent to 4.8 percent of the GNP. Offsetting this reduction, there was an increase in taxes on imports, reflected in relative increases in customs duties, in foreign aid (counterpart funds), and in "other revenues." The latter category, which is normally the receipts of administrative agencies, experienced a sharp increase from 1964 to 1967 due to the inclusion within this item of a perequation tax (an import duty) imposed in 1966. Thus, if all the taxes on imports are aggregated, they approximated two-thirds of budgetary revenues in 1967 as compared with only 47 percent in 1960.

There are several possible explanations for the relative decrease in internal taxes as a group during the period from 1964 to 1967. One could be the regressivity of the rate structures, resulting in a negative correlation with income.

---

*By comparison, revenues as a percentage of the national income in 1962 were at a level of 20.5 percent in Cambodia and 24.5 percent in Ceylon. In all other Asian countries, this ratio was below 20 percent; see Angel Q. Yoingco and Ruben F. Trinidad, Fiscal Systems and Practices in Asian Countries (New York: Praeger, 1968), pp. 255-256.

TABLE 4.5

Budget Revenues, 1960, 1964, and 1967[a]
(Amounts in VN$ Millions)

Source of Revenue	1960			1964			1967[b]		
	Amount	Percent of Total	Percent of GNP	Amount	Percent of Total	Percent of GNP	Amount	Percent of Total	Percent of GNP
Internal taxes	6,184.4	44.7	7.5	6,198.0	31.9	5.4	16,898.2	25.9	4.8
Customs	1,990.6	14.4	2.4	5,199.0	26.8	4.5	13,731.0	21.0	3.9
Foreign aid	4,480.5	32.4	5.5	6,359.4	32.8	5.6	21,577.3	33.0	6.1
Other revenues	1,177.2	8.5	1.4	1,649.0	8.5	1.4	13,085.0	20.0	3.7
Totals	13,832.7	100.0	16.8	19,405.4	100.0	15.9	65,291.5	99.9	18.5

[a]Excluding deficit financing of VN $12.6 billion in 1964 and VN $2.2 billion in 1967.

[b]Data are for collections as of March 31, 1968, which are close to final collections for 1967.

Sources: General Directorate of Taxation and the National Bank of Vietnam.

TABLE 4.6

Internal Tax Collections, 1960, 1964, and 1967

Kind of Tax	1960 Amount (VN$ Mill.)	1960 Percent of Total	1960 Percent of GNP	1964 Amount (VN$ Mill.)	1964 Percent of Total	1964 Percent of GNP	1967[a] Amount (VN$ Mill.)	1967[a] Percent of Total	1967[a] Percent of GNP
Direct	830.8	13.4	1.0	1,006.7	16.2	.9	2,857.3	16.9	.8
Indirect	3,189.9	51.6	3.9	2,492.8	40.2	2.2	4,798.5	28.4	1.4
Excise	1,434.7	23.2	1.7	1,810.1	29.2	1.6	6,253.5	37.0	1.8
Registration	729.0	11.8	.9	888.4	14.3	.8	2,988.9	17.7	.8
Totals	6,184.4	100.0	7.5	6,198.0	99.9	5.5	16,898.2	100.0	4.8

[a]Data are for collections as of March 31, 1968, which are close to final collections for 1967.

Source: General Directorate of Taxation.

Another is the generation of income by the American sector, which is reflected in the GNP, but which remains essentially nontaxable. Collections also weakened on specific (as compared to ad valorem) excises under inflationary conditions. And finally, there is the likelihood of a general deterioration in both tax compliance and enforcement during the period of the war.

Table 4.6 shows the trend of collections for the four categories of internal taxes. Each category shows rather dramatic increases in absolute amounts during the period from 1964 to 1967, which would appear impressive on a bar chart. But the more relevant indicator of strength during an inflationary period is the degree to which each category maintains its relationship to the GNP. In this respect, only excise taxes showed improvement. Direct taxes, without any essential changes in rates or structure, decreased from 1.0 percent of the GNP in 1960 to 0.8 percent in 1967. Indirect taxes decreased sharply in relative importance, in large part as a result of substitution of an austerity tax on imports (appearing as a customs receipt) for the production tax on imports (formerly appearing as an indirect tax). Some excise taxes also were converted into customs duties, but these were offset by increases in several other excises. Registration taxes were bolstered by a new tax on "super rent."

A basic dilemma arises when one turns to a consideration of prospective rather than past revenue performance. The crux of the dilemma is that there is no meaningful comparative norm by which to evaluate Vietnam. Even in 1960, before the outbreak of armed conflict, the economy received large amounts of American aid. These subventions, in fact, date back to the Geneva agreement. Therefore, South Vietnam during all of its modern history as a nation has been supported by significant and rising amounts of American aid. This aid, in turn, as it has been demonstrated, has had a significant impact on the character and structure of the revenue system.

Under these circumstances, what could be "normal" for the postwar period? As a first approximation, about all that could be expected in the short run is a return to the level of aid received in 1960, and also to the structure of revenues prevailing in that year. This would mean a return to a period in which there was an approximate balance between internal taxes and taxes on foreign trade, as compared to the distribution in 1967 of about one-third of budgetary revenues from internal taxes and two-thirds from taxes on foreign trade.

Historical experience among other nations is probably the best indicator for a look into the more distant future. A recent study indicates that a developing country in the process of transition into modernity first breaks away from the past by emphasizing taxes on the foreign trade sector. During a later stage of development, as there is more monetization, domestic production, and internal transactions, internal indirect taxes are developed. Finally, as a developing country emerges into modernity, there is a shift from internal indirect taxes to modern direct taxes.*

From this model, one would interpolate that Vietnam is currently in the latter stage of transition into modernity. Indirect taxes are relatively well developed, both on the foreign trade sector and internally. Modern direct taxes are in use, but are relatively underdeveloped. Undoubtedly, the emphasis on internal indirect taxes as compared to modern direct taxes is also due in part to Vietnam's French heritage. Where British influence has prevailed, as in Hong Kong and Malaysia, much greater emphasis has been given to direct taxes.**

Suggested Reforms of Current Taxes

The Taxation of Income

The Vietnamese system of taxing income is a schedular type which includes five separate and distinct taxes: (1) a tax of from 1 percent to 16 percent on wages and salaries; (2) a tax on profits earned by individuals and the self-employed at

---

*Harley H. Hinrichs, A General Theory of Tax Structure Change During Economic Development (Cambridge: The Law School of Harvard University, 1966), pp. 97-102.

**In the period from 1958 to 1962, South Vietnam obtained only 10 percent of government revenues from direct taxes. By comparison, this ratio was 21.3 percent in Malaysia, 27.7 percent in India, and 40.0 percent in Singapore; see Yoingco and Trinidad, op. cit., p. 252.

a rate of 16 percent; (3) a tax on profits earned by incorporated businesses at the rate of 24 percent; (4) a tax on dividends and interest paid by corporations at rates varying between 18 percent and 30 percent; and (5) a general income tax on all incomes received by individuals, with rates of from 1 percent to 50 percent. Another way of viewing the system is to say that there are four schedular taxes applied to four distinct categories of income--salaries, profits of individuals, profits of corporations, and dividends and interest paid by corporations--and that each of these separately taxed categories of income is then taxed once more, when received by individuals, under a personal or general income tax, levied at progressive rates and with respect to total income from all sources, including income not taxable under the four schedules.

Besides its many biases and discriminations, which have been detailed at length in previous research, the Vietnamese income tax has not even demonstrated the virtue of built-in flexibility. Revenues as a percentage of the GNP fell from 0.73 percent in 1960 to 0.46 percent in 1966, before rising to 0.58 percent in 1967. This improvement in 1967 is principally due to the institution of withholding on the wages and salaries of all employees on January 1, 1967, and the placing of corporations on current payment.

A new income tax bill was under consideration in 1968. Its primary aim is to improve the prospects for compliance. Other favorable features of the new bill are: (1) the taxation of capital gains with a relatively simple device for discriminating in favor of longer-term assets; (2) a provision for the carry-forward of losses, applicable to both individuals and corporations; (3) a provision for the revaluation of assets for depreciation purposes, necessary because of the degree of inflation; and (4) a requirement for the current payment of tax by individuals receiving nonsalary income.

Dramatic as would be the improvement under this bill, it has a few areas of weakness which could be reconsidered. And since the bill (will be) given close scrutiny at both the executive and legislative levels, it is opportune to make these known:

1. Rather than have a separate and lighter tax schedule for civil servants with a taxable income of less than VN$100,000

it (would be) preferable for the government to face up to the need for a salary adjustment. In other words, the salary adjustment (should be) accomplished directly rather than indirectly through the tax system.

2. The end result of rationalizing the taxation of corporate profits (will be) a somewhat lower tax burden on resident shareholders. Since most shareowners are foreign, this change is not important from a revenue point of view, but it will become more important as the Vietnamese ownership of corporations increases. This suggests the need to have a higher corporate tax than 30 percent, which is relatively low by Asian standards. It would also be desirable to have a second rate of tax lower than the standard rate for the purpose of encouraging new corporations.

3. Only Japan among Asian countries has a marginal individual income tax rate as high as 75 percent; other countries have rates ranging from 35 percent (South Korea) to 72.5 percent (India). In view of Vietnam's relatively weak tax administration capabilities, it seems self-defeating to have a marginal rate in excess of 50 percent.

4. It is characteristic of developing nations to give capital gains distinctly favorable tax treatment by an unduly low tax rate and by exempting them from income taxation if the assets are held until death. Vietnam has resolved the first problem by taxing gains through favorable but not unduly generous tax treatment, but has not resolved the second problem. Capital gains should be taxed as if realized at death under the income tax.

In the postwar development period, taxes on incomes must be strengthened and increased so that as gross national product rises, the revenues from this source will rise more than proportionately. This is mandatory if resources are to be transferred from private consumption to public investment use.

Registration Taxes

Registration taxes include a wide number of dissimilar taxes and fees, including taxes on the sale of property, contracts, transfer of vehicles, insurance premiums, gifts, an annual tax on corporations (mortmain tax), and others. As they exist at present, the laws covering this group are so obtuse that it is doubtful if even the administrators understand them, let alone the public. Many of the laws also lack any clear rationale for existence; they appear to represent a blind clutching for revenue in any direction which may conceivably be productive.

The registration taxes need thorough reform, rather than simplification, after the war. Some of the taxes need to be retained and strengthened, others need to be transferred to a more logical administrative unit, and still others need to be abolished. For this reclassification and sorting, it would be helpful, for tax policy purposes, if not for purposes of administration, to divide all revenues into direct, indirect, and other revenues. If this were done in Vietnam, all taxes on income and wealth would be classified as direct, all those on transactions and consumption as indirect, and those remaining as other revenues. This tripartite division may even be worthwhile for administrative purposes.

Business License Tax

A business license tax, the patente, is levied on individuals and corporations for the privilege of engaging in a trade, profession, or industry. Also, taxpayers have a tendency to construe the payment of the patente as a necessary prerequisite for operating a business. There are two parts to the tax. The first, which may be called the basic tax, is a specific levy determined by the type of business. The second, in addition to the basic tax, is a levy applied to the rental value of the business property, which is derived either from the actual gross contract rent or the gross rental value if the property is owner-occupied.

If one simply examines the structure and the application of the patente, the initial reaction is to condemn the tax as a feudal relic which should be eliminated as soon as practicable. The basic part of the tax is levied principally on the basis of external indications of capacity to pay, such as location and outward appearance of profitability. As a result, the basic tax assessments have scant relationship to any rational yardstick of ability to pay or economic activity, such as gross or net income. But the tax has one important virtue. Among the major taxes of Vietnam, the patente probably has the best score in compliance and enforcement. While many businessmen give token recognition to the income and real property taxes, either not bothering to file or paying a fraction of their tax liabilities, virtually every businessman pays the patente. Collection statistics bear out its unique administrative feasibility. Central government collections rose each year from 1959 to 1966, from VN$104.5 million to VN$317.4 million. This is an increase of 304 percent. The comparable increase for the income tax was 207 percent, while the property tax actually declined from VN$132.1 million to VN$80.6 million.

To encounter a tax which is particularly amenable to compliance and enforcement is so unusual that the possibility is immediately raised whether the patente, instead of being discarded, could not be modified in such a way that it could serve a permanent role in a tax system for postwar Vietnam. No amount of tinkering can really change the basic inequities of the patente. Therefore, if it is to be exploited it must be changed in some basic or significant way which is consistent with plans for a postwar tax system.

Anyone familiar with the Vietnamese tax system would at once agree that a basic requirement for the future is a broad-based consumption tax instead of the myriad miscellaneous bases currently in use. Of the tax methods available, the best ones are wholesale and retail sales taxes, a combination of these two, or a value-added tax. A retail tax is the better of the two sales taxes, but is made difficult to apply if many of the retailers are small. This raises the possibility of taxing large retailers and the suppliers of smaller ones. A value-added tax applies to all stages of production and distribution, but the tax is applied only to the gross sales less the cost of goods which were taxed when purchased by the firm.

No conclusive answer should be given to a choice among these alternatives without careful research. But if one thinks in terms of the ideal, a value-added tax has received strong support from public finance specialists. The long-run possibility of a value-added tax in Vietnam is also particularly appropriate for consideration because the existing production tax at 6 percent at the producer's level is a value-added tax, and attempts have been made to extend the tax to other levels of taxation. If a value-added tax is to evolve to all levels of taxation, however, it would be necessary, as a preliminary step, to develop a base of taxation which would involve gross income. A base of gross income would be necessary, too, for a sales tax. With these thoughts in mind, there arises the possibility of exploiting the patente as a transitional device toward the development of a broad-based consumption tax: simply convert the base of the patente from external indication of ability to pay to gross income.

If this were done, it is recognized that Vietnam would have, in effect, a turnover tax, which is to be avoided as a long-run solution. Therefore, the next stage in evolution, if the goal were a value-added tax, would be to permit the deduction of goods previously taxed, possibly first at the wholesale level and then later at the retail level.

One could immediately object that the substitution of gross income for the base of the patente is administratively impossible--that the tax has only been operative because the base is arbitrary and unclear, and that if an attempt were made to substitute a more concrete base in the form of gross income, businessmen would immediately become deceptive and evasive. There is no doubt that gross income would be more difficult to determine. On the other hand, it appears to be unduly pessimistic to hold that gross income could not be approximated by personal visits by enforcement personnel to each business establishment, giving them the authority to inspect the accounting records. Moreover, progress must be made toward developing a broad consumption-based tax if Vietnam is to emerge from the wilderness of capricious and arbitrary taxes assessed on a multitude of bases, and what better way is there than to use an existing tax, with a relatively good record of compliance and enforcement, as a means of making this progress?

Indirect and Excise Taxes

Indirect and excise taxes are actually two groups of consumption taxes, and the present distinction between them should be removed in tax collection and administration. The problem for the future is largely that of sorting through these taxes to determine which products should be subject to a general consumption tax applicable to most goods and services and which ones should be given special treatment.

The production tax, adopted in 1957, is Vietnam's first attempt at a value-added tax. Two clear mistakes are evident from examining the introduction of the production tax in Vietnam, and these should be rectified if the tax is to be improved. First, the exemption of small producers should have been retained, as it is demoralizing to have a law which is so broad that it is unenforceable. Second, the law should not have been restricted largely to physical transformation. Service industries also should have been included. In other words, the process of evolution should have been from the larger and more easily taxed firms to the smaller and more difficult ones, and the tax should have been applied to all productive activities.

Since service industries have not been included under the production tax, there is presented an unusual opportunity to expand the tax. In fact there is probably no better way of both raising revenues and improving the tax system than to expand the production tax so that it embraces all the larger firms in the service-producing sector. If this were done, it might be more appropriate to change the name of the production tax to, say, a business activity or an economic activity tax.

Judged on a revenue productivity basis, however, Vietnam's introduction of a value-added tax has been highly successful. Tax collections from the internal production tax rose from VN$349 million in 1960 to VN$2,510 million in 1967, which is one of the best production records in the tax system. This shows the advantage during an inflationary period of having a tax which is directly related to the price level.

Although the group of excise taxes includes several different products, it is dominated from a revenue point of view by liquor and tobacco products. Out of total collections from excises in 1967 of VN$6,189.8 million (exclusive of various fines, fees, and other miscellaneous items), alcoholic beverages accounted for 23 percent and tobacco products for 68 percent, or together for 91 percent of collections. These products, like all others subject to excises, are also subject to production tax. This use of the production tax seems to be an unnecessary administrative and bookkeeping complication which could be eliminated.

Because of inflation and increases in the tax rates, collections from liquor and tobacco (exclusive of import duties and the production tax) increased from VN$885.8 million in 1960 to VN$5,620.0 million in 1967, or by over six times.

Clearly, there is no need to encourage the government to tax these products more heavily. Tax burdens will also be increased by the relatively new surcharge of 20 percent.

In general, it would be desirable to change many of the excises from specific to ad valorem taxes, both to provide more neutrality in taxation among products as well as to prevent erosion of the base during inflation. This shift should be undertaken in the future, even though it will cause enforcement problems. It would be necessary, for instance, to audit the records for ad valorem taxes, while only a physical check of output is necessary for specific taxes.

There will be a broader role for excises to play in the future than is presently the case. As import substitution industries develop in Vietnam, some of the products inevitably will be of a luxury nature. These products will probably also be given the benefit of protective customs duties and tax relief. When these new industries are adequately established, however, the products should be brought within the excise tax system.

The Taxation of Real Property

Vietnam has a complicated system of property tax rates and bases covering urban land, buildings and improvements, and agricultural land (that is, rice or mixed cultivation land). Different tax schedules apply to the categories of land and real property, and rice land is taxed under a series of tax rates that vary according to the productivity of the land.

On January 1, 1968, the property tax was transferred to the cities, provinces, and villages. What was predominantly a central government source of revenue, only minor shares being received by the local governments, has now become entirely a source of revenue for the local governments. And what was formerly a centrally assessed and centrally collected form of revenue, except on smaller holdings at the village level, has now become a locally assessed and locally collected source of revenue.

Under the new scheme, the revenues from urban land and buildings are received either by the municipalities, or, in the case of a provincial capital, become revenues of the province. A tax on rice land and mixed cultivation land becomes revenue for the villages. Rates are determined by each local government within ranges established by the central government. As of July, 1968, little had been done to effect these changes, except that the local governments instead of the central government were receiving the property tax revenues.

Why were the changes introduced? Principally, the purpose was to develop democratic institutions below the central governmental level. The local levels of government at the municipal, provincial, and village levels historically have been almost completely dependent on subsidization by the central government. However, with the new constitutional provisions for elected representatives and self-government at the local level, it was felt that it was mandatory to give these governments at least one independent source of revenue. If this were not done, it was reasoned, local governments would have no real autonomy.

The motives for doing this are excellent, but there are grounds for uneasiness, nevertheless, in the transfer of the property tax to the local governments. The uneasiness arises because the central government itself apparently has not had the administrative capacity to develop the tax. And if the central government could not develop the tax, can the local governments do any better? Or will they do worse? The issue is of vital importance, because a well-administered and productive property tax at the local level is a mandatory inclusion in a revitalized tax system for postwar Vietnam.

In 1959, the property tax was assessed in the following manner:

> Among the major taxes used in Vietnam, the tax on real property is probably more in need of rehabilitation than any other levy. The tax breaks every canon of equity, convenience, productivity, and neutrality to an alarming degree. The basic law promulgated in the Fiscal Code is structurally unsound and archaic, while special decrees and arretes have supplemented the law capriciously. Weak assessment and collection, together with low rates, have resulted in the tax being a minor source of revenue at all levels of government. Nothing less than a major reform of the whole tax, together with its

administration, is needed to raise the levy to fiscal respectability.*

If the tax was weak in 1959, it is barely alive at the present time. The tax is, in fact, a casualty of the war. Of all the major taxes, the property tax is the only one that has experienced an absolute decline in revenues, despite inflationary conditions, with revenues falling from VN$109 million in 1960 to VN$76 million in 1967. To provide a yardstick, this is less revenue than is collected from the tax on insurance premiums, and is less than 20 percent of the revenue obtained from the tax on carbonated beverages.

In a very real sense, then, the central government is relinquishing little; certainly, VN$76 million will provide little fiscal autonomy to the local governments when compared to the total subsidization of these governments of over VN$3 billion annually. And the central government may even be getting rid of a headache--a tax which cannot be rehabilitated and made productive without a great deal of hard work. But the greatest danger of all is that the tax will continue to deteriorate; indeed, it is probable that the village councils, if given a free hand, would abolish the tax altogether. This cannot be allowed to happen, for the property tax is necessarily the main hope for improvement in local revenues, and increases in such revenues are essential to the success of local government.

How can these dire possibilities be avoided? One way is to give the local governments a more workable and structurally improved law. Testative suggestions along these lines have been made previously, but additional research needs to be done. Second, the local governments will require extensive technical assistance support in order to administer the tax effectively. One could advocate that this support should be provided by the Directorate General of Taxation, but this is obviously unrealistic, given the difficulties that this agency has been facing in keeping its own house in order. Therefore, if the property tax is to thrive in its new milieu, there is no other alternative but sizable foreign technical assistance.

---

*Milton C. Taylor, The Taxation of Real Property in Viet-Nam (Michigan State University Vietnam Advisory Group, July, 1959), pp. 1-2.

The Taxation of Agriculture

In the postwar period a great part of the national development effort will go to agriculture. It has provided the largest part of the gross national product in the past and will continue to do so in the future. Export earnings will come from raw and processed agricultural products, and much of the investment will go to this sector. Investment projects for the development of the Mekong Delta, for land settlement and irrigation in other regions, and for provision of all agricultural inputs are a substantial part of the total investment program. The purpose is to raise agricultural output, income, and exports. Consequently, it is reasonable to assume that a way must be found to tax agricultural income and output for development purposes.

An underdeveloped country, producing primary materials, has few alternatives but to tax the agricultural industry, simply because there is no other industry that produces the magnitude of surplus necessary for development purposes. A primary goal of tax policy is the allocative one of restricting consumption for public sector investment purposes. Because the populations engaged in all other industries do not produce a sufficient taxable surplus in the aggregate, taxing the agricultural industry is not a question of equity but of necessity, particularly if it is the special beneficiary of development expenditures.

Although this thesis is plausible, it is nevertheless difficult to subscribe to without some reservations. If development is essentially a matter of sacrifice, then it is markedly inequitable to impose most of the sacrifice on the rural low-income sector. If there is to be a sacrifice in the level of consumption, social justice and political stability demand that the sacrifice be borne by all. Since 1958, austerity for parts of the urban population has been conspicuous by its absence. It is particularly difficult under these circumstances, then, to defend the proposition that the agricultural industry should be taxed, unless the burden is also shared by a program of equal burdens imposed on the urban middle-income and upper-income groups.

Nevertheless, the output of agriculture must be taxed, and there remains the determination of the best means of accomplishing this. Obviously, this is a question of great importance, and one that requires for its resolution a comprehensive knowledge of Vietnamese institutions. All that can be undertaken here is to suggest various alternative methods of taxation, and to indicate which ones appear to be the more likely solutions. No conclusive answer should be given without further analysis, but the options briefly are as follows:

1. Vietnam already has a tax on land, but the revenues henceforth will be used for local government purposes. Moreover, it will be a laborious and slow process to rehabilitate this tax in the postwar period. Thus, some other alternative must be found to tax the agricultural industry.

2. Agricultural income is taxable under the income tax, but a fiscally productive income tax applicable to the agricultural industry would be impossible to administer except in the case of plantation agriculture.

3. There is a paddy transformation tax on the milling of rice, collectible from the millers, but it has encountered severe enforcement difficulties and has produced low revenue yields.

4. Export taxes are levied on most agricultural products and would pose few enforcement difficulties in the postwar period. However, because of the necessity of developing rapid increases in exports to earn foreign exchange, export taxes should be avoided. A principal liability of export duties, moreover, is that they subsidize the internal consumption of the exported products.

5. The mandatory collection and marketing of agricultural products by the government, which is undertaken in Taiwan and Burma, is capable of producing large volumes of revenue, but it would raise a very fundamental issue of the appropriate role of the government. With all of the extensive responsibilities faced by the government in the postwar period, it is doubtful that it should, in addition, substitute itself for an existing private market mechanism.

6. A possibility which has not been tried in Vietnam, and which appears to be particularly appropriate wherever public improvements are introduced, is betterment levies, or special assessments equated to benefit received. These may be particularly applicable in the Mekong Delta.

It is obvious that no single tax base would suffice for taxing the agricultural industry in Vietnam. Sifting through the alternatives, the combination of measures which appear to be the most appropriate as a first approximation is land taxes, betterment levies, and the application of the production tax to the internal consumption of agricultural products. The latter, in turn, would require an intensive effort to tax the processors (e.g., millers of rice) of agricultural products.

Improvement of Tax Administration

When particular proposals are made in Vietnam for the restructuring of the tax system, almost invariably there is a negative response. It is contended that a combination of administrative incapacity and taxpayer evasion would make the reforms impossible to introduce. To some degree this is a matter of rejecting the unfamiliar, and it is only to be expected, also, that professional tax administrators, already overburdened, do not welcome an increase in their work load. If tax reform depended on the ready acquiescence of tax administrators, there probably would be little reform. Nevertheless, it is also likely that the combination of administrative limitations, political procrastination, and the level of tax morality on the part of the public constitutes a much greater barrier to tax reform than the technical problem of devising a better tax system. It also appears to be a reasonable assumption in Vietnam that tax reform can only move as fast as the administration can be improved.

It is, therefore, highly relevant to ask the question of how administrative capacity can be improved. In the last analysis, this is simply a matter of the allocation of public resources. Any country, regardless of its level of development, could make significant progress in tax administration if it identified this problem as one of high priority and allocated resources accordingly. It is simply a matter of being willing to pay the price of, say, doubling the number of enforcement personnel, raising salaries, creating an elite group of personnel, installing better equipment, and so on.

If it is recognized that tax administration is a strategic area for the allocation of additional resources, how should the resources be used? The crux of the problem is to increase both the number and quality of personnel. To increase the number is a budgetary problem, but to increase the quality would require a massive training program for the great majority of the staff of the Directorate General of Taxation. What Vietnam needs is something comparable to the Japanese system of special colleges for the training of tax enforcement personnel on a continuing, long-run, and professional basis.

At the same time, it must be realized that a superior staff cannot be developed and retained unless salaries are upgraded. If the government is to stress the importance of tax administration, it follows that personnel in tax administration must be paid salaries close to the equivalent of what they could earn in private enterprise.

Summary of Tax Reform Measures

The conclusion is inescapable that the tax system of Vietnam is ill-prepared for peace. Vietnam began the war with a basically unproductive, inequitable, and inefficient tax system; it probably will end the war with much the same system. War finance has consisted of muddling through: increasing rates as a revenue-raising device, but not altering the basic structure of the tax system. But even raising tax rates has not prevented a deterioration in the general revenue productivity of the tax system. Unless a serious and continuous effort is made to improve the system, it will fail to contribute significantly toward any of the goals of a tax policy outlined previously.

Although the faults of the internal tax system are deep and extensive, and the system is so complicated that it is often difficult to understand fully, the broad outline of reform is apparent. The internal tax system should have three basic elements: (1) a modern system of taxation based on income and wealth; (2) a broad-based tax on consumption; and (3) a selected excise tax system for particular items of consumption. In principle, therefore, Vietnam could achieve its goals of tax policy with literally a handful of taxes rather than with the great variety of levies currently in use. One of the principal strategies of reform, therefore, is consolidation and simplification. Even if nothing else were accomplished, Vietnam's tax system would be immeasurably better if there were twenty taxes instead of about double this number.

Probably the weakest area is the taxation of income and wealth. A large part of this problem will be resolved if the income tax bill proposed in 1968 is adopted. Further improvements could be made to this bill, but they are minor as compared to the achievements which would result from enactment of the present bill. When this goal is accomplished, attention should be directed to a rehabilitation of taxes on real property and to a strengthening of death and gift taxation.

While it is mandatory to restructure the direct tax system, only slow progress can be expected in compliance and enforcement. Thus, no less important is the need to develop a single broad-based consumption tax instead of the multitude of levies currently applied on consumption and production. A beginning has been made toward this end with the adoption of a value-added tax--the production tax on the physical transformation of goods. Assuming that it is Vietnam's goal to develop a comprehensive system of value-added taxation, the production tax eventually could be extended to all levels of economic activity. An important thrust forward immediately could be made, with sizable revenue gains, by extending the tax to large firms in the service sector. Another means of working toward an extension of the production tax, and at the same time eliminating one of the worst taxes in the tax system, is to convert the patente to a base of gross income for many taxpayers. Eventually, this gross income tax could then be converted into a value-added tax.

Several items of consumption warrant special excise tax treatment, notably gasoline, tobacco, and liquor products, as well as a few others. Many of the products currently taxed on a unique basis, however, lack a compelling rationale for special treatment, and should be taxed under a broad-based consumption tax. Other products, like tobacco and liquor, have been fully exploited, although further improvement in their rates and bases is possible. Gasoline is seriously undertaxed.

When the need arises, it is always possible for a country to obtain additional revenue in one way or another. What is necessary for maximum progress, however, is to obtain this revenue in a way which is consistent with the evolution of an improved revenue system. Two conspicuous opportunities are apparent at the present time if attention is simply confined to the need for sizable increases in noninflationary revenue.

One is to extend the production tax to the service sector, and the other is to raise the tax on gasoline. After this is accomplished, additional revenues of the right type will be more difficult to obtain, but nevertheless relatively easy to identify. Attention should be directed to the patente, the real property tax, and the licensing of motorcycles. There are only two conditions necessary for progress in tax reform. One is to have a clear vision of the goal which is being pursued; the second is to exert an intelligent and responsible effort to reach it.

FOREIGN TRADE AND THE REFORM OF IMPORT DUTIES

Government revenues from foreign trade and the tax system on that trade have been separated from the discussion of the internal tax system because some of the functions are different, particularly in a development period, and because the future structure of the system of taxes on foreign trade should be markedly different from the present system and with quite different impacts on the economy in shifting resources to development needs.

There are two main objectives of a tax system on foreign trade: (1) to provide a major part of government revenues; and (2) to provide the appropriate incentives and protection so that exports will be promoted and efficient local production can substitute for imports. A third objective, which is very relevant to the system in Vietnam today, is to have a system that is simple to administer and apply and that is efficient. Vietnam's system is neither.

Typically, taxes on foreign trade, primarily import duties, are the major source of tax revenue for most developing countries. Reliance is placed on this source of revenue partly because in a period of development, imports tend to grow, and partly because less effort is required to obtain import duties than other taxes. The fact that foreign trade is channeled through relatively few ports in a country enables governments in developing countries to tap this flow of commerce for revenue with relative ease and with a minimum expenditure of resources. Some countries rely on customs duties for half of all tax revenues, and in most countries the proportion, if less than this, is still high. Korea in 1965 relied on import duties to provide 23 percent of its tax revenue and 16 percent of total revenue. In the same year, the Philippines raised 19 percent of its total revenue and nearly 23 percent of tax revenue from import duties, and Thailand relied on export and import duties to generate 40 percent of its total revenue and nearly 47 percent of its tax revenue. Taxes on foreign trade have provided Vietnam also with its largest source of revenue. In 1967 customs duties accounted for 11.3 percent of total revenue, but nearly one-third of total government revenue excluding foreign aid and Treasury advances. Customs duties are of great importance as the major source of taxes; in 1967 they accounted for 41.3 percent of all tax revenues. In addition, if the foreign exchange tax and perequation tax, which are levied on foreign trade transactions, are included, customs duties accounted for nearly two-thirds of total tax revenue in 1967. The foreign trade sector, then, has been carrying a heavy burden of responsibility in providing Vietnam with tax revenues, and this level of burden on the foreign trade sector can be expected to continue in the near future.

Customs duties in Vietnam are derived primarily from taxes on imports since only one export, rubber, has a levy placed on it. All duties are levied at ad valorem rates on the commodities. The tariff system of Vietnam is probably one of the most complex in the world, for there is not only a tariff rate on the dutiable imports but there are other taxes levied on imports, depending on the source of foreign exchange. These other taxes or duties--the perequation tax and austerity tax, on top of the regular import tariff--add to the complexity and inefficiency of the system.

The perequation tax is levied on imports which are financed with foreign exchange owned by the Vietnamese government, but it is not levied on imports financed under the U.S. Commercial Import Program (CIP). Apparently, the original purpose of this tax was to equate the prices of imports originating in countries other than the United States with the prices of those originating from the United States. Actually, the perequation tax has functioned as another tariff of a protective nature, and is equivalent to a multiple exchange rate on different commodities.

The perequation tax is levied at the time the import license is issued, at rates varying from zero to 215 piasters per dollar of value--the equivalent percentage rates being from zero to almost 270 percent. This tax is an effective revenue producer, for it provided 3.6 billion piasters in 1966, 6.3 billion piasters in 1967, and an estimated 11.0 billion piasters in 1968. Until 1968, the proceeds from this tax, as well as the economic consolidation surtax, were not included in the budgetary revenues but in the extrabudgetary revenues.

The austerity tax is levied simultaneously with the tariff on imports. As the name suggests, the tax is a wartime and antiinflationary measure. On April 1, 1968, there was a general increase in the coverage of the austerity tax, and the minimum rate was increased from 5 percent to 10 percent; the maximum rate is 210 percent of the cost-insurance-freight (c.i.f.) value of imports. Low rates apply generally to raw materials, and the rates are highest on luxury items.

The tariff rates on imports range from zero to 200 percent of the c.i.f. value of imports, seventeen different rates being levied. The very high tariff rates are on luxury items such as alcoholic beverages and automobiles. A disturbing fact is that there are tariffs levied on some raw material and other inputs for industry which may neutralize a part or all of the protection given to the final products of certain industries, essentially penalizing local production of those items. This important point is discussed later as a major item for reform of the system.

When the 17 tariff rates are combined with the austerity tax rates, there are 50 different rates of taxes ranging from zero to 304 percent. And when the perequation tax is added to the other two, there are 139 different tax rates on imports, and the rates range from zero to 555 percent of the import value. This proliferation of taxes, rates, and ranges results in a cumbersome system, one aspect of which is the fact that the same commodity is not always treated consistently in the application of duties and taxes. However, this is less important than the fact that the relative rates on different classes of commodities, such as raw materials, semifinished goods, consumer goods, capital goods, and so on, do not provide the incentives and protection that stimulate efficient local production to substitute for imports.

Table 4.7 reveals certain characteristics of the system of duties and taxes. From the table it can be computed that

TABLE 4.7

Distribution of Imports by Rates of Total Import Duties[a], 1967

Rate (Percent)	Value of Imports (VN$ Millions)	Percent of Total
Exempt	508	1.2
5 - 20	5,321	12.4
22.5 - 40	8,462	19.7
42.5 - 60	3,566	8.3
62.5 - 80	10,302	24.1
82.5 - 100	2,871	6.7
102.5 - 120	3,780	8.8
122.5 - 140	1,917	4.5
142.5 - 160	722	1.7
182.5 - 180	1,486	3.5
182.5 - 220	578	1.3
222.5 - 320	2,835	6.6
322.5 - 555	418	1.0
Total	42,766	100.0

[a]Includes austerity tax, import duty, and perequation tax.

Source: Director of Customs, Government of Vietnam.

in 1967 the average weighted duty (tariff, austerity tax, and perequation tax) was 83 percent. Of this amount, 42 percent is attributable to the customs duty plus the austerity tax, and 41 percent is the average for the perequation tax. Thus the division is almost equal between the two groupings, and the strength of the perequation tax is obvious.

Almost two-thirds of the imports by value had total duties of less than 80 percent (one-third having duties of less than 40 percent), but over a quarter of imports carried duties of more than 100 percent. A considerable portion of these import duties was generated from levies falling on industrial inputs. Of total imports (excluding food), about one-third were raw materials and semifinished goods and two-thirds were final manufactured products.

If import duties are to have appropriate incentive effects on local production without adverse effects on revenues, the rates of tax or duty must be computed not only on the final products but also on the goods and materials that go into the final product. There is a difference between the effective rate of protection and the nominal rate. The latter is simply the actual total rate of duty on the commodity in question. The effective rate is the rate on the final product after adjusting for the rates on the materials going into the final product. The effective rate is the rate of increase that could occur in the value added because of protection. Since inputs as well as final products may be imported, the effective rate refers to that part of the value of production which is produced domestically by local labor and capital.

If the weighted average tariff rate on inputs is lower than the tariff rate on the output, the effective rate of protection exceeds the commodity tariff rate. For example, if the tariff rate on the import of, say, finished furniture is 50 percent, with 30 percent of the value of the furniture in value added, and the rate on the wood, cloth, and other items necessary to produce furniture is only 5 percent, then the effective rate of protection on the final stage of furniture manufacture (i.e., the protection afforded the value added in furniture manufacture) is greater than the nominal rate of 50 percent. Greater protection is thus given to the domestic production of furniture than is indicated by the rate of 50 percent on the finished product.

This basic principle for the structuring of import duties is crucial for the reform of such duties in Vietnam in the postwar period if appropriate and efficient domestic industries are to be established. The issues involved can be illustrated by simple examples.

The assembly, and later the production of motorcycles and scooters, is one type of industry that could be established efficiently in Vietnam. At present the supply is largely imported; in 1967, these products accounted for 7 percent of total imports. The market is sufficiently large and the production processes are relatively simple; it is a prime example of an industry ready for domestic expansion.

If an import duty is placed on the finished product but not on any components, an assembly industry in Vietnam will be stimulated. The parts will be imported and only the final stages of production will be local. This is the usual way to start, since assembly of a finished product from imported parts is an easy step.

If duties are placed on some components, the local production of semifinished materials will be stimulated, although the degree of protection for the finished assembled product will be decreased. This is the normal process of expanding the local production of inputs into industrial products.

If import duties on the raw materials and components of a product are, say, 100 percent of import value and the duties on the finished product are only 10 percent, the simultaneous application of such duties will discourage the establishment of local production. The finished product may still be imported, and unless there are special resource advantages and favorable costs in the production of industrial raw materials and semifinished products, there will be no stimulation of local porduction of these products. In effect the difference in tax rates on industrial inputs and the finished product will act as a tax on production of the final product by domestic industry.

If the industry is one that produces primarily for export markets, a duty on the inputs to the industry is in reality a tax on domestic production, raises the price of the domestic product, and reduces its attraction in world markets. For example, high duties on small agricultural machinery and fertilizers may not stimulate low-cost domestic production but may raise the prices at which agricultural products have to be sold in export markets. This will put such products at a disadvantage in world markets, and would be unfavorable to the rapid expansion of exports which is essential to the growth and development of the economy.

The above four cases refer primarily to the relationship of import duty rates as between raw materials, semifinished products, and final manufactured products. The purpose is to find a relationship that will stimulate local production of both kinds of goods without penalizing the export industries. But it is also extremely important to remember that in every case the rates on commodities imported for domestic production of goods should not result in prices that are continuously higher than import prices of those goods. The protection of new or infant industries is justifiable, but after a period of five years the continued protection of high-cost domestic production would be disadvantageous to the whole economy. Our strategy of import duties is aimed primarily at helping to give birth to vigorous industries that can stand competition.

The present system of taxation on foreign trade has many defects, but the most serious one is its complexity, resulting from the layering of the several different taxes, not unlike the internal tax system. There is no advantage gained from such a system, but there is much confusion for the businessman and the taxpayer. The system is duplicative and therefore creates unnecessary additional work for an already understaffed and undertrained administration; and it provides opportunities for evasion and corruption. The first order of business should be either the abolition of the austerity and perequation taxes and their integration into the tariff structure, or an adjustment in the exchange rate in the case of the perequation tax.

For reform of the present system of import duties we recommend first that imports be classified into the following categories, which are related to development incentives:

1. Industrial raw materials; capital goods (machinery); and inputs for export industries.

2. Unprocessed or processed components for intermediate industries which draw investment into the country or provide considerable employment.

3. Components for final assembly in industries in which there is high value added in final production stage or in which there will be gains to the economy from the development of production of components for the finished commodity;

4. Consumption goods which cannot be produced relatively efficiently in Vietnam;

5. Semiluxury goods which cannot provide additional benefits to Vietnam if produced domestically;

6. Luxury goods. The category in which a good falls suggests the level of tariff to a certain extent. The first category should have minimal tariffs so that there is no disguised taxation on export industries and so that the importation of capital equipment is not discouraged. Tariffs on this category of goods could have more harmful effects to the economy than tariffs on any of the other categories.

The second category should be assigned tariffs with low rates depending on the degree of protection which is desired for the component produced at the next stage of production. A maximum degree of protection is provided by the absence of a duty. If less protection is required, a tariff at this point would reduce the effective rate of protection at the next level. It is important to remember that effective protection depends on the rate of tariff levied both at the input level and the final output level.

Goods in the third category offer excellent opportunities for the development of domestic industries providing the basic cost structure is favorable. The duties imposed will depend on a judgment as to how rapidly domestic production can be increased.

Category four might carry higher rates of duty than any of the first three. Exceptions may need to be made for commodities that are regarded as basic to the standard of living yet not obtainable domestically. Categories five and six obviously should bear increasingly high rates of duty, and for certain goods prohibitive rates might well be appropriate.

To some extent there is overlapping between these categories of goods, and the suggestions concerning rates are simply to rank them from low (categories one through three) to high (categories five and six). The objective in this chapter is to suggest guidelines for action and reform and not to attempt a detailed evaluation of each commodity class. The classification and treatment suggested are quite different from any applied in the existing system.

As mentioned in regard to the internal tax system, a larger share of government revenues should come from internal taxes in the future, but customs duties will still provide a significant part of the revenue even after tariff reforms on the above lines. It is reasonable to assume that for a time after the war the composition of imports will tend to remain heavily dominated by consumption goods. If the pattern is to be changed in order to shift more foreign exchange into the purchase of capital goods, the tariff structure must impose high rates of duty on consumption goods--primarily durables and luxury nondurables--and this should generate high levels of revenue in the early years of peace.

It may be useful to provide an idea of the likely magnitude of customs revenues in the early postwar period without going into the details of the composition of imports. We assume that the perequation tax will be absorbed in a reform of the foreign exchange rate, and that the austerity tax will be absorbed into the tariff duty reform. In the postwar period, annual imports in the range of US$500-600 million may be expected and they may go higher in the last part of the decade. Assuming that tariff rates will be adjusted upward on consumer goods to average at least 50 percent, that they will be 10-20 percent on capital goods, and that the latter will be at least half of total imports, the revenues from customs should range from US$160 million to US$210 million, with an average rate of 30-35 percent, about the same as they are now. This assumes, of course, that import demand is not adversely affected by the shifting of rates, any changes in exchange rates and monetary policy, or basic changes in national income. In fact, there surely will be shifts in import demand in response to these factors, so that the estimation of future revenues from foreign trade is subject to many errors. Detailed analysis of the level and composition of imports under different income, tax, and credit policies will be required in the early future.

THE BUDGET AS AN INSTRUMENT OF FISCAL CONTROL AND MANAGEMENT

Given the limitations and deficiencies of the public service as a result of war-induced strains, budget-making in Vietnam, although traditional in form, is a highly institutionalized, systematized process, providing in great detail for compilation and execution. If taken together with the policy statements which invariably accompany its presentation, it offers a fairly precise statement of government policy and its contribution to capital formation, as well as being a basic vehicle for internal planning and organizational control. It presents a detailed picture of past, present, and proposed work and the costs of that work under a refined classification system which, within administrative units, groups appropriations under specific objectives. The legislative processes leading to its adoption and promulgation are soundly based and provide some limited scope for subsequent flexibility by way of virement of funds between articles and chapters and by supplementary provisions in the course of a fiscal year; and its implementation is vested with a complex system of controls and cross-controls to ensure executive accountability and the preclusion of unauthorized expenditure.

The basic shortcomings of the budget are mainly those inherent in the traditional "line-item" presentation. That is, there is a concentration on developing and presenting information primarily intended for day-to-day administration and control to the detriment of forward planning, program selection, the establishment of priorities, and, where feasible, the assessment of cost-effectiveness.

In this section an examination is made of the national budget process and an assessment provided of the extent to which its presentation and format, and the procedures by which it is compiled and implemented, detract from its potential usefulness as a vehicle for channeling resources to their most efficient use in terms of economic growth and social progress. Such an examination would be incomplete and of limited value without an attempt also at a critical analysis of the budget process in central, provincial, and village governments with a view to evaluating its effectiveness at these different levels as a means of apportioning resources.

From this starting point we have explored the practical possibilities of moving toward a simple form of program and performance budgeting in Vietnam as an adjunct to budget preparation, to assist in the formulation of prime program objectives and to render the budget a more versatile management instrument. We conclude with a recommendation that progression to a program budgeting process should be initiated as soon as possible, at first in one selected area of government activity, as a pilot scheme capable of extension when experience has been gained and trained staff become available. Such a system has great potential usefulness in Vietnam in arriving at approximations of cost of future development programs and in determining, in the light of over-all needs, a reasonable allocation of public investment between economic development and the social services.

The National Budget

The budget for the calendar year 1967, used here for purposes of illustration, provides for a total estimated expenditure of VN$75 billion, balanced by equivalent, anticipated revenue. The dominant feature of the expenditure estimates is, as would be expected, the provision for military spending, which totals VN$42 billion as against total civilian or other expenditures estimated at VN$33 billion. About 60 percent of revenue is accordingly devoted to the pursuit of the war effort.

The budget is balanced by virtue of two titles of revenue: Title 16, foreign aid (U.S. counterpart fund), VN$30 billion; and Title 17, advances (i.e., loans from the National Bank), VN$17 billion. Their total is VN$47 billion. National resources in the form of taxes and administrative income amount only to VN$28 billion, or less by 15 percent than is required to support the civil program reflected in the budget. It will be noted that the revenue to be derived under Title 17, i.e., loans from the National Bank, appears as a balancing item and represents deficit financing, the extent of which, in the absence of forward planning and expenditure constraint, and in relation to the over-all public debt, its servicing and its contribution to inflation, has an undesirable open-endedness.

It is clear that the over-all expense to the government of countering guerrilla insurgency (which would total not VN$42 billion but VN$49 billion if the costs of the Security Department and the Department of Communications, Veterans and Youth were to be included, and which excludes the massive direct American expenditures for these purposes) is very greatly in excess of receipts from the sources of revenue capable of being exploited at present. Tax resources are predominantly and typically indirect, and there is a considerable need for more progressive taxation and for an enhanced contribution to public funds by a wider section of the population.

The estimates are clearly tabulated and classified in accord with administrative organization on the expenditure side and by type of receipt on the revenue side, and also by major activity, function, and economic character. For each administrative unit appropriations are made for specific objectives classified as to type of expenditure. There is, however, no clear-cut distinction between recurrent and capital expenditures.

Comparisons with preceding years are not particularly illuminating. A table giving actual revenues and expenditures for a recent year and an estimate revised in relation to actual performance would be useful for purposes of presentation and understanding. These appear below as Tables 4.8 and 4.9. No attempt is made to delineate capital revenues, i.e., those derived from the alienation (by sale or other method) of resources, although it is true that this source is not a significant element in the makeup of income.

An analysis of the 1967 expenditure estimates reveals that personnel emoluments, including pensions and allowances, are estimated to cost VN$45.75 billion, apportioned as follows: civilian staff VN$13.25 billion; military personnel, including directly employed civilian supporting staff, VN$32.5 billion. Expenditures on emoluments total 61 percent of the budget. Civilian emoluments alone, in relation to the VN$28 billion estimated to be derived from national resources, amount to 47 percent.

A breakdown of expenditures into recurrent or operating expenditures and expenditures of a capital or investment nature can only be attempted in approximate terms because of a lack of detail in the budget presentation. It seems probable, from examination of the available data, that recurrent operating expenditure is estimated to amount to VN$14.5 billion for the year and capital expenditures to VN$2.5 billion. The over-all position is shown in Table 4.8.

TABLE 4.8

National Budget, 1967
(VN$ Billion)

Revenue	Amount	Expenditure	Amount		
			Civil	Military	Total
National resources	28.00	Personnel emoluments	13.25	32.50	45.75
Counterpart funds	30.00	Recurrent expenses	6.25	8.25	14.50
Deficit financing	17.00	Capital investment	1.40	1.10	2.50
		AID and unallocated funds	12.25	-	12.25
	75.00		33.15	41.85	75.00

The large figure for unallocated and other funds in Table 4.8 requires explanation. The total, VN$12.25 billion, consists of:

VN$1.2 billion reserved for the subsidization of state owned enterprises.

VN$2.13 billion provided for special programs, the planning of which is incomplete but in respect of which there is a reasonable anticipation that funds may be required during the year.

VN$0.4 billion reserved for supplementary provision should chapters require increased funds or should new agencies be established during the course of the fiscal year.

VN$6 billion for "development and growth" programs.

VN$0.7 billion to meet unexpected expenses not anticipated, e.g., elections, damages to property, and so on.

VN$20 million for the acquisition of property, if required, and

VN$250 million unclassified but available in Title 17, Chapter 202, Office of the Prime Minister.

VN$1.53 billion for subsidies to provincial budgets and autonomous agencies.

Of these eight items, the largest quantitatively and the most significant in terms of budgetary influence is the VN$6 billion for the development and growth programs. This provision is to be found in 1967 in Title 32, Chapter 909, which is commonly known as the "American AID" Chapter. In addition to the VN$6 billion appropriated, a further VN$2 billion is also recorded as a "supplement" which is not reflected in the over-all budget and which, if expended, would have to be matched by a similar increase in counterpart funds. The projected expenditure under this chapter provides in close detail for all construction and development programs visualized for the year, and also presupposes the disbursement of the VN$2 billion supplement to give an over-all total for American AID programs of VN$8 billion.

The actual 1967 apportionment of expenditures between recurrent and capital outlay revised to include this additional expenditure, is as shown in Table 4.9.

TABLE 4.9

National Budget, 1967, Revised

Expenditure	G.V.N. Budget (VN$ Billion)	AID	Total	Percentage
Staff emoluments	45.75	0.5	46.25	60.0
Recurrent expenditure	14.50	4.5	19.00	24.9
Capital investment	2.50	3.0	5.50	7.0
Unallocated	-	-	6.25	8.1
			77.00	100.0

The effect of Title 32, it will be seen, is to concentrate in one chapter allocations which lend a sense of purpose to the budget as a whole. The divorce of this essential nucleus from the individual title estimates makes any assessment of ministerial policy objectives unrealistic unless a conscious effort is made to integrate and spread the Title 32 provision within the budget as a whole. Much greater general influence, it is felt, could be exerted on the entire budget, and program formulation and project selection could be very considerably improved if these funds were to be merged chapter by chapter with those provided for the individual administrative units of government, instead of being applied to specific projects. It is also apparent that direct capital investment in construction and equipment stemming from this chapter exceeds by 20 percent the total nonrecurrent expenditures envisaged elsewhere in the budget and is of an order of magnitude which to some extent dictates development patterns in the short and medium term.

The remaining items totaling VN$4.88 billion or 7 percent of the total budget are, strictly speaking, unallocated or reserve funds, earmarked it is truc for specific ranges of activity but illustrative of two shortcomings: a lack of flexibility in the budget structure and implementation, and an absence of even medium-term planning in those fields.

Inflexibility is most clearly demonstrated by the need to reserve VN$400 million for supplementary purposes. There is no mechanism whereby, as a continuous process during the fiscal year, supplementary funds can be created and released for unforeseen commitments, increased expenditures following revised or new policies, staff fluctuations, the creation of new agencies, and so on, other than by resort to this reserve under Title 31, overhead expenditures, or, should this reserve be exhausted, by the cumbersome and protracted process of presenting a revised budget to the legislature. A limited procedure for virement of funds between articles and between chapters exists which provides some degree of fluidity within agency allocations, but even this requires the administrative sanction of the prime minister.

Good government is a constantly evolving activity which cannot and should not be constrained financially within the confines of a single financial year. Changes of emphasis, the introduction of new policies, the extension of governmental influence and participation in new areas of endeavor should not have to wait for annual legislative sanction. Not only should administrators be given reasonable powers to transfer funds, but machinery should be created which could accelerate the provision of additional funds for approved changes in or extensions of policy. Long-term forward planning and a greater emphasis on programmatic preparation of estimates would go some way toward reducing the requirement for flexibility, but would by no means remove it. Such systems exist and could be adapted to local circumstances without loss of control or accountability.

Some observations follow concerning subsidies to local authorities, autonomous municipalities, and other bodies. There are some twenty-five autonomous organizations, largely public or in a combination of public and private ownership, in the industrial and commercial field. Many of these enterprises evade budgetary control while incurring deficits which become a charge on the national budget. This is particularly the case with pricing policies--the principal reason for their over-all losses. Without budgetary control and until they are brought into the context of national fiscal policy, there is no way of limiting the drain these enterprises make on the nation's resources. Then there are 53 provincial councils and autonomous municipalities which require subsidization. In 1967, the total revenues of these organizations amounted to VN$2.84 billion. Of this sum, VN$1.53 billion, 54 percent, represented central government contributions. This wholesale support, while necessary, does not appear to be predetermined to any great extent. It largely represents the shortfall between over-all expenditures and over-all revenues from sources other than central government assistance. Such an arrangement, instead of increasing the viability and independence of action desirable--within prescribed limits--in local authorities, increases and perpetuates their dependence on the central government.

Provincial Budgets

An anaylsis undertaken of the 1967 budgets of eight provincial councils in the IV Corps tactical zone provided the data shown in Table 4.10.

TABLE 4.10

Comparative Provincial Budgets, 1967
(VN$ Million)

Province	Revenue			Expenditure		
	Subsidies	Others	Total	Councils & Administration	Public Works & Reconstruction	Total
An Giang	25.75	6.45	31.7	17.12	14.58	31.7
An Xuyen	30.00	3.20	33.2	24.4	8.8	32.2
Chau Doc	27.1	6.90	34.00	18.48	15.52	34.0
Go Cong	24.40	3.60	28.00	16.6	11.4	28.0
Kien Giang	24.3	7.70	32.00	12.5	11.8	24.3
Long An	37.5	6.5	44.00	26.00	18.00	44.0
Phuoc Long	26.0	3.8	29.8	14.6	15.2	29.8
Tay Ninh	22.3	3.1	25.4	16.2	9.2	25.4

Since provincial revenues from local resources yield so small a percentage of the funds required to meet expenditures, there is a preponderant reliance on the central government subsidy in order to maintain even the present level of extremely modest services and works. Any development of badly needed facilities by the councils must depend either on a more vigorous and comprehensive system of tax collection, or an enhanced state subvention, or both. But the government subsidy is provided almost automatically as a balancing item, and is limited, it is presumed, only by the constraints imposed on over-all spending by the central government by considerations of national policy, particularly in relation to inflationary pressures.

The motives of those who defend this practice are understandable; they maintain that under present conditions provincial governments cannot be expected to raise adequate revenues and thus need constant reinforcement from central resources to maintain even a minimal degree of viability. But an opportunity to regenerate the activities of provincial governments and to promote a more positive approach to their responsibilities is being missed. While maintaining a minimum level of support necessary to perpetuate essential activities by provincial councils, consideration might well be given to the construction of a formula, adaptable for differing conditions throughout the country, whereby some element of inducement is built into the subsidy system. Simple formulas for the calculation of subsidies have been evolved in many developing countries. Basically what is needed is a combination of subsidy and grant related to population, geared to essential expenditures and responsibilities and variable in relation to revenues collected, the latter possibly on a matching basis.

There is need for a clearer definition of provincial government functions in relation to village government, and in particular, there is scope for the delegation to provincial councils of many central government functions on a repayment basis with a contribution to overhead costs. There is also a need for greater independence from central authority in the matter of staffing and staff remuneration. Establishments appear to be excessively large. Certainly the cost of revenue collection in salaries alone makes the incremental yield negligible. Salary increases are imposed by decree without regard to the ability of the council to meet the additional costs. This would be less deleterious to performance if wages and allowances were to be a factor clearly determinable and responding to change in a subsidy or grant-in-aid formula. As it is, the subsidy is equated to estimated deficit and any reduction in subsidy or any failure to realize local revenue targets or any imposed increase in wages and salaries is immediately reflected in the reduction in value of works and services performed.

Similarly the overburden of cost of the council itself--the salaries and allowances paid to members, the frequency of meetings, the extent of reimbursable travel--though modest in absolute terms, represents a substantial drain on limited resources and is to some extent imposed by permissive decree having no correlation with the level of central government assistance.

Village Budgets

The picture does not change much at the village level, other than in respect of subsidies which, generally, are substantially less in proportionate terms than those given to the provinces. An analysis of six village budgets in Dinh Tuong Province demonstrated that subsidies amounted to 35 percent of total estimated revenues (as opposed to 84 percent in the cross-section of provincial councils examined). Estimated expenditures on public works was 41 percent of total estimated expenditures (40 percent in provincial councils) and administrative costs 44 percent.

Perhaps the most significant aspect of the budgetary process at this level is the degree of control and surveillance imposed by the central and provincial governments. All village budgets require the approval of the province chief, and those which exceed a total of VN$1 million require the approval of the minister. Virtually every activity by a village council, whether of a revenue-productive nature or designed to enhance services, requires ratification at various higher levels. This rigidity of control engenders excessive accounting, places the emphasis more on the paper work which accompanies it than on implementation of plans, and overburdens the slender administrative resources of the villages.

Apart from the subsidy, the major sources of revenue-earning levies in the villages studied are derived from their markets, licenses to operate boats, and taxes on the occupancy of public land. A recent decree has transferred all rice-lands revenues to village budgets, but it is obvious that unless collections improve (and security considerations have a substantial effect on revenue potential in this regard) and realistic assessments or valuations are made of rice land (which may be politically impossible at the present time), villages are not going to benefit materially from this redisposition of revenues between central and local governments.

A revision of the division of functions between the various levels of local government is also required, but it may be thought premature to advocate increased responsibilities for village authorities until peace and stability return to the countryside.

Autonomous Agencies

A survey of the budgetary process as it affects selected municipalities would be useful, but for present purposes it is sufficient to note that municipalities, like provincial and village councils, require heavy and virtually open-ended subsidization by the central government. The state-owned enterprises, however, represent so heavy a burden on the national budget that further comment is necessary.

Investment by government in a miscellaneous range of industries has to some extent been necessary because of the reluctance of private investors to provide risk capital in the present circumstances. However, there is little discernible correlation between government investment and the potential of the industries concerned to contribute essentially to economic growth. The first conclusion which emerges, therefore, is that while this investment may be a legitimate activity for the government at the start and in present circumstances, in the future there should be an effort to reduce the utilization of scarce public resources for such purposes, to limit such public investment as may be desirable to selected enterprises which will contribute significantly to economic growth, and to provide incentives and inducements for private investment.

There are serious deficiencies in the accounting systems of many of the existing state enterprises, to the extent that operating costs are unknown and profit or loss margins incapable of calculation. Prices for services or end-products are thus determined arbitrarily, and the government lacks valid criteria for determining amounts of subsidies. These deficiencies go some way to explaining the very large sums of money reserved in the national budget but not specifically allocated for this sector of the economy. So long, however, as government is the unquestioning provider of subsidies to meet losses, and so long as there are no clear-cut development and pricing policies, there will be no incentive to the enterprises to operate efficiently.

The eventual implementation of Decree Law No. 019/820, which provides for a uniform budget, accounting, and audit system for these organizations, should go a long way towards improving the position when implemented, but the present situation represents most haphazard and inefficient channeling of resources.

The Budgetary Process and Resource Allocation

A well-established budgetary concept and process exists, but there is little recognition of the role of policy determination in this process. What then are the more fundamental inadequacies of the system in relation to the allocation of resources?

The first inadequacy, and one of prime importance, lies in the departures from the principle of comprehensiveness of the budgetary document. This departure may be summarized as a failure to include the affairs of autonomous national governmental agencies within the framework of the national budget, thus permitting them to escape budgetary control. In the same manner, the unbudgeted deficits of provincial and village councils are also absorbed, creating an open-ended commitment which it is the responsibility of government to meet.

There is an absence of data concerning actual and revised previous collections or expenditures which makes comparisons of growth and contraction in budgeted items difficult to assess. In addition, the practice of allowing a complementary or carry-forward period of five months in the following financial year, during which revenues received and expenditures made relating to the preceding fiscal year are debited or credited respectively to the accounts of that year, results in an operative cycle which renders early direct annual comparisons impossible and blurs what should be the clear outlines of the accounting period.

There is no clear-cut distinction between revenues or expenditures of a recurrent nature and those of a nonrecurrent or capital nature; neither is expenditure on emoluments delineated. The isolation of the major part of capital expenditures in a separate AID chapter renders any assessment of ministerial policy objectives unrealistic, detracts from the possibility of achieving any real degree of program formulation and project selection, and destroys the essential unity of purpose of the budget.

There is a lack of flexibility, preventing budget modification and expenditure variation during the year to enable programs to be adjusted and new policies or changes in emphasis of existing policies to be provided for. Comparatively large resources are therefore sterilized by the need to reserve block sums for possible supplementary provision for governmental agencies during the year.

At all levels there is tax delinquency and inefficiency in collection, wasting resources which could otherwise be harvested and directed to productive public use. At the local government level, both provincial and village, these failings are at present exacerbated by security considerations, and there is an apparent overstructuring of administration which in many cases makes the incremental gain from revenue negligible or even negative in relation to costs of collection. What resources are available tend to be dissipated on administrative overheads to the detriment of programs productive of services and public works.

Subsidization of local authorities is not geared to essential expenditures and responsibilities; it provides no inducements for enhanced revenue collection or economic disbursement of resources; and as a balancing item in most of such budgets, merely increases their dependence on central authority for even minimal viability. A clear-cut, practical definition of functions and responsibilities is needed which would permit greater scope for delegation of functions under a grant-in-aid system. For management purposes, the budgetary process possesses flaws which must inevitably lead to inefficient allocation of scarce resources. Nevertheless, whatever criticisms can be made of existing budget policies and processes, they should be viewed in the context of the recent constitutional changes, military and ideological conflicts, a background of war, and the ever-present paramount demands for financial support of the armed forces. That developmental and economic planning are secondary considerations in these circumstances is not surprising.

Recommendations for Change

The examination of the traditional budget presentation contained in this chapter exposes the limitations of the present system and reinforces the arguments for modification and change in the budget process. The degree by which the budget fails to provide for the precise allocation of scarce resources between the various priorities, and the extent to which resources may be sterilized through lack of planning or may be used for unproductive purposes, point to a clear need for a more sophisticated appraisal of competing needs and a more accurate and comprehensive approach to allocation. It is these deficiencies which the following recommendations are intended to repair.

1. The format of the estimates of revenue and expenditure should be revised to provide for a clear differentation between recurrent and capital expenditures, and clear comparisons should be made with previous years.

2. The previous recommendation will involve dispensing with the supplementary accounting period. Increased flexibility would assist in this, but really all that is needed is a simple revote procedure to re-provide funds in the subsequent year for approved expenditures which were not realized in the year in which they were due; there is no essential distortion of revenue if it is credited in the fiscal year in which it is received.

3. The AID chapter funds should not be divorced from the individual title estimates. Merging of these funds could improve program formulation and project selection.

4. Greater flexibility should be introduced by controlled statutory delegation of authority down to the level of department

heads for small amounts and in conformity with approved policies.

5. Control and limitation of subsidization of local authorities and the provision of incentives to revenue collection by them should be introduced by means of a grant-in-aid formula related to population, geared to essential expenditures and responsibilities, and variable in relation to revenues collected.

6. A clearer definition of provincial government functions in relation to village government should be provided, and the scope for further delegation of central government developmental activities to provincial councils on a repayment basis with a contribution to overhead costs should be explored.

7. In both provincial and local government there should be greater independence from central control in the matter of staffing, staff remuneration, estimate preparation, and expenditures generally.

8. The transfer to village treasuries of more of the revenues they now collect for government is desirable.

9. A review of the types and incidence of taxation at the province and village levels should be undertaken to obviate the multiplicity of items and services which attract tax and which increase administrative costs to the point of being uneconomical.

10. Decree Law No. 019/820, which provides for uniform budget, accounting, and auditing systems for state-owned enterprises, should be implemented in full as soon as possible.

We believe that these measures would be helpful in improving the value of the budgetary process as an instrument intended primarily for day-to-day administration and control; it is not, however, suggested that they would by themselves remove the fundamental weakness of the budget, which is its failure to reflect adequately and to assist in forward planning, program selection, the establishment of priorities, and, where feasible, the assessment of cost-effectiveness. It is therefore proposed that, as an adjunct to budget preparation, gradual steps should now be taken in the direction of program budgeting.

It has been advocated on more than one occasion that the budgetary system of Vietnam should be abandoned and replaced in entirety by a system more suited to the current needs of the country. It is our opinion that such a step is not only impracticable but also unnecessary. A well-tried, soundly based system which is understood in its complexities by those who operate it has been evolved. The reduced numbers of trained, experienced budget personnel resulting from the war, and the limitations of the civil service as a whole from the same cause, make it most desirable that the existing framework be retained. Improvements can be made to it but, most importantly, a complementary technique should be evolved which, used in conjunction with the existing line-item presentation, will provide a basis for major program and policy decisions which the present system does not permit.

No dramatic change is contemplated or recommended. It is not possible to radically alter a deeply established system in a short period. What is proposed is that progress toward a program budgeting process should be initiated as soon as possible in one area of governmental activity, very much as it was in the United States, where it was originally confined to the Department of Defense. There should be, in fact, a pilot scheme in one agency.

The Joint Development Group has published a working paper, "Towards a Program Budget in Vietnam," which describes in some detail the nature and advantages of program budgeting, and there is no need to repeat it here. Perhaps the most succinct description of program budgeting is contained in a U.S. Congressional committee paper, as follows:

> The PPB system is one more step in a continuing endeavor to make the budgetary process a more versatile and helpful instrument of the President and his principal advisors. As its name suggests it is an effort to tie forward planning to budgeting via programming...
>
> The traditional budget has been prepared and presented in terms of objectives of expenditure or "inputs." In this form the budget has not shown the link between agency spending and agency purposes--between the resources an agency uses and its missions and tasks or outputs. By linking resources to purposes, inputs to outputs in a program

> and by planning ahead for several years, the program budget is expected to contribute to better appraisal by decision makers of what a budget cut or increase would mean in terms of an agency's program--the goals to be pursued and the goals to be sacrificed or deferred.

The working paper "Towards a Program Budget in Vietnam" endeavors to apply the principles and practices advocated in this system first to one branch of a Government of Vietnam ministry in a simple, hypothetical illustration. It then structures a partial program budget for a major ministry containing ten separate agencies. What emerges is a clear indication that the budget of one ministry, at least, would respond readily to programmatic analysis and restructuring, and that there are other ministries as well in which budgets would also lend themselves without undue complication to such treatment.

Of course there can be no question of immediate implementation of such a system. Such techniques take time for installation and require an educational and training program to familiarize staff with new procedures. Continuing studies would be needed to improve and refine the suggested adaptations in individual agencies. But it is a target worthy of consideration during the transition to peace, when a more stable, more capably staffed administrative machine can be brought to bear on the matter. Extension, thereafter, would be a conscious step in a direction in which some expertise had been gathered but would still be subject to personnel availability and training.

The postwar development of Vietnam should not be impeded by deficiencies in administrative techniques, such as budgeting, when processes are available which would help in the acceleration of economic growth through wise and carefully analyzed use of resources. In this context program budgeting has an important role to play, and the opportunity should not be lost to lay a foundation for it now, so that it can be expanded in the period of transition to peace and become fully effective in the postwar period.

CHAPTER 5 EMPLOYMENT, MANPOWER, AND SKILLS

Several studies of manpower problems have been undertaken in Vietnam, and some are still in progress, but most of them are concerned with specific and short-term issues. For example, much work has been done on the implications of current military and paramilitary activities, and the potential impact of recruitment policies on the availability of labor for military contractors, private employers, and agriculture; and careful studies and projections have been made of the requirements for and effects on manpower of direct American military employment.

Less attention has been paid to long-term postwar manpower problems. These include the redeployment policies required to meet a possible reduction in numbers of military personnel and a consequential reduction in employment opportunities in the construction and other industries which support the military effort, if there should be an end to the war. Recommendations for such policies require first an assessment of the dimensions of the problem: how many men, for instance, will be retained by the armed forces; how many and by what stages men will be released to civilian life; what their capacities will be for nonagricultural employment and to what occupations they are naturally inclined; to what extent labor that is surplus to the military effort can be absorbed by programs of reconstruction and development, including those described in this report; how far the population shifts which have occurred during the war will become permanent, and what rural resettlement and rehabilitation programs will be needed for the mass of refugees who crowd the cities; and, finally, what training facilities and administrative and organizational arrangements will be required to make such policies effective.

In very general terms, the dimensions of the immediate problem are seen as follows:

First, there is an army of up to 800,000 men which, during the transition to a secure peace, perhaps five years, will probably remain at approximately that figure. For such men as may be released and do not return to their original pursuits, alternative civilian employment will have to be provided; for the majority who remain in uniform, productive employment should be found in the intervals between periods of active military duty.

Second, there is a refugee population of well over a million; many of these persons will need assistance in reconstructing their rural lives, and others have learned new trades, have left their villages for good, and will prefer employment in the cities.

Third, there is the rising generation; the majority, coming into the labor market from the primary school system, will not necessarily be inclined toward agriculture nor be particularly well qualified to benefit from secondary and higher education even if sufficient facilities existed. There are also about 35,000 students who complete their secondary education each year, and 6,000 or more professional but inexperienced men who graduate from the universities. All will expect to find work, and if they do not will then constitute a potentially dangerous body of discontent.

Fourth, there are suggestions in favor of a reduction in the numbers occupied in the public services--easily the largest employer in the country--which, if implemented for the sake of desired economy and efficiency, will certainly aggravate the potential unemployment problem, unless alternative work is found for those civil servants who lose their places.

Finally, there are the Viet Cong. When peace returns it will be of very great importance, both politically and economically, that they too be absorbed into the economic life of the nation.

The general shape of the immediate problem is now visible: possibly as many as 900,000 people will have to be provided either with assistance to re-establish themselves in self-employed agriculture or with opportunities as wage and salary workers in peacetime public construction programs, such as housing and roads; in the service industries; in private manufacturing industry; in plantation and forest industries. In addition, it will be most desirable to find productive uses for another 600,000 to 800,000 people who may still be in uniform.

These are formidable numbers. The task of finding productive employment for so many in a short term of perhaps the first five postwar years could be daunting. It is none too soon to start thinking in definitive, practical terms of the programs necessary to stabilize, utilize, organize, and remunerate at reasonable levels so large a force of men and women.

In this chapter a closer look at the problem is taken, and an attempt is made to establish a reasonably accurate estimate of its potential magnitude in all sectors of the economy in the first five years after the war. On the basis of manpower requirements for the public programs described in this volume (for water control, transportation, resettlement, and so on), and also of the requirements for private industrial projects and housing, as far as these are known, a first tentative estimate of the potential demand for labor is made. Indications are given of where the labor force can most conveniently and profitably be employed, and where programs might be needed to make productive use of any surplus labor, until such time as existing manufacturing industry revives, investment in new industry takes effect, and the service industries expand to the point where the need for such projects will substantially diminish or, it is hoped, disappear.

THE PRESENT DISTRIBUTION OF THE LABOR FORCE

A number of estimates of the labor force and its distribution have been made since 1954. In 1955 a United Nations Economic Survey Mission estimated the economically active population of South Vietnam at 42 percent of the total (the range of participation rates in Asian countries being set at from 31.7 percent to 51.6 percent). Since the estimated total population was then 12,067,000, if this participation rate was correct, it suggests a labor force of 5,068,140.

TABLE 5.1

Distribution of Labor by Sector, 1960 and 1966

Sector	1960	1966
Agriculture (general)	3,982,000	3,965,000
Plantations	61,000	26,000
Fishing	191,000	254,000
Mining and quarrying	1,000	2,000
Manufactures and handicrafts	124,000	168,000
Construction	50,000	131,000
Commerce, banks, and insurance	206,000	134,000
Transport and communications	145,000	149,000
Electricity, gas, water, & sanitary services	3,000	4,000
Government employees		
Public administration	309,000	330,000
Armed forces	--	680,000
Other services	35,000	67,000
Domestic servants	100,000	115,000
U.S. sector (excluding construction)	--	80,000
Total labor force	5,207,000	6,105,000
Total population	14,072,000	16,500,000

The suggested distribution in 1955 was 90 percent in agriculture (a residual figure), and 4.5 percent in the armed forces and the auxiliary forces. Subsequent studies by the International Labor Organization indicated a reduced participation rate, 39.4 percent, and an economically active population of 4,750,000.

Surveys of employment in industrial and commercial establishments were made by the Ministry of Labor in 1960 and 1966, and in 1960 a census was also undertaken of the agricultural population in 27 provinces. The 1960 surveys resulted in estimates very different from the previous ones: a labor force of 6,475,000 and a participation rate of 47.4 percent. There is no doubt that in this instance the residual figure assumed for agricultural employment was greatly exaggerated. When these figures were revised, however, to take account of the agricultural census, which demonstrated that 85.3 percent of the population were engaged in agriculture, the estimate of the total labor force was reduced to 5,207,000 and the participation rate to 37 percent.

In 1966 a U.S. AID estimate of civilian employment by type of activity indicated a total civilian labor force figure of 5,618,000, and, when the 680,000 men serving in the armed forces were included, a participation rate of 38.2 percent. There was some variation between these results and those produced by the Ministry of Labor, but adjusting the figures to 37 percent participation rate, we have re-estimated employment by sector and provided a comparison with the 1960 figures, as shown in Table 5.1.

ASSUMPTIONS AND PREMISES

Because of the obvious uncertainties concerning the transition from war to peace, statistical projections for the postwar period must rest on a variety of premises and assumptions. The first, and most obvious, difficulty is that a confident prediction cannot be made of when the period will start or of the duration of a possible transitional period in which, though there may not be open warfare, some parts of the country may continue to be disturbed. The projections which follow cover an arbitrarily selected period, 1968-73, and most of our conclusions relate to that time frame. It is also assumed that a cease-fire agreement will be effective to the extent that armed combat and terrorism will stop, or at least will be considerably reduced, and that the population will be reasonably secure in the country as a whole, even though attempts may be made by the insurgents to maintain or acquire political control in particular localities.

Other assumptions are that the political and economic programs of the government of Vietnam will continue to offer its citizens an individual freedom of choice, with no coercion in the exercise and implementation of manpower plans; that the existing political and economic forces in the country will not be drastically or abruptly changed; and that whereas general conditions will tend to be continuations of conditions as they exist today, there will be a degree of economic advancement and an improvement in general affluence as the measures we advocate and the programs which are now being designed are implemented in agriculture, in infrastructure, and in industry. It is not assumed that in these first five years Vietnam will reach a stage of self-sustaining economic growth, but it is assumed that there will be significant progress toward a viable economy.

THE SCOPE OF THE EMPLOYMENT PROBLEM

By 1973 the population of Vietnam may be 20 million, and under extreme conditions, the labor force, now estimated at a little over 6.1 million, might at that time total 9 million persons. If this were to happen, the economy would be required to create work at the rate of 500,000 new jobs a year in order for full employment to be maintained. However well-balanced and expanding the economy might become, it would be impossible for it to sustain a growth rate of these dimensions. In that case, by 1973 unemployment in Vietnam would be widespread and serious. The extreme conditions postulated are simply that the population and the proportion of the economically active part of it will grow at maximum rates during the first five postwar years.

Such growth rates are not altogether inconceivable. The population is said to have increased at an average estimated annual rate of 2.6 percent over the last few years. Such doubts as have been cast on the accuracy of this figure, by experienced observers in medical and social fields, suggest that the average annual increase may be much higher, particularly in Saigon. It is not, therefore, impossible that at least for a time after the end of the war, the rate may rise to over 3 percent and will stay high until family planning programs achieve wider acceptance and become effective. History offers many examples of dramatic increases in birthrates following extended wars.

The current rate of participation of the population in the labor force is thought to be about 37 percent. An increase in this rate may well occur with the end of the war and the removal of the restrictions on mobility imposed by it: 45 percent of the present population is currently in the age group 15-25 years, and if the participation rate were to reach even 46 percent, the kind of widespread unemployment suggested above could very well occur.

We do not consider it likely, however, that the participation rate will reach 46 percent. A rate of 40 percent would be more in keeping with expectations and with experience elsewhere. It may, indeed, be lower than that to begin with, as many women now in employment return to being housewives. At 40 percent, and assuming a population growth rate of 3 percent, the labor force would total about 8 million by 1973--an increase of 2 million, representing 400,000 new employment opportunities required each year. If the population growth rate remains at the presently assumed 2.6 percent and the rate of participation stays constant at 37 percent, then the labor force will approximate 7,150,000 in 1973, and there will be an average annual requirement for over 200,000 new jobs. This is the absolute minimum that will be required.

These are the parameters, and it is probably reasonable to assume that the annual growth rate of the labor force will fall somewhere between them: a figure of 300,000 new jobs required a year seems to be a reasonable basis for the formulation of manpower projections and policies.

There are, of course, two interrelated problems: the immediate postwar task of finding employment for refugees and labor that is surplus to military requirements (as the work associated with the war effort diminishes), and the longer-term necessity for meeting the employment requirements of a labor force expanding under the dual influences of a high birthrate and a higher and more effective degree of participation.

The most important first step toward solving the long-term problem is an effective program of family planning, for the size of the labor force is a direct function of the size of the population. The reasons why population containment is essential in Vietnam are not typical of most other Asian countries, where such controls are needed primarily to limit the number of mouths to be fed. Vietnam should be in a position to export foodstuffs within five years, but it must expect serious unemployment, and it cannot expect standards of living to rise, if the population grows at an uncontrolled rate. Secondly, it may be desirable to consider restrictive child labor legislation for economic if not social reasons. Over 15 percent of the population is in the 10-15-year age group; almost 10 percent is in the 15-20-year age group. Taken together they comprise perhaps one-quarter of the labor force. Their participation during the current period of labor shortages is advantageous to the economy, but, if serious unemployment sets in, then it will be more desirable that heads of households and other adults be given preference. While this proposal cannot be extended to agriculture, where traditionally the entire family lends assistance during planting and harvesting, it is certainly applicable to certain selected industrial occupations.

Similarly, changes in the educational system could have a significant long-term impact on the size and composition of the labor force. For example, compulsory universal education up to the age of 16 would eliminate an appreciable number of young people from the labor force. Obviously, this would require investments in education which may not be practicable for many years to come; but at least some changes could be made in the educational system which would yield greater numbers of more readily employable school leavers and graduates. The present ratio of students pursuing general academic studies to those following technical courses is 156 to 1, yet the most serious labor shortages are in the technical occupations. It is important that the nation's education and training system be as responsive as possible to the needs of the economy. We would venture to suggest that in Vietnam it is not. The subject is further pursued in Chapter 11.

Last, something will have to be done to prevent what is quite likely to happen in postwar Vietnam: a shift from rural underemployment into urban unemployment. The urban drift is no new phenomenon, but it tends to be exaggerated, at least initially, in the developing countries. All feasible measures should be taken to discourage and reduce the movement of people into the cities, for when unskilled people arrive in them they tend to form hardcore pockets of unemployed and unemployables, which, once formed, are extremely difficult to absorb as productive labor. Solutions range from increasing the attractiveness of farm life (through rural electrification schemes, for example, or the development of community institutions) to expounding the simple truth that if agriculture is modernized, and acceptable levels of production are achieved, most people will, in fact, be better off on the farm. This teaching has not, as a matter of fact, been very successful in either the developed or the developing countries, but it is true, and it has to be tried.

REDEPLOYMENT: THE IMMEDIATE PROBLEM

The problems of redeployment fall into four distinct but related categories: demobilization; the interruption of the industrial and service activities which support the war effort; possible reductions in the public services; and the rehabilitation of refugees. Overlaying these problems of redeployment, of course, are those associated with the new generation coming for the first time onto the labor market, as discussed above.

The Armed Forces: Demobilization

It is conceivable, although it may not be probable, that security conditions within five years after the cease-fire will be such that a sizable demobilization of the military forces will be feasible. Should this be so, demobilization of any significant number of troops will have to be approached with caution in view of its potentially disruptive impact on the economy. The great majority of military personnel are unskilled in civilian occupations, and should be prepared as realistically as possible to perform usefully and productively as citizens before they are released.

Within a time frame of five years this is not a very likely contingency. Our hypothesis is that for a number of years after the cease-fire the security forces will, of necessity, be maintained at a high level; indeed, as allied forces are increasingly withdrawn, there may well be an initial increase in establishment levels. For the Vietnamese armed forces to provide their own logistic support, it is estimated that the temporary addition of up to 70,000 men will be necessary. In addition, there are proposals to increase the Republic of Vietnam naval and air forces by over 30 percent, as responsibilities for the riverine fleet now manned by the U.S. Navy and the logistic support given to the U.N. Air Force are transferred. Another 30,000 men could be absorbed in these activities. Limited releases of individuals possessing particular skills will be necessary and desirable, but such individuals will present no employment problems; their skills will be urgently and immediately required in reconstruction, in private industry, in government, and generally in the provision of managerial functions.

In Chapter 4 we state a case for substantial and progressive demobilization in order to release financial resources for investment; and it is recognized that serious political and social problems may occur if the armed forces are kept at existing levels for any length of time after the fighting has stopped. However, whatever the economic arguments, and however strong they may be, the political realities of the situation in Vietnam make wholesale demobilization unlikely. These opposing viewpoints can only be reconciled, and far from completely at that, by providing that the armed forces, when not actively engaged in security operations, should be used for economically productive purposes and should play a significant role in the formation of fixed capital.

Selective demobilization is essential and should be possible. With information provided by the General Headquarters of the Armed Forces, we have prepared, in an as yet unpublished working paper, a breakdown of military occupations and the number of men engaged in each category. No detailed classification exists, and the figures may not be completely up to date and reliable, but they indicate the reserves of skilled labor available in the armed forces, and what skills selective demobilization could release to the economy.

The armed forces numbered about 623,000 troops at the end of 1967, and it was planned that their numbers should reach 800,000 by the end of 1968. Some 73,000 men, roughly 10 percent of the establishment, are classified under more than 150 skilled or specialized occupations (Table 5.2).

TABLE 5.2

Armed Forces: Professional and Technical Skills

Category	Number
Engineers and engineering technicians of various grades	14,040
Skilled construction workers	1,670
Maintenance (various)	8,082
Communications	4,927
Artisans	3,593
Medical (all grades)	7,493
Administration	14,378
Drivers	12,830
Other	5,671
Total	72,684

Very few of these men would fail to find civilian employment suitable to the skills they use in the Army. That they cannot all be released is obvious; the armed forces require such services. But in a peacetime environment many--possibly up to 50 percent--could probably be spared, particularly those who have vital civilian functions to perform; medical aidmen, nurses and doctors, communications experts, and those with technological skills in construction and equipment-handling and maintenance.

In the immediate postwar period, the armed forces can act as a safety valve to some extent, drawing in and providing employment for up to 100,000 potential job-seekers. There are also said to be plans to strengthen the security forces by a considerable expansion of the National Police, which may absorb another 50,000 men. Provided they are capable of being trained, none of these 150,000 men need possess special skills.

The alternative hypothesis is that demobilization will occur at a steady, but comparatively rapid, pace in order to reduce the budgetary burden of a large standing peacetime army. If this is to happen the problems of redeployment will be much more difficult. A reduction to the level of, say, the standing army in 1955, immediately after the Geneva agreement, would release more than 500,000 men to the labor market, possibly at the rate of at least 100,000 a year. Although this possibility may be unlikely, it must be taken into account when the demand for labor in the postwar period is assessed, and when the creation of job opportunities is being considered.

Under either hypothesis, it is hoped that the armed forces will participate fully in the tasks of economic reconstruction and development after the war. It is essential that their important assets in manpower and skills, which would otherwise represent an unproductive expenditure of a very large share of the country's limited financial resources be employed in a positive, productive economic role whenever they are not required for active military purposes. We envisage their uses as being similar in nature to some of the labor-intensive development projects suggested later in this chapter, but the selection of work will be determined more by the localities in which garrisons have to be maintained than by the type of project. Thus the Army might well be employed on the construction of flood control works, drainage works, and navigation canals in the less secure delta provinces, while wage workers are employed on the same works in the secure ones; on new road construction for the expanding timber industry, and for land development and resettlement in the less accessible provinces which are, by definition, also the most disturbed ones; and, of course, serving soldiers should be afforded the same training opportunities as will be available to civilians. It would be advantageous, if it is possible, to regroup Army units so that the men will have the attraction of working for the defense and improvement of their own regions, even, perhaps, of their own localities. It is important, however, that the armed forces should not compete with or reduce the demand for labor in the civilian sector. They should avoid, wherever possible, activities which the private sector has the capacity to undertake. In the industrial sector, it is certainly our firm opinion that there are no development activities that could not be carried out better by private enterprise, if given a relatively free hand and some financial support.

War-Related Activities

The U.S. presence and that of allied nations in Vietnam has led to an abnormal increase since 1965 in the manpower utilized in support activities for their armies. As of June 30, 1968, U.S. government forces and agencies employed 127,418 Vietnamese citizens, 49,989 of whom were unskilled workers (Table 5.3). Most were employed by the U.S. Army, but a substantial number were working for contractors engaged in military construction, including 27,182 who are described as skilled or semiskilled workers. The war, as is well known, has generated a great deal of employment in the construction industry. In Saigon alone, where there were 22,557 construction workers in 1964, there were 69,584 in 1966, including those employed in the U.S. sector. In 1968, throughout Vietnam, 69,000 workers were engaged in civilian construction in the urban areas, largely to meet the temporary demand for accommodation created by the large numbers of foreigners brought into Vietnam by the war.

Another activity which has developed rapidly during the war is transportation. In Saigon transportation workers increased from 88,345 to 113,646 between 1964 and 1966. Throughout Vietnam, there are probably some 175,000 persons working in this field.

In the service industries, employment in Vietnam doubled between 1960 and 1966; and in addition to those accounted for in official statistics, a very large though unknown number of people are earning their living in one way or another, partly or wholly, by providing a variety of services to foreign troops, as peddlers, in restaurants and bars, and so on.

TABLE 5.3

Occupations of Vietnamese Citizens Employed by the U.S. Sector, 6/30/67

Occupation	Number
Total employees	127,418
Executive and managerial	45
Professional, technical and related	8,224
Medical and health	677
Engineers	206
Technicians	1,038
Natural scientists	18
All other	6,285
Clerical	15,917
Secretaries, stenos, and typists	4,056
Record keeping clerks	2,914
Office equipment operators	504
All other	8,443
Sales	949
Skilled and Semiskilled	52,294
Construction trades, - journeymen	23,216
Construction, helpers and junior grade	3,966
Mechanics and repairmen, journeymen	3,718
Mechanics and repairmen, helpers and junior grade	1,107
Machinists and welders, journeymen and helpers	676
Drivers and heavy equipment operators	7,173
Power and water plant, operators and attendants	862
Protective service	632
Other service	2,230
General foremen, not elsewhere classified	178
Other	8,531
Unskilled	49,989
Service	18,553
Guards and watchmen	4,682
Kitchen and dining room	13,187
Service station attendants	684
Other unskilled	
Janitors, cleaners, maids, and caretakers	3,632
Laborers, material handlers	27,296
Laundry	508

When the war ends and there is a reduction in allied establishments in Vietnam, fairly widespread redundancy can be expected in this sector, but we do not expect a serious problem. It is quite improbable that all the agencies of foreign governments will close down suddenly and completely, and some residual employment will be perpetuated. One major source of potential unemployment will arise from the 50,000 or so unskilled materials handlers and service workers, such as guards and kitchen staff. Some of these will find employment outlets in domestic service, others as laborers in reconstruction activities: but men directly engaged in war-related construction can be redeployed in peacetime reconstruction work without much difficulty, and in transportation there will be greatly increased activity once the restrictions on travel imposed by lack of security are removed.

Public Administration

A total of 330,000 civil servants, or 5 percent of the existing labor force, is employed by the government of Vietnam. It is said that suggestions have been made for reducing the number, possibly by as much as one-third, in the interests of greater efficiency and budgetary economy. Given its essential role in the implementation of postwar plans, certainly the public service should not be regarded as a source of employment padding; and in certain areas, though not in all, there are signs that the numbers of public servants now employed are in excess of those required for efficient operation of the government machine.

We question, nevertheless, whether a substantial reduction in force is a practical possibility. In many ways the postwar responsibilities of government will be greater than they are now. There will be expanded activity in many areas of the public service, as the economic development programs now being prepared are put into action and as increased economic activity throughout the country creates additional needs for official supervision and support. That there are redundancies in some branches of government is obvious; but it is likely that any reduction in employment in these branches will be more than compensated for by increases elsewhere. (We have already referred to the possibility of a large increase in the National Security Police, not necessarily correlated with a reduction in the armed forces.) Alternative employment for capable civil servants will be provided in regional development authorities and boards in the provincial and local government, as increased responsibilities, for instance the administration of appropriate public works projects and social services, are transferred to these local authorities. There does not, therefore, appear to be cause for alarm in a reorganization of the public service insofar as the possibilities of its releasing large numbers of men into the labor market are concerned. Reorganization in the interests of efficiency is obviously most desirable.

Refugees

On July 31, 1968 official sources stated there were 1, 122, 958 registered refugees, both in camps and reception centers and outside them (Table 5.4). More than half were in the I Corps Tactical Zone, mainly in Quang Nam and Quang Ngai provinces. There were nearly 300, 000 refugees in the II Corps Zone, but in III and IV Corps the numbers were more moderate and manageable (50, 000 and 115, 000 respectively). Numbers fluctuate considerable depending upon the location and severity of the fighting at any one time, but in I Corps a regular pattern is appearing: in a twelve-month period, about 1 million people register as refugees, roughly 700, 000 of these return to their villages or are otherwise resettled, and about 300, 000 continue in refugee status, adding to the build-up of previous years. This pattern is not untypical of the rest of the country.

Almost all the refugees are farm families displaced by the war from their native villages. Many are simply awaiting an opportunity to go hom and will do so when the war ends. Others have acquired new skills and found employment in urban areas, in an environment which they now probably prefer. These will wish to stay, and for those who stay, but are not gainfully occupied, jobs will have to be found.

Numerically, the refugees constitute the most serious of the postwar employment problems. In succeeding sections of this chapter a tentative assessment is made of the extent to which an expansion in agriculture will provide employment for them, and of the job requirements for the remainder. Though a confident prediction is impossible, it is not overoptimistic to assume that 75 percent of the refugees will

TABLE 5.4

Status of Regular Refugees, 7/3[illegible]/68

Location	In Camp	Out Camp	Location	In Camp	Out Camp	Location	In Camp	Out Camp
I Corps			II Corps			IV Corps		
Da Nang	7,994	25,000	Dalat	0	0	An Giang	1,386	846
Quang Nam	131,897	75,822	Binh Dinh	74,965	105,225	An Xuyen	68	4,000
Quang Ngai	92,347	102,428	Binh Thuan	12,334	893	Ba Xuyen	0	8,227
Quang Tin	47,553	18,692	Cam Ranh	0	0	Bac Lieu	371	231
Quang Tri	43,184	37,642	Darlac	35,412	2,782	Chau Doc	0	1,144
Thua Thien	46,901	19,317	Khanh Hoa	0	0	Chong Thien	958	3,144
			Kontum	10,132	12,566	Dinh Tuong	175	9,584
Total	369,876	278,901	Lam Dong	914	0	Go Cong	145	1,325
			Ninh Thuan	3,185	0	Kien Hoa	0	0
III Corps			Phu Bon	5,207	0	Kien Giang	980	38,000
			Phu Yen	41,142	0	Kien Phong	0	5,096
Bien Hoa	0	0	Pleiku	7,146	0	Kien Tuong	33	33
Binh Duong	9,500	0	Quang Duc	0	0	Phong Dinh	0	2,000
Binh Long	4,528	0	Tuyen Duc	4,631	0	Vinh Binh	0	6,307
Binh Tuy	0	0				Vinh Long	0	10,345
Gia Dinh	4,310	0	Total	195,168	122,133	Sa Dec	0	11,900
Hau Nghia	720	112						
Long An	259	1,274				Total	4,116	102,202
Long Khanh	5,082	2,185						
Phuoc Long	14,200	0						
Phuoc Tuy	0	7,740						
Tay Ninh	652	0						
Vung Tau	0	0						
Total	39,251	11,311						

National Totals

In Camp	608,411
Out Camp	514,547
Total:	1,122,958

Source: Refugee Division, Civil Operation and Revolutionary Development Support (CORDS).

wish to return to their farms; and in other chapters of this volume programs are suggested for helping them to do this or to relocate themselves in other areas if that is what they prefer. Assuming a total of 1,200,000 refugees remaining at the end of the war, with 37 - 40 percent of them economically active and the rest dependents, some 480,000 job opportunities will be required, up to 360,000 of which will be farming on lands either abandoned during the war or to be opened up in new land development projects. The balance of, say, 120,000 will need work in reconstruction, in the service industries, in commerce, and in the industrial sector generally.

THE DEMAND FOR LABOR IN THE IMMEDIATE POSTWAR PERIOD

Agriculture

There is no doubt that when peace returns the first effort must be to reestablish as many refugees as possible in agriculture. The solution to this particular problem of surplus manpower will not lie, at least during the first five years, in the expansion of industry, which, in the short and medium term, will not be able to provide work for anything like the number of people to be accommodated. The function of industrial development as we see it is not just to create work for the sake of work, but to provide a broader base for the economy and to increase national production and income. In the long run, of course, the net effect of sound industrial growth will be an increase in over-all national employment through the achievement of higher levels of national wealth; but in the early years, before investment and industrialization have had time to take effect, the numbers of workers employed in manufacturing will not be very large. If, in two years' time, the total number of jobs in manufacturing were to be tripled, rising from 120,000 to 360,000 (which is most unlikely), the effective result of the additional 240,000 jobs would be the equivalent of a mere 6 percent increase in employment in agriculture.

In spite of the publicity given to industrial damage in the Tet and May offensives of 1968, it is in agriculture that the greatest losses to the economy have been occuring. Large areas of arable land have been abandoned, in many places plantations have been neglected or destroyed, and extensive hectarage may have been rendered infertile, at least temporarily. In 1964, a relatively secure year, official figures suggest that 2,291,600 hectares yielded a first crop of rice; only 2,052,840 hectares were cultivated in 1966. In 1967 and 1968 even more rice land was abandoned, as farmers were forced to leave to find greater security in urban areas. There are no precise and reliable figures available, but it is not unlikely that the present hectarage of abandoned riceland is about 250,000 (net of land brought back into production as the security forces clear areas of enemy, and refugees return to their villages). If land previously under other crops is included, the area of the losses will approximate 300,000 hectares.

On the broad assumption that one hectare can provide for the subsistence of a family, such an area is capable of providing a livelihood (though at subsistence level, not a good one) for 84 percent of the probable number of refugees who will need work after the war. In practice, of course, since yields and fertility are not uniform, there will be wide variations in the size of farm required to yield reasonable farm incomes, but improved practices and increased inputs will raise income levels; and it is not unreasonable to take the view that if indeed 300,000 hectares of abandoned land are available, and if other profitable opportunities in agriculture (such as those we describe later) can be provided, then the essential problem of the refugees concerns only those of them who have come to the cities and do not wish to leave.

Bringing new land into production depends to a large extent on comprehensive water storage, water control, and irrigation projects. These will take time to implement, in some cases as long as twenty years, but some additonal land can be expected to be brought into production in the first five years--possibly as much as 100,000 hectares, including land development projects in the highlands. If resettlement schemes are to be properly organized, administered, and financed, the process of resettlement will be gradual, not swift and sudden. But even in the early postwar years, some opportunities can be created for those refugees who still want to be farmers but have no farms to go to. At the start we envisage only a few thousand families a year being accommodated, but as the larger irrigation and settlement projects are implemented, a target of 10,000 families a year will not be unreasonable.

Our attention has also been called to the land expropriated from French proprietors and large Vietnamese owners in 1958, much of which, probably 400,000 hectares, has not yet been distributed. In fact this land does not appear to be a significant source of employment: about half of it is presently under Viet Cong control, and no doubt redistribution, even if irregular and illegal, has already been accomplished. Nearly all the rest is occupied and worked by squatters and when titles are distributed they should clearly be given first consideration. Only a marginal contribution to the resettlement of refugees in agriculture is likely to be made by these lands.

Forestry

The forest resources of Vietnam will provide a ready source of employment. Forests damaged by shellfire, bombing, and defoliation will need rehabilitation. Reforestation, particularly the planting of pine and eucalyptus around Dalat and Phan Rang as a base for a pulpwood industry, and logging and other extractive activities can utilize the services of up to 60,000 workers, exclusive of those who will be engaged in timber processing industries.

It is clear that in agriculture and forestry together there will be opportunities to provide employment for all the refugees who wish to return to the rural areas, and also some scope for relieving the pressure on the land of those regions where population is most dense and standards of living are consequently low.

Construction

The construction industry employed 131,000 people in 1966. In 1968 probably 150,000 were so occupied, more than half on construction directly related to the war effort. As war-related construction activity declines, it can be expected that private construction and public works will together absorb most of the workers laid off. Extensive programs have been established for repair of the main road network, bridges, and railways. For the Mekong Delta, proposals have been made and a project could soon be ready for implementation consisting of the construction of polders, lock control structures and pumping stations, and the dredging and widening of canals, as the first stage of a comprehensive system of water control for purposes of agricultural development. This one project may provide steady employment for up to 5,000 workers.

It is not possible at this stage to state with any degree of precision the size of the labor force which will be required for postwar reconstruction. It will be considerable, although the adoption of labor-intensive reconstruction techniques cannot be recommended as a matter of deliberate policy if they should be found to result in unacceptable cost-benefit ratios. Labor-intensive operations should be reserved for activities which may be found necessary to bolster faltering employment levels.

In the construction industry, including publicly financed works, there is an important role for private Vietnamese contractors. The employment of private contracting capacity can be particularly beneficial to a developing country; it enlists the management and technical skills of the private sector for public purposes; it encourages the private sector to acquire and invest in capital equipment; it leads to the accumulation of new investment capital from profits; and, as has been demonstrated elsewhere, it usually gets the work done more efficiently and at lower cost.

Industry

We have assumed a labor force of 120,000 workers in manufacturing establishments in 1966, and if account is taken of cottage industries, a figure of 168,000 is possible. Of the 120,000 regular wage earners, 60,000 are employed in the most important manufacturing activities, mainly in the Saigon area; this is the high productivity group and the employment base on which major industrial expansion will occur in the future. The other 60,000 work for small, family-sized businesses, scattered throughout the country.

Manufacturing will not absorb very much surplus labor in the immediate postwar years. It cannot, at least at the start, provide opportunities for employment comparable with those offered by agriculture. Industrialization is a long process in which valuable employment effects will not be felt for a number of years. We estimate 1978 employment in industry (i.e., assuming the scale of investment described in Chapter 9) as 250,000-300,000. In the first five peacetime years, employment in manufacturing will do well to achieve half of this objective, say 150,000 jobs, only 30,000 more than the present estimate.

Trade and Commerce

At this stage it is almost impossible to predict what employment patterns will emerge in the trade and commerce sector. There are too many imponderables. Some disruption is certain to occur in those activities which provide directly or to a great extent for the needs of foreign troops or personnel, but a significant reduction in the purchasing power of the population generally is not envisaged. Indeed, as capital investment is made in reconstruction, and as the value of increased agricultural yields and industrial processes enter the market, the buoyancy of trade should be maintained. In banking and insurance circles there will almost certainly be an increase in activity.

A PROJECTION OF EARLY POSTWAR DEMAND AND SUPPLY

Given wise use of resources, sensible planning, and the necessary financial inputs, there should be no insuperable difficulty in finding effective employment for the refugees, the presently unemployed persons (who are few), and those for whom the end of the war will imply an end of the work on which they are presently engaged. This conclusion rests on a set of assumptions, of unproven validity, certainly, but reasonably acceptable in the existing circumstances of Vietnam. The two safety valves are the armed services and rural rehabilitation. Assuming (1) continuing high levels, possibly, even, increases, in mobilization, and (2) sufficient financial resources for rural rehabilitation and resettlement, serious unemployment in the immediate postwar period is unlikely to occur. There is no alternative to rural rehabilitation and it must be a major objective of immediate postwar policy. Should there be, contrary to the first of these assumptions, any substantial demobilization, then the organization of programs planned to absorb surplus labor will be necessary. There is ample scope for these in many parts of Vietnam.

In summary, the immediate postwar manpower problem begins to look like this:

There will be 900,000 economically active persons looking for new work very shortly after the war ends. The majority of these, about 480,000, will be refugees; there will be at least 200,000 recruits to the labor force from the rising generation; there may, though we think it unlikely, be 100,000 temporarily redundant civil servants after possible reform of the public services; some 40,000 men now employed in the U.S. and other foreign sectors may be released from their engagements, and as many as 75,000 men and women now occupied in war-related construction activities will be out of work, though not all of them immediately.

Even if some selective demobilization of men with skills is possible as allied support is withdrawn, there may be a net increase in the armed forces and in the National Police of 100,000 men. Whatever the numbers, perhaps 100,000, of redundant civil servants, they will in effect be reassigned to other public services. Of the refugees, 410,000 will be resettled on the lands they have abandoned or relocated in new resettlement schemes, 60,000 can find work in forestry, and 10,000 in new and expanding industries. There will be an increase in construction activities as infrastructural reconstruction and rehousing gets under way, and this increase could not only accommodate the 75,000 who will be released from war-oriented construction but could possibly provide employment for a further 25,000 men. There will also be an increase in trade and service activity which may provide work for yet a further 20,000 or more. There will still be some 40,000 to 60,000 persons for whom productive work may have to be created, possibly in labor-consuming programs until normal economic growth is resumed.

THE LONG-TERM DEMAND FOR LABOR

It is a reasonable expectation that labor availability will grow at a rate of about 300,000 a year. It is possible that, given a continuing state of security in the next five years, the political and budgetary difficulties of maintaining a large standing army will be such that demobilization will become essential. Should the numbers of the armed forces be reduced by 50 percent over three years, a further 400, 000 men would become available for civilian employment during this period.

Agriculture, once again, would be the main source of employment. It has been suggested that greater use of high-yielding varieties, more extensive application of fertilizer and insecticides, the increased practice of double-cropping arising from improvements in water control, and greater diversification of crops will demand more work to sustain production. This is true, but it may not involve a significant increase in the agricultural labor force. The degree of underemployment in agriculture has been estimated at between 30 percent and 60 percent. New practices will help to reduce agricultural underemployment and will also help to increase farm incomes, but we do not think that there will be an appreciable demand for additional labor, other than at harvest times. It may be that this seasonal demand will bring into being a pool of urban-based migratory labor, engaging in casual work in off-periods but earning a supplementary income from providing assistance in rural areas during harvesting, and this could form a useful addition to the labor force. But for many years to come, probably as much as 80 percent of the economically active population will continue to depend primarily on agriculture, and new areas must be brought into cultivation to accommodate them.

In this volume there are proposals for water control, irrigation, and land reclamation projects throughout Vietnam which will not only lead to increased yields and crop diversification but will also put new lands under production. In the five northern provinces alone, a thirty-year water development program is suggested which will eventually extend to 410, 000 hectares of land (Chapter 12). Similar opportunities present themselves, though to a lesser extent, in the Central Highlands and the coastal lowlands of II Corps. In the Dong Nai Basin it is possible that very large areas can be put under crops as the hydroelectric potential of the Dong Nai River is developed and water storage for irrigation is provided. The program of water control proposed for the Mekong Delta is intended to make possible the exploitation of the full agricultural potential of that important region.

In all, it would not be unduly optimistic to predict that these programs may make an additional million or more hectares of farmland available; but this will be over a long term, probably in excess of thirty years. In such a period, population growth in the agricultural sector will be such that even an increase in farm areas of this size will fail to satisfy demands. In the short term, employment in reconstruction projects planned to absorb surplus labor will provide for labor in the urban areas in the critical period between the end of the war and the time when expanding industry, commerce, and services will create other employment opportunities. However, there seems to be no escape from the conclusion that in the long run, although Vietnam may be able to feed its growing population, unless effective measures are taken to limit population growth, it will do so only at the expense of reduced standards of living.

THE DEMAND FOR PROFESSIONAL SKILLS

Previous sections of this chapter are concerned principally with unskilled, semiskilled, and agricultural labor requirements, but the opportunities described will not be realized unless adequate managerial and technical skills are available to provide direction and control. "As a rule the rate of accumulation of strategic human capital must always exceed the rate of increase in the labor force as a whole. The rate of increase in scientific and engineering personnel may need to be at least three times that of the labor force. Sub-professional personnel may have to increase even more rapidly."*

As recently as 1967 it was estimated by the Directorate General of Planning that almost 6,000 additional professional, subprofessional, and skilled workers were required at that time to meet existing needs. Over the next three years, it was thought, these requirements would more than double.

A preliminary breakdown of projected requirements is provided in Table 5.5. This projection has not taken into

---

*Frederick H. Harbison: Human Resources Development Planning in Modernizing Economies, 1962.

TABLE 5.5

Estimate of Skilled Manpower Requirements for 1968-71

Sector	Pro-fessional	Subpro-fessional	Skilled	Total
Administration	90	177	26	293
Post office and telecommunications	19	187	123	329
Agriculture (including animal husbandry)	825	926	1,212	2,963
Mechanics	89	238	1,072	1,399
Marine	16	38	85	139
Aeronautics and rail-roads	45	224	1,035	1,304
Public works	129	272	76	477
Industry	87	92	184	363
Electricity and electronics	188	257	523	968
Mining	25	23	53	101
Chemistry	76	91	29	196
Construction	84	29	26	139
Economics and finance	145	345	15	505
Food industry	13	29	29	71
Forestry	118	143	-	261
Law	209	252	-	461
Banking	9	-	-	9
Fishery	129	143	123	395
Management	70	78	20	168
Statistics	58	98	91	247
Sociology	41	64	-	105
Health	245	310	-	555
Radio and television	10	17	60	87
Teachers	805	355	-	1,160
Vocational training	82	62	-	144
Other	294	172	245	711
Natural science	54	5	-	59
Total	3,955	4,538	5,043	13,536

account the additional requirements of development programs in the postwar period. Industrialization alone will require many more engineers and managers than there now are. The present system of education in Vietnam is not adapted to the formation of men of this type in adequate numbers; the most serious educational deficiencies are in the technical and vocational fields, and though several studies have been made and numerous recommendations presented, there has been little opportunity during the war to act on them. Technical and vocational schools should be given top priority, even at the expense of faculties of law and letters, and the sooner this can be done the better. For some types of skills there are presently no training facilities whatever in Vietnam; but there are, of course, many Vietnamese who possess these critical skills residing in foreign countries, and a conscious effort should be made to persuade them to return. If they do not, then Vietnam will depend far more than is desirable on importing skills from overseas in the years following the war. Adult education and in-service training should be encouraged. In short, a rationalization of the educational system in terms of economic requirements is urgently needed, and if an immediate program of reform is to be carried out a far larger budgetary allocation for technical and selected professional training will be necessary.

THE INSTITUTIONAL FRAMEWORK

Manpower planning as an organized national process has achieved few successes which can be directly applied to new situations. But it has been developing an improving methodology and an extensive record of effort and of results. The clearest lesson this record offers is that the process of planning must not be separated from the process of implementation. This dictum applies to all organized human activity, but particularly to human resources planning, which is a multidimensional, multiinstitutional function penetrating all aspects of national life. Any manpower planning process which is not accomplished in conjunction with the implementing authorities will be incomplete and ineffective.

We believe, then, that the basic steps in the process of human resources development in Vietnam should be the establishment of an organization having high status, its chairman reporting directly to the prime minister and consisting of key ministers and a small permanent staff of professional planners. It should be the task of this organization to develop and specify the government's manpower plans. In another chapter we have advocated a National Institute of Planning. It would not be inappropriate for human resources development planning to take place under the aegis of this institute in order to achieve the degree of coordination with other aspects of economic planning which will be essential to its success.

The other institution vital to the proper implementation of any manpower organization is an effective national employment agency to help workers find employment and employers to find workers. We shall be developing this theme in a future work in which we hope to make detailed recommendations. This theme has been developed in a separate report in which specific recommendations concerning a job placement service are made.*

---

*Development and Resources Corporation Report: Labor, Employment and Skills, October, 1969.

CHAPTER 6 INSTITUTIONAL DEVELOPMENT

Recent political developments suggest that operational economic development plans in several sectors may be needed rather soon in Vietnam and it is timely to consider what capacity there is in the Republic to design and implement such plans. The end of the present war will not be the first occasion on which Vietnam has embarked on a program of economic development. Since independence, successive governments have prepared plans and projects intended to secure the exploitation of Vietnamese resources in the interests of the Vietnamese people. Thus two separate five-year plans were drafted in 1956, one intended for implementation in the years 1957 to 1961, and the other in the years 1962 to 1966. A one-year plan was prepared in 1966. They were not necessarily bad plans, but usually their objectives were to alleviate specific conditions, particularly those arising from the war, not to promote steady and continuing economic growth; and, in the event, implementation of previous plans has consistently fallen short of the intentions of their authors, leaving a legacy of disillusionment and cynicism of which the Joint Development Group has been made aware though it does not in any way share in it.

Development plans and policies (including those presented in this book) are significant only to the extent that they result in actions being taken which will provide better living for the ordinary men and women of the nation. The fact is that though the war may be won, the peace cannot be kept without economic progress; and plans and policies do not achieve economic progress by being written, but by being applied. The plans ought to be sensible and realistic ones, so the men who make the decisions (and who are not themselves expected to be experts in economics or engineering or agriculture or finance) must be able to command objective and disinterested advice from people who are expert in these matters; and since their decisions have to be carried out, they must also command men and organizations that are capable of doing this honestly and efficiently.

The questions addressed in this chapter are simple ones. It is a matter of establishing (1) who will consider the choices, establish the priorities, and make the decisions, (2) who will provide the advice on which good decisions can be made, and (3) perhaps most important of all, who will actually do the work. At the present time the institutional resources of Vietnam, confused and weakened by the war, leave a good deal to be desired in all of these respects.

In the sections which follow, the formation of the existing National Planning Council is reviewed and a recommendation is made for the establishment of a National Institute of Planning and Development. The implementation of development is considered broadly; activities at national, regional, and local levels are discussed in relation to the formation and capabilities of existing and future institutions under which development programs can be advanced.

THE NATIONAL PLANNING COUNCIL

Since independence the history of development institutions in Vietnam has been one of frequent and sudden change, suggesting either that the search for satisfactory solutions has been difficult, or, possibly, that although it is easy to create institutions on paper it is not so easy to find the right men to staff them and make them come to life. A Directorate General of Planning was created as early as 1955, but with an increasing tendency in later years toward personal and centralized government the office operated under the direct authority of the president and appears to have lost any capacity it may at first have had to provide disinterested and objective advice. This particular department of government still exists, of course, now within the prime minister's office and therefore without the constraints placed upon it by previous regimes; but the scope of its activities and its capacity to perform a useful development planning function have diminished, possibly because of a shortage of qualified staff, but perhaps primarily because in recent years, when resources have been mobilized for the single purpose of winning the war, no priority has been given inside the government to the prospects for economic development after the war is won. Since 1966 the functions of the Directorate General of Planning have been discharged in practice by the Joint Development Group, a body which has no official status and an uncertain span of life. Whatever the reason the capacity and prestige of Directorate General of Planning have shrunk to a point at which it is presently incapable of any significant influence on development decisions.

This does not mean that there was no planning of any kind for long-term development before the establishment of the Joint Development Group. Many ministries have planning directorates or services, and so of course have Electricity of Vietnam and other autonomous or semiautonomous agencies, including the National Bank. The programs described in Part II of this volume have in some instances drawn heavily from these services. But, with the possible exception of the National Bank, development planning of this sort has inevitably been narrow and sectoral, concerning itself with particular ministerial or departmental functions rather than with the entire range of national development, and with immediate wartime problems instead of continuing economic progress. In a period when the resources devoted to development have been insignificant (as described in Chapter 4) and when there has consequently been little prospect that plans could be implemented, planning within the ministries and other agencies has also been necessarily academic. Commonly, the result has been simply catalogues of unrelated projects and aspirations, prepared without reference to the total resources likely to be available or to any priorities within a national development program.

Proposals for remedying this situation were submitted in a report presented to the Central Committee for Administrative Improvement in December 1966. The establishment of a small high-level planning council was recommended and so was the reorganization and strengthening of the Directorate General of Planning to enable it to serve as the council's secretariat. The first of these recommendations has been implemented, though not in the precise terms in which it was made, by the setting up in June 1968 of a National Planning Council. This sits under the chairmanship of the president and consists of five permanent members, two of them ministers, and of such other ministers, officials, and private citizens whose presence may be deemed desirable from time to time for the discussion of particular subjects. It is in the National Planning Council that the power of decision in matters of economic and social development now appears to lie and will presumably stay. The council's functions are to determine the general strategies and priorities of all public development programs, to keep a continuing watch on progress, and to adjust policies according to changing circumstances.

The second recommendation, designed to provide the council with an executive staff capable of preparing programs and projects for consideration by the council, and of supervising the implementation of programs after they have been approved, has not been implemented. If the Joint Development Group's understanding is correct, the intention was to absorb the Directorate General of Planning and other governmental agencies into a Commissariat General of Planning whose commissioner general would simultaneously act as secretary general of the National Planning Council and would thus provide the link between planning, decision, and implementation. Apparently it has not been possible to proceed with this intention. As a result the Directorate General of Planning has been left exactly as it was, and the National Planning Council has been left without the tools it needs to discharge its important functions.

AN INSTITUTE OF PLANNING AND DEVELOPMENT

As it now exists, the Joint Development Group cannot supply the need for planning and development. It is not a permanent organization, it has no official status (though it has intimate and mutually beneficial relationships with the prime minister's office and several ministries), it is dependent for its existence partly on annual appropriations by the legislature and partly on arrangements with the U.S. government. In these circumstances it has not been able to attract the full-time services of Vietnamese citizens of caliber to a task which, however important and absorbing, does not offer them prospects of lifetime and rewarding careers. With the help of the ministries of government, the technical divisions of U.S. AID, and numerous other agencies, the Joint Development Group is able to present, for the first time for many years, a general review of the prospects for the economy in the ten years following the end of the war which, it is hoped, will provide an acceptable framework within which detailed development planning can proceed and decisions can be taken. But this has been a limited function, useful for present circumstances but not of enduring and permanent value in meeting future and changing needs and opportunities. The Joint Development Group in its present form is not equipped to provide the National Planning Council and the government with continuing, almost perpetual, authoritative counsel on the variety of matters which will require decision as events unfold. Something new is wanted, and the Joint Development Group believes that now is the time, before the group's own existence comes to an end, to create it.

In a series of memoranda prepared in the middle of 1968 we advocated the establishment of an Institute of Planning and Development, and this recommendation and the arguments used to support it are here repeated. It is now generally recognized, by responsible officials in the Government of Vietnam as well as in the government of the United States, that there is a need for an organization which can undertake substantive economic and technical studies and provide advice on major policies to the government.

The principal criteria for such an organization are as follows:

First, it should be a permanent group, one that would not exist at the pleasure of a particular official or by virtue of a particular and not necessarily enduring policy.

Second, as a corollary to the above, it should be an apolitical body, so that it can preserve some independence in its approach to problems and give judgments and advice unaffected by political expediency.

Third, it should be a thoroughly professional body of technical and economics personnel, with sufficient incentives of all kinds to its staff to persuade men of the highest qualifications and competence to make a career of development planning and implementation.

Fourth, while it should be linked somewhat closely to decision-making in the government, and particularly to the National Planning Council, it should not be so closely linked that it would be in the position of having to undertake task order assignments to provide justification for decisions which have already been taken.

These criteria can be summarized by saying that the proposed group should be permanent, professional, and reasonably independent. The question arises of how to find an institutional arrangement consistent with the experience of Vietnam into which to fit such an organization. One alternative (which has in fact been discussed inside the government after presentation of the memoranda referred to) would be to transfer the Postwar Planning Group directly to a government office--perhaps a Ministry of Planning or a Ministry of Development--and to make it an integral part of that office. This would, unfortunately, make the group subject to any reorganization that might later occur, and more importantly, would deny it the degree of independence and permanence necessary for effective action. A second alternative would be to create a private but nonprofit corporation on the lines of the Brookings Institution in the United States, the Getulio Vargas Foundation in Brazil, or the Center for Development Studies in Venezuela. There are some attractions in all of these models, but there are also disadvantages: the agencies named are not in fact closely involved in development planning for all sectors of the economies of their countries, there is no cultural experience with this type of unofficial operation in Vietnam, and there is the general improbability that any device which works in one country will, without substantial modification, work equally well in another.

Our preference is to seek a solution which will be more familiar in its arrangements to the kind of society that is evolving in Vietnam, and it will probably be found somewhere between the two alternatives described above. The following proposals are advanced to provide a basis for discussion.

1. We recommend the creation by decree of an Institute of Planning and Development. The particular name does not greatly matter; but the one suggested implies that the institute would have functions somewhat broader than research and planning, as it should, and that it could also assist in supervising the implementation of development programs after they have been approved. There are precedents in Vietnam, in the National Institute of Statistics and the National Institute of Administration, for the establishment of such an agency, though it is hoped that the proposed Institute of Planning and

Development would be granted a somewhat greater degree of autonomy than either of these institutions.

2. The institute would report directly to and would supply research and advisory services to the National Planning Council, the body from which major policy decisions will come. The major share of its work and the greater part of its income will be derived in this way from the government, and its primary concern will be with development problems internal to the Republic. However, it is most desirable that the institute should also have authority to contract separately with external agencies such as the Asian Development Bank and the Economic Commission for Asia and the Far East (ECAFE) for basic economic and technical studies, particularly those which concern any Vietnamese interest in regional economic integration. The institute should additionally be authorized to negotiate directly for grants and other forms of assistance with the United Nations and with private foundations overseas.

3. It is suggested that the institute's staff should consist of four classes of personnel. First there should be a group of from six to eight very senior staff members, including a director, who would be remunerated not on the basis of civil service salary scales but in accordance with the rewards that men of like quality have come to expect from private industry or from the existing state-owned enterprises. This would be an elite group, the members of which would undertake major responsibilities for directing independent research on important problems. The composition of the group might vary from time to time, but changes should not be so numerous or frequent as to impair the continuity and cohesiveness of the institute's activities. Like other members of the institute's staff, these men would be expected to devote their full energies to the institute's purposes and would not be free to engage in other business. Second, there should be a professional group of permanent people at the level of senior civil servants. Third, there should be a provision for "senior fellowships," tenable for periods of approximately one year, available to civil servants, faculty members from the universities, and men from private business and industry, who would pursue selected research topics during the duration of their fellowships and then return to their previous occupations. Finally, there should be provision for lower-level and younger professional men, recent graduates from the universities, serving the institute as research assistants and acquiring practical

professional experience while they do so. These assignments should be limited in numbers so that they would be prized.

4. The institute will not be able to carry out its responsibilities to the National Planning Council and the government unless its personnel policies are militantly on the side of merit, and appointments, promotion, and seniority should be based on performance, not merely on past degrees, current status in the university community, and hierarchical rules. Merit and performance can only be demonstrated by quantitative, policy-oriented research.

5. The institute should have a Board of Trustees which would meet twice a year to consider the merits and content of the research program and make recommendations for promotions within the institute or for the release of staff members who have not performed adequately. The membership of the board (perhaps nine in number) might appropriately be derived in equal proportions from (a) members of the Cabinet, (b) the private sector, and (c) outstanding representatives of the legislature and the universities.

A high-level professional organization of this type should be able to attract financial support and technical assistance from overseas foundations. Some preliminary estimates of costs for the institute have been prepared, and these indicate that capital costs would be in the range of US$120, 000 (almost entirely the cost of constructing and equipping suitable premises) and that annual operating costs might be from $130, 000 to $150, 000. An additional budget allowance would be required for a limited input of foreign advisers during the formative years. If the Joint Development Group's recommendation in favor of the establishment of this institute is accepted in principle, we would propose in the following six months to take the following steps:

1. Preparation, for consideration by the president and prime minister, of a paper describing in detail the functions and organization of an Institute of Planning and Development. This would include personnel policies for the appointment and removal of staff, and provisions for the control of the institute through the Board of Trustees.

2. Negotiations with interested parties both inside Vietnam and overseas for the financing of the institute's operations.

3. The drafting of a decree establishing the institute. The need is now urgent, and the sooner this can be done the better.

IMPLEMENTATION OF DEVELOPMENT PROGRAMS

It is recognized that within a national plan of development there will be regional, local, and communal interests to be served and regional as well as national sentiments to be satisfied. Not only substantial political advantages but also faster economic progress and increased administrative efficiency are likely to result from the decentralization of the direction and control of the development effort; the objective is to give the ordinary men and women of the nation familiar knowledge of what is intended and what is happening, a voice in the kind of decisions that will be necessary at local levels, and an opportunity to control the ways in which these decisions are carried out. Here and elsewhere in this book we recommend that considerable responsibilities for economic development and for the provision and maintenance of social services be placed upon representative, self-governing, and democratic organizations in the regions, provinces, and villages of the country.

The Role of Saigon

It is not implied that a policy of decentralization can be followed for the entire range of activities which make up an integrated development program. Most of the matters treated in previous chapters require decisions which can only be made at the highest level in the executive and in the National Assembly; and many, perhaps most, of the matters treated in subsequent chapters are presently within the functions of the regular ministries of the government and their departments and services. The principal responsibility for turning approved policies into operational plans must be borne by these ministerial offices. While their capacity to perform development functions satisfactorily has been weakened by the military draft and by the limitations of a public service system which is in need of extensive reform, these defects are not inherent and irremediable; and institutional development in Vietnam should not be a matter of depriving the regular agencies of government of the functions which are natural to them for the sake of untried and unfamiliar innovations. These functions would not necessarily be discharged more efficiently simply by providing the same men with new titles. To a large extent institutional development implies equipping the ministries with the men and the resources and with the all-important sense of purpose that leads to efficient performance.

The principle that should apply is that what can be done best by the ministries and other governmental agencies in Saigon should be done in Saigon, but that what can be done best in the regions and the villages, by the people for themselves, should be done in the regions and the villages, with whatever support and assistance the ministries may be able to provide, but without the kind of interference and control which vitiates local purpose and initiative. A policy of decentralization can be applied to a good many development activities, both those of a ministerial character and others, and it is most desirable that this should happen.

It is most desirable because Vietnam is now entering upon a period of movement and change which, in the perspective of history, will be infinitely more important than the period of waste, destruction, and strife that has preceded it. This kind of movement simply cannot be accomplished entirely out of offices in Saigon; it will take place in the fields and forests and factories, and it cannot be accomplished in the end by statesmen and civil servants, however wise and devoted they may be, but only by the great mass of the people, spontaneously identifying their own self-interests with those of the nation and applying their energies to secure it. In the next ten, and for that matter, in the next twenty or thirty years, this movement will involve a mobilization of human resources, spontaneous instead of compulsory, for peace and production rather than for war and waste, but every bit as total and complete as mobilization for the armed forces has been in the last few years.

The problem therefore is one of getting ordinary people interested and involved. We do not subscribe to the belief that the people need to be taught what their problems are or where their interests lie. There has been ample evidence during the war of their skillful and swift adaptability to change, and of their readiness to invest cash and effort in improvements which offer assurance of better living. With the exception of the great infrastructural works brought about by military requirements, probably the single most important development of recent years has been the purchase by over 100, 000 small farmers of 4-5 horsepower pumps and motors, an investment accomplished entirely from their own savings, without cost or trouble to the government, which has directly increased the production of particular crops with which these same farmers were quite unfamiliar a few years ago. People who can demonstrate this degree of capacity for self-improvement in time of war are unlikely to be resistant to new economic opportunities when the war is over; and though well planned and well-managed development plans are obviously necessary, some economic progress--perhaps a great deal--can be made simply by the removal of the multitudinous restrictions on human economic activities which have been introduced for military reasons. A particular example of such a restriction, one that has deprived the economy of several million dollars in foreign exchange and has deprived many hundreds of families of useful and profitable occupations, is mentioned in Chapter 8. A useful task will be reviewing all such remaining restrictions and recommending which of them ought now to be dispensed with.

Nevertheless, even if some progress and some improvement can be made in this way, the Vietnamese people will not be able to exploit their economic opportunities to the full unless they can be brought to believe that the government's programs are intended to serve them, that the projects set out in these programs are really going to happen, and that their participation is necessary and will be welcomed. Ultimately the success of the development effort will depend on the degree of understanding, enthusiasm, and participation it will attract from the communities it is intended to benefit in the country's towns, villages, and hamlets. In Vietnam, as in any other country, it is undeniably difficult for any agency of the central government, situated in the capital, restricted by bureaucratic procedures, and unavoidably remote, to reach out to the rural areas and inspire and foster this kind of local enthusiasm. If it can be done at all it can only be done by organizations which the people recognize as their own; and in the period of postwar development, organizations which they recognize as their own will be wanted both in the regions and at local levels. These will be the agencies that will turn into action substantial sections of the development plan, including those sections of it which are most meaningful to the ordinary people of the land.

Regional Implementation of Development

Three major geographical areas of Vietnam which lend themselves to programs of regional development, and possibly two others, are identified in Chapter 12. Each of the three, the five northern provinces, the Central Highlands, and the Mekong Delta, has problems and opportunities peculiar to itself, though the opportunities of one may sometimes complement the problems of another. Each, for historical as well as geographical reasons, is now in a stage of development which sets it somewhat apart from the rest; and in each the inhabitants appear to have a distinct sense of their identity within the nation as a whole. It is substantially for this reason that special regional development programs are recommended in Chapter 12: the content of these programs is not, in fact, so very different from that of national programs lying within the functions of the ordinary agencies of the central government, but the presentation of these programs in a regional context offers the best hope that they will become credible to the people they are intended to help. It is within the regions, and within the provinces, villages, and hamlets of the regions, that a community of interest is most clearly visible and popular participation in the development effort is most likely to occur.

In Chapter 12 we have also suggested the regional organizational arrangements we believe to be appropriate in each case. They need not follow an identical pattern, indeed it is far preferable that each should be tailored to fit the peculiarity of the regional circumstances. In the five northern provinces, where the most pressing and immediate problem, the resettlement of the refugees, will, it is hoped, be of short duration, the device already adopted by the government--the appointment of a Commissioner for Development to supervise and coordinate ministerial activities--may well be sufficient to secure the efficient execution of the regional development program. In the Central Highlands and the Mekong Delta, where programs are contemplated extending far beyond the normal ten-year horizon of this study, more permanent and elaborate organizational arrangements are needed. This may also prove to be true in the coastal lowlands of the II Corps Tactical Zone, for which the beginning of a possible regional development approach is being planned, and in some of the provinces surrounding Saigon, for which regional development has still to be formulated.

Although the pattern will not be identical, some characteristics of regional development authorities will be common to all.

1. In previous discussions on this subject these agencies have occasionally been referred to as "autonomous" or "independent." This has been an error. Essentially the function of these bodies is the management within an area of those projects of a national plan which are of particular significance to the area. Regional development authorities in Vietnam will be answerable to the government (which retains over-all responsibility for implementation of the national plan) and to the legislature (from whom a substantial proportion, at least, of the income of the authorities will be derived). At the very least the government will wish to retain control over appointments to the governing boards of the regional authorities, and the legislature will wish to satisfy itself that the moneys allocated for regional projects are properly spent and accounted for. In these circumstances, to speak of "autonomy" or "independence" is misleading.

2. Within these obvious limitations, however, all regional development agencies should be given the utmost liberty in the conduct of their day-to-day business, operating more in the style of private corporations than in that of government departments, and applying personnel policies that will attract to their services men of talent and ability.

3. The headquarters of any regional development authority should be set up within the area it is intended to serve; and members of the governing board should be appointed on merit, but also with a view to those communal interests, whether they be technical, religious, or political, which are dominant in the region. Some consultation, perhaps of an informal nature, would be advisable with regional interests and with appropriate members of the legislature before appointments to the boards are made, and if it is considered necessary to appoint some representatives of the central government to the boards, these should be men with local affiliations and should not be so numerous as to constitute a majority. If these bodies are to attract and employ regional energies and loyalties for development, then they must be given a distinctly regional appearance. On the other hand, the professional employees of the boards should be appointed solely on the basis of capacity without regard to their origins.

4. The financial requirements of the regional development programs are very large. In the Mekong Delta, for example, probably the equivalent of US$400 million in the first ten years after the war will be needed; in the five northern provinces almost US$200 million for the development of water resources and about US$50 million for the resettlement of refugees, in addition to other projects of lower but still substantial cost. In the main, these large financial requirements can only be met from budgetary allocations made by the government with the approval of the legislature or from grants and loans by external financing agencies: but the regional development authorities ought, in addition, to have some local source of revenue which they would be free to apply to projects of social and economic development in consonance with the general objectives of a national development plan but selected by themselves. In the Mekong Delta, for example, the most likely regional source of income will be water charges contributed by local development associations to meet the costs of irrigation water-supplies and drainage.

5. It should be made clear that the regional development authorities are not intended to supplant the ministries of government in their ordinary field activities, but rather to coordinate and support the ministries' work within each region. There may be certain projects of such significance--for example, the construction of water control works in the Delta region--and of such concern to more than one ministry as to warrant their being undertaken by an authority on its own account, but the general intention is that the regional development programs will be implemented by the development authorities and the ministries under such cooperative arrangements as may suit each case.

With the exception of the Mekong Delta program, the regional development programs set out in Chapter 12 are still in a very preliminary stage of preparation. In some cases they represent rather an accumulation of ideas and policies, and extensive engineering surveys and investigations as well as feasibility studies will be required before operational development plans take shape, financing can be sought, and construction started. At the present time and in present conditions of security the opportunities for action are still limited.

In these circumstances there may be an inclination to defer the establishment of regional development authorities until after the war. We do not recommend this course: the assumption on which we have proceeded so far is that, wherever and whenever circumstances permit, development programs should be set in motion without waiting for peace to return to the entire country. Such opportunities as exist should be taken; and even under existing conditions, the legislative processes necessary to the development program can be got ready and initiated. The early establishment of regional development authorities is therefore strongly recommended; they can represent regional needs, direct and contribute to the elaboration or amendment of the programs suggested in general terms in Chapter 12 (so that in their final form these will be more truly representative of regional opinions), start to assemble their staffs, educate public opinion, and, most important, provide a demonstration in their regions of the seriousness with which the postwar development program is to be undertaken. We believe that an early announcement by the government of an intention to plan a substantial proportion of its development program within a regional context and the establishment for this purpose of regional development authorities in appropriate geographical areas will help considerably in restoring stability and facilitating progress when the war is over. Specific recommendations concerning the constitution, functions, and powers of regional authorities for two such areas are presented in Chapter 12.

The Village Councils

It is unrealistic to suppose that a Central Highlands Development Board or a Mekong Delta Development Authority or a Commissioner for the Northern Provinces will be able to reach and assist every one of the millions of families on whose participation the successful implementation of a development program will ultimately depend. A function suggested for one regional agency in Chapter 12 is the promotion of local associations of farmers to construct and operate local systems of water control and promote the development of agriculture; a function suggested for another is technical and financial assistance to village councils for the construction and maintenance of such amenities as farm-to-market roads, village primary schools, water supplies, and public health facilities. It is these modest manifestations of the development process, intimately affecting the daily lives of the mass of the people, that will make the development program meaningful to them at the start and will, it is hoped, secure their involvement.

The involvement of the people is not merely desirable; it is absolutely essential to economic and social development. It should be recognized at the start that resources are limited, and that, from its own resources, and with even the most generous assistance from overseas, the government of Vietnam simply cannot hope to meet the manifold needs and aspirations of every one of the country's 2,500 villages and 13,000 hamlets. These needs and aspirations--in agriculture, education, public health, and transportation, among many others--are by no means unreasonable ones; they represent important aspects of the objective of all development, more prosperous and enjoyable lives for the mass of the people; and they ought to be supplied. But the state itself cannot play the part of universal provider, and for it to attempt to do so after the war would only result in the dilution of the development effort to a point at which any thoughts of economic independence within ten years can be abandoned.

How, then, shall these desirable local improvements be brought about? The state cannot realistically do much more than create and encourage the institutions and agencies, official and voluntary, through which works of local development will be undertaken, and it cannot finance these local works to a greater extent than its resources and its major national commitments will permit. The financial assistance it is able to offer, preferably through the regional development authorities, may be considerable, but it will not be 100 percent of the cost. In the end, local needs cannot be fully supplied except from local resources mobilized and organized by representative local institutions; and it would be quite misleading to represent to the mass of the nation that any development plan will automatically satisfy its increasing expectations without any effort and cost on its own part.

Since the elections of April, 1967, representative local governments have been installed in rather less than half the villages of Vietnam, but some form of local government exists in most of the others. The elected village councils represent an attempt to restore a valued tradition of local self-government which began to decay in the colonial period and almost disappeared in the period of personal rule and increasingly centralized government which followed independence. It is not easy to restore an ancient institution and adapt it to modern purposes, especially in time of war, and the village councils of today are not well equipped to supply economic and social services of a standard their constituents have come to expect. Some of the more important projects of economic development, for example the construction and operation of local systems of water control, or the operation of electric power services, are almost certainly beyond the capacity of the village councils, and new organizations will be needed for these particular purposes. New local organizations for such purposes are described subsequently in this volume.

The reforms of 1966 and 1967 were undoubtedly a useful first step toward the reestablishment of an effective system of local self-government. The elections which followed at least gave the councils more appearance than they previously possessed of being representative and responsible local authorities. In a good many cases, though certainly not in all, the elections were successful in putting into office candidates who commanded the respect of their communities and who, within the narrow limits of their powers, can be relied upon to serve the public interest. Nevertheless, it cannot be said that these reforms have as yet resulted in a system of effective local government responsive to the needs of local development.

One reason, of course, is the continuance of the war, especially the Communist offensives of early 1968, which created widespread if temporary insecurity in areas in which security had been good enough for the holding of elections only a year before. But other reasons are inherent in the system and in the status of the village governments, and are only susceptible of correction by legislative action and administrative reform. Decree 198 of December 24, 1966 is liberal compared with previous legislation, but it gives village councils very little freedom of action to initiate and carry out development works and very little power to control their own finances. The approval of the government at ministerial level is still required for budgets, construction projects, and equipment purchases exceeding VN$1 million, for all taxes and fees the village councils may wish to impose, and for any loans and subventions, such as those it might wish to negotiate with a regional development authority. The approval of the central government at the level of the province chief is required for almost everything else. It is most unlikely that local initiative will spring up and flourish in these restrictive conditions. The village chiefs and councils appear to be answerable more to the government than to their constituents, and it is doubtful whether they are yet fully aware of the extended powers of local self-government implicit in the reforms of 1966, or whether they are ready to take advantage of them.

The capacity of these local authorities to provide works and services for their people is also limited for financial reasons. Out of more than 2,500 villages in Vietnam there are very few which have budgets exceeding 1 or 2 million piasters (say, US$8,000-15,000). An authoritative opinion has been given that without central government subsidies only 75 villages are capable of supporting the costs of their own administration, and that fewer still command the resources to make modest improvements in the services supplied to their constituents. These viable villages are invariably the places with large and profitable markets, in other words, the province and district capitals in which central government services are concentrated and there is consequently less of a void for local authorities to fill. The recent transfer by the central government to the villages of its share of the taxes collected on real property--another welcome step in the right direction--has not made the villages prosperous overnight. The taxes on farm land are unpopular, difficult to collect, and unproductive; where they are collected, at the obsolete rates at which they are imposed they bring in very little, frequently less than the costs of collection.

It does not really matter what form of organization is used to mobilize public participation in the development program so long as it is familiar to the community and commands its confidence. In some villages of the Mekong Delta, tenant farmers' unions have been able to supply useful services to their members, in social welfare and public health facilities as well as in the distribution of fertilizer supplies; in three provinces model rural electrical cooperatives have been set up and are producing and supplying domestic power to their members; under joint arrangement between U.S. AID and the Ministry of the Interior, committees of responsible citizens have been formed in a number of places in an effort to persuade villages to examine their problems and to seek their own solutions to them; in connection with the development of the Mekong Delta, the Joint Development Group proposes the establishment in every village of a voluntary association of water users which will concern itself with increasing the productivity of the village lands. All these activities represent or are intended to represent public participation in particular aspects of social and economic development; but in the long run it is the regular agencies of local government, the village councils, which should bear the major responsibility for making improvements and supplying services to the communities of the rural areas.

This is, in fact, the course the present administration has already embarked upon, and the principal purpose of this part of our study is only to suggest that the local government reforms introduced in 1966 have not yet succeeded in restoring the traditional autonomy of the villages or inspiring local initiatives, and that bolder measures should be considered. For the time being, security is still the most important consideration in the countryside, and this is not, therefore, the ideal time to recommend any diminution of central government controls over local government. However, it is assumed that it is still the intention to hold local government elections in the remainder of Vietnam's villages as soon as conditions permit, and it is not premature to at least consider what other reforms might be introduced into the local government system when peace returns.

The following observations may serve for a basis for discussion.

1. The organizational structure created by Decree 198 of December 24, 1966 appears to be unnecessarily complicated and extravagant for a simple system of local government based on villages of a few thousand hectares and from 5,000 to 10,000 inhabitants. One might question, for instance, whether there is any need at this level of government for a separation between the executive functions discharged by the village administrative committee and the deliberative functions discharged by the village council. One might also question whether there is any need for separate elections in both hamlets and villages, since the members of the village councils are derived from the hamlets and each can represent in the village the interests of the hamlet from which he comes.

2. As the legislation now stands, village councils appear to be expected to maintain administrative staffs sometimes in excess of their needs, and very frequently in excess of their means. The business of the smaller councils is modest, and could probably be discharged quite easily by one or two properly trained and adequately remunerated professionals, permitting a reduction in administrative costs and larger expenditures than are now normal on public works and services.

3. In any new legislation there should be an attempt to define in some detail the governmental functions which belong exclusively to the village, those which belong exclusively to the central government, and those which are shared, and should therefore be exercised by the villages by arrangement with higher authorities. The villages can and should provide for their own administration, that is, for the remuneration of their administrative staffs, for the maintenance of public buildings and equipment, and for the purchase of supplies, without financial or other controls or interference; and there should be no question of any subsidy for these services. Because the villages appear to give considerable priority to primary education, they should have some specific functions in that field, certainly the construction and maintenance of school buildings and possibly the payment of teachers' salaries or at least a contribution toward them. There are obvious functions for local authorities in public health, for if the village does not concern itself with the cleaning of public streets, markets, and public places, then nobody will; and the villages can almost certainly do more than this: they can construct and maintain village water supplies, construct and operate (under supervision) village health centers, and play a useful part, subject to professional direction from staff of the Ministry of Health, in the control of endemic and epidemic diseases. They ought to be given some precise functions in agriculture as well, for this is where the best prospects for raising the living standards of their constituents are to be found.

4. Some central government staff working in the rural areas, teachers of the Ministry of Education and extension agents of the Ministry of Agriculture, might well be seconded to or placed under the administrative control of local authorities while remaining subject to the technical direction of the ministries. Such men are intimately connected with the progress of the rural people; and they might perform their duties better as servants of the village councils than they do as central government officials remotely controlled by the provinces and Saigon. It would not be unreasonable for the villages to supplement the salaries of these men from their own resources: and it is certainly most desirable that the burden of cost of such services as primary education should not fall entirely upon the central government after the war. As we point out in Chapter 11, it is most unlikely that in the next ten years the government of Vietnam will command sufficient resources simultaneously to invest in development and operate a full range of social services.

The village councils already perform a useful function in the maintenance of vital statistics and should continue to do so; but some form of association with the National Institute of Statistics is necessary, and it is possible that the institute, as the agency of the central government, ought to reimburse the villages for at least part of the costs involved in this service. Some local authorities, though not all, already provide postal services between their villages and hamlets and the Post (Mail), Telephone and Telegraph (PTT) offices in province and district capitals. This is simple and easy to do, and provides a service to the public which is probably greatly appreciated. But it can hardly be an exclusive village function, since in places where the volume of business is sufficient the PTT ought to provide offices of its own and supply all the services that commonly go with them. This is the kind of thing that some villages might do by agreement with the ministry concerned and even under contract to it. Certain public works should be put entirely under the control of the villages, for example the construction and maintenance of primary schools and health centers (already referred to) and also markets, transport parks, local government offices, and local roads. But villages should not be expected, as some now are, to meet any part of the cost of central government installations established in village council areas for central government purposes.

5. The village councils might perform some functions in land reform, though this would have to be within the general framework of national policy and it is recognized that the subject is a controversial one. They already maintain records of land ownership (though these are mainly for purposes of taxation and are in need of updating) which could usefully be expanded to include information concerning land use, tenancies, and rents. Whether the councils as at present constituted are appropriate agencies for the registration of titles and the adjudication of disputes between landlords and tenants is debatable, but worth debating.

6. The village councils now possess scarcely any control over their own budgets, and this is perhaps the most serious deterrent to the development of local initiative. Obviously the central government has a part to play, and it cannot be expected to transfer revenues and provide subventions for particular works without exercising any control whatever. As a minimum the central government will wish to carry out a regular

audit of local government accounts; and it will also wish to retain powers to amend budgets and otherwise intervene in the administration of village affairs (even to the extent of deposing a council and ordering new elections) on a complaint subscribed to by a sufficient number of citizens. But generally the relationship between the representatives of the central government and the representatives of the villages should be based upon encouragement, advice, and help rather than upon regulation and control.

The particular functions suggested for local authorities in this section obviously do not represent an exhaustive catalogue of what they can do in the extensive and varied fields of development. But they are enough for any village to choose from, having regard to its capacity and needs, so as to provide its constituents with the kind of works and services they consider most important to them. Let it be recognized that in a majority of cases villages will not, for some years, be able to carry out the works they want without some financial assistance from the government; in no case, however, ought there to be subventions amounting to 100 percent of the cost. The only acceptable qualifications for assistance are a contribution from the village's own resources and an undertaking to provide for the recurrent costs of operation.

The village's contributions may be modest at the start, but local involvement in the development process is what is important. If the development strategies and programs suggested in this study are ever to take effect, then they must be made popular ones to which the people as a whole will subscribe and in which they will participate to the fullest possible extent of their capacities. In the present state of local government budgets and prospects, there are some who think that the rational course is to abandon local government and local development entirely, at least until peace and security return. This, in our view, would be a mistake. Even in the poorest places there is at least a skeleton of a local organization, and in the course of time it will get some flesh on its bones. The poorer councils might be well advised to concentrate for the time being on performing a few simple tasks well; if they succeed in this, public confidence will grow, and they may then be able to talk frankly to their constituents about all the work that is waiting to be done and all the taxes it will cost. Public confidence, the acceptance by the people of Vietnam that it is within their own power to shape their future, is what the development program is all about.

PART II PROGRAMS FOR ECONOMIC DEVELOPMENT

CHAPTER 7 AGRICULTURAL DEVELOPMENT

South Vietnam is primarily an agricultural nation; it has been so categorized for many years and the probability is that agriculture will continue for some time to be the keystone of the local economy. It is variously estimated that from 70 percent to 80 percent of the population is currently involved directly in the production of crops, animal products, and fisheries products. Apparently, there are about 2, 000, 000 farm units and over 250, 000 fishermen making up Vietnam's agricultural sector. Agriculture has been by far the principal source of exchange earned through exports. Rice and rubber have been the major export commodities, although since 1964 the balance on rice has become negative. In recent years the agricultural sector has been contributing about one-third of the national income reported for South Vietnam. This fact alone is indicative of the basic problem of the agricultural sector. Vietnamese farmers making up 70 percent to 80 percent of the population but accounting for only 33 percent of the national income are generally an economically disadvantaged group.

Prices of agricultural products as a group have nearly tripled since 1964. The agricultural price index for 1967 was 410. 3 (1957-59 = 100), compared with 145. 6 in 1965 (Table 7. 1). Plant products advanced to 389. 6 but animal products moved up even more rapidly to 465. 9. Meanwhile, over-all production has been mostly stagnant during 1965-67 and has not improved over the 1959-61 level. The agricultural production index for 1967 was 101. 1 (1959-61 = 100) compared with 106. 7 in 1965 and 96. 5 in 1966 (Table 7. 2). Although the trend is downward, plant products increased slightly from 1966 to 1967, but this was largely due to the adverse effect of flood damage on the 1966 output. Animal products continued to hold their ground, however, and reached 148. 7 in 1967. With production showing no significant gains and inflationary forces exerting strong pressures on the local economy,

TABLE 7.1

Indexes of Agricultural Prices, 1964-67

(1957-59 = 100)

	Agricultural Price Index			
Product	1964	1965	1966	1967
Rice	125.2	142.5	237.4	438.5
Rubber	74.9	75.4	98.7	110.9
Tea	148.1	163.2	190.4	267.9
Coffee	84.9	77.9	68.4	68.8
Corn	147.5	160.5	251.3	470.5
Sugar cane	132.1	121.3	203.9	294.3
Tobacco	101.1	92.4	150.3	288.0
Sweet potatoes	133.4	165.1	329.3	400.0
Manioc	112.4	162.5	337.9	401.1
Peanuts	151.7	176.4	308.1	398.9
Coconuts	172.4	198.8	315.7	568.4
Plant products	120.3	135.4	222.9	389.8
Buffaloes	156.0	186.4	367.1	526.5
Cattle	132.1	156.9	320.4	422.3
Pigs	133.9	159.4	295.4	435.9
Chickens	181.8	238.3	454.5	603.8
Ducks	173.2	222.1	435.9	600.3
Chicken eggs	180.0	239.1	396.1	549.0
Duck eggs	221.6	279.6	468.0	691.7
Animal products	142.7	173.2	323.4	465.9
Agricultural products	126.4	145.6	250.0	410.3

Source: Ministry of Agrarian Reform and Agriculture.

TABLE 7.2

Indexes of Agricultural Production, 1964-67

(1959-61 = 100)

Product	Agricultural Production Index			
	1964	1965	1966	1967
Rice	106.1	98.7	88.8	95.9
Corn	161.8	154.2	124.5	115.4
Sweet potatoes	136.6	126.2	111.7	115.3
Manioc	132.2	108.1	128.3	119.9
Peanuts	152.7	136.4	144.0	141.1
Soybeans	146.3	158.4	277.0	207.0
Mungo beans	170.4	168.6	204.6	283.6
Pineapples	125.7	106.1	85.6	81.6
Black pepper	156.2	157.6	114.6	122.4
Sesame	101.5	63.5	57.1	71.0
Rubber	96.3	84.1	64.2	55.2
Tea	118.9	130.6	115.2	92.6
Coffee	106.0	109.4	95.1	103.6
Coconuts	104.0	108.8	95.5	96.3
Tobacco	100.8	104.9	95.6	109.3
Sugar cane	114.9	119.0	101.9	83.8
Plant products	108.3	100.9	90.6	94.7
Buffaloes	160.9	289.7	310.9	267.5
Cattle	116.4	175.9	182.5	196.2
Pigs	104.6	127.0	114.7	126.9
Chickens	199.6	198.2	178.0	175.1
Ducks	133.7	142.9	147.7	159.5
Animal products	131.3	149.6	140.5	148.7
Agricultural products	111.0	106.7	96.5	101.1

Source: Ministry of Agrarian Reform and Agriculture.

it is not surprising that the prices of agricultural products have been spiraling upward. The fact remains, however, that farmers as a group are obviously at the lower end of the income scale in South Vietnam.

There is no doubt that agricultural prices would have advanced even more rapidly during the years 1966-68 if the government had not engaged in certain price control activities. Rice is the principal item subject to price manipulation. It is difficult to say just how much of the failure of the plant products production index to keep abreast of the same index for animal products is attributable to the disincentives of price controls, but a number of uncontrolled commodities have registered production gains while rice has lost ground. Many of Vietnam's farmers operate largely on a subsistence basis and thus have little to sell; however, the great majority do make some sales, and they are very conscious of returns and are subject to price incentives or disincentives.

The foregoing comments and observations are intended to establish the setting in which the planning efforts for agriculture are being conducted and to indicate certain of the factors that underlie policy considerations in this sector of the South Vietnamese economy. In this chapter attention will be focused on (1) description of the current situation in the agricultural sector; (2) prospective needs for agricultural products in South Vietnam; (3) a production strategy; (4) prospective agricultural production; and (5) delineation of the major elements in a program for agricultural development during the interim period and over the longer term after the war.

CURRENT STATUS OF AGRICULTURE

As a preface to the more analytical and technical discussion of the major elements to be considered in an agricultural development program for South Vietnam, it is appropriate first to scan the current situation with particular reference to output and trends. This section is a very brief summary of the situation of some of the major products or groups of products that make up the bulk of the nation's agriculture.

Rice

Due mostly to the devastating effects of the war, which has created a shortage of farm labor and displaced many agricultural workers, the production of paddy has fallen from an average of 5 million tons during the period from 1960 to 1964 to 4, 668, 400 tons in 1967-68 (Table 7. 3). Before World War II, Vietnam was a large rice exporter, but since 1945 exports have decreased sharply; yet a significant quantity of rice was exported each year until 1964. The three-year average of rice exports from 1961 to 1963 was 200, 000 tons, valued at VN$700 million. The exports in 1963 alone amounted to 320, 000 tons of rice valued at VN$1. 25 billion. In 1964, South Vietnam still exported about 50, 000 tons of rice, but since 1965 large quantities of rice have been imported. By 1967 imports totalled 749, 000 tons, valued at over VN$8 billion.

Rubber

Rubber production has suffered more than rice from war destruction. Battles have taken place on many plantations. The shortage of labor and the lack of care of the trees reduced the yield sharply. On the other hand, the price of natural rubber has decreased significantly on the international market during the last few years. Exports of rubber from 1955 to 1964 averaged more than 70, 000 tons, but they fell to about 38, 000 tons in 1967. The downward trend of both areas under cultivation and production is evident in Table 7. 4.

To help the rubber plantation owners to survive these difficulties, the government has reduced the export taxes from 40 percent of the f. o. b. value to 20 percent, then to 1 percent.

Tea

In general, the tea producers in Vietnam have met the same problems as the rubber plantations. High costs of production and processing and the deteriorating international market for Vietnamese tea have been the main factors that have influenced both production and exports.

TABLE 7.3

Rice Production, Export and Imports, 1960-67

Crop Year	Area (ha)	Production of Paddy[a] (MT)	Calendar Year	Import or Export Milled Rice[a] (MT)
1960-61	2,318,000	4,955,000	1961	155,700 Export
1961-62	2,353,000	4,607,000[b]	1962	86,370 "
1962-63	2,479,000	5,205,000	1963	338,480 "
1963-64	2,538,000	5,326,000	1964	48,000 "
1964-65	2,562,000	5,185,000	1965	271,000 Import
1965-66	2,429,000	4,822,000	1966	434,000 "
1966-67	2,295,000	4,336,000[b]	1967	749,000 "
1967-68	2,295,000	4,668,400	1968	500,000[c] "

[a]Ratio of conversion of paddy into milled rice is 3/2.

[b]Flood damage was severe during the crop season.

[c]Preliminary.

Source: Data on area and production are AESS annual estimates by the Ministry of Agrarian Reform and Agriculture.

TABLE 7.4

Rubber Production and Exports, 1963-67

Year	Planted Area	Exploited Area	Production	Export
	(ha)		(MT)	
1963	142,770	72,630	76,180	68,926
1964	134,700	72,530	74,200	71,630
1965	129,660	64,925	64,770	58,161
1966	126,340	56,720	49,455	48,899
1967	120,000	53,600	42,000	37,704

Source: AESS annual estimates, Ministry of Agrarian Reform and Agriculture.

To help maintain the export of black tea to the London market the government in 1967 subsidized every kilo of black tea exported by an average of 50 VN dollars. Yet the annual exports of about 2,000 tons in previous years have fallen to a little above 1,000 tons in 1967. Exports in 1968 were expected to be even lower.

Tea production in 1967 was about the same as in 1962 but exports were down by almost 50 percent (Table 7.5)

Other Crops

The over-all production of other crops, substantially all of which are used in-country, remained more or less the same for the three years 1965-67. There are a few outstanding exceptions to this generalization; for example, vegetable production increased from about 133,000 tons in 1965 to 192,000 tons in 1967, while the production of sugar cane decreased significantly from over 1 million tons in 1965 to 770,000 tons in 1967.

TABLE 7.5

Tea Production and Exports, 1962-67

Year	Area (ha)	Production	Export
		(MT)	
1962	9,350	4,540	1,931
1963	9,310	4,730	1,995
1964	9,650	5,380	2,148
1965	9,685	5,903	2,341
1966	8,150	5,210	1,863
1967	7,500	4,500	1,047

Source: Ministry of Agrarian Reform and Agriculture.

Livestock and Fisheries

Livestock and poultry population decreased only slightly during the 1965-67 period (Table 7.6). The production of fish and shrimp has been increasing. The catch of sea fish in 1965 was 289,000 tons, while that of 1967 was more than 319,000 tons (Table 7.7).

Imports and Exports

Traditionally, the three most important exports of Vietnam are rubber, rice, and tea. However, beginning in 1965 rice has been imported. Current agricultural exports are rubber, tea, peanuts, copra cake, and duck feathers (Table 7.8).

Imports of agricultural products have been increasing in recent years due largely to the increase in demand and decrease in production as a result of the war. Imports now include some of the products Vietnam exported before the war, such as rice, pork, and chicken (Table 7.8).

TABLE 7.6

Livestock and Poultry Population, 1965-67
(thousands)

Item	Population 1965	1966	1967
Buffaloes	733	751	665
Cattle	1,101	1,013	1,033
Pigs	3,373	3,254	3,185
Chickens	22,242	19,980	19,657
Ducks	13,484	13,939	13,742

TABLE 7.7

Fishery Products, 1965-67
(metric tons)

Item	Production 1965	1966	1967
Sea fish	289,000	287,450	319,500
Fresh-water fish	57,000	64,710	59,500
Shrimp and others	29,000	28,340	31,700
TOTAL	375,000	380,500	410,700

Source: AESS and Directorate of Fisheries annual estimates, Ministry of Agrarian Reform and Agriculture.

TABLE 7.8

Exports and Imports, 1965-67

Product Traded	Trade Average, 1965-67 Quantity (MT)	Value (VN$ thousands)
Export		
Rubber	46,921	1,065,541
Tea	1,750	84,473
Peanuts	3,165	22,777
Copra cake	5,104	13,698
Duck feathers	553	37,053
Import		
Rice and Broken	436,900	8,815,544
Cotton and cotton thread	21,519	1,034,252
Milk	120,363	618,616
Sugar	30,369	1,155,289
Frozen pork[a]	7,299	30,942
Frozen chicken[b]	1,582	174,936
Corn	300	44,614

[a]1966 and 1967 average.

[b]Data for 1967.

PROSPECTIVE NEEDS FOR AGRICULTURAL PRODUCTS

In looking forward over the period of 1970-90, it is impossible to forecast with any real precision or in detail the probable total needs of Vietnam for all agricultural products. Despite the limitations involved, an estimate of in-country needs based on anticipated population growth and involving commodities now being produced can be computed, and it can be a reasonably satisfactory factual basis on which to begin the planning of an agricultural development program. It is when estimates of exports, import displacement, and new products enter in that the forecasting becomes an even less precise estimate, with little other than past performance and opinions of future prospects available to serve as guidelines.

In Table 7.9 the probable in-country requirements for crops, livestock, and fish from 1970 to 1990 are listed. These estimates are based for the most part on the highest levels of per capita disappearance in 1962-67 and thus do not reflect changes that may, or possibly should, occur in the consumption pattern of the Vietnamese people during the next twenty years. Based on this projection alone, production needed in 1990 would exceed the 1967 output by about 150 percent for crops, 120 percent for livestock, and 90 percent for fish. Certain commodities now produced in some volume, such as sugar cane and tobacco, where import displacement is an important factor, would move up much more rapidly if the indicated self-sufficiency is attained. The same is true of those items that have been declining in recent years; e.g., manioc, sweet potatoes, and pineapple. Rice alone would be somewhat more than double the 1967 output.

It is with much less certainty that estimates are suggested for possible exports and/or displacement of certain imports. In this context, "imports" refers only to commodities not now produced in any volume in the country; thus, sugar and tobacco are listed in Table 7.9. Despite the probable inaccuracies inherent in such forecasts, it is necessary to consider the possible needs for these purposes when over-all agricultural development in Vietnam during the 1970-90 period is under review. In Table 7.10 such an estimate is made. It covers all of the commodities that are now or have in the past been a factor in the export trade, plus several items currently produced that may have an export potential. It also includes several commodities now imported that are believed to be adapted to more extensive in-country production. Omitted entirely from Table 7.10 are those new agricultural products that have not yet been produced commercially in South Vietnam but which may still be potentially important.

Rice is the principal crop in South Vietnam. The export of 2,500,000 metric tons (paddy basis) in 1990 indicated in Table 7.10 would, if achieved, represent a substantial increase over the levels previously attained, even prior to World War II when Vietnam was a significant exporter of rice.

TABLE 7.9

Projection of In-Country Needs for Major Agricultural Products,[a] 1970, 1980, and 1990

Product	Estimated Annual Per Capita Disappearance[b] (kg.)	Projected In-Country Disappearance[c] 1970 (MT)	1980 (MT)	1990 (MT)
Rice (paddy)	325.0	5,957,900	7,701,200	9,954,750
Corn	3.0	54,996	71,088	91,890
Sweet potatoes	19.2	351,974	454,963	588,096
Manioc	25.4	465,633	601,878	778,002
Peanuts	2.0	36,664	47,392	61,260
Mungo beans	1.2	21,998	28,435	36,756
Soy beans	0.5	9,166	11,848	15,315
Yam beans	0.9	16,499	21,326	27,567
Sugar cane	137.8	2,526,150	3,265,309	4,220,814
Vegetables	11.3	207,152	267,765	346,119
Pineapple	4.1	75,161	97,154	125,583
Bananas	15.0	274,980	355,440	459,450
Tree fruits	17.2	315,310	407,571	526,836
Watermelon	2.8	51,330	66,349	85,764
Tobacco	0.71	13,016	16,824	21,747
Tea	0.22	4,033	5,213	6,739
Coffee	0.23	4,216	5,450	7,045
Coconuts	9.7[d]	177,820[d]	229,581[d]	297,111[d]
Buffaloes and cattle	11.6	212,651	274,874	355,308
Hogs	18.6	340,975	440,746	569,718
Chickens and ducks	6.3	115,491	149,285	192,969
Eggs	69.6[e]	1,275[e]	1,649[e]	2,132[e]
Fish, all types	25.2	461,966	597,139	771,876

[a]Only the major commodities produced regularly for consumption primarily in Vietnam are included.

[b]Based mostly on highest levels of disappearance during the 1962-67 period. Disappearance and consumption are not synonymous; e.g., disappearance includes amounts used for seed, lost through spoilage, damaged by rodents and insects, and so on.

[c]Reflects a population growth rate of 2.6 percent per year as estimated by the National Institute of Statistics.

[d]Number of nuts, in thousands.

[e]Number of eggs, in millions.

TABLE 7.10

Estimated Quantities[a] Required for Export or Displacement of Imports, 1970, 1980, and 1990 (metric tons)

Commodity	Estimated Quantity 1970	1980	1990
Rubber	60,000	80,000	100,000
Rice (paddy)	none	1,500,000	2,500,000
Tea	2,500	4,000	6,000
Duck feathers	750	900	1,200
Peanuts	7,500	10,000	12,500
Oil cake	10,000	15,000	20,000
Cinnamon	250	1,000	2,000
Pepper	60	350	400
Kenaf and jute	2,500	12,500	25,000
Duck eggs	2,000	2,500	3,000
Kapok	1,000	1,750	2,500
Cotton (lint)	30,000	40,000	50,000
Corn and sorghum (feed grains)	50,000	150,000	200,000
Medicinal plants	3,000	4,000	5,000
Sesame	500	1,500	2,500
Roots and tubers (cassava, etc.)	2,500	25,000	50,000
Live buffaloes	500	1,500	1,500
Fish products	2,500	6,000	10,000

[a] These quantities are additional to those listed as required to meet domestic needs in Table 7.9. Only commodities that are now or have been produced in Vietnam are included; this excludes several new items, such as oil palm, castor beans, grapes, that may have considerable potential.

It is impossible to predict with any accuracy either the supply of rice that will be available for export or the need for rice on the world market during the next two decades. Historically, North Vietnam has been a market for rice from the South, but in recent years the North has made some gains in rice production and if it adopts the improved practices now gaining increasingly wide acceptance, then it may continue to approach self-sufficiency in rice. Mainland China as a market for rice from South Vietnam is highly uncertain because of political complications. For some time to come it is likely that India, Indonesia, and possibly Japan will be buying quantities of rice. Malaysia, Singapore, Hong Kong, and Ceylon are also potential markets. The complication, however, is the probability that all rice-producing countries will be increasing their productivity (even Japan had a surplus in 1968), with a currently unpredictable impact on the world market. Population will continue to increase and thus step up the need for rice and other foods. But it is difficult to predict how the population growth will equate with the food supply, to say nothing of the purchasing power situation. Rice exports are expected to be resumed by the 1980's and would again be very important to South Vietnam if they reached the projected 2,500,000 tons of paddy in 1990; this would be equivalent to 25 percent of the estimated in-country needs at that time.*

For many years rubber has been a major export of South Vietnam and an important source of foreign exchange. Production has been in the 70,000-80,000 ton range several times during the past fifteen years. It is now little more than half that level. The future of rubber as an export crop is obscured by the international market situation, in which synthetic rubber is an increasingly serious competitor; and by the downward trend in prices for several years. There has been a recent upturn in prices which may be maintained because of forecasts for natural rubber consumption. To regain the production level of the early 1960's, the rubber plantations will need extensive rehabilitation. Whether this outlay is economically justified is a concern of the industry and government alike. In view of the substantial investment in this industry and its importance to the local economy, it is essential that all possibilities of revival and even expansion be examined

---

*"The International Market for Rice," JDG Working Paper (unpublished).

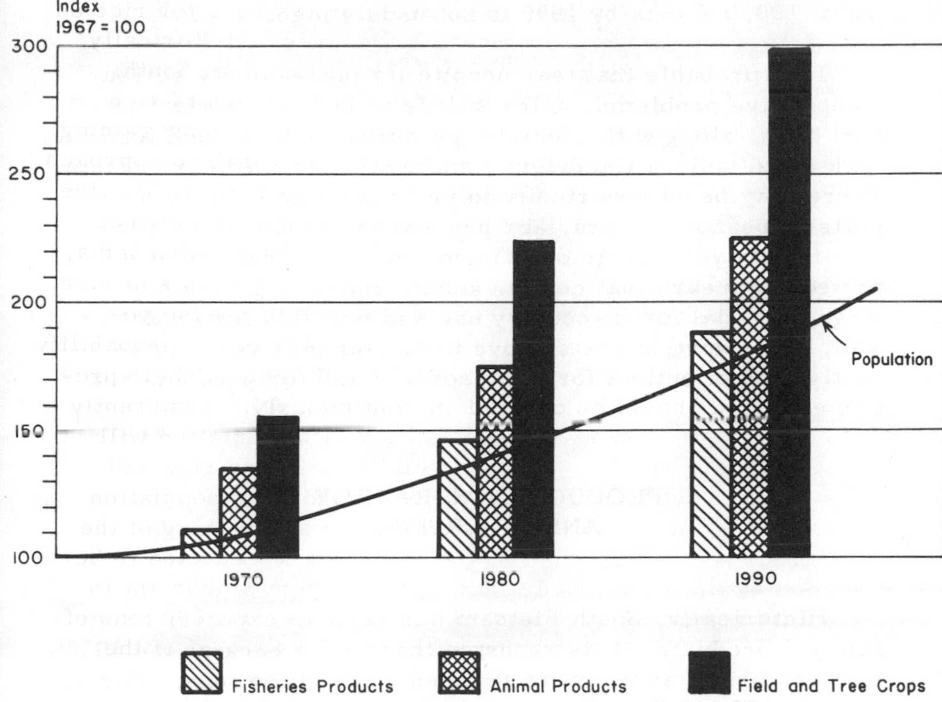

Note: Production needs include domestic requirements and export shipments and are based on a simple aggregate of the products involved, expressed in metric tons. Population estimates assume a constant annual increase of 2.6 per cent.

ESTIMATED POPULATION AND AGRICULTURAL PRODUCTION NEEDS IN SOUTH VIETNAM, 1970–1990

Figure 7–1

thoroughly. If the industry regains momentum, then an output of 100,000 tons by 1990 is not unduly high.

It is probable that tea, despite its increasingly serious competitive problems, will continue to be an important export item, along with specialty products such as duck feathers, duck eggs, spices (including cinnamon), and medicinal plants. There may be an opportunity to increase significantly the exports of peanuts, copra, and processed cassava during the next twenty years. Among the commodities that are now imported it appears that cotton, kenaf, and feed grains have a large potential for in-country use and possibly for export as well, if production costs prove to be competitive. The investigation of outlets for new products and for products not now exported should be carried on continuously.

PRODUCTION STRATEGY AND PRIORITIES

Historically, South Vietnam has been an exporter of agricultural products. It is reported that as far back as the 1930's rice exports in some years reached 1.5 million tons. During and after World War II this trade declined greatly but even in the early 1960's the nation derived a considerable amount of exchange from the sale of agricultural commodities, principally rice and rubber. As late as 1963 the value of such items exported exceeded the value of agricultural products imported. Beginning in 1964, when South Vietnam started importing rice, the flow was reversed, however, and by 1966 the adverse balance was almost 10 to 1 on these products alone. Nevertheless, agricultural products have been and continue to be the principal exports; from 1963 to 1966 they accounted for over 90 percent of the value of all exports leaving South Vietnam.

With the decline in output of agricultural products in the war situation, accompanied by strong inflationary pressures, the outcome in the form of rapidly rising prices was virtually a foregone conclusion; in fact, the price level on agricultural products would probably be even higher if the government had not restrained the price of imported rice. Along with the emergence of Vietnam as a net importer of agricultural commodities in which the nation had previously been at least self-sufficient (such as rice, pork, poultry, animal feed), there has occurred a marked increase also in receipts of the usual import items; e.g., cotton, cereals, sugar, milk, and tobacco. Despite the rapidly advancing prices of agricultural products produced locally, there is little evidence to show that farmers are achieving an improved income position relative to the nonfarm sector. One complicating factor, of course, is the refugee problem, involving as it does many thousands of farmers or would-be farmers, many of whom are trying to subsist by producing small quantities of produce.

Population growth is another important factor accounting for the upward spiral of agricultural prices in recent years. While 1967 production had declined to about the level of 1959-61, population was up almost 20 percent over the earlier period. The gap was filled largely by imports, rice making up the bulk of the shipments. By 1970, population is expected to be some 29 percent above the 1960 base and, assuming a constant 2.6 percent rate of growth, South Vietnam will have more than 30 million people by 1990, which is over twice the 1960 estimate. In the light of these demographic prospects, there will be an acute need for increasing quantities of food and other farm products. Agricultural production, which historically is heavily weighted on the food side, will need to be accelerated rapidly, first to catch up with population growth and then to keep up with or move ahead of the increase in the numbers of people to be fed.

Increased productivity is generally the central theme of an agricultural development program. The intended corollary of increased productivity is a strengthening of the national income and improvement in the economic well-being of those engaged in this activity, particularly the farmers. In the circumstances prevailing during the 1965-68 period, it is perhaps obvious that South Vietnam's agriculture must be made more productive, and it is at this point that a major effort is required. It is equally evident that first priority in such a program should go to increasing the output of those commodities already being produced in the country primarily for domestic consumption but which are currently in especially short supply because of the war conditions. Rice, sugar, and tobacco are among the items in this group. Greater quantities of animal products and fish are also needed to improve the diet of the Vietnamese and to exert a moderating influence on the price spiral that has been particularly noticeable in protein foods.

Next in priority is attention to those commodities that have been and still are exported in some volume but have suffered a severe setback during the war. Prime examples of these products are rubber, tea, duck feathers, duck eggs, fish, cinnamon, and copra. These export commodities are important sources of foreign exchange and the trade channels for them are already established. Careful study of the export market prospects is an absolute prerequisite to initiation of a program aimed at stimulating production of products intended primarily for export.

A third group of commodities deserving early attention is made up of products currently imported in volume that may have a production potential in Vietnam. Cotton, kenaf, feed grains, grapes, and baby chicks are examples of such items. Some of these commodities have been produced in Vietnam on a very limited scale but there is need to explore fully the possibilities of displacing these imports on a broad front, wherever it is considered economically feasible to do so. By reducing such imports, Vietnam would save foreign exchange and also add to the national product by increasing the productivity of the agricultural sector.

Finally, there should be constant attention to the search for new products that may have a potential for export or for domestic use. On the basis of experience in other areas of the Far East, this category might include such items as processed cassava, palm oil, milk, seeds, processed fruits, citronella, and mushrooms. Castor bean, cocoa, and silk have also been suggested. Research and experimentation are basic requirements in the process of discovering and developing new agricultural products for Vietnam. Both time and money are needed in the continuing exploration of both the production and the marketing of these commodities.

In determining priorities for emphasis in an agricultural production program, there are no absolute criteria that apply to any group of commodities or even to any one item. Rather it is a case of using reason and exercising judgment as to what can and should be done given the factors affecting the commodity or commodities involved. On this basis it appears that Vietnam must give primary attention to becoming self-sufficient in those products that are already a part of its agriculture and where economically justified, to reviving its export trade in those commodities that it has been selling out of the country. In so doing the initial objective will be to provide the food needed by the Vietnamese people and to either earn or save foreign exchange. Aside from the apparent need for such production, this course of action is indicated by the existence of expertise in both production and marketing and by the fact that the necessary physical plant is already available in varying degree.

AGRICULTURAL PRODUCTION PROSPECTS

Along with a consideration of prospective needs for agricultural products in Vietnam during the next decade, it is equally necessary to examine the production potential of the nation. The Agricultural Section of the Joint Development Group now has under way a detailed and comprehensive study of the resources available to support agricultural production. Upon completion of this work it is expected that there will be sufficient information available to permit an objective evaluation of the production potential by areas and by commodities. This will contribute importantly to the planning of a long-range program for the agricultural sector of the economy.

These studies were reported in the form of working papers by members of the Agricultural Section and by experts contracted by the group. The subject content of the specific studies ranged from fisheries, livestock, soil fertility, agricultural extension needs, to detailed studies on the potential for those crops ecologically fitted to Vietnamese growing conditions. The papers discussed existing conditions, present programs and emphasized future, postwar needs for the subject studied. Over 30 of these papers have been published in limited numbers in both English and Vietnamese as an aid to discussion and planning.

As a preliminary step in the planning process as it relates to production prospects, it is perhaps appropriate to summarize the outlook as seen by technical experts in the field of agricultural production. Several officials of the Ministry of Agrarian Reform and Agriculture are members of the Agricultural Section of the JDG. The discussions of crops, livestock, and fisheries that follow represent a free translation of views expressed by these ministry officials on prospects for Vietnam's agriculture in the next decade. To a limited extent the statements also include suggested actions required to realize the production potential of each commodity group.

Neither this section nor the one on prospective needs for agricultural products is to be considered as representing the "agricultural plan" of the Joint Development Group. It is intended that both production needs and production prospects will be essential ingredients of the more definitive program in which specific objectives will be listed along with suggested implementing action considered necessary to achievement of the goals.

Out of the total 17 million hectares in South Vietnam, only 3 million hectares are planted to rice, annual crops, and tree crops. The remaining hectarage consists of forests and poor soils. However, approximately 2 million of the remaining 14 million hectares do have an agricultural potential.

The main groups of soils found in South Vietnam are listed in Table 7. 11.

TABLE 7. 11

Soil Groups: Uncultivated Land

Soil Group	Hectarage
Red	2, 000, 000
Slightly acid sulfate (the Plain of Reeds)	1, 055, 735
Very acid sulfate	618, 400
Saline (Ca Mau area)	468, 035
Organic (U Minh area)	142, 520
Gray podzolic (eastern region and Central Highlands)	1, 890, 000
Mountainous	6, 200, 000
Alluvial	2, 347, 590
Total	14, 722, 280

Although most of the alluvial soils are now planted to rice, annual crops, and fruit trees, the application of new techniques of production plus water control will greatly increase yields. Only a part of the red soils of the Central Highlands and eastern region are under cultivation, as is the case with the gray podzolic soils of the eastern region. Their use will be expanded in the postwar period; it is estimated that over 1 million more hectares of this land will be utilized by 1990. Although large hectarages are in problem soils, such as the acid sulfate soils of the Mekong Delta and Plain of Reeds, and the saline soils of the Ca Mau area, these areas will probably be very little exploited in this century. The organic soils of the U Minh area, on the other hand, will be used in the postwar period when water control is achieved.

The climate of South Vietnam allows for year-round cultivation; it is variable enough to produce not only tropical crops but also subtropical and temperate crops in highland areas. South Vietnam has the potential to be a very important producer of animal protein--chickens, ducks, swine, buffaloes, and cattle. But to do so will require a greatly expanded feed-growing industry.

With a coastline of over 2,500 kilometers and numerous inland fishing facilities, Vietnam has a tremendous potential for fish production.

To live up to its agricultural potential, development plans must be carefully considered and supported by the government. The postwar economy will remain primarily based on the agricultural sector. Attention must be directed now to possible means of generating capital for the resettlement of abandoned lands, to the development of new lands, to industry based on agriculture, and to the modernization and expansion of the fishing industry.

Crop Production

Rice

Rice is by far the most important agricultural commodity in Vietnam.* After the war, South Vietnam should be in a position to quickly attain the production level achieved before 1963. Moreover, it should be possible to produce sufficient rice for export in spite of the high local demand presented by an increasing population. This can be accomplished by

1. Increasing the cultivated area of rice. Because of wartime insecurity, many farmers have had to flee their home lands. Upon the cessation of hostilities, a large percentage of these refugees will no doubt return to their villages and resume agricultural activities. For this reason, it is likely that the area devoted to the cultivation of rice may return to its former level. Thus, during the postwar period, 200,000 to 300,000 additional hectares will no doubt be planted to rice again, bringing the country's total from approximately 2,200,000 hectares to 2,500,000 hectares.

2. Intensive use of land. Rice production can also be increased by planting two rice crops a year on the same land. In the coastal areas of central Vietnam, this is now being done extensively (the third and eighth lunar month's crops), but only one rice crop a year is the practice in the Mekong Delta. With the anticipated water control for this region, a good portion of the area will be able to engage in double cropping of rice. Although the exact area that can sustain a double crop is not known, it could conceivably be from 500,000 to 1,000,000 hectares.

3. Increasing yields. A direct effect of water control in the delta will be the changes in the pattern of rice culture resulting in higher average yields. With flood control and drainage, the yields in the floating rice-area would be raised from 1.0 to 1.5 tons per hectare to 2.0 to 3.0 tons per hectare, using the double and/or single transplanting system. The double

---

*"Potential for Rice Production in Post-War Agricultural Economy," JDG Working Paper (unpublished); and <u>The Production and Marketing of Rice</u>, Working Paper No. 4, JDG, October, 1967.

transplanted zone with adequate drainage would be able to shift from an average of 2.0 tons per hectare to 2.5 to 3.0 tons per hectare.

Average yields are being increased also by the use of improved rice varieties. Thus far, the newly introduced IR-8 and IR-5 varieties are being readily accepted by the farmers and, when properly handled, provide yields ranging from 4 to 6 tons or more per hectare (per crop).

Considering the factors of improved varieties and water control, it is conceivable that by 1980 the country's average yields for the rainy season rice crop would be raised from 2.1 to 2.9 tons per hectare. The irrigated dry-season crop should be at the level of 3.9 tons per hectare. Under these conditions the in-country and export requirements projected for 1980 could easily be met. In 1990, it is expected that the average yields would be at least 4 tons per hectare for both the dry and wet season. The in-country and export requirements would thus be met using the same area for the wet season as used before, but increasing the dry season area by 100,000 hectares (Table 7.12).

Annual Crops

In order to obtain a balanced agricultural economy, one not based on rice alone, diversified cropping of annual crops will assume great importance in the postwar years. With the greater need for animal protein, the livestock industry will require feeds such as corn, sorghum, and leguminous forage crops. Peanuts and soy beans will provide oil for humans and feed for livestock. Table 7.13 lists the hectarage and yield level needed to satisfy domestic demands for several annual crops by the year 1980. For all of these crops, high-yield strains are now in the country and new ones will no doubt be received later. The crop production program will be based not only on the widespread use of the new high-yield varieties but also on water control, fertilizing, and insect and disease control programs.

TABLE 7.12

Projected Rice Production and Requirements, 1980 and 1990

	Rice Production					Rice Requirements		
	Rainy Season		Dry Season					
Year	Hectarage (million)	Av. yield (T/ha)	Hectarage (million)	Av. yield (T/ha)	Total (million tons)	In-Country (million tons)	Export	Total
1967	2.3	2.1	N/A	N/A	4.7	5.9	-1.2	5.9
1980	2.5	2.9	0.5	3.9	9.2	7.7	1.5	9.2
1990	2.5	4.0	0.6	4.0	12.4	9.9	2.5	12.4

TABLE 7.13

Estimated Area and Yield Required for In-Country or Export Substitution Needs for the Major Upland Crops, 1980

Crop	Total Req. (M/T)	Est. Av. Yield (T/ha)	Hectares Needed	Present and Prospective Production Locations
Peanuts	57,392	1.6	35,870	Tay Ninh, Binh Duong, Bien Hoa
Sugar cane	3,265,309	40.0	81,632	Binh Duong, Quang Ngai, Hiep Hoa, Tuy Hoa
Tobacco	16,824	1.3	12,941	Bien Hoa, Phan Rang, Nha Trang, Quang Nam, Quang Ngai
Manioc	626,878	12.0	52,240	Mekong Delta, Binh Dinh
Corn (feed)	50,000	1.6	31,250	An Giang, Chau Doc
Sorghum (feed)	100,000	4.0	25,000	Phu Bon, Mekong Delta
Soy beans	11,848	1.5	7,897	An Giang, Chau Doc, Phan Rang
Kenaf	12,500	1.0	12,500	Mekong Delta
Sweet potatoes	454,963	11.0	41,360	Mekong Delta

Vegetable crop production has an almost unlimited potential in South Vietnam and practically all existent vegetables can be successfully grown in the country.* If prices can be made competitive, and if a preservative industry can be established, South Vietnam would become a major supplier of vegetables to other oriental centers.

The production of the crops listed in Table 7.13 would make it possible to expand the present processing capacity now devoted to these crops. This increased output will require more sugar factories, feed mills, and oil extraction plants as well as bag manufacturing and tobacco curing plants. In addition, fiber processing plants will be needed to handle the raw kenaf. As a general rule, the new processing plants should be as near to the raw material as possible.

The processing of peanuts, soy beans, and other oil seeds within the country will make available a valuable oil cake as a by-product. The oil cake will be an excellent, cheap protein supplement for livestock feed. Moreover, if the processing plants are efficiently run, they would be a tremendous asset to the productiveness of the agricultural sector.

Tree Crops

The postwar period will undoubtedly also show a development of or an expansion in fruit crops such as mangoes, citrus fruits, plums, cherries, and jackfruit as well as in the industrial tree crops such as coconuts, oil palm, cocoa, tea, coffee, pepper, and possibly even rubber (see discussion below on rehabilitation of rubber plantations). Bananas and pineapple, although not tree crops, offer postwar opportunities. The Joint Development Group has prepared a series of working papers (unpublished) on most of the tree crops referred to here.

Miscellaneous Crops

There are several crops that can be grown on small landholdings with high financial returns, and these crops should assume export importance in the postwar period. These are

*Vegetable Production Problems in the Dalat/Tuyen-Duc Areas of South Vietnam, Working Paper No. 27, (JDG, September, 1968).

specialty crops, high enough in value to warrant air shipment to markets all over the Orient. The Dalat area produces a strawberry of unique flavor. The straw-mushrooms can be grown in small areas by specialists.* Black pepper is also labor-intensive but yields high average returns. These three are but examples of agricultural crops that could be raised economically by small farmers.**

Livestock Development

South Vietnam is not only capable of producing more rice and other crops, it is also in a position to produce more livestock and livestock products such as pigs, chickens, ducks and eggs. With the anticipated production increase of rice, feed grains, and oil seeds, the feed problem, one of the major factors limiting livestock development, should be resolved. Since the climate and other environmental features of the Mekong Delta provide one of the world's best regions for duck raising, this is one facet of livestock development that is considered to have a great potential. Hogs, chickens, and cattle have also shown wide adaptability to the various climatic zones found in the country. Since the importation of milk and milk products was of such high magnitude in 1967, dairying should be investigated. The Central Highlands, where the climate appears to be suitable for dairy cattle, seems to be a logical site for the initial efforts. The following comments represent some of the goals and thinking of livestock experts attached to the JDG.

Production Targets

It is estimated by some experts in the ministry that by three years following cessation of hostilities South Vietnam could show a 30 percent to 40 percent increase in swine production, a 60 percent to 70 percent increase in chickens, and a 90 percent to 100 percent increase in ducks and egg production. These increases will not only permit greater local consumption

---

*"Potential for Mushrooms Production in Post-War Agricultural Economy," JDG Working Paper (unpublished).

**Vegetable Production Problems in Dalat/Tuyen-Duc Area, Working Paper No. 27, (JDG, September, 1968).

of livestock products but will also allow South Vietnam to resume exporting pigs, frozen pork, ducks, eggs, and egg powder.

According to the same authorities, ten years after cessation of hostilities the increase over current levels for hogs should be 80 percent to 100 percent, for chickens 100 percent to 120 percent, and for ducks and eggs 200 percent to 220 percent.

Since agriculture in the future may be partially mechanized, the number of buffaloes and cattle is not expected to increase very much. Three years after the cessation of hostilities, it is estimated that the increases will be only 15 percent to 20 percent for buffaloes and 30 percent to 35 percent for cattle. Ten years later, there should be a further 25 percent increase for buffaloes and 70 percent to 80 percent for cattle. During this period, dairying should be investigated thoroughly, especially in the Central Highlands, where the climate appears to be suitable for this type of endeavor.

Improvement of Livestock Breeds

Hogs. There is a need to import foreign breeds of hogs* in order to improve native ones by crossbreeding. The breeds which have given good results in the past are Yorkshire Large White, Danish Landrance, Yorkshire Middle White, and Duroc. During the first two years, about 2,000 boars should be imported annually. More artificial insemination centers would contribute greatly to the improvement of swine production.** In addition to the four existing centers, six more should be established within the next three years and sixteen more centers within ten years. Each center will have two or three subcenters. The main center will take care of the purebred boars and carry out the laboratory work. The subcenters will receive only the semen and carry out the artificial insemination in the surrounding areas.

---

*Swine Raising Development Program in Vietnam, Working Paper No. 22, (JDG, April, 1968).

**"Livestock Improvement with Special Reference to Needs for an Artificial Insemination Program in Vietnam," JDG Working Paper (unpublished).

Chickens. Foreign breeds of chicken* which have shown good results under South Vietnam's environment should also be imported. The suitable breeds are New Hampshire, Rhode Island Red, White Leghorn, and Barred Plymouth Rock. In addition, parent stock for the production of broilers or layers should be imported. During the first two years after the cessation of hostilities, 50,000 purebred baby chicks and 50,000 chicks as parent stock would need to be imported annually; thereafter, 25,000 of each in the third year.

Beef Cattle. Approximately 150 head of imported male cattle for crossing with native females should be introduced within three years. Under South Vietnam's environment the crossing of the local breed Phu Yen with Santa Gertrudis imported from the United States has given very good results.

Dairy Cattle. The dairy cattle industry should be investigated and upon favorable results should be established over the next three years in the Central Highlands, in the vicinity of Saigon, and in other areas. Dairy cattle of one to one-and-one-half years in age need to be imported for the project.

Ducks and Buffaloes. South Vietnam already possesses good breeds of ducks** and buffaloes. Good breeds of buffaloes are found mainly in the provinces of Quang Ngai and Quang Tin, and of ducks in the Mekong Delta. For this reason, it is not necessary to import foreign breeds, but selection within the local breeds of buffaloes and ducks is recommended.

Improvement of Livestock Feed

In addition to rice and its by-products, corn, sorghum, cassava, soybean oil meal, coconut oil meal, peanut oil meal, rubber seed oil meal, and fish meal are needed for making animal feeds. The Republic of Vietnam produces fish abundantly and low-cost fish could be used for processing fish meal, a nutritive feed supplement for swine and poultry. In the meantime, until local production of feed grains has been developed,

---

*Broiler Production in Post-War Vietnam, Working Paper No. 25 (JDG, June, 1968).

**"Duck Production Potential in Post-War Vietnam," JDG Working Paper (Unpublished).

corn and other supplementary feedstuffs will have to be imported. It is expected that feed needs could be met locally within two to three years.

As local production of feed grains develops, more feedmills should be established. There should be at least three more with a daily production capacity of 50 to 100 tons each, and approximately 40 small mills with a capacity of 10 to 20 tons each set up in the various provinces. There are now only two feedmills in the Saigon area and one under construction in Phong Dinh Province.

Production of Vaccines

The National Institute of Bacteriology and Animal Diseases in Saigon has conducted research over the past twelve years and has produced vaccines* necessary for the prevention of contagious diseases in livestock. During eleven months in 1967, the institute has produced vaccines for the control of rinderpest in buffaloes and cattle (648,740 vaccines), cholera and pasteurellosis of hogs (481,875 vaccines), and Newcastle disease of chickens, fowl plague, and fowl pox (5,086,310 vaccines).

Provincial mobile units must be established in order to perform vaccinations in the more remote villages. More vaccines and especially antibiotics for the control of livestock diseases will have to be produced using imported or local raw materials and more research is required to improve the quality of the vaccines.

Training of Livestock Specialists and Extension Workers

In Vietnam, there are very few livestock specialists capable of working with livestock and animal diseases. In Japan, which has the same livestock population as Vietnam, the number of livestock specialists is sixty times more than in Vietnam.

---

*Protection of Farm Animals Against Contagious Disease in Vietnam, Working Paper No. 21 (JDG, April, 1968).

To meet the need for technicians,* during the next three years 100 Vietnamese specialists should be sent abroad for at least one year of training. In addition, 500 specialists should be trained locally in animal disease control and livestock raising for a period of three to five years.

More training facilities should be provided in the colleges and technical schools of agriculture. Short-term training courses for farmers, training of livestock cadres, and the preparation and publication of simple, nontechnical pocket books on livestock raising are necessary and would be highly beneficial.

Fisheries Development

Lying along the continental coast of southeast Asia, the Republic of Vietnam, with a coastal length of 2,500 kilometers, abounds in a wide variety of marine fish. The numerous internal ponds and rivers in the Republic of Vietnam provide an additional resource in the form of inland fishing.

Fish and fish products provide the Vietnamese with a major source of protein which is much cheaper than meat. Moreover, it is more readily available and relatively easier to produce.

Present Situation

The fishermen are very skillful, but like many farmers in Vietnam and other countries, they have been very reluctant and skeptical about modernizing their traditional customs and practices. As a result, the fish catch has been far below its potential. Furthermore, the lack of training facilities, a poorly organized marketing structure, an inadequate transportation system, insufficient capital, and insecurity have all contributed to restricting the development of the fishing industry.

In spite of the above-mentioned factors that have limited the development of the fishing industry, fish production has

---

*"Postwar Extension Programs Needed in South Vietnam," JDG Working Paper (Unpublished).

increased over the years. Although limited in degree, the motorization of boats, improvement of fishing gear and methods, application of new techniques in pond fish culture, and training of fishermen and cadres have contributed to increasing production from 121,000 metric tons in 1955 to 410,700 metric tons in 1967.

Postwar Action

The development of fisheries in the postwar period will greatly contribute to the national economy by providing employment and investment opportunities. The investment opportunities can be classified as those requiring limited capital and those requiring substantial investments.

Examples of the projects requiring relatively limited capital would be the increase in areas of farm fish ponds and the establishment of fish ponds in the brackish-water coastal areas using milk fish. At the same time, private-sector fish hatcheries should be encouraged to produce fish fry for stocking purposes. Farmers and fishermen will need training to improve their fishing skills, and fish marketing needs modernizing.*

For the long-range picture, substantial investments will be required for deep-sea fishing craft, the establishment of canning factories and processing plants, the building of modern fish landing facilities complete with storage buildings, and the development of efficient transportation and marketing.**

Program for Development of Offshore Fishing

The JDG has under study a plan for the first three postwar years aimed specifically at increasing offshore fishing through investment in motorized boats. This program is being encouraged through a joint research project of the Food

---

*Present Situation and Possibilities of Post-War Development of Inland Fisheries in the Mekong Delta, Working Paper No. 42 (JDG, December, 1968).

**A Description of Ocean Fish Marketing in Saigon, Working Paper No. 24 (JDG, June, 1968).

TABLE 7.14

Plan for Postwar Development of Offshore Fishing

Gross Tonnage and Type of Boat	Daily Catch (Tons)	Number of Fishing Days/Year	Yearly Catch (Tons)
First Three Years			
75 tuna net boats, 25T	2	250	37,500
45 trawlers, 50 T	2	250	22,500
18 trawlers, 90T	3	280	15,120
10 tuna clippers, 120T	4	280	11,200
		TOTAL	86,320
Additional Seven Years			
175 tuna net boats, 25T	2	250	87,500
105 trawlers, 50T	2	280	58,800
42 trawlers, 90T	3	280	35,680
25 tuna clippers/ trawlers, 120T	4	280	28,000
5 tuna clippers, 300T	8	280	11,200
		TOTAL	221,180
TOTAL increased production			307,500

and Agriculture Organization and the government of Vietnam, under which the development of marine fisheries in the South China Sea is being investigated. An extended program would cover the balance of the ten-year period after the war (Table 7.14)

In total, it is estimated that the fish catch could be increased by 300,000 tons per year on completion of the programs under study. This would produce in total an offshore catch of 700,000 tons per year. The estimated cost of the program outlined above is VN$4 billion; the increased catch would be worth about VN$6 billion each year.

At present, there are 270,000 fishermen in the country; the average annual catch is about 2 tons per fisherman. With the improved techniques discussed above, the annual fish catch may, during the first three years, be doubled to 4 tons and reach 12 tons per year within ten years after the cessation of hostilities. Compared with Japan, where the annual catch is 23 tons per fisherman, South Vietnam's performance is still far behind, but it is making encouraging progress.

The production of fish products could be increased substantially by following the points mentioned above. If steady development is continued for ten years after the cessation of hostilities, total production will reach the level of 800,000 metric tons, assuming inland fishing is increased to 100,000 metric tons per year. This would be sufficient to meet future domestic needs as well as export requirements.*

PLANNING AND IMPLEMENTING THE PROGRAM

The long-range plan for postwar agricultural development in South Vietnam will revolve mainly around the matching of the prospective needs for agricultural products with the production capability of the nation. In such a plan it is essential that appropriate attention be given to the means of implementing

*"Offshore Fisheries Development Required in the Post-War Period in South Vietnam" JDG Working Paper (Unpublished).

it once the objectives and priorities are established. The intent of the Agricultural Section of JDG is to focus attention on suggesting specific goals and recommending the programs and projects considered necessary to accomplish the objectives. This would then round out the initial stage of the planning process for agricultural development.

In this section, several projects or elements that will have a major impact on the agricultural development program are briefly discussed. A study and review of the various branches of agricultural activity are an integral part of the planning process and provide the factual basis for many of the decisions to be made on both the content and the implementation of the plan.

Land Development and Settlement

The objective of agricultural development is increased production and the improved standard of living this will provide for farm families. In Vietnam increased production will come about partly by the better use of lands already under cultivation and partly by the expansion of the area cultivated, that is by opening new lands for development and settlement.

Programs of the latter type will not be innovations in Vietnam. Between 1958 and 1962 very large areas of new land were developed for agriculture by the Commissariat for Land Development, and about 60, 000 families were installed on them. The majority of the new settlements were in the eastern region (the provinces of Binh Long, Phuoc Long, Binh Duong, and Tay Ninh), the Central Highlands (Pleiku, Kontum, Quang Duc, and Phu Bon), and the Mekong Delta (An Xuyen, Kien Tuong, and Kien Phong), though there were also smaller movements of people from the heavily populated coastal plains of Quang Tri and Thua Thien into the foothills of the Annamite Range in the same provinces.

The history of the program, insofar as it applied to the Central Highlands, is described briefly in Chapter 12; but both in the Central Highlands and in the other principal regions, there were some failings as well as successes. The land development projects of 1958-62 provided new lives for a good number of the refugees who entered Vietnam from the North after the Geneva Convention: they did introduce people and economic activities to areas which had previously been empty and unexploited; and they resulted in increased crop production. Some of the new settlements appeared to take hold and would probably have prospered had not increasing insecurity in the countryside compelled the settlers to remove themselves to safer areas in the vicinity of the towns. When the settlers did this they did not necessarily become idle; today intense agricultural activity in the vicinity of Ban Me Thuot in Darlac Province is partly the result of the 1958-62 land development programs.

The failures were sometimes associated with the neglect of essential precautions which will have to be faithfully observed if similar programs are undertaken after the war, as we believe they should be. There is no point, obviously, in implanting people on poor or patchy soils unsuitable for extensive cultivation of the particular crops they are expected to grow. The soils of those regions which offer the best apparent prospects for expanding the area under cultivation are not homogeneous but very mixed; and no settlement project should be sited without a careful soil survey to determine the areas best suited to cropping, those which should be used for housing and other purposes, and the land-use problems that are likely to be encountered. There is no point either in moving people in the dry season to sites which lack a perennial source of surface water, or on which subsoil water resources do not exist or have not yet been exploited.

There are still considerable areas of unoccupied land which probably satisfy these conditions, though they are by no means as extensive as the maps may suggest. They occur mainly in the same regions which attracted the attention of the Commissariat for Land Development in 1958-62, that is to say, in the provinces of the III Corps Tactical Zone which constitute the hinterland of Saigon, and in the Central Highlands. There are still large areas--almost 2 million hectares--of unoccupied and unexploited land in the Mekong Delta, but for reasons to be described these do not offer as good prospects for early postwar development as the other two.

The hinterland of Saigon, including parts of the basin of the Dong Nai River, presents attractive prospects for the resettlement of families from the heavily populated lowlands of central Vietnam. Although there has not yet been a full examination of all the possibilities of this eastern region, areas of good but as yet unexploited soils totaling 80, 000 hectares have already been identified. These occur principally in the areas of Bau Tram, Ba Mien, Bu Xa Lung, Bu Ban, Xuan La, and north of Vinh An. These lands, and probably others as yet to be investigated, are suitable for a variety of tree crops, including rubber, and also for field crops with a commercial value, such as peanuts. The proximity of Saigon will facilitate the marketing of farm surpluses and the distribution of supplies, including fertilizers, insecticides, and small farm machinery. The agricultural potential of the region has not been compromised by the practice of shifting cultivation.

In the Central Highlands, the settlement problems are different; they are concerned principally with providing opportunities for highland families to adopt settled and progressive agriculture. These opportunities occur principally in the development of small and medium-sized irrigation projects in the basins of the Sre Pok and Se San rivers. The possibilities for this kind of development might eventually embrace from 100, 000 to 150, 000 hectares; they are described in Chapter 12, where proposals are also made for a program of agricultural education and assistance intended to introduce new cultural practices and new crops into traditional farming systems and so improve the conditions of highland families. Apart from the irrigable areas, at least 20, 000 hectares of land presently under secondary forest in Darlac, Quang Duc, and Phu Bon provinces have been identified as having soils sufficiently good to support substantial increases in farm production, though the long dry season and lack of perennial surface water will be inhibiting factors.

Over much of the Central Highlands, steep slopes and shallow soils will prevent development for agriculture, and there are very extensive areas which should be left in permanent forest. In total the opportunities for land development and settlement, in spite of a far greater over-all land area, may not be as extensive in the highlands as in the eastern region, and in Chapter 12 we offer the opinion that at least at the start they should be exploited primarily for the benefit of the indigenous population.

The problems and potentials of the Mekong Delta are entirely different from either of the other two regions discussed here. Undoubtedly, very large increases, and diversification as well, can be achieved in farm production by systems of water control for the 2 million hectares of delta lands, which are already being cultivated. This has the highest priority in a delta development program; it has already been the subject of considerable study, and a project for water control in lands already cultivated is presented in Chapter 12.

At various times attention has been drawn to areas of equal extent in the delta, also approximately 2 million hectares, which have not yet been brought under cultivation, and certain tentative suggestions for their development have been advanced. The Joint Development Group can only recommend that the subject be approached with caution because of doubtful soil conditions.

The mangrove swamp areas, although they may remain undeveloped for a relatively long time, could possibly be used for fish-pond operations. However, before this can be realized a very precise survey should be carried out to determine the potential sulfate acidity of the area.

In the long term, Vietnam may find itself with a need to develop the more difficult lands of the delta; some research of a basic nature might be initiated, but the Joint Development Group does not see any prospect of actual development in these areas in the next ten years.

Both in terms of satisfying human needs (especially of those refugees who do not go back to their own villages) and of increasing agricultural production, there is every justification for resuming the land development and settlement programs as soon as security returns to the rural areas. As mentioned earlier, careful selection of sites is essential. Settlement at any site selected will demand substantial investment, in the clearing of forest lands, in land preparation (including, where appropriate, irrigation, drainage, and leveling), in housing, in supplying seed, tools, and livestock, in transportation costs, in communal amenities such as schools and public health facilities, and in maintaining the settlers until the time of their first harvest. In Chapter 12 it is proposed that up to 40,000, mostly highland, families could be settled in the Central Highlands in a period of ten years after the war; in the provinces of the III Corps Tactical Zone we suggest that 20,000 to 30,000 families could be accommodated in a comparable period. This would be an ambitious and sufficient program for the immediate postwar period.

Research, Extension, and Training Programs

Research

The Joint Development Group feels that with respect to agriculture, emphasis in the immediate postwar period should be placed on applied rather than on basic research. Applied research produces more rapid results and can be carried out by technicians with lower degrees of skills than can basic or pure research. When scientists are available and their programs can be supported by the economy, basic studies can be initiated. Immediately in the postwar period, research efforts of the Ministry of Agriculture should be directed at the following four programs.

Soil Surveys. South Vietnam has many unexploited natural resources, such as uncultivated acid sulfate soils, organic soils, and in particular, the uncultivated gray podzolic soils. These soils vary in fertility level depending upon location. To determine clearly the exact location of soils suitable for cultivation, soil survey maps for the area under consideration should be completed. These surveys would provide data for future land development and would be basic for land resettlement. To conduct this work, several soil survey teams will be required. One soil survey team at least should be stationed in the Mekong Delta to map the acid sulfate and organic soils; another in the eastern region to survey the gray podzolic soils; and another in the Central Highlands to determine the limits for agricultural development.

Crop Production. Although crop yields in South Vietnam are traditionally very low, the use of fertilizers and improved varieties is leading to greatly improved yields. There are available, either in Vietnam or in other areas of southeast Asia, improved varieties of most crop plants. These should be field tested to measure their adaptability to Vietnamese conditions, and extensive variety trials should be set up in the different climatic zones on various soil types. Hybridization is a time-consuming sophisticated method for plant improvement requiring higher technical skills than are needed at the immediate postwar level. With a build-up of trained manpower after a few years, it will be applied to the various adapted crops. At the same time, as the introductions are subjected to varietal trials, studies should be carried out to ascertain the most effective kinds and application rates of fertilizers required for the major tree and field crops grown on different soil types. A continuing search needs to be conducted for crops that may have a potential in Vietnam but which are not grown at present. Data needs to be obtained on the water requirements of plants, especially with respect to the timing and amount of water required for irrigation. Pathologists and entomologists need to pay strict attention to the control of diseases and pests affecting the important field and tree crops, and to ascertain the correct dosage and methods of application of the many agricultural chemicals on the market.

Livestock. The Ministry of Agriculture's specialists feel that the primary livestock interest should be directed at determining the most suitable pure breeds and crossbreeds of hogs, chickens, and cattle for the varied climatic belts found in the country. Equally important, they feel that real attention needs to be directed at the livestock feeds industry and the testing of new feedstuffs and forages. They further feel that the problem of animal health, especially the stabilization of vaccines, has priority for study.

Fish. The concerned officials of the Ministry of Agriculture feel that with the advent of new technologies of insect control, toxicity problems may affect aquatic life. They feel that investigations ascertaining the effect of pesticides (to be used on rice and other crops) on fish in paddy fields, ponds, and canals should be initiated with the view of selecting pesticides that will be nontoxic to fish and other marine life. They feel that applied studies on spawning induction need to be carried out for those species that do not reproduce in confined waters.

Extension

The results of the research on agricultural matters must be disseminated to farmers by extension workers if it is to have any effect. In addition, new techniques in agriculture need to be brought to the attention of farmers. There are various techniques that can be effective in extension work, notably the conducting of demonstrations, meetings, and other educational activities at the sites of improved villages. Radio (and television) has the power to reach farmers who do not often have ready access to printed material and can thus be a most effective means of communicating ideas.

The "improved village" concept under which extension workers can demonstrate new techniques, appears very sound and additional improved villages should be established. For the future, a minimum of one improved village per province is suggested. Through technical training and observations at the improved villages, farmers are more likely to apply new techniques in their home villages than if they were simply visited by an extension agent. Results obtained from the provincial improved villages could be applied to other communes and hamlets in the area or be employed in planning and implementing regional programs such as the one proposed for the Mekong Delta. Extension needs in the postwar period will be complex and have been the subject of two studies under the auspices of the Joint Planning Group.

Training

Training is necessary to support extension and research programs. Because of hostilities, many agricultural technicians have been drafted. Indeed, in many directorates, it is estimated that from 50 percent to 70 percent of the technical people are now in the military. Those remaining are often either females or more elderly men. It is hoped that upon the cessation of hostilities, the drafted technicians and specialists will be allowed to return to their former directorate or service. Retaining of these returnees in new and old techniques, as well as updating their technical knowledge, will be necessary.

In the past, there has always been a shortage of adequately trained personnel for both research and extension. Therefore, aside from retraining the ex-soldiers, additional workers for both branches will have to be trained in order to reach the expanded level of output planned for the immediate and long-range future.

To meet educational needs, training programs should be implemented at several levels.

1. Primary: Agricultural teaching should be introduced at the primary level, since approximately 80 percent of the population is directly involved in farming.

2. Secondary: Those secondary agricultural schools now in existence should be strengthened and additional ones developed.

3. College: The University of Can Tho should be developed as the main center for agricultural education for the delta, and the College of Bao Loc developed to handle the needs for the other regions. And, of course, the College of Agriculture of the National University should continue its training of agriculture specialists.

Additional training could be provided at the National Rice Production Training Center, as well as in short courses developed at various agricultural experiment stations, demonstration centers, and improved villages.

To meet an immediate pressing need to train farmers, the Ministry of Agriculture and U.S. AID are proposing that the Cooperative Research Training Center (CRTC) at Gia Dinh be turned into a National Agricultural Training Center. The top provincial agricultural officers in the various disciplines could be brought to this center for special training. These officers would return to their respective provinces and conduct training programs at the cadre level in specific subjects, such as artificial insemination and maintenance of equipment.

To assist with the manpower needs for the training program, an effort should be made to bring back the Vietnamese students who are now living abroad and have some training in agriculture. They can be of invaluable immediate assistance.*

Agricultural Credit

It is generally granted by agriculturists that credit in adequate amounts and on reasonable terms is one of the major facilitating factors in any effort to increase production. The importance of credit in an agricultural development program is not always recognized by legislators and other public officials, and implementation through government-sponsored programs is often inadequate or poorly designed for accomplishing the task at hand. If agriculture in South Vietnam is to develop as intended during the postwar period, it is clear that credit in greatly increased amounts and tailored to fit the peculiar needs of the agricultural sector must be readily

---

*"Agricultural Extension Requirements in Post-War Vietnam," JDG Working Paper (unpublished).

available to substantial numbers of farmers and fisherman and to private dealers, cooperatives, and others who are engaged in marketing or supplying inputs.*

At present, there are three sources of organized credit available to finance Vietnam's agriculture; the regular commercial banks, the dealers and merchants who provide goods and services to agriculture, and the government-sponsored agencies such as the ADB and CCVN. Other important sources of agricultural credit include the less formal arrangements with relatives, friends, and neighbors. Generally speaking, the commercial banks are interested only in loans to private dealers or perhaps to large producing units such as plantations. They have preferred to concentrate their activities in the urban centers and have been reluctant to extend their services into rural areas. Thus, the commercial banks have been doing only a very limited job of providing agricultural credit. They have not yet provided funds for producer organizations such as cooperatives and other associations. In Chapter 3, there is a more detailed discussion of commercial banking in Vietnam.

Dealers and merchants have over a time provided a large part of the credit used by Vietnamese farmers and fishermen and they have also financed one another through a trickle-down process. In many cases, this credit has consisted of loans in kind that usually result in a very high interest rate. Credit extended by dealers and merchants is highly personalized and involves an absolute minimum of formalities. In the legal sense, the loans are largely unsecured. It is very common for one dealer to help finance another; e. g., Saigon merchants advance funds to provincial dealers, who then provide the same service to buyers at the district and country level.

So far as government-sponsored agricultural credit is concerned, only the ADB has, thus far, made a significant contribution in the form of an on-going, aggressive program. The ADB itself was established in 1967 as the successor to what had previously been known as the National Agricultural Credit Office (NACO). NACO had been operating since the 1950's

---

*"Rural Credit Requirements in South Vietnam," JDG Working Paper (unpublished).

but had never become an important part of the agricultural credit system of South Vietnam. At its peak in 1959 and 1960, the NACO made loans of just over VN$1 billion per year but by 1965, the total for the year was down to VN$150 million. In revitalizing the agricultural credit program of the GVN, the ADB had set up 40 provincial offices by the end of 1967 and its resources totaled VN$3.5 billion at that time. So far as the CCVN is concerned, its contribution to agriculture has consisted mostly of financing rice dealers, but there is evidence that its interests are broadening.

Throughout southeast Asia there is a surprising amount of agricultural credit provided by relatives, friends, and neighbors. These personal loans are usually for small amounts and for a short term, but in the aggregate they are important. Studies in Thailand and South Vietnam indicate that over half of the loans from this source are interest free. Such loans will undoubtedly continue to be an important but declining factor as the agriculture of South Vietnam becomes more commercialized. At the present time, little is known about the total agricultural credit situation in the nation. It is impossible, short of undertaking farm surveys, even to estimate with any reasonable accuracy the sources and amounts of credit used at any particular time. A good beginning has been made on a farm credit survey in South Vietnam, under sponsorship of the Joint Development Group. An initial survey in five representative provinces has been completed and the results give some indication of certain aspects of rural credit in the nation. This survey is being extended to other sections of the country; when completed, it is expected to provide information needed in evaluating more completely the agricultural credit situation in South Vietnam.

In 1967 the ADB made loans totaling almost VN$1.8 billion to 85,000 families; in 1968 the loan program was substantially larger. Over-all, however, the ADB has probably not been serving more than 4 percent to 5 percent of the farmers and fishermen in the nation, although in certain provinces where special programs are centered, the number receiving ADB loans may be as high as 15 percent of the total. ADB credit consists mostly of loans for short terms and special purposes with heavy emphasis on rice and livestock production. In principle, these loans are made under the supervised credit precepts which underlie the operating policy of the new bank. It is difficult, however, to provide a full measure of supervision and guidance in the present situation of limited manpower and restricted security.

Looking ahead over the next ten years to the future agricultural credit needs of the nation, it appears that by 1980 the total loan funds required to provide solid support for the production effort may be as much as VN$30 billion (1967 price base) per year. This estimate is based upon aggregate loans to producers, dealers and semipublic organizations, and so on, equaling 10 percent of the value of the projected agricultural production needed to meet in-country and export requirements. At this level the credit would cover the cost of some 25 percent to 50 percent of the direct inputs entering into the production of most crops, livestock, and fish. Various assumptions can be made as to the share of the agricultural credit that the public sector (such as ADB and CCVN) should provide. A reasonable goal might be 50 percent, which would call for perhaps VN$15 billion annually (1967 price base) in loans of this type by 1980. To cover the normal carryover of loans having longer terms, it would be necessary to provide additional funds--perhaps VN$5 billion, or a total of VN$20 billion for current loans and carryover. This projection of credit needs assumes no great increase in the rate of capital accumulation among the agricultural population in general.

Agri-Business Units

Although agricultural-based industries are included in the chapter on industrial development, there are some aspects of agri-business that have a direct bearing on agricultural development. In this context, the emphasis is more on integration and commercialization of production than on industrial development in the usual sense of the word.

Despite the distinct probability that agriculture in Vietnam is not likely to shift quickly toward general commercialization from its present semisubsistence character, there are indications that some producers are moving toward establishment of larger-scale, integrated units. In the rubber industry, where the plantations are dominant, this pattern is already established on a broad front. Several proposals have been offered recently for setting up poultry and hog enterprises in Vietnam that would be comparable to the broiler and pork units in the United States and elsewhere. These proposals involve varying degrees of vertical integration of the production and marketing processes. The same approach has been suggested in the fishing industry; it is proposed that large, ocean-going vessels serve as the base for integrated units. Cooperatives or other associations would in some cases perform the integrating function for the smaller production units.

Generally, integration of production and marketing not only steps up output, it also leads to greater efficiency and lower costs. In Vietnam a limited number of such units, particularly in livestock and fisheries, should be established so as to determine their potential contribution to the agricultural development program in the postwar period. Credit is usually a key factor in such enterprises, and present sources of funds do not appear to be well adapted to agri-business needs. This deficiency can and should be corrected.

Provision of Needed Production Inputs

Ready availability of needed inputs and services at fair prices is a major factor in any program to develop the agriculture of a country or region. For this reason, increasing attention is being given to the present structure through which inputs and services are provided and to the possible improvement of the system. A study of this subject has just recently been completed in the delta region by the Simulmatics Corporation, which was under contract to U. S. AID. The summary that follows draws heavily from the Simulmatics report.

In Vietnam the distribution of such inputs as fertilizers, pesticides, seeds, fishing gear, and motors is primarily a function of private dealers, although there are a few cooperative or semiprivate associations that play a relatively minor role in the system. Contrary to popular belief, the inputs are widely available and marging of profit are very low, so low, in fact, that dealers cannot afford frills such as advertising and field services. Although these dealers are not innovators in the market development sense, they are very adept at responding quickly to demand once it becomes apparent. They have also proved to be remarkably flexible and resilient in the face of the rapidly changing economic and security situation. Some of the prejudicial attitudes toward dealers in agricultural inputs has stemmed from the belief that this activity is a Chinese monopoly. Although many of the dealers in this trade do indeed have a Chinese background, there is evidence that ethnic Vietnamese are increasingly becoming involved, and this is apparent throughout the nation. In the countryside, it is easy for new dealers to become involved in the sale of agricultural inputs, and outlets spring up very quickly when and where the opportunity or need becomes evident. It is apparent that at this level and in the economic sense there is nothing approaching a monopoly in the distribution of fertilizer, insecticides, seeds, fishing gear, and motors; in fact, competition is described as being "fierce."

At the Saigon/Cholon level, however, the distribution of the major inputs needed in agricultural and fisheries production is in fact concentrated in the hands of a few importers, wholesalers, associations, or government agencies. Fertilizer, for example, has recently been imported only under government auspices, although this policy was changed in 1968. Insecticides have been subsidized and distributed in generally inadequate quantities by the Ministry of Agrarian Reform and Agriculture. Motors, fishing gear, and seeds are mostly handled by private distributors. There is some tendency on the part of the government to channel agricultural inputs at the first stage (Saigon/Cholon and provincial levels) through semipublic or cooperative associations such as the Central Labor Union (CVT), the Central Farmers Association, and the National Federation of Agricultural Cooperative Associations (NFACA). In the country, however, the private dealers are said to be the dominant element in the distribution of the agricultural inputs.

On the basis of actual experience in the field, it is fair to say that in present circumstances and in the short run, the simplest and most direct approach to providing Vietnamese farmers and fishermen with additional inputs and services is not only to allow the private sector to continue expansion in this field but also to encourage such action through a more sympathetic attitude towards the dealers and merchants engaging in this business. This observation runs counter to suggestions by some officials and advisors who advocate "new" channels of distribution, principally cooperatives and associations of one sort or another. With margins as low as they are reported to be, it is quite unlikely that the new organizations relying on hired help can compete effectively with the private dealers. The problem is also compounded by the fact that substantially all of the business expertise is rather firmly attached to the private sector. This is not to say that cooperatives and associations should not be encouraged; it is merely recognition of the potential contribution that may be expected from the private sector with a minimum of outside support. Group buying on a pool basis is a sound beginning in cooperative action and some farmers and fishermen are already working together in this way. This activity should be encouraged on a broad front.

There has been some sentiment for government-operated supply depots through which agricultural inputs would be distributed. To involve the government in this type of business would seem to be both unnecessary and undesirable. The experience in insecticides is perhaps a good example of how government participation may lead to unexpected results; in this case, by subsidizing only a part of the supply needed, the government program has made it almost impossible for dealers to provide on a competitive basis the balance of the supply needed by farmers. One direct result has been adulteration as a means of meeting the subsidized price of government stocks. If the trade must be subjected to control, there are other less cumbersome and costly ways of policing the situation. Credit is vital in making production inputs more readily available. It is here that the government can and should provide more assistance to both farmers and dealers.

It is not anticipated that there will be a serious problem in distributing fertilizers, insecticides, seeds, motors, and other inputs needed in Vietnam during the postwar period, providing there is a consistent policy of minimal restrictions on trade in and prices of such goods and services coupled with joint effort by the government and distributors, both private and semipublic, to achieve the desired levels of acceptance and use by farmers and fishermen in the nation.

Prices and Price Policy

Prices have a very strong bearing on both the production and the marketing of agricultural crops. It has been amply demonstrated that farmers in less developed countries respond to a price incentive just as they react to it in the more advanced areas. With the partial removal of price restrictions on pork in 1967, there was a noticeable upturn in hog production in South Vietnam despite wartime impairment of feed supplies, labor, transportation, and so on. In Thailand, the continued depression of the farm price of rice because of the export premium (tax) and the low ceiling price on pork are undoubtedly holding production of these products below levels that would otherwise prevail. The current surplus of rice in Japan is directly attributable to the artificially high price guaranteed to farmers. Examples from countries throughout the world attest to the efficacy of the price incentive as an inducement to greater production and the use of improved practices; conversely, low prices to farmers are an equally effective deterrent to production.

Problems inherent in price programs are often difficult to solve, as is illustrated by the price situation on rice imported by South Vietnam in recent years; on the one hand, it is believed advisable to hold down the price paid by consumers, while on the other, it is hoped that farmers will increase their production--but the paddy price is not always sufficient to induce the farmers to take the action necessary to step up production. To reach the levels of production required to meet prospective needs for agricultural products, it seems obvious that there must be a reasonable price incentive on all commodities. This is particularly true if Vietnamese farmers are to move toward commercial farming at a more rapid rate.

Prices also play a vital role in the export of agricultural products. The continuing inflation of prices in South Vietnam is rapidly leading to a situation in which the local products are priced out of the international market under official rates of exchange. In such circumstances, barring further devaluation, there is likely to be more and more demand for export subsidies or other special concessions aimed at bolstering the return from commodities shipped out of Vietnam. Exports of tea are now heavily subsidized and while this item alone is no serious drain on the public funds, the situation would be much different if, say, a million tons of rice were involved, as may well be the case if domestic production increases along the lines indicated.

A number of alternatives are usually available for consideration by policy-makers and others who may be involved in in planning and administering programs that affect agricultural prices. In some cases, the best course may be to free trade and let prices seek their level in the market; in other circumstances, however, more direct intervention may be necessary. Support prices, purchase programs, subsidies, import and export restrictions, and even price controls are among the measures often used to influence prices. Careful study of the peculiarities of each situation, as well as the effect of action or inaction on the commodity involved and on other related elements, is essential because of the very delicate nature of the price mechanism and the many interrelationships that exist in this field.

Farm Size and Family Income

In any planning related to agricultural development, there are always questions about the income level of farm families and the scale of operation which, in turn, has such a strong influence on the income of the farm unit. Administration of public programs such as those in land reform and credit can be used to influence farm size and, consequently, farm income per operating unit. Farm units in South Vietnam are small, averaging about 1.35 hectares, and income is generally low--VN$16,700 per farm family of 5.5 persons, in 1963-64. Although there are no later data available on farm income as such, it appears that average income in 1967 may have been about VN$60,000, which would be reasonably well in line with the change in prices of farm products since 1964. Even at VN$60,000, however, the per capita farm income would still have been less than VN$11,000, which is well below average for the nation.

Vietnam has four major groups who will almost certainly be affected directly by policy on the size and income of farm units: (1) refugees who must be relocated; (2) members of the military who may elect to enter or return to agriculture; (3) urban workers whose employment may cease with the return of peace; and (4) farm families on units that are not capable of producing an acceptable level of living.

Many of these people will be most reluctant to enter, return to, or continue on in farming if to do so means living at a bare subsistence level. At the same time, it is unlikely that parity between rural and urban incomes can be established quickly--it has not been achieved in the United States or in most other developed countries.

It is suggested that a realistic approach in Vietnam may be to select as a goal an income level that is both equitable and attainable and then to develop as rapidly as practicable farm units that will provide such an income. From the standpoint of both economic well-being and political stability, this procedure is far superior to setting up large numbers of additional uneconomic units that can lead only to intensification of rural poverty. At the same time, in the absence of alternative employment opportunities, it is imperative that farms be made available to large numbers of people in the groups listed above. There will undoubtedly be great pressure to care for as many people as possible without regard for economic soundness of the individual units.

The relationship between farm sizes and family incomes is, of course, a valid concern of the Joint Development Group. The difficult question of land reform, with its strong political and social overtones, is not; it is the concern primarily of the minister of agriculture and agrarian reform. Land reform is nevertheless relevant to the discussion of agricultural development, in that present programs of redistribution of large holdings may be expected to result in a particular pattern of land tenure, and this, in its turn, will have effects both upon levels of production and the standards of living which Vietnamese farm families will be able to achieve.

These effects may be quite different from those the land reformers expect. A slogan such as "Four acres and a cow" may have been appropriate for Ireland in the nineteenth century but is entirely unattractive for Vietnam in the twentieth. Land reform has important economic implications, as well as political and social ones, and the fragmentation of large holdings for its own sake, regardless of its consequences on production and farm incomes, is something to be avoided. Land reform in this narrow sense is, nevertheless, commonly accepted as a panacea for all the troubles of the developing countries. It has numerous advocates in the developed ones, which have, as a matter of interest, usually followed quite a contrary process, achieving immense increases in farm production by the consolidation of small holdings into large factory-type enterprises, with heavy capital investment in plant and machinery.

In Vietnam there are crops which lend themselves to development by small holders, and others may be introduced. There are relatively few crops of sufficient value and sufficiently sought in world markets to provide a farmer and his family, be they tenants or proprietors, with a good living from

1.35 hectares, which is the size of the average farm in Vietnam today. There are other crops, already cultivated, like sugar cane, or capable of being introduced, like oil palm, which usually cannot be grown economically and competitively except in holdings of from one thousand to several thousand hectares. Land reform should not be carried so far as to make such profitable enterprises, potential employers of labor, impossible.

The intention at this point is not to decry a program which may have become a political necessity and which, well administered, might produce political profits. It is simply to point out that if the program aims merely at creating fifty small, uneconomic farms where there was formerly one large profitable one, then it leaves a good deal to be desired. A high level of production on the farm is surely as important an objective, for owners and sharecroppers alike, as a sense of proprietorship is to the latter alone. In many cases in Vietnam the solution to rural poverty may be found in an efficient, well-organized farm labor force earning wages far superior to the scanty returns which many farmers now obtain from their small holdings.

What the Joint Development Group suggests is that land reform is not a subject on which the options should be limited by dogmas and ideologies. The solutions may vary from place to place and from crop to crop. Where, in particular cases, it is indeed desirable to reduce or abolish large land ownerships, it may be possible to achieve efficiency in production by the organization of producers' cooperatives or by other joint action aimed at achieving economies of scale. Where, in other cases, agricultural development requires substantial inputs of capital and modern management, enlightened employers may replace the traditional landlords. We question the wisdom of breaking up holdings in land to a point at which neither owners nor tenants can possibly make a living from them; preferable objectives are fair rents for farm tenants, fair wages for farm labor, and higher production from the land for all. If these objectives can be achieved, the desire to parcel out what is left of the large estates might become less urgent.

Improvement of the Marketing System

Few subjects in the field of agriculture evoke stronger opinions than the question of efficiency in marketing. In South Vietnam, the marketing system is a favorite whipping boy among critics who blame middlemen and others involved in marketing for most of the problems of farmers and fishermen. To what extent such criticism is justified cannot be determined objectively at the present time because so little is known about costs and margins and even about the details of structure and services. It is often alleged that group action by farmers and fishermen in the form of cooperatives, associations, or unions would lead automatically to lower marketing costs and higher returns to producers. This allegation should not be taken literally without some important qualifications. It is not the purpose here either to vindicate the existing marketing system or to advocate a reorganized or different system; rather the intent is to point out certain aspects of the marketing situation that are often overlooked and to suggest marketing research that is essential to an objective evaluation of the system.

In Vietnam, the marketing of agricultural products (including fish) is largely a function of the private sector. It is often said that these activities are dominated by Chinese and it is probably true that many of the dealers are indeed ethnic Chinese. The Chinese have no real monopoly in either the marketing of agricultural products or the sale of inputs, however, because to an increasing extent, ethnic Vietnamese are becoming involved in this segment of the economy. This is particularly evident at the provincial and country level. Regardless of ethnic background, the real question is whether dealers and handlers are performing a useful and necessary service and whether they are being paid a reasonable amount for services rendered. This question cannot be answered with any certainty at present because the studies needed to back up judgment have not yet been undertaken. There is more evidence of concentration in fish marketing, and this situation deserves early investigation. Some critics decry the fact that the marketing system in Vietnam is not "modern." This observation in regard to marketing is about the same as saying that Vietnamese agriculture is not commercialized. It is unrealistic to expect a highly sophisticated marketing system in a setting of subsistence or near-subsistence farming. The present market structure has developed over a long period of time and is generally well attuned to the pattern of agricultural production now prevailing. This is not to say that dealers cannot and do not attempt to take advantage of their superior bargaining position in their buying activities. What is apparent is that given the state of technology in agriculture, the marketing system is providing the service required to move the products of the farms and fisheries into consumption. With the information currently at hand, it is impossible to state with any certainty that the system is inefficient or that either the private sector or semipublic organizations (cooperatives, associations, and so on) can do a significantly better job at less cost. Generally speaking, if there is sufficient competition among dealers, the more aggressive and efficient will set the pace and force others to match the performance or lose out. Where competition does not exist because of collusion or other factors, then government action to control price and/or margins or to support farmers' and fishermen's organizations may be required to improve the producers' position and to assure a reasonable charge for marketing services.

In a number of cases, the indigenous market structure in several less developed countries has demonstrated remarkable flexibility and adaptability in adjusting to rapid changes in agricultural production. Field corn and kenaf in Thailand and bananas in Taiwan are outstanding examples in recent years; in Thailand, the private sector was wholly responsible, and in Taiwan, it was entirely the semipublic (cooperatives). It is not the question of private versus semipublic approach that is important, it is the obvious ability of the structure already at hand to expand and adjust, providing obstacles are removed and proper encouragement is given. In Vietnam, it is entirely reasonable to assume that the marketing system can and will make similar adjustments to meet developing needs in the postwar period, providing restrictive action is not present, credit becomes more readily available, the government undertakes to develop with dealers a cooperative approach to industry problems, and the long-range outlook for investment becomes more favorable. The government can do much to facilitate this growth and development of the market structure for farm and fisheries products without itself becoming involved directly in buying and selling or providing facilities.

Farmers' and Fishermen's Organizations

In South Vietnam, it is fair to say that farmers' and fishermen's organizations have made only limited progress despite a considerable amount of effort to stimulate their growth and development. These organizations include farmers' associations, agricultural cooperatives, a tenant farmers' union, fishermen's cooperatives, and a fishermen's union. Ostensibly, all have one common objective--to further the economic and social well-being of their members. Both government and foreign assistance (U. S. AID mostly) has been and is being given to these activities, but the fact remains that they are still a relatively minor element in the agriculture of Vietnam. Reasons for this are many; it suffices at this time to mention only the security situation, lack of managerial skills, limited capital, and the failure of members to identify closely with their organizations.

Distribution of farm and fishing supplies has been a large part of the business phase of these associations. Marketing is still a minor activity. The government has endeavored to bolster such organizations by channeling government-sponsored credit and government-financed supplies through them to their members. The multipurpose farmers' associations tend to be more broadly based than the cooperatives, most of the latter being organized along commodity lines (rice, tea, livestock). The tenant farmers' union and the fishermen's union engage in certain business activities, particularly in supplying production inputs and a limited amount of credit, in addition to their main purpose of safeguarding and furthering the welfare of their members. It is estimated that there are about 140 agricultural cooperatives and some 70 to 80 fishermen's cooperatives in South Vietnam. Approximately 70 farmers' associations have been set up. Both the cooperatives and the farmers' associations reflect the uncertainty of the wartime period in that many units are either temporarily dormant or even disbanded. Some will undoubtedly be revived as soon as the hostilities cease. A few new organizations are being formed in spite of the currently unfavorable conditions; several are in refugee centers.

Farmers' and fishermen's organizations have a part to play in agricultural development, and they deserve to be encouraged in those situations where a need for their activities is apparent and they are in a position to provide efficient service for their members. As a prelude to more formal cooperation, it is suggested that both farmers and fishermen may gain valuable experience and improve their economic position through group buying and selling. JDG Working Paper No. 26, on fertilizer distribution, provides a further insight into the activities of farmers' organizations in Vietnam.

JDG Working Paper No. 27, on vegetable growing problems, makes proposals for future farmers' organizations.

Rehabilitation of Existing Plantations

Rubber

The most important plantation crop in Vietnam is rubber. It accounts for a large portion of foreign exchange generated by exports. The rubber plantations are under two types of ownership: Vietnamese and foreigners--primarily French and Belgian. In 1965, there were approximately 30,000 hectares in which the units were less than 500 hectares in size and 70,000 hectares in units of 1,000 hectares and over. There were very few plantations ranging between 500 to 1,000 hectares. Those less than 500 hectares in size are owned by Vietnamese. Thus, the foreigners dominate the industry (in terms of hectares and output).

As pointed out in the section above dealing with the present agricultural situation, rubber production has been undergoing a steady decline. The security situation, with attendant reduction in yields, the destruction of trees, and the lack of labor have brought about the widespread abandonment of plantations.

Yields have also been declining. In 1960, the average yields were approximately 1,000 kilograms per hectare (kg/ha), and in 1967, they were down to about 700 kg/ha. On the other hand, in Malaysia, on plantations of 500 hectares or less, the average yields were 700 kg/ha in 1960, while in 1967, the average yields had increased to 1,000 kg/ha. In short, the rubber industry is in a very bad state, getting progressively worse as hostilities continue.

In the postwar rehabilitation, there are a number of unpredictable factors that the rubber industry, and particularly the foreign investors, will have to ponder. Among these are the future price for natural rubber, government policy, land ownership, and alternate and perhaps more lucrative sites for future investments. However, if it is assumed that the price of rubber in the next twenty years remains about what it is today (that is, assuming current price rises are maintained), that hostilities cease, and all other things remain equal, the future for rubber looks fairly promising.

A rehabilitation program for rubber should take the following five lines of approach.

1. It should aim at obtaining a return from the land while replanting. In view of the fact that many trees have been abandoned for as much as eight years, they are no doubt in a state of low productivity due to lack of management, disease, and insect damage. Furthermore, many of the trees are old and their ability to provide sustained high yields is very questionable. Therefore, a large-scale cutting-out program should be undertaken to remove the trees in this condition. This would involve approximately 40,000 hectares, and would represent a substantial loss in income even though tree yield was low. The rubber logs would have a market value for firewood, and according to the Rubber Research Institute a greater return could be had if they could be sold to make paper, as is now being done in Japan (or for plywood, for which experiments are now being conducted in Malaysia).

Additional returns could be had by interplanting the young rubber clones for three years with annual leguminous crops. The intercrop, aside from providing an income for the plantation, would be highly beneficial by contributing to meeting needs for human and livestock consumption.

2. It should aim at increasing the output per acre. Increased output per unit area can be accomplished by planting and/or replanting with high-yielding rubber clones. There are commercial clones available which can produce 2,500 kg/ha, although there are experimental clones that can give as high as 3,500 kg/ha. The available commercial clones would produce 2.5 times as much as the average yields of 1,000 kg/ha obtained in 1960. The use of fertilizers would also be helpful for old as well as new rubber. The application of fertilizers has given a 30 percent increase in yields after a three-year period.

3. It should aim at reducing the cost of production. The cost of production could be greatly influenced by increasing efficiency of tapping. At the present time, tapping costs account for 50 percent of the cost of one kilo of rubber. By utilizing the continuous flow system and applying hormones, production costs should be greatly reduced.

4. It should aim at improving rubber quality and the marketing situation. By improving the quality of rubber produced, it would be possible to receive a higher return per kilo than is now being received. High quality rubber always commands a higher price than ordinary grades. This would require the revision of present processing techniques, and the adoption of and adherence to a specific quality standard. Moreover, the processed rubber should meet the needs and requirements of the manufacturer, which is for small, standard-quality bales. The industrial potential is discussed more thoroughly in Chapter 9.

In regard to marketing, the possibilities for processing rubber products locally should be studied. There is a wide margin between raw rubber (40 piasters/kg) and processed rubber products (150 piasters/kg). It is estimated that between 30 and 40 percent of the rubber produced could be utilized locally. The local processing industry would ensure a market for a large percentage of production and provide for the employment of additional persons. The economic benefits could be distributed between producer, consumer, and processor.

5. It should aim at expanding small holdings. It is believed that the Central Highlands and eastern region are probably the best areas for growing rubber. In these regions, it would probably be wise to promote the development of a small-holders' industry. The small holdings, not having the heavy overhead that the large plantations have and possessing a much greater degree of flexibility, could possibly make an efficient producing unit. Such small holdings, of course, are only viable if central processing facilities are available, either on a cooperative basis, or as a commercial service.

With the utilization of modern techniques, a small-holder could handle 6 hectares of rubber. Since it takes six years before he begins to receive returns, he could interplant with annual crops for the first five years. This would provide an annual income until the rubber begins to produce.

With good management and the utilization of technical inputs, the small-holder should be able to receive 1,500 kg/ha. At 40 piasters a kilo, the gross would be 60,000 piasters a hectare, or 360,000 piasters for 6 hectares per year at 1968 prices.

Tea

At the present time, tea is an important crop for both the local and export market. However, production has been dropping over the years because of widespread abandonment of plantations. The indications are that the demand for tea on both the local and export market will remain fairly stable and therefore, tea production appears to have good prospects for the future. In the postwar era, efforts should be made in five directions, as follows.

1. Replant some of the abandoned plantations. To date, approximately 3,000 hectares of tea have been abandoned. The better strains of tea stumps on some plantations could be revived by simply pruning the stumps and foliage to a convenient harvesting level (reestablishing a plucking table.) However, many of the stumps should be replanted with the high-yielding varieties now in the country. At present, the average yields are around 600 kg/ha. Some efficient farmers are getting 1,000 kg/ha, but there are clones in agricultural stations that can produce as much as 4,000 kg/ha.

2. Expand the area under production. There is land available in Blao and Quang Duc which is quite suitable for tea. These areas might be better for tea than for other crops.

3. Improve the fertility status of the soils. The tea estates are in the highlands on red latosols which are inherently low in organic matter and not particularly fertile. Thus, if a livestock industry could be encouraged and expanded in the area, the manure could be used for adding organic matter to the soil and increasing the water-holding capacity of the soils. Inorganic fertilizer, in the amount of 100 kilos of nitrogen per hectare, would also be required. During the development of the plantations. leguminous cover crops should be grown and they could be cut and used for livestock feed.

4. Encourage resettlement in the highlands. Although insecurity has been responsible for part of the labor shortages in the highlands, in general the area is normally short of manpower. Therefore, it would be expedient to encourage resettlement in areas where the labor could be used effectively. Moreover, the demand is for female harvesters (pluckers) which would round out employment of a family unit. Present wages average 5 to 6 piasters a kilo, and the average load plucked is approximately 30 kilos per day.

5. Study feasibility of a small-holders' industry. It is felt that the industry could benefit by the development of small units of approximately two hectares. At present, about 50 percent of the holdings are about 30 hectares and larger. The remaining half ranges in size from 1 to 10 hectares. Since tea is a labor-intensive industry, a family could make good use of the available labor in a small unit. The more industrious and diligent farmers could produce the high-quality product. For example, in Kenya, the small holdings produce the high-quality tea while the plantations produce the average grades. This is mainly because a good farmer can easily control the extent and degree of harvesting and provide the tree stumps with the needed care and attention, if he is interested.

Coconuts

Although coconuts are usually grown in very small units of from 1/2 hectare to 3 hectares, the nut is in the aggregate an important tree crop. It is important because, before 1965, copra was exported and in 1967, 2,000 tons of copra was imported for the soap industry. Output has declined because of labor shortages, reduction in yield (from a prewar 4,500 to a current estimated 3,000 nuts per hectare), and destruction of trees due to war activities.

As soon as possible, the small-holder industry should be encouraged and supported by (1) making high-yielding strains available to farmers for replanting; (2) providing loans or grants for replanting and the purchase of fertilizers; (3) developing an effective extension program for improving the status of production; and (4) assisting in improving the marketing of copra so that farmers can receive better prices for their produce.

Postwar Agricultural Mechanization

Mechanization of Vietnam's agriculture* is at a very low level, having changed little over the centuries. The motive power for field work is primarily the buffalo and cattle. Planting, weeding, harvesting, and threshing are almost

---

*Post-War Requirements for Farm Mechanization in Vietnam, Working Paper No. 43 (JDG, December, 1968).

exclusively performed by hand labor. Farms are very small and the average farmer is poor; both factors are obstacles to mechanization.

However, smaller items such as water pumps and mechanical pesticide sprayers are gaining fairly wide acceptance, the demand far exceeding the supply. These should be constructed in Vietnam in greater numbers in the postwar period.

With the more extensive and intensive agriculture planned for the postwar period, mechanization of a more serious sort will become mandatory. The farm animal population even at present does not provide enough animals to perform farming functions. Tractors will be required in developing new farm lands, in leveling fields, for digging canals and ditches, and in seed-bed preparation. Harvesting will probably continue to be done by hand in most cases, but threshing will be done by using small pedaled or power-driven portable threshers. The more intensive use of land and the resultant harvesting during rainy seasons will require drying facilities to reduce paddy, corn, or sorghum to a moisture level at which it can be stored.

In addition to a very great need for multipurpose tractors, threshers, driers, pumps, and spraying equipment, there will exist a real need for technicians capable of operating and maintaining equipment. There will also be needs for agricultural credit to permit purchase of the equipment in the first place. Courses should be set up as soon as possible to school technicians in the operation and maintenance of equipment.

Land Capability of Forest Land

During the past ten years or so, a large though undetermined amount of land has ceased to be cultivated, primarily because of insecurity. In the postwar period, these previously cultivated lands will logically be resettled first. However, it is estimated that in the twenty years following peace there will be a sizable conversion of land now classified as forest to agricultural use. Needed now are estimates showing how much of the forested public domain will be required for agricultural expansion, and how much of the unneeded land will have to be reforested. Land capability studies will answer these questions by a consideration of existent vegetation, soil and water conditions, and economic factors. Maps are being prepared to identify all forest reserve, agricultural reserve, and forested areas that could be converted to agricultural use within twenty years. A more complete treatise on forestry is contained in Chapter 8; and see also Working Paper No. 17, Preliminary Report on Forestry.

CHAPTER 8 FORESTRY

A preliminary report on forestry published in January 1968,* contained general recommendations concerning the reform of forest policies and forest management in Vietnam and made suggestions for the promotion of specific forest industries. Certain of the recommendations were regarded as controversial, and the report inspired some useful criticism and comment. We understand that these recommendations have since been taken under active and serious consideration by the ministry and other interested governmental agencies. The preliminary report has been widely distributed and additional copies can be readily supplied. In this chapter we are not repeating the conclusions we reached earlier or the arguments we used to sustain them, except to the extent necessary to explain and illuminate the account of subsequent work. The Joint Development Group believes that the conclusions presented in Working Paper No. 17 were valid ones.

Vietnam's principal interest in its timber resources in the next ten years lies in the promotion of the wood-based industries--logging, saw-milling, plywood and veneer manufacture, and wood pulp--to supply domestic and overseas markets, thus reducing imports and earning foreign exchange. The economic importance of the country's timber resources will make apparent the need for efficient administration and research, including such elements of these as forest inventories, forest protection, and reforestation and management plans. Recommendations for particular wood-based industries are presented in Chapter 9, and the importance of forest assets to the economies of the principal regions of Vietnam is described in Chapter 12.

---

*Preliminary Report on Forestry, Working Paper No. 17 (JDG, January, 1968).

Since November, 1967, the work of the Joint Development Group in forestry has been carried out in very close cooperation with the governmental agency principally concerned, the Department of Water Resources and Forest Administration in the Ministry of Agriculture. A postwar planning committee consisting of senior officers of the department has been established, and ministerial instructions concerning collaboration with the Joint Development Group were issued. It was under the auspices of this committee and by individual members of it that the studies described in this chapter were actually carried out.

CURRENT STATUS OF FOREST LAND

The following description of forest lands, which may be more comprehensive than previous descriptions applied in Vietnam, is being used: "All lands with trees whose crowns cover more than 20 percent of the area and are not used primarily for purposes other than forestry."

In Working Paper No. 17 it was stated that there are 12 million hectares of land in Vietnam to which this description may correctly be applied. Subsequent studies made by the Joint Development Group, using a U.S. Army map showing twenty different vegetative types, confirm that this figure is approximately correct. Descriptions are available of each type of vegetation, and tables have been constructed showing their distribution province by province. Although the details may be less correct than the total figure arrived at for forest land, the study has been useful in identifying the larger areas of valuable forest in which commercial exploitation is likely to take place after the war.

About half of the total area of forest land has individual trees of sufficient size for industrial use. The country's forests are overwhelmingly tropical hardwoods, with a great variety of species, some of them worthless, but others among the world's most prized. In value and volume the most important of them belong to the dipterocarp family, a group of species with an established place in world markets. Typically these are large, dominant trees which produce many seedlings and grow fast, traits which simplify the management of a dipterocarp forest and usually make replanting unnecessary.

The economic importance of the tropical hardwood forests of Vietnam is considered in Chapter 12, in the context of regional development programs, but a brief description of the physical resources available is appropriate here as well.

The five northern provinces (the I Corps Tactical Zone) alone have 1, 600, 000 hectares of forest cover, rather uniform in that almost all is high forest with several canopies and dense undergrowth. This forest undoubtedly has large volumes of high-quality timber. However, owing to the difficulties of the topography, resulting in high logging costs, and the distance of the forest from the principal centers of population on the coast, the forests of the region have remained largely unknown and unexploited.

The five provinces of the zone traditionally imported their timber supplies from North Vietnam, and since 1954 have been doing so from the south.

Further south, the seven provinces of the Central Highlands (Kontum, Pleiku, Darlac, Phu Bon, Quang Duc, Tuyen Duc, and Lam Dong) have a high proportion of forested land, about 4 out of a total of 5 million hectares. In contrast to the forests further north, these forests are not uniform, five major classes presenting various problems and opportunities.

In Kontum and Quang Duc there are extensive areas, about 1, 800, 000 hectares, of high-quality timber, but they are remote and often on difficult terrain. They are not as likely to be exploited in as early a future as the forests further south and east, and are therefore suitable for forest reserves. Of more immediate interest are 1, 500, 000 hectares of more open forest, which forms the dominant cover of Pleiku, Phu Bon, and Darlac; of particular interest are 180, 000 hectares of coniferous forest in Tuyen Duc and the neighboring provinces.

These pine forests present silvicultural problems very different from those of the tropical rain forests, but very similar to those of the southeastern United States. Fire and grazing are two of them, and a third is how to regenerate the extensive, even-aged stands of a single species. Because of their long fibers, rapid growth, and accessibility, the pine forests offer an excellent opportunity for the manufacture of sulfate pulp for domestic use and export.

Darlac, Quang Duc, and Tuyen Duc have between them about 100,000 hectares of grassland, formerly under forest, and capable, as trials have proved, of growing trees again, but probably more suitable now for development as livestock ranges. Finally, in scattered blocks there are 500,000 hectares of forest land with an undergrowth of bamboo, the largest block lying just north of Kontum city. The interest in bamboo is for paper pulp, since its fine long fibers can be used to add strength to those of the tropical hardwoods. While not as valuable as those of the conifers of Tuyen Duc, bamboo fibers have special qualities which suggest that this type of forest may eventually be a useful source of material for a pulping industry, and should be placed in reserve for that purpose.

In the six provinces of the III Corps Tactical Zone which lie nearest to Saigon, there are still 500,000 hectares of forest land, including a large block of mangrove. The hardwood forests contain some commercial timber, but the timber values of these areas are becoming less important. However, the other five provinces of the zone lie on the Mekong Terrace, in a belt from the sea to the Cambodian frontier and northward to the Annamite Range, and within this area of 2,000,00 hectares there are at least 1,500,000 hectares of high, dense forest, besides smaller areas once under dense forest but in which the state of the forest has been affected and changed by human activity. The Mekong Terrace presents the best opportunities in Vietnam for exploiting and growing tropical hardwoods. Forestry operations of all kinds are easier and cheaper than further north; the natural composition of the forest is favorable, in that there is a high proportion of species belonging to the valuable dipterocarp family.

The forest lands of Vietnam include over half a million hectares of mangrove, mostly in An Xuyen and Kien Giang provinces in the Mekong Delta and in the provinces immediately east of Saigon. The mangrove forests grow upon very poorly drained saline and acid soils, unsuitable for agriculture without costly preparation. This type of forest consists of about twenty species of trees and shrubs which form a dense tangled evergreen mass. The species are all highly specialized, and adapted only to the tidewater flats, where they stabilize the soils and gradually build up firm ground. In the westernmost part of Kien Giang and in adjacent areas of Chau Doc, there are 190,000 hectares of tram (Melaleuca) forest, and large areas of tram also occur in the Plain of Reeds. The tram is a small fast-growing tree which grows upon the higher, less saline but still flooded sites, and is widely planted by the people of the countryside.

Mangrove and tram do not produce industrial wood, but both supply excellent firewood and charcoal and have long been exploited for these products. Large quantities were formerly shipped to Saigon and Singapore, but with increasing insecurity and diminishing markets this trade has now almost ceased. Although it may eventually recover somewhat, the long-term trend will be downward, for charcoal and fuelwood are economically inferior goods the demand for which will decline as incomes rise and other fuels become available. In this sense, neither mangrove nor tram forest presents an economic opportunity. The bark of the mangrove has been a source of tannin extract in the past, but this can no longer be thought of as an economic opportunity either. Tram, on the other hand, is greatly esteemed by rural communities, providing not only fuel but also building poles, framing and foundations for their houses, and shade.

At the present time most of the logging taking place in Vietnam is on the Mekong Terrace. Loggers are also at work on the more level portions of the Central Highlands, particularly in Tuyen Duc and Darlac provinces. Presently accessible and operable forests probably amount to only 2,500,000 hectares of the total, and it is significant that by far the greater part of the country's sawmill capacity is in the Saigon area (including Gia Dinh and Bien Hoa). In all five of the northern provinces, despite their natural forest wealth, only two sawmills are in active operation, and they work only sporadically at that.

Two basic principles have governed forest policy in Vietnam. The first is public ownership of almost all forest land and the second is close control over exploitation. The forest laws distinguish between the forests which are now protected but can be made available at some time for farming, and those which are permanently reserved for timber. Each forest district has an allowable cut, for which logging companies bid and receive licenses. In general, policies have been cautious and restrictive; and in the result the production of the country's sawmills has never approached the country's needs for industrial wood, which are estimated at about 1 million cubic meters a year.

The forest situation today displays those problems which are common to developing countries in the tropics and elsewhere, and also other problems arising from the war. Among other effects, the war has made it impossible for employees of the Forestry Administration to travel in the forest and perform their regular duties of preventing trespass and enforcing cutting regulations and other conditions of licenses. In practice forest guards are now confined to their offices in provincial capitals, and for all practical purposes control over exploitation has ceased. Many of the staff of the Forestry Administration have been drafted into the Army.

The long-range effects of defoliation are not fully known. They will certainly include a loss of growth and perhaps a change of composition toward other species which may be less or more valuable. Less doubt exists regarding the effects of bombardment. Shrapnel has become a common ingredient of Vietnamese logs and can seriously lower their value, especially for export. Finally, military operations have made logging more difficult and dangerous and explain, to some extent, a production of logs far below the country's needs and the sawmills' capacity.

Another effect of the war is possibly beneficial. It has caused many people to move out of the forest toward the coast and the urban centers. To this extent, they have cleared less forest for shifting cultivation, and this system of agriculture has had less impact on the forest than it would have done in time of peace. In the neighborhood of Ban Me Thuot, for instance, where large numbers of people have concentrated in the search for security, forest fallows are reported to be becoming shorter, and there is a growing interest in the use of fertilizers to maintain yields.

SURVEYS FOR POSTWAR DEVELOPMENT

Since its establishment in November 1967, the committee on postwar development planning in the Department of Water Resources and Forestry Administration, in cooperation with the Joint Development Group, has devoted its attention to three specific subjects. These have one thing in common: all have some long-term economic significance, and all, if the appropriate measures are taken, can result in benefits to the economy even in existing conditions. Although major developments in the wood-based industries will have to await the end of the war, every opportunity for progress at the present time, however small, should obviously be seized. The three subjects examined are Timber supplies for the Mekong Delta, the state of the sawmilling industry, and the production and export of cinnamon.

Timber Supplies for the Delta

The Mekong Delta is the only major geographical area of Vietnam which is not heavily forested and which cannot supply its own requirements for industrial wood. The population of the delta numbers more than 6 million, and it may be expected to increase rather rapidly after the war. Current and normal demands for sawn wood alone in this region amount to about 160, 000 cubic meters annually, and will increase rapidly in a period of agricultural and industrial development.

The delta already has the sawmilling capacity to supply its present needs, but in fact it does not do so. There are 60 sawmills in all, the largest concentrations being at Long Xuyen (21), Rach Gia (13), and Can Tho (10), and they have a combined capacity of 240, 000 cubic meters a year. In 1967, if official statistics are correct, they received between them 12, 300 cubic meters of logs, and cannot have worked at more than 5 percent of their capacity. At full capacity the delta sawmills would keep 1, 200 men in employment and would add VN$960 million annually to the gross domestic product.

Of the log supplies which reached these sawmills in 1967, 7, 000 tons came from inside Vietnam and 5, 300 tons came from Cambodia. Markets for Vietnamese wood products and sources from which Vietnam might draw additional supplies to feed its wood-based industries are discussed in Working Paper 17. When, for instance, safe and passable roads can be built into Laos, Laotian logs may be expected to move eastward either for shipment through Da Nang or for processing at that place, in either case bringing benefits to the economies of both countries. From Cambodia there are two possible trade routes: one, between the provinces of Tay Ninh, Binh Long, and Phuoc Long (which have some of the richest forests in Vietnam) and the border, would give access to similar forest areas in Cambodia; this route is presently closed and there is no prospect of reopening it until peace returns. The second is by the Mekong and Bassac rivers into the delta; this is the route by which logs from Cambodia are presently arriving.

The rivers are the most important present and future routes for delivering log supplies to the sawmill industry of the delta. In part this is owing to the natural advantages and low costs of transportation by water, and in part owing to the fact that the delta, and especially the Trans-Bassac, is inconveniently situated with regard to Vietnam's own commercial forests. It is easier, cheaper, and more certain to bring logs down the waterways from Cambodia than it is to deliver them overland by truck; and as long as there are equitable exchanges, with Vietnamese produce and manufactures moving in the other direction, it is in everybody's interest that former trade relationships should be resumed.

The frontier has been closed and the regular normal trade in logs stopped since 1963. However, four provinces, Kien Giang, Chau Doc, An Giang, and Phong Dinh, are still being permitted to meet their needs for sawn lumber from Cambodian log supplies, and the limited traffic which persists is being carried on without the formalities of import licenses and currency controls. This is a commendably pragmatic approach to a difficult situation. In 1968, imports from Cambodia are expected to be 10 percent higher than the 1967 volume of 5,300 cubic meters. The trade is not merely sanctioned, it produces revenue, since an import duty of 20 percent of controlled Cambodian log prices and a quarantine tax of VN$10 per cubic meter are being levied at the frontier.

The logs reaching delta sawmills in this way come mostly from the Cambodian province of Kampsang Cham. The species most commonly represented are sao (Hoppea spp.) and dau (Dipterocarpus spp.), both very acceptable in Vietnamese markets. The logs are of consistently good quality, which is not always true of Vietnamese logs originating from areas of military activity.

Cambodian log prices at the frontier and delivered to sawmills are subject to some distortion, and comparisons are difficult. Different currencies are in use at both official and free market rates: the Cambodian system of log measurement results in calculated volumes 70 percent greater than Vietnamese standard measurements; and though duties are levied on the basis of controlled Cambodian prices, importers claim that the prices actually paid considerably exceed the latter. However, the costs of a cubic meter of sao sold in Can Tho appears to be roughly as follows:

Cost at frontier	$VN3,429.00
Taxes	495.00
Transportation to Can Tho	30.00
Dealers' profit (20%)	790.00
	$VN4,744.00

Outside the four favored provinces a sawmill can only obtain a Cambodian log by arrangement with a sawmill or dealer operating inside them, and appears to pay an additional 20 percent markup for this consideration. Inside the four provinces large consignments of logs are allocated among sawmills by lot, and no operator can know ahead of time what logs he will actually receive or what he will have to pay for them. In this complicated process the opportunities for unofficial and irregular payments are numerous.

True prices and profits are therefore almost impossible to discover, but in the case of logs reaching sawmills outside the four provinces, profits may be as high as 60 percent of original costs. Nevertheless, prices of Cambodian logs delivered to delta sawmills still appear to be almost VN$800 cheaper per cubic meter than logs of comparable quality from domestic sources. Though the prices and profits of Cambodian logs are higher than they ought to be in the delta, at least the trade persists, and it is believed that if the trade were liberated, so that a bigger market could be supplied, both prices and profit margins would fall. In the event, the delta sawmills would operate closer to capacity, an incentive would be provided for the operators to expand and modernize their enterprises, and the public would get sawn timber at reasonable instead of exorbitant prices.

A policy of admitting greatly increased log imports from Cambodia may appeal as a temporary measure at a time when sufficient domestic supplies are not available. We believe, for several reasons, that it would be a correct policy for the long term also, even when the Vietnamese economy is operating normally and Vietnamese forests are being more fully exploited.

First, and as mentioned above, imports of Cambodian logs will help to keep lumber prices down, not only in the delta but in Saigon as well. More mills will be established; more employment will be created and more people will buy and use wood. There will be unusual demands for lumber in the period of reconstruction after the war and it is hoped that they can be met at reasonable cost. The effects of lower prices on domestic industries will not be deleterious but beneficial; they will result in a growing market and the Vietnamese sawmilling industry will be able to grow along with it.

Second, imports of logs from Cambodia will enable the sawmilling industry to close the gap between the country's needs for sawn wood (estimated at 1 million cubic meters in 1967) and domestic production of saw logs (205,000 cubic meters, from which 133,250 cubic meters of sawn wood were produced). In part the deficiency is being met by importation of sawn lumber from other countries. There should be no need for this when Vietnamese sawmills are idle.

Third, the case for expanding log imports in the long as well as short term rests upon Vietnam's increasing capacity to process and export manufactured goods. The Mekong Delta possesses many of the elements necessary for successful industrial development--a sound agricultural base, labor, low-cost water-borne transportation, installed capacity and established manufacturers. The sawmilling industry in the delta lacks none of the essentials except the raw material to work with.

Finally, the more that can be done now to resume normal trading relationships between Vietnam and her neighbors, the more likely is it that profitable regional exchanges of goods and services will develop after the war and that economic and political stability can be established in a southeast Asian context. For an outward-looking economy this is important.

The Vietnamese Sawmill Industry

The previous section of this chapter made recommendations concerning one aspect of the sawmilling industry in a particular region. In the course of 1968 the situation and problems of the industry were reviewed as a whole and a report has been published.* The facts and proposals which follow are drawn almost entirely from this report.

Sawmilling is a relatively uncomplicated process, often the first industrial activity to appear in an area, and it leads naturally to the development of other wood-based industries. It is flexible regarding size of units, skills required, and location. With little capital investment and simple technology, it can supply a versatile commodity which enters many parts of the economy at various levels and in various forms and can often substitute for materials which would otherwise be imported. Vietnam's needs for sawn wood are likely to grow rather steadily; and because they can be met mainly from a natural resource, this growth need not make excessive demands upon the country's holdings of foreign exchange.

At the present time sawn wood is scarce and expensive. Large volumes required for military needs have been imported, and the general public has either had to pay extremely high prices or resort to substitute, frequently inferior, materials of foreign manufacture. Neither the industry nor government policies toward the industry has yet been able to provide answers to the problems of higher demand and restricted log supply created by the war. Information on which more suitable policies might be devised has been unreliable and inadequate.

The study of sawmills undertaken in cooperation with the Joint Development Group was designed to correct this deficiency. In a first phase it covered the capital area (including Bien Hoa and Gia Dinh) and 110 operating sawmills. (There are in the same area almost as many which do not operate.) In a second phase an investigation was made of mills in 14 provinces. Specific facts, therefore, are now known about 80 percent of the licensed sawmills in the country, representing almost the entire capacity of Vietnamese industry to process wood efficiently. On the basis of the information acquired concerning the characteristics and problems of the sawmilling industry, it is now possible to suggest ways of raising output and meeting Vietnam's needs for sawn wood.

---

*Report on Sawmills in Vietnam, JDG Working Paper No. 59, December, 1968.

A notable characteristic of these enterprises is their large number and small capacity, even in an industry in which small capacity is common. The country has 500 licensed sawmills and probably several hundred more that are not licensed. Of the former, only 300 are actually operating and most are doing so sporadically. Of this number, 54 are capable of sawing 300 cubic meters a month; 120 are capable of 200 cubic meters a month; and the balance are only capable of 100 a month. The total capacity of the 300 active sawmills is 633,600 cubic meters a year.

In fact, these sawmills produce far below capacity. For example, in 1967 they sawed 205,000 cubic meters of logs into about 133,250 cubic meters of lumber. Their first problem, then, is a remarkable one; capacity is unused (and necessarily so due to insufficient log supply) at a time when market demands are largely unsatisfied.

A second characteristic of the operating sawmills is the extreme irregularity of their operations. On a comparison of capacity and production we may assume they work one-third of the time. However, since even the inactive mills produce occasionally and a certain number of unlicensed mills are also processing logs, the actual production of the mills studied may be closer to 20 percent of their capacity.

The degree of mechanization is very low. In a typical mill only the head-saw works by power, with perhaps one edger and a cut-off saw. Invariably logs and sawn wood are moved by human labor. The machinery installed is almost always antiquated and poorly maintained. The motor is often an army surplus jeep motor, and other items consist of odds and ends put together in response to an immediate need and not well coordinated. The usual horizontal band saw has notable advantages, but speed is not among them. With seven workers, it can process about six cubic meters a day.

For the most part, the owners of these sawmills are small farmers and tradesmen with few resources and limited knowledge of either the technical or commercial aspects of their business. Often they are people displaced by the war from their regular occupations who have taken up sawmilling as an alternative means of livelihood. Only a few have the skill, interest, and resources to become efficient producers. For this reason, although a program of financial assistance to the industry is warranted (possibly by Agricultural Development Bank loans for investment and operation), such a program should be selective as to the recipients.

At present the excessive number of mills in comparison to the supply of logs renders each an inefficient production unit. To some extent this inefficiency is concealed by currently high log prices. A sawmill profit of VN$1, 000 a cubic meter does not appear excessive when the log itself has cost VN$7, 500 a cubic meter and lumber costs VN$16, 000. In fact such profit includes the hidden costs to the owner of stoppages from lack of logs and breakdown of machinery. The public is paying for this; and the workers pay too, in irregular employment and low wages. Sawmills operate so irregularly that they probably do not justify even the modest investments made in them.

The problem of log supplies is discussed in some detail in Working Paper 17. It is compounded of Viet Cong extortion, military operations, poor roads and equipment, excessive official regulation, and irregular restraints and exactions. The weak financial position of most of the operators prevents their stocking enough logs to keep operating when deliveries are held up. They have no incentive to improve their machinery and increase the rate of output, and prefer to work slowly with the equipment on hand. If they do borrow money to purchase logs, it is at 5 percent interest a month. At this rate delays in deliveries can be ruinous, and there are many examples of bankruptcies as a result. When, in these circumstances, a sawmill changes hands, the new owner operates on the same disadvantageous terms. The industry needs not only logs and adequate machinery but also unencumbered equity capital. In sawmilling, working capital requirements should usually at least equal the fixed investment.

An excessive number of intermediaries are involved in the logging and sawmilling business. Between forest and mill a log may often have four or more owners and three separate licenses, and will be subjected to at least two legal taxes and possibly a number of unauthorized payments. These complications too contribute to delays in delivery and high prices.

The objective of the study described in the preceding paragraphs is clear. It is to raise the output and lower the cost of sawn wood so that it can meet the requirements arising from national reconstruction. Because alternative materials, including wood-based panels and paper, are often more difficult to obtain than sawn wood, and because the needs for building materials will be great, a production level of 1 million cubic meters is a minimum target. Counting both licensed and unlicensed, and operating and nonoperating sawmills, Vietnam may already be approaching the capacity to achieve this output. Tay Ninh alone, for example, has 59 mills, of which not one is presently operating. As stated already, the capacity of the industry has outstripped its supply of logs.

Several measures are suggested: first, a review of existing legislation concerning logging and sawmilling, to legitimize a good many straightforward commercial and industrial activities which the law in its present state appears to prohibit; second, a reorganization of the sawmilling industry, to reduce the number of operating enterprises but ensure that those which do operate do so full time. In meeting the country's demands for lumber, the industry could and should employ 4,000 men steadily, instead of offering them one day's work a week. Third, steps should be taken to encourage and assist the mills outside Saigon. The industry is well suited to operate in provincial capitals and smaller towns, and would be a useful source of employment in such places.

The most urgent problem, log production, has administrative aspects that should be dealt with at once. Procedures for licensing and taxing are cumbersome and subject to abuse. The Ministry of Finance has already proposed that logs be measured and royalties collected at the sawmills. Both Sabah and the Ivory Coast, large and successful timber producers, follow this procedure. In Vietnam, if measurement of the logs presents difficulties the procedures can be simplified still further by having royalties collected as a production tax instead. Simultaneously we suggest the granting of credit by the Agricultural Bank to encourage the more skilled and responsible owners to keep a supply of logs on hand and to use their machinery to better advantage. Increased efficiency will justify a more liberal policy toward imports of machinery, spare parts, and even logs.

Cinnamon

The cultivation of cinnamon has been examined in great detail by a member of the committee with long forestry experience in Quang Ngai, the province responsible for the greater part of Vietnam's previously flourishing trade in cassia bark.*

Many varieties of the cinnamon tree grow in tropical Asia, and it is the bark of the Royal Cinnamon tree (Cinnamomum lowerei; in Vietnamese, Que) that is most esteemed and most readily accepted in American markets. The tree is a dominant component of the high tropical rain forest: it grows at a variety of elevations, from 100 to 2,500 meters, but is exacting in its other requirements, preferring temperatures not in excess of 26° C., a relative humidity of from 84 to 86 percent, a rainfall of at least 2,500 millimeters spread over at least 140 days a year, and well-drained, red-yellow podzolic soils. Consequently, the area in which cinnamon occurs in Vietnam is a restricted one: the tree grows best in a zone of about 3,600 square kilometers, where the provinces of Kontum, Quang Ngai, and Quang Tin meet. In this zone it is hardy, prolific, and fast growing.

Highland farmers, especially those of the Cua and Sedang tribes of Quang Ngai, cultivate the trees with seemingly little special care or attention. Salable bark is produced at three years, but quality as well as yields of bark improve with age, and at thirty years a tree may be 40 centimeters in diameter and produce about 50 kilograms of dry bark, worth about VN$7,500 to the producer. The possibilities of increasing production in the area best suited to the cultivation of the cinnamon tree are almost unlimited, though obviously there is a limit to the quantity of this specialized product that world markets can absorb.

Buyers bargain for standing trees, and dry, sort, clean, and pack the bark. At this stage the bark is worth about US$2.00 a kilo, f.o.b. Saigon. Enquiries made by the Joint Development Group in the United States indicate that at this sort of price the American market can absorb all the bark

---

* Engineer Phan Dinh Lan, "The Production and Export of Vietnamese Cinnamon," November 1968.

that Vietnam can presently produce. Our enquiries in Vietnam indicate that if exports were permitted and the traditional trade were resumed, exports would have reached 1,500 tons, worth US$3 million in foreign exchange in 1969, and that by 1980 the trade would probably amount to US$10 million a year. Such figures represent a not inconsiderable proportion of total export values in recent years, and provide an instance of support for the forecasts of exports advanced in Chapter 2.

In fact, there is at present no trade whatever in this available and valuable commodity, and overseas buyers have been compelled to turn their attention to other sources of (reputedly inferior) supplies in Indonesia and Ceylon. Traffic in cinnamon bark was prohibited by the military authorities in 1965 on the ground that it constituted trading with the enemy, and the order then made has never been reviewed and rescinded. We recommend that it now be reviewed by the interministerial committee on resource denial in order to determine whether the damage the order inflicts upon national economic and social interests may not be greater than any military purpose it may serve. The danger of Vietnam's permanently losing a profitable market to competitors in Indonesia and Ceylon is a real one, while denying a valuable cash crop outlet to these rural communities is unlikely to strengthen their allegiance to the government of the country.

The export of the bark should be permitted, possibly under certificates of origin, and export licenses issued by the representative of the Ministry of Economy in Da Nang, if some form of control is still considered desirable; marketing cooperatives should be organized to assist the producers in their dealings with buyers; loans be granted to producers to promote new plantings; and an experimental station should be established in Quang Ngai with a view to improving methods of cultivating the tree and preparing the bark. Finally, an investigation is needed of the feasibility of grinding the bark and distilling the essence in Vietnam instead of overseas, so as to secure for the economy the considerable added values which these operations afford.

FOREST POLICY AND FOREST TAXATION

The preceding sections of this chapter illustrate the range of economic and social factors involved in the exploitation, in the national interest, of forest resources.

With the increasing growth of commercial and industrial activity, demands upon these resources will become even heavier than they are already under the stimulation of war. The policies, laws, and regulatory procedures which at present govern the forest industries were not designed to meet such demands; they were designed in an era when the products of the forest were mostly charcoal and fuelwood, and it seemed that the most desirable, and readily accepted, objective was to conserve the country's forest resources in their natural state. Today, the mere protection of natural resources from change is no longer an acceptable program; on the contrary, the forests must be turned into economically productive units, serving and supplying the most progressive sectors of Vietnamese society. Within the next ten years the country's demand for industrial wood, as a material for technically advanced industry and for international trade, will more than double. Of the three major industrial developments examined in some detail in Chapter 9, two concern the beneficial exploitation of the forest resource.

An objective discussion of how present policies affect production will touch on some sensitive points, and the agency principally concerned cannot be expected to propose or approve reforms that infringe upon well-established, if irregular, practices and prerogatives. Nevertheless, forest policy is a matter of significant national interest, not of the interest of a single government department. In wartime, and after the war, the overriding purpose of the forest authorities should be to see that a valuable public resource is put to good use. In contrast to such a purpose, there is now an acute shortage of industrial wood, though all the elements of production--material, men, and machinery--are present. If this situation cannot be corrected by the agency responsible within the framework of existing laws and policies, then there is something wrong with those laws and policies, or with their application, and they ought to be changed.

Fortunately, the urgent need to revise the basic premises of existing forest policy and to make them conform to economic realities appears to have been recognized. By direction of the minister of agriculture, conferences have already been held inside the Forestry Administration to decide what should be done. We suggest only that the revision of forest laws and policies should concern not only professional foresters, but also industrialists, economists, and businessmen, and that the opinions of the latter also should be sought and taken into account before definitive recommendations are submitted to the legislature.

Whatever new policies emerge from this activity, it is certain that the management of the nation's forests after the war will demand more manpower and more specialized skills than the Forestry Administration can at present command. Management in the future will involve much more than the routine enforcement of controls, the safeguarding of trees, and the collection of taxes. It will also involve, as examples, the highly specialized functions of carrying on silvicultural research and conducting forest inventories. In order to develop such capabilities Vietnam will have to develop adequate training facilities of its own, as well as draw upon those of its friends overseas.

Arrangements have already been made for the College of Agriculture in the University of Saigon to be assisted by the University of Florida in agricultural and forestry education. As far as forestry is concerned, it may not be easy to attract good candidates to present themselves for what has hitherto been regarded as a rather narrow and restricted field of public service. We make the recommendation that the university's Forestry School should in future provide in its curriculum not only for aspirants to the civil service but also for people whose interests lie in the development of private forest industries. We believe that in this way students of broader abilities and interests will be attracted to equip themselves for professional forest careers.

In Working Paper 17 some tentative recommendations were offered concerning specific actions to adapt forest policies and procedures to the needs of an increasingly industrialized society in the postwar period. One of these was proposed for immediate implementation--the reform of the complicated present system of taxation, in which royalties, license fees, production taxes, and similar dues are levied on a variety of different occasions between the felling of a tree in the forest and the time when it reaches the consumer as sawn wood. The recommendation was that all these dues should be replaced by a single production tax charged at the sawmill, and the belief was expressed that this would encourage production without resulting in loss of public revenue. Indeed, we thought a substantial increase in public revenue would be entirely possible.

The proposal was a controversial one, but there has been an exchange of views between the ministers of agriculture and of finance and a decision to simplify the taxation system, at least to the extent of collecting production taxes only on the finished products of the sawmills. In addition, action has been taken to reduce the number of check points at which log trucks are inspected by the Forestry Administration, and to simplify the bidding procedures by which standing timber is now offered for sale. Licenses to cut timber are now more easily obtained than formerly, and trucks can move more easily from the forest to the sawmills. Additional action to ease previous restrictions on the industry is being considered in cooperation with military and national police authorities; and the collector general of taxes has proposed that charges levied at the sawmills include also timber royalties and license fees, and that employees of the Forestry Administration be posted at the sawmills to assist in supervision. If this proposal is accepted and is effective, logs which have hitherto been escaping taxation altogether will begin to pay their share.

These are all welcome steps in the right direction, but they have not thus far been effective in greatly increasing the output of industrial wood, or in preparing the way for greater needs after the war. The facts are that since 1963 the price of lumber has risen 800 percent, and the officially recorded cut of logs has fallen from 315,000 cubic meters to 205,000 cubic meters (in 1967). In 1968, the average monthly figure was a little under 20,000 cubic meters, about a quarter of the country's estimated requirements. Obviously, military operations are in part responsible for this decline, but they are not by any means wholly responsible for it: existing policies of sale, taxation, and control are also responsible for the scarcity of lumber because they have not been adjusted to wartime realities. There have been no basic changes in the forest laws since 1932, long before Vietnam achieved its independence.

PLANNING FOR FORESTRY DEVELOPMENT IN 1969

The Joint Development Group will assist to such extent as may be desired, in the review of basic forest policies referred to in this chapter. In addition, arrangements have been made with the Committee for Forestry Research in the Department of Water Resources and Forestry Administration for four types of investigation, all closely related to the wood-based industrial developments described in Chapter 9. These investigations may be regarded as a further step toward implementation of the projects.

1. References are made in Chapters 9 and 12 to the prospects for the manufacture of plywood (and later other wood products) in the five northern provinces. A study has evaluated the capability of the region's forests to supply these industries. Particular attention will be paid to the available quantities and location of logs suitable for the manufacture of plywood of export grades.* The study extends to logging costs, explores methods of reducing logging costs, and defines the road construction requirements for the extraction and transportation of logs from the most suitable areas. An estimate is made of the rate at which the forests of the northern provinces can supply logs to a plywood mill at Da Nang, describing species and qualities, and the probable costs, capital and operating, of a logging operation and of transportation.

2. A comprehensive program of forestry work will be established. The principal objective will be to rehabilitate the nation's forests after the neglect and damage of the war years, and to provide for the services and infrastructure necessary to meet demands upon forest resources when the war is over. Rehabilitation of the forests, it may be said, will require a great deal of manual labor and should be a valuable source of employment in the difficult transitional period.

---

*The Capability of the I-Corps Forest and the Problem of Wood Supply for Plywood Milling in Da Nang, Working Paper No. 58 (JDG, August, 1969).

3. A new country-wide program is needed for the establishment and protection of a new system of forest reserves and national parks. The vegetation studies made in 1968 will be useful for this purpose, as will continuing land-use studies planned in cooperation with other services of the Ministry of Agriculture.

In a first phase the effort should be to identify, describe, and justify areas which should be kept permanently under forest to the exclusion of other uses. Examples of such areas to be investigated in this way might include the Bac Mah Range southeast of Da Nang (which has possible potential for a tourist industry), two areas in the highly productive Mekong Terrace, and the mangrove forests of Ca Mau and U Minh. Maps will be prepared for all areas recommended for reservation, together with programs and cost estimates for development in each case.

In a second phase, detailed management plans need to be prepared for two reserved forests on the Mekong Terrace, one in Tay Ninh and the other in Binh Tuy. The plans should include full descriptions, time schedules, and estimates of cost to bring these forests up to full production as rapidly as possible after the war. The work in these areas, which will also serve for purposes of demonstration and research, should indicate the dimensions of the problems of forest management in the country as a whole. As suggested elsewhere in this chapter, the forests of the Mekong Terrace offer the most favorable present opportunities for the intensive management of tropical hardwoods.

4. Finally, plans for reforestation are needed for the pine forest areas of Tuyen Duc and the plain of Phan Rang. As a start, under joint arrangements by the Forestry Administration and the Forestry Branch of U.S. AID's Division of Domestic Production, a training course for appropriate officers of the Forestry Administration will be provided in photo-interpretation and in the making of forest inventories. By photo-interpretation a determination will be made of where and how much reforestation will be necessary. The work will proceed concurrently with studies by an Australian expert in reforestation, whose services the Australian government has already agreed to supply under the auspices of the Colombo Plan.

These plans for reforestation, of course, are intended to support and supply the pulp-manufacturing industry proposed in Chapter 9. They should be given a high priority in postwar forestry programs.

Successful completion of these four projects will provide Vietnam with a firm base from which rational development of the forest industries may thereafter proceed.

The Joint Development Group's involvement in this case has been largely to define the vital role of forestry in the economic development of Vietnam and to suggest and encourage the most profitable lines of study. The acquisition of planning capacity in the Forestry Administration itself is probably the most valuable result to date of the Joint Development Group's forestry activities.

CHAPTER 9 INDUSTRIAL DEVELOPMENT

THE STRUCTURE OF EXISTING INDUSTRY AND THE EFFECTS OF THE WAR

Because of the war and the inadequacy of available statistical data, it is a matter of some difficulty to obtain a clear picture of the present structure of Vietnamese industry. Only one characteristic is obvious: almost the entire manufacturing capacity of the country is concentrated in the area of Saigon and Bien Hoa. Small manufacturers and cottage industries are numerous indeed, but their total number can only be approximated. Some businesses are licensed and some operate without licenses; and of those which are licensed, some make returns to the authorities and some do not.

National Institute of Statistics figures indicate that in 1960 there were 7,398 manufacturing companies in Vietnam employing 59,306 workers. About 70 percent of these companies were situated in the southern part of the country, employing 88 percent of the industrial work force. No less than 3,123 companies (42 percent of the country's total) were in Saigon, Gia Dinh, and Bien Hoa, employing 36,493 (61 percent) of the workers.

In 1966, 1,783 manufacturing companies and 12 electric power producers submitted returns to the Ministry of Economy and almost all were situated in the area of Saigon/Gia Dinh. The same is true of a catalogue of 1,390 manufacturers published by U.S. AID in 1967. Although none of these investigations claim to present a total picture of the country's industrial situation, there is no doubt that they correctly reflect an overconcentration in the capital area. Today Vietnamese industry is certainly no more evenly distributed than it was in 1960: indeed, it is probably even more heavily concentrated upon Saigon and its environs, for this is where the great majority of the new businesses opened since 1960 have established themselves. Although more accurate data than now available are needed, it is safe to assume generally that what is known of industry in Saigon/Gia Dinh and Bien Hoa accurately reflects the state of industry in Vietnam as a whole.

Structure

Capital Investment

To gain some notion of the present industrial sector in Vietnam, the Joint Development Group's industrial section has accumulated and analyzed information from a variety of sources. Included are capital structure, investment, and employment data from the returns submitted to the Directorate of Industry by public and private agencies engaged in industrial activities; credit data, credit policies, and business results from the General Federation of Industries and from the individual companies; and data on state-owned or joint state-private, enterprises from the commissioner for public corporations and the director general of budget and foreign aid.

This analysis has covered more than 700 manufacturing companies, both large and small, including almost all Vietnamese manufacturers of any size and importance. It is believed that the results are properly representative of the manufacturing industry as a whole, particularly those concerning capital structure, investment, and employment. Information on production and sales is less reliable, because firm owners regularly understate these figures in order to evade taxes.

With this exception, the data presented in Table 9.1 are believed to give a reasonably accurate account of the importance and structure of the seven principal groups of industry.

The performance of those industries in groups 3, 4, and 5 in Table 9.1 are in strong contrast to each other, though all display approximately the same level of capital investment. The chemical industry obviously has been less affected by the war than the others. Groups 6 and 7, both demanding high technical skills in the workforce, represent the lease developed of all Vietnamese industries. Nevertheless, the sales performance of the mechanical and metal products group is extraordinarily high in relation to capital investment when compared with

TABLE 9.1

The Structure of Industry, 1967
(Millions of VN Piasters)

Industry Group	Capital Invested	Value of Machinery	Work Force[a] (persons)	Sales	Remarks
1. Food, beverages, tobacco	8,159	3,585	17,300	34,575	Excluding Binh Duong, Quang Ngai, and small-scale sugar mills.
2. Textiles	5,768	1,859	18,000	4,660	
3. Paper, leather, rubber	2,758	1,233	3,650	1,506	Excluding sawmills
4. Basic and processed chemicals	2,653	1,024	9,310	5,064	Excluding An Hoa-Nong Son complex
5. Glass, ceramics, cement	2,562	1,449	3,960	1,405	Excluding handicrafts
6. Mechanical and metal products	1,508	363	5,050	5,065	
7. Electrical	520	159	3,320	990	Excluding electrical generation
Total	23,928	9,771	60,590	53,265	

[a]Excludes, in addition to enterprises referred to in the remarks column, the large number of small businesses which operate without licenses and therefore are not included in official statistics. These may employ as many as 60,000 additional persons.

the paper, leather, rubber, and even the textile industries. There is a simple reason for this: the large volumes of consumer commodities, especially motor-bicycles and scooters, imported since 1966 to flood the market with goods and counter inflation. In 1967, sales of motor-bicycles and scooters totaled no less than VN$2 billion.

The most important industries in each group were as shown in Table 9.2. In terms of invested capital, the order of importance of these industries is as follows:

Cotton weaving and spinning	VN$4,200 million
Beverages	3,500 "
Paper	2,400 "
Tobacco	2,100 "
Cement and products	2,000 "
Pharmaceuticals	1,500 "

With the exception of beverages and tobacco, all of the industries in the above list have been established in Vietnam since 1958. Moreover, the beverages and tobacco industries, though of older foundation, have been completely reequipped during the same period. A common characteristic of the six most important industries, therefore, is that all have modern plant and machinery.

Another common characteristic is that all, with the single exception of the cement industry, depend for their production upon imported basic or semiprocessed raw materials. Specific data on the materials used by these industries are not available, but foreign exchange requirements can be deduced from import figures in recent years and company estimates of requirements in 1968. They are as follows:

Cotton weaving and spinning	US$8 million
Beverages	8 "
Paper	9 "
Tobacco	14 "
Pharmaceuticals	7 "
	US$46 "

This US$46 million does not, of course, represent the entire foreign exchange requirement of Vietnamese industry for raw material imports, but only that for five of principal industries. The Directorate of Foreign Trade in the Ministry

TABLE 9.2

Major Industries by Amount of Capital Investment, 1967
(Millions of Piasters)

Industry	Capital Investment
Food, beverages, tobacco	
Beverages	3,500
Tobacco	2,100
Seasoning sauce	1,000
	Seasoning powder (530); Sugar (180); Canned food (80)
Textiles	Cotton weaving and spinning (4,200); Synthetic fiber weaving (820); Jute bag weaving (230); Blanket weaving (160).
Paper, leather, rubber	Paper (2,400); Bicycle tires and inner tubes (170).
Basic and processed chemicals	Pharmaceuticals (1,500); Basic chemicals (430); Plastics (390); Soap (150).
Glass, ceramics, cement	Cement (2,000); Glass (230); Plaster and cement products (290).
Mechanical and metal products	
Mechanical construction	670
Motor-bicycle assembly	160
Sewing machine assembly	200
Metal wire, nails	120
Aluminum products	60
Electrical	Radio assembly (190); Electric cable (160); Batteries (50).

TABLE 9.3

Classification of Manufacturing Firms by Type

Industry Group	Industry	Distribution of Capital Investment (Percent)		Distribution of Capital Investment by Sector(Percent)		
		Partnerships	Individual & Family Businesses	State Enterprises	Mixed Enterprises	Private Enterprises
Food	Beverages	99	1			100
	Tobacco	100				100
	Seasoning sauce	1	99			100
	Seasoning powder	92	8			100
	Sugar	100		100		
	Canned food	100				100
Textiles	Cotton weaving & spinning	100			42	58
	Synthetic fiber weaving	72	28			100
	Jute bag weaving	100			43	57
	Blanket weaving	100				100
Paper, leather, rubber	Paper, tires & tubes, shoes	99	1	51	34	15
Basic & processed chemicals	Pharmaceuticals	64	36			100
	Chemicals	100				100
	Plastics					100
	Soap	88	12			100
Glass, ceramics, cement	Cement	100		100		
	Glass	76	24		60	40
	Plaster & cement products	71	29			100
Mechanical and metal	Mechanical construction	100				100
	Bicycle & motor bicycle assembly	33	67			100
	Sewing machine assembly	58	42			100
	Wire, nails					100
Electrical	Radio assembly	47	53			100
	Electrical cable	100				100
	Batteries		100			100

TABLE 9.4

Classification of Industrial Enterprises by Capital Investment (VN$ Million)

Industry Group and Branch	No. of Enterprises	Capital Structure Under 10	11-50	51-100	101-500	Above 500
FOOD						
Canned food	4	2	2	-	-	-
Milk	1	-	-	1	-	-
Seasoning sauce (approx.)	400	400	-	-	-	-
Flour and confectionery	2	2	-	-	-	-
Seasoning powder and glucose	4	1	1	-	2	-
Edible oil	3	-	3	-	-	-
Alcohol and beverages	4	-	2	-	1	1
Tobacco	3	-	-	1	1	1
Sugar	1	-	-	-	-	1
TEXTILES (Industrial)						
Cotton spinning, weaving and dyeing	8	-	-	2	3	3
Synthetic fiber weaving	15	3	5	6	1	-
Jute	2	-	-	1	1	-
Blankets (Handicraft)	1	-	-	-	1	-
Cotton weaving	137	132	4	1	-	-
Woolen knitwear	39	37	2	-	-	-
Socks	9	9	-	-	-	-
Knitted underwear	19	19	-	-	-	-
Elastic braid	11	11	-	-	-	-
Towels	20	20	-	-	-	-
Miscellaneous	11	11	-	-	-	-

(Cont'd)

TABLE 9.4 (Cont'd)

Industry Group and Branch	No. of Enterprises	Capital Structure Under 10	11-50	51-100	101-500	Above 500
WOOD, PAPER, LEATHER, AND RUBBER						
Plywood	1	-	1	-	-	-
Writing and printing paper and paperboard	7	2	1	1	1	2
Corrugated cardboard	3	-	3	-	-	-
Paper pulp	1	-	-	-	1	-
Leather products	22	21	1	-	-	-
Footwear	105	103	1	1	-	-
Tires and tubes	6	2	2	2	-	-
Tire and tube retreading	3	1	2	-	-	-
CHEMICALS						
Chemical products	4	-	1	2	1	-
Toothpaste	7	6	1	-	-	-
Paints	22	21	1	-	-	-
Plastics	104	97	5	2	-	-
Matches	1	-	1	-	-	-
Soap	21	19	1	1	-	-
Printing ink	5	5	-	-	-	-
Pharmaceuticals	85	60	18	5	2	-
GLASS, CERAMICS, AND CEMENT						
Glass	15	10	4	-	1	-
Ceramics and earthenware	5	2	3	-	-	-
Cement products	45	42	2	-	1	-
Cement	1	-	-	-	-	1

Industry Group and Branch	No. of Enterprises	Capital Structure				
		Under 10	11-50	51-100	101-500	Above 500
METAL						
Aluminum products	60	60	-	-	-	-
Lighters	4	4	-	-	-	-
Wire and nails	4	2	1	1	-	-
General mechanical construction	4	-	1	-	3	-
Foundries	15	11	4	-	-	-
Sewing machines	12	6	5	1	-	-
Motorbicycle and bicycle assembly	15	12	1	2	-	-
Scooter assembly	2	-	-	2	-	-
Watch assembly	5	2	3	-	-	-
Welding rods	2	-	2	-	-	-
2- and 3-wheel vehicle accessories	11	10	1	-	-	-
ELECTRICAL						
Electric fans	3	2	1	-	-	-
Dry-cell batteries	6	4	2	-	-	-
Other batteries	2	-	2	-	-	-
Electrical fixtures	1	1	-	-	-	-
Electric wire and cable	2	-	1	-	1	-
Electric bulbs	2	2	-	-	-	-
Radio assembly	15	12	3	-	-	-
Transformers	1	-	1	-	-	-

of Economy states that total authorizations for the release of foreign exchange for importation of industrial raw materials amounted to US$69.75 million in 1967, about 65 percent of the total, therefore, being absorbed by these five branches.

Type of Enterprise

Most industrial enterprises in Vietnam have a single or family proprietor, and relatively few are partnerships. In terms of invested capital, however, the partnerships are clearly more important than businesses operated by single proprietors. (Table 9.3).

Investment is greatest in those branches in which the state participates. These include the sugar and cement industries, both with 100 percent public ownership. In the cotton, bag, paper, and glass industries, there is substantial public participation as well as private investment.

The state's total investment in industry has reached a figure of VN$5,723 million, no less than 24.2 percent of total investment in industry in 1968.* Table 9.4 provides a breakdown of investment by size for each branch of the seven principal groups of industries.

The Effects of the War on Industry

The war has had its effect on manufacturing as it has on other forms of economic activity. Some industries have actually benefited: the production of beverages, tobacco and canned foods, for instance, has increased considerably in the last few years (Table 9.5).

On the other hand there are several branches of industry which appear to have grown rapidly between 1961 and 1965 but have fallen off since. Mainly these are branches concerned with the production of certain construction materials such as bricks and tiles, asbestos cement, and roofing materials.

On the whole, industrial activity has increased for two principal reasons: (1) the increased size of the armed forces

---

*Source: director general of the budget.

TABLE 9.5

Wartime Increases in Manufactured Products, 1958-67

	Production			
Product	1958	1961	1964	1967
Beer and carbonated drinks (hectoliters)	812,000	774,000	1,500,000	2,108,000
Tobacco (tons)	3,400	4,232	6,071	12,400
Canned food (cans)	(650 T)	2,800,000	3,453,000	4,767,000

and the presence of large numbers of allied troops, and (2) the movement of the rural population into and towards the cities. In combination, these factors have provided markets sufficiently large to enable most manufacturers to work to full capacity, so providing an incentive for them to invest in modern facilities in order to increase production. Until 1965 consumer purchasing power in Vietnam was low, but with the arrival of the allied forces there is no doubt that there has been a substantial increase in working class incomes. Demand for consumer nondurables and other goods has climbed to unprecedented levels, as can be seen from Table 9.6. The liberal importation policy adopted in 1966 gave rise to an immediate and extraordinary increase in the volume of certain imported commodities, but the increase was not fully sustained in 1967. There have been consistent increases, however, in some essential consumer nondurables, such as sugar, textiles, and wheat flour. Consumption of milk products and cement, on the other hand, appears to have fluctuated considerably since 1965.

Consumption of goods manufactured from semiprocessed materials (for example, plastics and pharmaceuticals) has grown very rapidly indeed (Table 9.7). In the case of pharmaceuticals there has been more rapid growth than Table 9.7 indicates. In 1958 almost the whole of the foreign exchange allocated for imports of pharmaceuticals was used for importing finished products; in 1968 half of these foreign exchange

TABLE 9.6

Consumer Nondurables: Production Plus Imports, 1958-67
(Tons)

Product	1958	1961	1964	1965	1966	1967
Sugar	67,052	95,003	92,312	101,000	139,781	179,619
Milk	15,600	20,000	26,000	29,408[a]	51,650	23,779
Wheat flour	38,352	62,905	63,966	78,706	110,011	87,072
Cotton and rayon	--	12,603	12,508	15,080	16,327	NA
Synthetic fabrics	--	7,377	7,557	6,705	9,339	NA
Cement	284,253	367,648	512,722[b]	615,410	499,800	657,033

[a]The Foremost Company began production at the end of 1965; production as follows: 1965, 25,766 cases; 1966, 355,703 cases; 1967, 343,452 cases.

[b]The Ha-Tien Cement Company began operations at the end of 1963. Annual production: 1964, 75,305 tons; 1965, 189,284 tons; 1966, 141,000 tons; 1967, 181,033 tons.

Source: Constructed from data supplied by the Department of Customs and the National Institute of Statistics.

TABLE 9.7

Foreign Exchange Expenditure:
Plastics and Pharmaceuticals, 1958-66
(US Thousands)

	Expenditure				
Commodity	1958	1961	1964	1965	1966
Plastics	1,831	3,062	4,625	5,184	7,468
Pharmaceuticals	12,394	11,989	10,930	13,403	14,553

Source: U.S. AID.

requirements was used for the purchase of raw materials for manufacture in Vietnam.

Table 9.8 sets out the percentage increases in production, taking 1962 as a base year, for those industries which appear to have benefited substantially from the circumstances of the war.

A number of other branches of industry, on the other hand appear to have made relatively little progress in recent years, probably because the markets in which they sell their products have become increasingly confined to the cities. They include textiles (except for blankets), rubber products, glass and ceramics, basic and processed chemicals (excluding pharmaceuticals), and seasoning sauce. Many of the companies engaged in these activities have encountered difficulties in obtaining supplies as well as in distributing their products. As can be seen from Table 9.9, where production has increased in recent years the increase has usually been insignificant or unsustained.

Finally, there are a number of branches of industry on which the effects of the war have been definitely depressing; i.e., the production of ethyl alcohol, jute bags, cane sugar, pulp and paper, vegetable oils, natural silk, and coal.

Production of ethyl alcohol, for instance, has fallen off sharply purely as an effect of the fall in rice production. In

TABLE 9.8

Growth of Selected Branches of Industry, 1963-66: I
(1962 = 100)

Industry	Production 1963	1964	1965	1966
Tobacco	111	120	148	171
Beverages	120	148	182	189
Cement	a	100	251	178
Seasoning powder	100[b]	288	221	478
Blankets	225	224	479	628
Oxygen	120	136	172	195
Acetylene	126	142	183	214
Plastics	190	183	358	445
Electric fans	152	109	182	207
Batteries	137	118	378	691
Radio assembly	106	127	120	265
Scooter assembly	180	110	134	850
Motor-bicycle assembly	140	184	220	790
3-wheel vehicle assembly	174	119	162	660

[a]Production started late 1963.

[b]Production started May 1963.

Source: National Institute of Statistics.

TABLE 9.9

Growth of Selected Branches of
Industry, 1963-66: II
(1962 = 100)

	Production			
Industry	1963	1964	1965	1966
Nuoc nam (fish sauce)	105	94	112	132
Seasoning sauce	112	130	105	92
Cotton spinning	102	178	163	186
Cotton weaving	189	168	173	190
Rayon weaving	171	122	207	185
Bicycle inner tubes	208	354	248	182
Glass	101	128	117	129
Ceramics	120	110	87	88
Soap	88	84	104	112
Paint	98	107	148	108

comparison with the 1965 figures, it fell by 10 percent in 1966 and by a further 34 percent in 1967.

Cane sugar is another casualty: production in small cottage industries was at an average annual level of 35,000 tons in 1962-65, and dropped to 24,000 tons in 1966 and to 10,000 tons in 1967. The output of the Hiep Hoa sugar refinery, 13,000 tons in 1961, was only 1,900 tons in 1966.

Most of the raw materials for the paper industry are imported, and production increased steadily through 1966, but then the shortage of such local materials as bagasse and rice straw began to be felt; COBOGIDO, a newly established pulp milling enterprise, could operate only sporadically, and this in part was responsible for a drop in the production of its paper-making affiliate, COGIDO, which continued into 1968. In all three cases cited, the ill fortunes of the industry were direct results of the insecurity of the countryside and the consequent fall in farm production of rice and sugar cane.

Vegetable oil and silk manufacturing have been affected similarly. Taking 1962 as the base year for vegetable oil, the production index was less than half in following years, except for a brief recovery in 1965:

1962	1963	1964	1965	1966
100	43	37	54	45

The natural silk manufacturing industry is in a similar situation. In part it depends on imported supplies and in part on domestic sources for its raw materials. In the early years of the war, production increased steadily, but 1966 figures were only 50 percent of the previous year's and in 1967 and 1968 the position of the industry continued to deteriorate, the principle cause being the shortage of local silk.

Although they have been severely depressed by the war, these industries have not completely ceased to function, and there is still some production. This is not true of the An Hoa Nong Son industrial complex, which is not operating at all. In 1965 and 1966, production of coal at Nong Son was only 2 percent of planned output, and in 1967 and 1968 the mine was inactive. The record since 1956, in tons of coal produced, has been as follows:

1956	2,101	1962	77,000
1957	12,366	1963	104,090
1958	20,080	1964	76,955
1959	19,929	1965	2,511
1960	27,310	1966	3,000
1961	57,351		

INDUSTRIAL RECOVERY IN THE EARLY POSTWAR PERIOD

As has been seen in the previous section, since 1958 only a few industries, principally producers of consumer nondurables, have been able to develop and expand with little or no adverse effects from the war. Others--timber, paper, leather, rubber, glass, ceramics, mechanical and electrical--have encountered considerable difficulties in this period, particularly since 1965. These difficulties are mainly related to raw material supplies, credit, manpower, and marketing and distribution.

Several important existing industries have recently suffered considerable damage and destruction, resulting in a drop in their productive capacity.

These difficulties will have to be overcome if the nation's industrial base is to be rebuilt and the capacity of existing industrial installations is to be restored.

The length of the period of recovery will depend on the type of industry, official policies toward industry, and the drive and spirit of the manufacturers themselves. If all goes well, this period could be as short as three years. During this period the main efforts would be directed to:

1. Complete reconstruction and repair of industrial installations destroyed or damaged by the war.

2. Bringing into production half-completed projects such as the Quang Ngai sugarmill (which would take at least two years).

3. The revival of industries depressed by the war.

These should be the three priority activities during the recovery period.

Reconstruction of Damaged Installations

The two Viet Cong offensives of 1968 inflicted damage on a number of industrial installations in Saigon and its suburbs. From documents submitted to the General Federation of Industrialists and the Ministry of Economy by firm owners, total damage has been estimated at VN$5 billion. Hardest hit was the textile industry (estimated damage, VN$4 billion); next were the paper and food industries VN$206 million and VN$134 million respectively). Fourteen other industries reported losses and damage of varying amounts up to VN$100 million. It is improbable that in all cases the actual damage suffered was as extensive as the manufacturers have reported, but it certainly was significant in the textile industry, the production capacity of which dropped by 30 percent.

Some companies have started to repair their installations, but most are awaiting assistance from the government. The

Reconstruction and War-Risk Insurance funds will permit a few manufacturers to start reconstruction shortly, and it is assumed that the work will continue until completion. In many cases, however, there will be an inclination to defer reconstruction until peace is assured.

According to the Credit Service of the Industrial Development Center, up to September 1968, a total of VN$1,131 million in Reconstruction Funds had been issued in loans for replacement and repair of buildings, machinery, and equipment and for importation of raw materials lost in the 1968 offensives. The funds have been provided by U.S. AID and the national budget, and a balance of VN$1,048 million was still available for distribution as of September 30, 1968.

Partly Completed Projects

Partly completed projects are of two types: those in which implementation has actually started but has been held up, and those which have been approved but have not actually been started.

With the exception of the An Hoa Nong Son industrial complex, there is no reason why the projects of the first type should not be resumed and carried to completion once peace is restored. In the Bien Hoa area there are several cases in which the factory buildings were constructed some time ago but mechanical facilities have not yet been purchased and installed. For two large projects, the Quang Ngai Sugar Company and the An Hoa industrial complex, machinery and equipment have been purchased but because of security conditions have not yet been assembled and installed. As a general rule (again excepting the An Hoa enterprise), almost all partly completed projects could be finished and put into production within a period of 12 to 18 months from the end of the war.

In addition to three large publicly owned enterprises (Quang Ngai, Binh Duong, and An Hoa), there are 27 privately financed projects that were approved in the years 1965, 1966, and 1967 and are still in various stages of completion. They represent a total planned capital investment of VN$3,574 million.

In 18 of these 27 cases, investors have carried the work to a point at which they have been able to apply for foreign exchange to finance importation of machinery and equipment. Together these 18 projects represent a capital investment of VN$1,650 million, or 46 percent of that of all uncompleted private projects. The remaining 9 are less advanced and have gone no further than preparation of invitations to bid. Of these the most important are the Vietnam Sugar Company's refinery project (over VN$900 million) and VIKYNO's agricultural machinery project (over VN$500 million). These may take another two years after peace returns to come into production.

Two years after peace is restored, therefore, is the maximum period for the completion of all industrial projects, public and private, on which work has already started, excepting the An Hoa industrial complex, which is a far more difficult problem and will be considered separately below.

Projects of the second type, which have been approved but in which no steps whatever have been taken toward implementation, must also be taken into account. A good many investments approved in principle by the Ministry of Economy or authorized by the Investment Commission as long ago as 1965 or 1966 are still entirely on paper. There are three probable reasons for this. First, intensification of the war has resulted in reduced confidence on the part of private investors; Second, though some of the projects may be profitable, stiff competition is expected within certain industrial branches. In some cases, approval has been given to as many as seven different projects of precisely the same type at precisely the same time. In an uncertain market situation, the short-term prospects for a multiplicity of identical projects are far from promising; Third, the 1966 devaluation of the piaster increased investment costs beyond the expectations of some investors at the time approval was sought. This, of course, applies particularly to the projects proposed in 1965 and early 1966.

Lack of data prevents an estimate of the exact number of projects which have received approval in principle from the Ministry of Economy but have not been carried further. Many must have been abandoned. Some indication can be found in the figures showing authorizations issued by the Investment Commission given in Table 9.10.

Given suitable credit policies and appropriate incentives after the war, it is our belief that many of the appropriate companies which have deferred their investment decisions will resume these projects and carry them out.

TABLE 9.10

Projects Authorized by the Investment Commission, 1965-67

	Investment Authorization		Unrealized Projects	
Year	No.	Capital Investment (VN$ Millions)	No.	Capital Investment (VN$ Millions)
1965				
1966				
1967				
Total				

Revival of Depressed Industries

A great deal of existing Vietnamese industrial capacity was installed during the war in areas where security has been good. It has taken advantage of growing consumer markets and government assistance; and, during the early war years at least, a large number of these new enterprises made good progress. Since 1965, however, there has been a reversal in many cases. Since the offensive of Tet 1968, some businessmen appear to have lost their confidence; industrial enterprises, as well as public services, have lost skilled labor to the draft; and, perhaps most significant of all, some Vietnamese enterprises have not been able to face the competition of a flood of imported goods admitted to control inflation.

Some of the depressed industries rely on the rural areas for the supply of their raw materials and have been deprived of these supplies by the military situation. Examples are cane sugar, vegetable oil, silk, and coal. We may assume that with peace, supplies of raw materials will be resumed reasonably early.

Cane sugar and natural silk deserve considerable attention. The former will save foreign exchange, the latter will earn it. Both employ a large workforce and will absorb some of the surplus labor in the countryside in the postwar period. Both have been deprived of their sources of raw material by insecurity in the rural areas.

In 1967 sugar consumption in Vietnam was approximately 180, 000 tons but only a very small part of this came from local cane. Most of it, approximately 170, 000 tons, consisted of imported raw and refined sugar. Only two cane sugar mills have actually been installed (Hiep Hoa and Vinh Phu), and both are small. In addition, some sugar is produced in family operations of a cottage industry character. As the fighting has grown fiercer, many sugar cane plantations have been destroyed and at present production of cane is severely limited.

The Quang Ngai, Binh Duong, and Bien Hoa mills and refineries should all come into production within a reasonable delay after the end of the war. Special attention must be given to supplies of cane. From 1958 to 1966 the cane-producing area consisted of about 30, 000 hectares, remaining more or less constant during the period. Production yields, however, always have been low. The world average is 5. 5 tons of sugar per cultivated hectare, but in Vietnam average yields have been less than half of that, with only 2. 5 tons per hectare. Improved cultivation methods might easily increase production two or three fold. If, in the first years of peace, all of the refinery projects are carried out, and yields can be increased, sugar production, including the output of the small family producers, might exceed 200, 000 tons per annum. Production of this order would result in very substantial savings of foreign exchange.

As for the silk industry, before World War II, there were about 5, 500 hectares in central and southern Vietnam devoted to the cultivation of mulberries. Because of the present conflict only one-fifth of that area is still being so used, and yearly production is only 30 tons of silk. A hectare of mulberry bushes can be made to yield approximately 500 kgs. of silk, so to meet the country's current demand for silk (2, 000 tons per annum), a minimum of 4, 000 hectares would have to be cultivated.

Even at currently high silk prices, world markets could absorb an additional $40 million worth of silk a year. In the reestablishment of this industry, it is therefore important that the export possibilities be taken into account. Some Japanese interests have recently mentioned the possibility of their providing assistance for silk production in Vietnam.

There have been previous plans to develop the silk industry but because of the war they have not been implemented. When security is restored, both central Vietnam and the highlands will be suitable for this kind of development. Mulberries grow quickly, and the industry does not require a large capital investment. For farmers, the breeding of silkworms can be quite a lucrative activity.

Other branches of industry among those now depressed may fairly put the blame on the free importation policy introduced in 1966. These include small textile firms and those engaged in the manufacture of spare parts and accessories for sewing machines, motorbicycles, and two and three wheel scooters.

Small-scale textile manufacture is not likely to flourish even when peace is restored. Many small textile companies have now gone out of production. Because of their labor-intensive character and their suitability for establishment in rural areas, handicraft activities in textiles were at one time encouraged and assisted by the government. However, because of the primitive equipment used, the quality of finished products was often very inferior. This is essentially a noncompetitive activity and it can be only a matter of time before the whole of Vietnamese textile manufacture is in relatively large, properly organized industrial operations. People now involved in small textile enterprises (for instance unbleached cotton fabrics and mosquito netting) might be helped into other activities with better prospects, such as silkworm breeding and natural silk production.

On the other hand, workshops manufacturing parts and accessories for assembly industries should develop fairly rapidly, helping the establishment of a viable mechanical industry in Vietnam. Taking into account all the foreign exchange spent on importing scooters, motorbicycles, and sewing machines since 1965, efficient assembly operations and the manufacture of parts in Vietnam are not only desirable but essential. Recent import figures are as shown in Table 9.11.

Before June, 1966, there was a steady expansion of domestic manufacture of parts and accessories for these types of goods, although most of the companies engaged in these activities were small and the quality of their products was not the best. Domestically manufactured parts accounted, in fact,

TABLE 9.11

Imports, Three Mechanical Products, 1965-68
(US$ Thousands)

Commodity	1965	1966	1968
Sewing machines	983	3,880	5,431
2 and 3 wheel scooters	3,421	14,216	3,034
Motorbicycles	3,337	20,229	20,172

Source: Foreign Trade Directorate.

for a rather high percentage of the total f.o.b. price of each finished unit, ranging from 15 percent of the total for scooters to 30 percent for sewing machines and motorbicycles.

To revive this branch of industry and to ensure that it operates efficiently, two conditions appear to be necessary. First, the small and scattered firms engaged in assembly activities should be persuaded to regroup themselves into a few large companies. Financing, either by the Vietnam Development Bank or by private investors, could be influential in this development. Secondly, importation should be restricted to a limited number of types of scooters, and the foreign manufacturers concerned should be asked to provide technical assistance for domestic assembly of their products and domestic manufacture of an increasing number of parts.

If the existing assembly industries can be improved, then this branch of industry should, eventually, be able to expand into assembly and manufacture of parts for refrigerators, air conditioners, household appliances, and other consumer durables. Promotion of such labor-intensive industries will increase Vietnamese resources in technical skills and play an important role in early postwar development.

A LONG-RANGE STRATEGY FOR DEVELOPMENT OF INDUSTRY

The previous sections of this chapter have examined in some detail the present structure of the Vietnamese manufacturing sector and the difficulties which it faces in the initial postwar years. Although these problems are the most obvious today, there are other longer-range problems which must be anticipated in order to assure a logical and proper pattern of industrial growth during the next ten years. It is suggested in this section and those to follow that several important decisions (should be made now) to foster this logical development of the industrial sector.

Most of the present policies affecting industry have been designed in a wartime situation which has added innumerable complications to the normally difficult problems of development. Despite the considerable efforts of the government and U.S. assistance programs, policy planning has, by necessity, been aimed at ameliorating the more immediate problems, and little time has been available to consider policies which should be adopted in the postwar period. It is felt strongly that the approaches toward industrial development characterizing efforts since 1965 are unlikely to produce the desired long-term results, even though (at least before the Tet offensive) in the short run they have tended to accelerate manufacturing growth. The proper mix of fiscal, monetary, tariff, interest, savings, and financing policies must be identified at an early date and employed effectively in the coming period, or a high-cost industrial structure undoubtedly will result.

Even these efforts will not automatically produce a competitive industrial structure, for the path of development in the 1970's will be difficult indeed. Appropriate policy is a necessary but not sufficient condition for growth. It must be supplemented by unsparing efforts in the public and private sectors in order to become effective.

Two general routes for the future are open to Vietnamese manufacturing: (1) high protection, leading to high production costs, inefficient use of resources and, ultimately, stagnation; or (2) development in the key sectors of efficient, relatively capital-intensive industries which are based on relatively high labor productivity and low input costs and are more or less competitive internationally.

The first approach characterizes past development in the Philippines and most of the Latin American economies. The second path is now being followed by several rapidly growing countries, including Japan, Taiwan, Israel, Hong Kong, and, most spectacularly in recent years, Korea, a country which has successfully surmounted many of the problems which face Vietnam. This particular choice will be up to the policy-makers, not the entrepreneurs, be they foreign or national. Based on present knowledge of past development experience, one can only urge strongly that the government of Vietnam give serious consideration to the second alternative. While this path will be difficult to follow at times, and many compromises will have to be made, it is still the right goal.

The major conclusions which emerge from the Joint Development Group's study of future Vietnamese manufacturing and its relationship to the rest of the Vietnamese economy are as follows:

1. Highest priority should be placed on the production of inputs to the agriculture sector at the lowest possible price to the farmer, and production should be delayed (or in rare cases subsidized) until such time as markets build up to a point where production can be attained at or below the c.i.f. import price without duty. Within the agricultural sector, preference must be granted to products which will tend to lower production costs of potential or actual agricultural exports.

2. Production of most major basic commodities should be permitted only when production costs can, or will in a reasonable period of time, approach world competitive prices (without duties). This will in general require (a) large, economical plant sizes; (b) low material input costs; (c) realistic interest rates; (d) appropriate tariff policies to stimulate rapid market growth prior to plant operation; (e) adequate financing; (f) tax incentives; (g) adequate technical know-how and managerial capabilities (often available only from abroad through joint ventures and so on); (h) clearly defined and realistic investment policies; and (i) careful sectoral planning, preferably through joint efforts of the public and private sectors.

3. Within the manufacturing sector, priority should be placed on (a) the product categories in which costs can be reduced to the point where exports can be expanded rapidly; and (b) institutionalization of the export process.

4. Industrial promotion and financial assistance efforts can and should be selective. In some sectors, such as handicrafts and refugee-based textile and apparel production, a labor-intensive approach will be necessary initially. Thus a dualistic attitude toward manufacturing must emerge. Different incentives will be needed for the low-productivity and high-productivity sectors. Nevertheless, the simple principle must emerge that whatever is worth doing at all in the manufacturing sector is worth doing well. Furthermore, policies should be developed whenever possible that will automatically permit the private sector to work toward solutions that are in the mutual interest of the national economy, the private sector, and the individual segments of the society.

5. Entrepreneurship should be encouraged, provided with technical assistance where necessary and desired, and aided through joint ventures with foreign firms, but the process must be guided wisely to avoid excesses. The tools are already available for program implementation, but difficulties remain in the planning process itself.

There is no reason why the disadvantages resulting from the present insecurity cannot be used to advantage in the early planning process. In particular, the fact that the private sector has tended to defer investment decisions, while highly undesirable on the whole, has served in numerous cases to postpone certain unwise investments, particularly those which would have resulted in uneconomic plants that could only hinder early postwar development. The postponement of these investments now allows them to be reassessed in light of new forecasts for the postwar period and a fresh definition of investment goals. With investment at a virtual standstill, this is the time to reexamine past plans and adapt them to future requirements. It is the objective of this study to assist that process.

The most obvious tendency of past industrial development in Vietnam has been toward a proliferation of small plants which, if faced with the free entry of competing imports, could not survive. The argument invariably heard from entrepreneurs, and public officials in favor of these small plants, is the foreign exchange savings that can be achieved from them.

It should be noted that Vietnam does not have a short-run foreign exchange problem, but it does have a massive one in the long run. From the experience of far too many developing countries, it can be said with considerable certainty that the small plant philosophy, based on profitability at high protection levels, is invariably going to lead to greater long-run foreign exchange costs. In fact, many of the small plants now under consideration are notably capital-intensive, with large foreign exchange requirements for equipment and manufacturing inputs. It is entirely possible that the net effect of their postponement could be an additional reduction in short-term foreign exchange costs. At any rate, a primary objective of industrial development must be growth in foreign exchange earnings through efficient import substitution and exports. The small-plant philosophy is at variance with this objective.

A second failing in previous industrial planning is the tendency for project analyses to be conducted in narrow financial terms instead of in terms of broader economic considerations. For most projects, the price of competing imports is taken as the price paid in the Vietnamese market, including import duties and taxes. This artificially high price is then taken as the upper price limit for the locally produced item, and the viability of the project is judged on the basis of the excessive revenues which result. The result, of course, is a viability assessment which has no relationship whatever to international standards of production efficiency. Such practices must stop if high-cost industries are to be avoided.

As recommended in the discussion of assembly industries, one way to avoid construction of small plants is to discourage excessive numbers of competing units from being started in any one industrial sector, each separately uneconomic but which together might form an economic operation. An example is the production of nylon in Vietnam from imported caprolactum, for which two plants are now in the planning stage, each with a production capacity of 2.5 tons of nylon per day. The minimum economic plant size for nylon production is 10 tons per day, so that even together these plants could not result in a single unit which could be competitive with imported nylon. The most appropriate path for this industry to follow would be to postpone investment in both projects and let the market for nylon develop until it reaches the size where a single minimum economic unit can be supported. To do otherwise can only result in higher input costs to the textile sector, which already labors under a high cost-structure.

The objection usually raised to the construction of only one plant is that monopolistic control will result. This can be prevented by a flexible and realistic import policy, through which the actuality or threat of import competition can prevent monopolistic pricing and other excesses.

In summary, the following major items of strategy are recommended for long-term development of industry:

1. Production of key items should be postponed until future markets (say in five or six years) can justify economically sized plants,

2. Imports should be permitted at relatively low duties to develop markets for those products which in future can be manufactured at low cost,

3. These low duties should be continued after domestic production begins to insure low-cost and quality production by domestic plants.

The over-all objective should be to adopt those policies and incentives which can assure the installation of the right plants at the right time, a process far more complicated than it sounds. The following sections of this chapter examine the product areas in which this strategy can have the greatest impact and the institutional structure which will be required to carry it forward.

A TEN-YEAR PROGRAM FOR INVESTMENT IN INDUSTRY

This section focuses on what the Vietnamese manufacturing sector should look like in about ten years and an industry-by-industry strategy for attaining a strong, competitive industrial base in the 1970's. By 1978, if present population trends are maintained, Vietnam will have a population of about 24 million; and a reasonable expectation is that around that time, value added in manufacturing should reach the equivalent of about US$500 million, roughly twice what it was in 1968.

In order to facilitate the rather difficult process of forecasting the future structure of Vietnamese industry, the Joint

Development Group undertook a study of the historical experience of Korea, the Philippines, Taiwan, and Thailand.* Taking into account the existing structure of Vietnamese industry, the availability of resources, agricultural requirements, probable world market conditions, and realistic levels of investment, and using the experience of the four countries as a guide, projections have been made of feasible levels of fixed investment and production for each sector of Vietnamese industry in 1978. In using data from the other four countries, differences in population density, climate, land characteristics, raw material availability, comparative advantage, and aggregate market sizes have been taken into account.

None of the four countries studied can serve as a complete model for Vietnam. All at one time or another have adopted policies contrary to those recommended in this study. Each has shown excellent development in some sectors of industry--evidenced by rapidly increasing output and expanding exports--where appropriate policies have been followed. There have also been serious setbacks where the reverse was true; for example, the chaotic development of the fertilizer, pulp and paper, and coke sectors in Taiwan, of the pulp and paper, chemical (at least at the start), fertilizer, flour milling, and steel sectors in Korea, and of the chemical, mechanical, textile, and many other sectors in the Philippines and Thailand. It is as important for Vietnam to avoid the shortcomings of other nations as to learn from their successes.

The strategy proposed in this study does not depend (except for investment scheduling) on when the over-all level of US$500 million in value added is obtained, but rather on reliable considerations of aggregate market sizes, economies of scale, and production costs.

Projections by Industrial Sector

This section presents a (subsectional) and product development strategy based on an analysis along the lines described. While it is recognized that each projection and strategy recommendation should be studied further and modified where

---

*A Long-Range Development Program for Manufacturing in Vietnam, Working Paper No. 41 (Joint Development Group).

necessary, it is suggested that each be given serious consideration in the next stages of planning.

Tables 9.15 and 9.16 present a summary of the projections and strategy recommendations and should be read in conjunction with the text that follows. Table 9.15 indicates feasible levels of value added, value of sales, and production levels for each major product category in 1978. Table 9.16 presents the estimated total fixed investment required up to 1978 to reach these levels and a rough estimate of how this investment might be phased over an eight-year period. The result is a forecast of capital investment requirements in industry ranging from US$108 million in 1970-71 to US$303 million in 1976-77. The estimated total investment required in the eight-year period is US$749 million, the approximate amount needed to bring value added in manufacturing beyond US$500 million per annum. Once again, it should be noted that this level of output may not be achieved until later than 1978, in which case the investment estimates will be spread out over a longer period of time.

For purposes of future planning, it is felt that whether political stability comes by 1970 or later, the essential features of this program should remain basically the same; the same mistakes need to be avoided and the same policies need to be implemented. The present illustrative design for 1978 or 1980, or whenever the value added by manufacturing in Vietnam approaches US$500 million, will require time to develop and implement policies and time to design for plants and markets of economic size. An early start should be made.

Manufactured Food Products (ISIC 20)

In most of those manufactured food products for which substantial Vietnamese exports might be achieved in the late 1970's, economies of scale are very important. World competitiveness will depend on the costs of agricultural production, manufacturing, processing, transport, and distribution, together with production and export organization and product quality and standardization. Preliminary considerations of Vietnamese climate and land quality, historical trends in processed agricultural production and exports in comparable countries, and economies of scale suggest that plant size and production costs are particularly important for the major products listed below.

Predominantly Export	Export & Domestic Markets	Domestic Markets
Fruit and vegetable canning (pineapples, mushrooms, vegetables, etc.)	Sugar, fats and oils Animal feeds Fish processing Monosodium glutamate	Dairy products Flour milling Starch

Major markets would be land-short areas, such as Singapore and Hong Kong, and developed countries, including particularly the United States and Japan.

Economies of scale appear to be less important in other manufactured food products with export potential such as (1) fish sauce; (2) vegetable (soy) sauces; and (3) rice milling. However, even in these products, detailed micro-economic studies are required before exports are considered.

The development of agricultural processing is of course dependent primarily on the agricultural program considered in Chapter 7. The main purpose of this analysis of manufactured food products is to suggest where coordinated agricultural and manufacturing planning is essential.

Without proper planning, it is possible that traditional inefficiencies and proliferation of small plants will be built into flour milling, sugar processing and refining, fruit and vegetable canning, and meat processing, particularly where no exports are contemplated. Inefficiency and proliferation merely increase the cost of these products to domestic consumers, the total investment requirements, and the foreign exchange costs of imported capital goods. Large production units, with high labor productivity, should be the goal for these products.

An excellent start has been made in some Vietnamese food processing sectors such as dairy products. Nevertheless, considerable support is needed in the 1970's for such sectors as meat processing, a comprehensive sugar program, processing of fats and oils, and animal feeds. Progress is currently being prevented by insecurity, particularly in such fields as sugar and meat products. The need now is to develop a rational approach to each subsector and to plan ahead for each crucial element.

Timing of investments is particularly difficult to estimate. It is clear that investments in such products as sugar, flour, dairy processing, and meat processing should develop in units of approximately $10 million each (perhaps as low as $5 million), but it is not possible to estimate when agricultural output and markets will permit this. Where inputs are imported, as in flour milling or sugar refining, the timing of the agricultural program is of less importance. A considered estimate of the investment schedule is shown in Table 9.16.

Food technologists and product planners should acquaint themselves with historical and current developments in the four countries studied in Working Paper No. 41, especially insofar as this concerns economies of scale, production costs, and major errors. Special studies are warranted of the major export markets. The future of a food-processing industry in Vietnam can be bright if some of the more apparent handicaps can be overcome and close coordination with agricultural planning can be achieved.

It can be said with some confidence that for many years the domestic market for canned food in Vietnam will be inadequate to support, by itself, a viable canning industry, and export markets must be sought. Several small canning operations exist now, but their methods are primitive and product quality is unsatisfactory.* They use imported and even second-hand**cans, illustrating one of the primary requisites for establishing a canning industry in the country: the domestic manufacture of cans from imported tinplate. Already, the real or potential demand for cans in Vietnam for soft drinks, beer, oil products, and dairy products may be approaching the level where the present limited can production could be expanded, and studies of this possibility are already proceeding in U.S. AID. These studies should be coordinated with planning for the food-processing industry.

---

*Lee Shiu, Survey Report on Development of Food Processing Industry in Vietnam (Chinese Agricultural Technical Mission, May, 1965).

**U.S. AID Task Force on Industrial Development, Planning Paper No. 2 (November, 1968).

The climate and soils of Vietnam permit cultivation of a wide range of vegetables and fruits which could be developed into processed exports, provided that low costs and high product quality can be achieved. (Similar opportunities exist for fish exports, and the following comments apply equally to that sector.) Nevertheless, it is the feeling of the Joint Development Group that the present level of farm prices is so high that the country could not today compete in world markets in any product area. Labor costs have little effect on the canning process itself, which is relatively capital-intensive, but the cost of the raw agricultural produce is a major item in total costs and must be kept as low as possible.* The feasibility of the industry, therefore, will hinge on the whole structure of farm prices, and no attempt should be made to develop large food processing units until this basic problem is solved. A fuller discussion of this matter is presented in Chapter 2.

A successful export-oriented food-processing industry cannot be developed without considerable assistance from overseas, and it was recommended that during 1969 one or more firms with successful experience in world markets should be engaged to undertake a preliminary design for the industry. The first, and most important, item will be an analysis of world markets for food products, followed by a detailed agricultural and industrial plan to develop those specific product lines which can be grown in Vietnam and have the greatest opportunities for success in the postwar period. At the start, the attempt should not be to develop a broad range of products, but to concentrate on high quality production of a limited number. Taiwan has been eminently successful in mushrooms, for example, last year overtaking France as the world's leading mushroom producer, just ten years after its first exports.** There is no reason why Vietnam cannot become equally successful in selected products in future years, but it will be necessary to utilize foreign expertise

---

*United Nations Conference on Trade and Development, E/CONF. 46/P/8, <u>Possibilities of Establishing Food Processing Industries in Developing Countries for Export</u> (January, 1964).

**<u>Far Eastern Economic Review,</u> September 26, 1968, p. 604.

if this is to be done. A series of joint ventures between Vietnamese interests and experienced foreign firms will provide the fastest route to success in this field.

Beverage Industries (ISIC 21)

The beverage industry is already developing well and natural forces are adequate to permit a reasonable level of development in this sector through the private sector. Special incentives do not appear to be required. The major issues appear to be the timing of import substitution in inputs to the sector (malt, soft drink concentrates, hops, barley, tin cans, and cork) and development of a long-range tax policy. Import content appears to equal about 15 percent of value added at market prices and 25 to 30 percent of value added at factor cost (excluding indirect taxes). Economies of scale and/or agricultural production will dictate when further import substitution will be feasible, and relatively complete domestic dependence for all inputs except tinplate should be possible by the mid-1970's. A study would appear to be required of the relative merits for the economy of different types of beverage containers (tinplate, glass, paper). Finally, it should be remembered that this sector provides a substantial source of public (national and local) revenue, and appropriate tax programs should be developed; at the present time taxes on beverages are only a moderate percentage of sales and possibly could be increased. Some of the tax proceeds of the sector might eventually be set aside for export expansion.

Tobacco Manufactures (ISIC 22)

As with beverages, the tobacco industry is well developed and serves as a major tax base. Modernization is already in progress and natural market forces should bring about steady development. In terms of the national economy, the major problem is the large dependence on imported tobacco, and the desirability of increasing domestic production of tobacco is indicated. Some exports might ultimately be contemplated.

Taxes from tobacco were about 4.7 billion piasters in 1967, a significant source of revenue to the government. Again, a long-range tax program needs to be developed.

Textiles (ISIC 23)

In ensuring an efficient, low-cost textile industry, the crucial subsectors are cotton and synthetic spinning, weaving, and finishing. The experience of Colombia, Taiwan, and Korea all emphasize how important it is that the pace of the basic industry be set by a few large, efficient, automated, and integrated firms which ultimately can compete in international markets.

In recent years, and particularly in 1967, considerable modernization and expansion have occurred in spinning and weaving operations. Approximately one seventh of all new manufacturing investment in 1965-67 took place in this sector. Continued efforts are needed to ensure the development of a competitive industry based on low input costs. Emphasis must be given to the high quality standards demanded by both Vietnamese and foreign markets. The demand of domestic markets for high-quality textile goods has been illustrated clearly by the increasing competition felt from more expensive but higher quality French, Japanese, and other imported goods since import restrictions were relaxed in 1966. This situation is a dramatic demonstration of the problems inherent in allowing domestic industries to build up behind protective walls: standards are bound to fall (and costs to rise) without competition from the outside, and the end result of continued protection is wastage of scarce resources.

Another problem of Vietnam's textile industry is low productivity of both capital and labor. At least one existing mill was averaging one-third idle time during the first half of 1968. Obviously, the problems of the war are acutely felt, and the industry deserves much praise for what it has accomplished in recent years with so many difficulties. Nevertheless, much hard thinking is required now if a competitive industry is to be attained in the postwar period.

Particular care is required to assure competitive input costs in the synthetics sector. Capital costs per unit of output are high for the production of all major synthetic inputs, particularly for rayon, nylon, polyester, acrylic, and polyvinyl chloride (PVC). The suggested strategy for ultimate production of these inputs best illustrates the philosophy of this study. Domestic production of each should be delayed until market growth permits an efficient plant size. Where market growth will permit this within a reasonable time horizon, import duties on inputs should be kept low to stimulate and speed the growth of demand. Nylon and rayon are two principal examples of where this philosophy could be successful.

It is recommended that current plans to install two nylon plants, capacity 2.5 tons per day each, and one rayon plant, capacity 10 tons per day, be reconsidered in light of the above comments. These particular projects should be deferred. When projected markets for, say, five years ahead are large enough, a decision should be taken to construct much larger plants than those presently contemplated. The simultaneous installation of the two nylon plants, together having only half the capacity of a single economic unit, is certainly not consistent with the recommendations of this study, and the postponement of all three projects owing to the effects of the war has some advantages; the continuous stepwise expansion of synthetics in Korea and Taiwan actually impeded sound development of the textile sector in those countries, and Vietnam should be warned by their experience.

Production of synthetic and mixed fabrics and apparel goods in Vietnam, given the patterns of demand, should be encouraged where self-sufficiency ultimately can be achieved. Nevertheless, export expansion is also a long-range goal, and potential growth in the sector should not be compromised by premature manufacture of inputs.

Apparel and Footwear (ISIC 24)

Rising incomes will result in a steady growth in this sector, especially as regards high-quality ready-made goods. Some exports might be achieved eventually, if wages can be held to competitive levels, quality and standards be maintained, the industry modernized, and export activities formalized.

Wood and Wood Products (ISIC 25)

The wood products sector is one of real potential growth because of the abundance of raw materials, both coniferous and hardwoods. Security does not permit expansion at this time, but immediate planning is desirable. Important subsectors are hard board, particle board, plywood, veneer, and sawn wood. Modern mills of economic size are required in each case, and exports could augment domestic markets and help to establish low-cost industries at an earlier date than domestic sales alone would allow. Wood-short countries such as Japan provide markets.

Major nonwood inputs to the sector, such as resins (phenol-formaldehyde, urea-formaldehyde, and so on), can later be produced from imported chemicals, and eventually backward integration in resin manufacture will occur.

The importance of forestry development has been described in Chapter 8, and a specific plan for the development of a plywood industry is presented below in this chapter.

Paper; Pulp and Paper Products (ISIC 26)

The war has prevented the development of an integrated pulp, paper, and paper products industry, but considerable progress has taken place in recent years as regards paper and paper products. The crucial problems are (1) the production of chemical and mechanical pulp for paper and newsprint, and (2) the integration of pulp and paper production. Economically sized pulp and newsprint units must produce a minimum of 100,000 tons per year, and 200,000 tons per year would be a better target if an efficient export trade is to be achieved.

Thus, in the near future, massive exports must be ensured to justify plants of economic size. Future planning strategy should aim at tying down export markets, possibly through equity investments, at avoiding installation of mills that are too small, and at providing for ultimate integration of paper and paper products manufacture with pulp facilities.

A specific proposal for the pulp industry is made in the section headed "Three Projects for Immediate Consideration."

Rubber and Rubber Products (ISIC 30)

If the natural rubber industry revives after the war, it will be easy for Vietnam to achieve almost complete self-sufficiency in natural rubber products. The natural rubber content of vehicle tires will remain high, and some product exports might be possible eventually.

Domestic markets do not appear to be large enough for the production of synthetic rubber until after 1977. Polybutadene production from imported butadene may be feasible by about 1975, but this possibility should be reevaluated about 1972 in the light of new technology at that time. Domestic production of fillers and chemical additives for tire production should eventually be feasible.

Chemical Manufacture (ISIC 31)

Chemical production will develop either through forward integration from raw materials (salt, limestone, petroleum, liquid petroleum gas and petrochemicals, and others), or, more generally, through backward integration based on imported inputs. Product prices can be held down by not manufacturing inputs too rapidly and by initiating only those projects in which imported inputs can be processed efficiently. Economies of scale are important for all chemical products, and the strategy indicated for each product area is outlined in Table 9.15.

Because of the large size of present and estimated future markets, ammonia and urea production must receive the highest priority. This subject is covered in some detail below.

At a later date, when markets develop, certain chemicals can be produced from domestic raw materials at low cost, for example, soda ash, caustic soda, and ammonium nitrate explosives. Here, economies of scale are important. Market development should be encouraged through low import duties, but at the present time investments would not be justified.

Most organic chemical products, such as plastics, should be developed from imported intermediates when market sizes permit. Priority should be given to the use of low duties to encourage consumption of products such as PVC for which an economic scale of operation is eventually probable.

Export potentialities are greatest in urea and mixed urea fertilizers, urea animal feed, urea-based resins, and chemicals based on raw material, such as naval stores (turpentine and rosin) and fats and oils.

As far as the An Hoa ammonia plant is concerned, thought should be given to the feasibility of using the equipment for thermal power and steam generation (if it is still intact) at An Hoa. The sulfuric acid plant (if that is also still intact) is a self-sufficient one and could be located in the Saigon area for sulfuric acid production. The problem of An Hoa is considered more extensively in the section "Three Projects."

Petroleum and Coal Products (ISIC 32)

Plans for a petroleum refinery in Vietnam were started in 1964 with the formation of the Vietnam Refinery Company, shareholders being the government of Vietnam, SOFIDIV (now the Vietnam Development Bank), Esso, Shell, and Caltex. For a variety of reasons, the project as originally conceived (capacity 22,500 barrels a day) has been delayed. Deteriorating security and other complications of the war have been principal reasons for this delay. It is obvious that a refinery will not be built until security improves, and in the meantime the need for a fresh look at the whole problem is evident.

Previous discussion of the project has always been based on consideration of the domestic market for petroleum, oils, and lubricants (P.O.L.), with reexport only of heavy fuel oil. It is the feeling of the Joint Development Group that, in the light of growing Asian markets for which refinery capacity does not exist at present, the possibility of a larger refinery, which would export other finished products, should also be considered. The economics of a reexporting petroleum operation, probably located at Nha Trang and combined with supertanker operation, warrants serious study.

One likely reason why this has not previously been considered feasible is the relative insecurity of Vietnam compared with other Asian locations. It is probable, nevertheless, that even for a refinery oriented solely toward the domestic market, the interested foreign companies whose technical and financial assistance is essential will not be able to participate until security reaches a level that would be required anyway for an export-oriented operation. The government, therefore, would appear to have little to lose in raising its sights on this project somewhat higher than a relatively small domestically oriented refinery. If the larger unit can be achieved, the price of domestic P.O.L. will be lower.

One procedural problem which seems to have delayed the project thus far is the absence of a final decision on a site for the refinery. It is recommended that this decision be made at an early date, for, until it is, further planning will be difficult.

It should be borne in mind that refinery technology is changing rapidly, and a final decision on a refinery leading to engineering design probably will have to be delayed until it is apparent that security will allow final project implementation within a two-year or three-year period.

The use of coal resources other than as fuel for thermal power appears unlikely, unless higher quality deposits are located by future exploration (see section "Three Projects" below).

Nonmetallic Minerals (ISIC 33)

Economies of scale in cement and flat glass production are critical. Flat glass production should be postponed until per capita income rises significantly and a broad market develops. Cement planning is probably second only to fertilizer planning in terms of priorities. A detailed long-range cement program should be developed, including clinker grinding facilities near major markets as well as facilities for production of building materials in which cement is a component. Cement plants can be added in US$10 million or larger units, and clinker grinding in lower cost increments. At present, some clinker grinding is feasible, based on imported clinker, but this program should be integrated with a definitive cement production program. Improvement of the technical management of the present public cement monopoly and long-range production and market planning are both badly needed. Sale of existing capacity to the private sector (to be repaid from profits, with prices controlled by import duties) might stimulate both.

Additional exploration for nonmetallic minerals is warranted, with particular emphasis on their quality.

Base Metals Manufacture (ISIC 34)

Economies of scale are critical for steel, aluminum, and copper metal production, and the development of these units should be postponed for several years. Backward integration from aluminum and copper products should and will develop slowly, with one unlikely exception--massive production of aluminum from imported bauxite or alumina.

Comparison with Korea, Taiwan, and the Philippines suggests that by the time Vietnam's manufacturing value added equals $500 million (perhaps 1978), the country will be consuming about 250,000 tons per year of basic steel. This is approximately the size of a direct reduction furnace (using oil or gas as the reducing agent, rather than coal). Technological developments in direct reduction should be followed closely through about 1975, at which time an investment decision might be possible. Unless iron ore is located, ore or pellets will have to be imported, probably from Australia. Meanwhile, rolling might be developed in the early 1970's, using imported billets and skelp, but the rolling facilities will have to be designed carefully or they probably will become obsolete when an integrated mill begins to operate.

For some time, scrap will be a major source of Vietnamese steel, based on electric furnaces if cheap power is available. Scrap is an important resource in Vietnam and its use should be planned wisely. Small inefficient units should not be financed with public funds, and current plans should be postponed until a long-range plan for the metals sector is developed.

Metal Products (ISIC 35)

Care should be taken not to finance a proliferation of structural metal, wire, and pipe mills. One, or at most two, efficient and flexible producers will be needed in each category, and mills should be designed for 1978 markets. Some lines of equipment in the structural metal mills and an efficient pipe mill could be added later in the period. In any event, the structural metal mill should be integrated with rolling facilities.

Low-cost metal products are essential to rapid development of all of the following sectors.

Machinery, Excluding Electrical (ISIC 36)

Production in selected lines will expand with assembly of a number of items of common usage, such as water pumps and agricultural tools. This is already occurring. Backward integration may take place as demand grows, with an increasing number of parts being manufactured domestically.

Special technical knowledge and adequate markets will both be required for complex machinery; technological assistance should come from licenses or joint ventures with foreign firms. Markets can be developed by low input duties where future manufacturing opportunities are greatest.

Detailed planning for the machinery sector could begin after 1972, including planning for production of certain consumer durables, the production of which would not be well advised at present. As with many other sectors, high quality standards will be important.

Electrical Machinery and Equipment (ISIC 37)

Economies of scale are important for all electrical equipment and machinery not now produced in Vietnam, except for simple assembly operations. In general, for communications equipment (radios, television, telephone and switching equipment), models and makes of equipment should be limited and an assembly program developed, with backward integration into manufacture of parts as technological ability improves and markets expand. Planning for consumer durables should be deferred until the mid-1970's.

Transportation Equipment and Vehicles (ISIC 38)

Manufacture of major auto and truck components and assembly should be deferred. Detailed planning can start about 1975, although some manufacture of truck bodies, of three-wheeled trucks, and possibly of bus bodies could start at an earlier date.

Assembly and production of cars and vehicles (if limited to a few makes and models) might be contemplated by 1980. Preferably, the makes and models of trucks and cars imported in 1970 and after should be limited to these makes and models, in order to facilitate component spare parts production. This will be difficult to enforce in the absence of long-range production plans, but it is most desirable to control the number of models of cars and truck and bus chassis whenever possible. Agreements with foreign manufacturers therefore should be negotiated in the early postwar years. Car imports and ultimate production might be limited in general to small cars in order to conserve foreign exchange.

Bicycles and motorcycle assembly and expanded manufacture of parts can proceed rapidly because of present demand levels; but, again, makes and models should be limited, and joint ventures should be sought.

Present shipbuilding capacity should be adequate for the domestic fleet, and could eventually supply ocean-going fishing vessels as well. Technical assistance will be required for the latter.

Production of railroad equipment is not contemplated. It is unlikely, on world-wide trends in countries of similar stages of growth, that railroad transportation will play a major role in the postwar era.

Miscellaneous Manufactures (ISIC 39)

As per capita incomes rise in, say, five years after the war, natural market forces will permit development of many miscellaneous products on a substantial scale (plastic household goods and toys, signs, jewelry, watch assembly, and many other goods). The number of models of items such as watches needs to be limited, and this might best be done by appropriate tariff policies. Detailed planning for the sector should be initiated early in the postwar period.

Investment Summary and Schedule

The investment schedule for bringing about a manufacturing-added value exceeding US$500 million at market prices is estimated to be as shown in Table 9.12.

TABLE 9.12

Estimated Peacetime Investment Schedule for Manufacturing-Added Value Over US$500 Million

Period of Investment	Investment (US$ Millions Equivalent)
First two peacetime years	108
Second two peacetime years	164
Third two peacetime years	174
Fourth two peacetime years	303
Total	749

(Details are shown in Table 9.16.) These estimates assume that substantial exports will be attained, and in this case value added in manufacturing will be about US$593 million in 1978, the year chosen for the study projections. If such exports are not attained, value added will reach only US$523 million by 1978, and the level of total investment during the 1970-77 period will drop to about US$641 million.

With successful development of exports, foreign exchange requirements for fixed capital will total about US$443 million for the eight-year period, or, without exports, US$377 million. A rough breakdown of foreign exchange requirements by subsector is included in Table 9.16.

In summary, fixed capital investment requirements for the 1970-77 period will be as shown in Table 9.13.

TABLE 9.13

Fixed Capital Investment Requirements, 1970-77
(US$ Millions)

Investment Component	Domestic Markets and Exports	Domestic Market Only
Total fixed investment	749	641
Foreign exchange component	443	377
Value added 1978 (annual rate)	593	523

Some first-priority decisions requiring immediate attention involve large expenditures in the first two years of peace. These are concerned with the following branches of manufacturing industry:

1. Fertilizers
2. Cement
3. Textiles and apparel (selective)
4. Fruit and vegetable canning and other food products
5. Plywood manufacture
6. Pulp and paper (for investment in 1972 and 1973, but early action is desirable)
7. Fish and fish products processing

Decisions should also be taken, as a matter of second priority, concerning:

8. Sugar production and refining
9. Meat products
10. Textiles and apparel (including synthetics)
11. Pharmaceuticals
12. Fats and oils processing
13. Flat glass manufacture
14. Initiation of an oil refinery project
15. Minor transport vehicle assembly

Important investment decisions that probably should be delayed until well into the 1970's are:

16. Basic iron and steel production
17. Synthetic fiber raw materials
18. Plastic raw materials
19. Soda ash
20. Nonferrous metals
21. Heavy metal products
22. Heavy machinery
23. Most electrical machinery and equipment
24. Production of vehicles and vehicle components
25. A second round of sugar production and refining
26. Meat processing for export

For the major products listed in Table 9.15 as exhibiting crucial properties of economies of scale, it is important not only to prevent installation of plants that are too small, but also to design capacities for what demand will be in 5 to 6 years after a plant first goes into production, rather than for demand in the first year or two. For example, in oil refinery design it is cheaper in the average developing country to design the refinery for 7-8 years in the future (2 years construction plus 5-6 years). The exact period will depend on the interest rate and economies of scale, but the 5-6 year rule appears to be applicable for the major products listed in Table 9.15. This rule is relevant even when foreign exchange is considered as well as total cost.

It will be necessary to allow imports when investment decisions are postponed, but the over-all foreign exchange cost (discounted in the long run) will invariably be less if the goal is large production units than if small plants are built and small-capacity additions are frequently made. It is our conviction that if Vietnam wishes to develop a competitive economy by the end of the 1970's, the policies outlined in this chapter are the ones it should follow.

THREE PROJECTS FOR IMMEDIATE CONSIDERATION

The Production of Nitrogen Fertilizer

Previous studies have examined the question of the production of nitrogen fertilizer in detail, including long-term recommendations for developing a fertilizer industry.* Our intention here is not to duplicate the works of others but to supplement them and support the case for an ammonia-urea fertilizer complex in the Mekong Delta. It has been pointed out in the aforementioned studies that, given world prices for the finished products and raw materials, production of phosphatic and potash fertilizers in Vietnam is not justified, and these fertilizers will not be considered here.

Markets for Nitrogenous Fertilizers

Nitrogenous fertilizer distribution (and, presumably, consumption) in the 1967 and 1968 crop years totaled 54,000 MT and 62,000 (estimated) MT respectively (nitrogen content). These figures are below the 1967 Tennessee Valley Authority (TVA) projections, but despite the effects of the war are considerably higher than those of previous years. Continuing growth in nitrogen consumption is expected, with several factors contributing now and in the future to the upward trend: (1) the recent opening of distribution channels and relaxation of price controls; (2) the introduction of improved rice varieties, IR-8 and IR-5; (3) maintenance of a favorable rice/fertilizer price ratio; and (4) the establishment of a credit system by the ADB to finance the needs of the agricultural sector.**

---

*J. R. Douglas, Jr., John A. Burnett, Jr., and William N. Sutherland, South Vietnam: An Evaluation of the Fertilizer Industry (Tennessee Valley Authority, 1967); J. R. Douglas, Jr., Follow-up Report on South Vietnam's Fertilizer Industry (Tennessee Valley Authority, 1968).

**Ibid.

The 1967 TVA report projected 1972 nitrogen consumption at 130,000 MT, rising to 180,000 MT by 1977. There is every likelihood that these estimates will be exceeded, particularly in light of the proposed water control program in the Mekong Delta, the first effects of which could be felt by 1975. The addendum to the TVA report points out that fertilizer use could double or triple in a very short period of time, and the Joint Development Group shares this optimism. The 1972 and 1977 estimates therefore will be taken as minimum figures for purposes of this analysis.

Allowing four years for feasibility studies, plant construction, and attainment of adequate security, it is likely to be at least 1973 before fertilizer production could begin in Vietnam. A plant should be designed to satisfy consumption estimated for about six years after start-up (or 1979), so that construction of a complex with a capacity of 200,000 MT of nitrogen per annum would not appear unreasonable. With urea as the source of nitrogen, an equivalent ammonia-urea complex would have a capacity of about 430,000 MT of urea per annum.

Urea Production

The 1967 TVA report recommended completion of the An Hoa/Nong Son industrial complex, which would provide a portion of nitrogen fertilizer requirements, and further recommended that consideration be given to a second ammonia-urea complex to be built in the Mekong Delta, with a capacity of 297,000 tons of urea per annum. In the 1968 TVA addendum, the delta complex was again suggested for consideration, and a firm recommendation was made that a bulk blending and bagging facility be installed as soon as possible at Can Tho to serve as the first stage in building up a Vietnamese fertilizer industry at that location. The Joint Development Group concurs with the 1968 recommendations, but suggests that a realistic time schedule for initiating urea production, plus the previous estimates of nitrogen consumption, indicate that a much larger ammonia-urea complex should be considered; that is, about 430,000 metric tons of urea per annum. An additional reason for considering a larger complex is the fact that the future production of urea at An Hoa, for reasons that are described further below, is unlikely.

None of the above statements are meant to suggest that a smaller delta ammonia-urea complex would not be economic. All evidence points to the contrary, as illustrated in Table 9.14.

TABLE 9.14

Average Production Costs, Urea, by Rate of Return and Production Rate (US$ pcr MT)

Rate of Return[b] on Investment	Average Urea Production Costs[a] 500 Mt/day (160,000 Mt/yr)	700 Mt/day (231,000 Mt/yr)	900 Mt/da (297,000 Mt/yr
8%	96	76	65
12%	106	84	71
16%	116	91	76

[a]Computed from TVA cost estimates.
[b]Strictly speaking, rate of profit, since interest at 6% has been included in the cost figures.

The most recent c.i.f. price of imported fertilizer in Vietnam (without subsidies) has been US$100 MT, having fallen as low as US$92 in 1968. The average price on a year-round basis is not expected to go below US$95. Thus, for any of the rates of return shown in Table 9.14, average production costs at 700 Mt/day (231,000 Mt/year) would be below the lowest probable import price. Consumption is expected to exceed 231,000 Mt before 1972, so that the fertilizer complex should probably be economic from the very beginning (1973), even if consumption were to fall below the TVA estimates by as much as 30 percent.

In the light of postwar uncertainties and possible problems of capital availability, there may be attractions in considering implementation of the delta complex as recommended by the TVA, that is on a scale of 297,000 tons per annum. Nevertheless, it is quite possible that future domestic demands for nitrogen will support an ammonia-urea complex perhaps 50 percent larger than the one under discussion. At the higher level of production, resulting unit costs could be significantly lower.

It is suggested, therefore, that development of the fertilizer industry proceed along the lines of the 1968 TVA recommendations, but that feasibility studies be carried out for both the 900

TABLE 9.15

Projection of Major Manufactures, 1978, and General Strategy for Development

(In parentheses: total output if substantial exports attained)

ISIC	Sector	Value Added (US$ Millions)	Value of Sales (US$ Millions)	Amount per year (MT thous.)
20-39	Total Manufacturing	523(593)	1325(1527)	
20	Food Products	71(93)	170(230)	
	Sugar processing and refining (priority)	20(30)	40(60)	270(400)
	Fruit and vegetable canning (priority)	1(12)	3(31)	(45)
	Dairy processing	5	16	70 (processed milk)
	Meat processing (priority)	1(2)	3(6)	200(400)
	Fats and oils (see chemicals) (priority)	3(6)	9(18)	70
	Starch	1	3	10
	Rice milling	10	33	
	Flour milling (wheat)	5	20	200
	Animal feeds (priority)			130

(Con't)

TABLE 9.15 (Con't)

Importance of Economies of Scale	Export Potential	Remarks on Development Strategy
Critical for exports	Competitive market	Minimum plant investment $10 Million; depends on agricultural program, U.S. quotas, and achieving world competitive position.
Important	Substantial markets	Requires modern processing plants, coordinated agricultural program (pineapples: 1 million std. cases; mushrooms: 200,000 std. cases.)
Important	Doubtful	Requires a global meat and dairy program, plus efficient plants. One modern plant already installed.
Important	Possible markets	Requires global plan. Large, modern meat processing and freezing, and by-product recovery.
Important	Possible markets	Requires large modern solvent extraction units.
Moderate	Possible markets	
Important	None	Large efficient mills would reduce price to consumers.
	Limited	Requires careful coordination with agricultural programs.

ISIC	Sector	Value Added	Value of Sales	Amount per year (MT thous.)
		(US$ Millions)		
	Fish processing and salting			30 (minimum)
	Tea processing			
	Miscellaneous, mono-sodium glutamate, yeast			
21	Beverage Industries	45	96	
	Wines, spirits, beer	40		
	Soft drinks	5		
22	Tobacco Manufactures	50	90	
	Cigarettes	47	84	
23	Textile Manufactures	50	152	
	Cotton Textiles and fabrics	27	94	70(80)
	Spinning (yarn) (priority)	10	31	50
	Weaving (priority)	13	51	
	Finishing (priority)	4	12	
	Synthetic and rayon textiles & fabrics	8	24	
	Spinning			15
	Fabrics (priority)			
	Silk fabrics			
	Wool textiles and fabrics	3	10	
	Yarn	2	7	1
	Fabrics	1	3	
	Jute and other bags	4	12	
	Knitting mill products	4	13	
	Twine	2	8	2

(Con't)

TABLE 9.15 (Con't)

Importance of Economies of Scale	Export Potential	Remarks on Development Strategy
	Limited	(Fish catch estimated at 500,000 T/Y).
		20,000 T/Y of tea processed.
		5,000 T/Y MSG, and 2,000 T/Y yeast.
	Limited	Natural competitive forces should develop sector. Efficient competitive units needed. (Beer production estimated at 400,000 hl, other alcoholic beverages 800,000 hl).
	"	
	None	
	None	Tobacco production estimated at 30,000 T/Y. Cigarettes: 20 billion units per year. Efficient production units will automatically result.
Critical	Limited	Large efficient integrated plants required. (250,000 continuous spindles vs. 100,000 existing). 200 million meters, 10,000 automatic looms.
"		
"		
"		
Important	Limited	
"		
		75 million meters.
	Limited	2,000 meters.
	"	
Important		
		2 million meters.
	"	
	-	
	-	

ISIC	Sector	Value Added (US$ Millions)	Value of Sales (US$ Millions)	Amount per year (MT thous.)
24	Apparel, shoes	18	48	
	Men's clothing	6	17	
	Women's clothing	2	5	
	Underwear	4	14	
	Leather shoes	3	7	
	Shirts (ready made)	(Incl. above)	10	
	Dresses (ready made)	(")	2	
	Rubber and canvas shoes			
25	Wood and Wood Products	19(23)	65(80)	
	Sawn lumber	11	46	
	Plywood, veneer	5	14	
	Hardboard, particle board	- (4)	- (12)	
26	Furniture	5(7)	13(18)	
	Chairs, desks, beds, chests, etc. of wood	4(6)	11(16)	
27	Paper, Pulp, and Paper Products	26(38)	51(67)	
	Pulp, newsprint	6(18)	17(46)	90(270)
	Chemical pulp	4(12)	12(30)	60(150)
	Newsprint	2(6)	5(16)	30(120)
	Paper, writing, wrapping Paper, Kraft	5	20	100
	Paperboard, boxboard, containers	5	14	30

(Con't)

TABLE 9.15 (Con't)

Importance of Economies of Scale	Export Potential	Remarks on Development Strategy
Moderate	None	Large efficient units should eventually develop.
	"	
Moderate	"	2 million dozen.
"	Possible	Requires careful planning of cattle and leather sectors (650,000 pairs men's, 1,700,000 pairs women's, 550,000 pairs children's).
"	None	1.5 million dozen.
"	"	0.5 million dozen.
		3 million dozen.
	Good	Includes some wood and plywood exports in estimate.
Moderate	"	Production estimate 1 million cubic meters.
Important	Competitive	30 million square meters.
Critical	Difficult Entry	
Not Impt.	Feasible	Requires modern industry, good design, and standards.
	"	" " " " " "
		Estimate of $19 million value added includes some exports.
Critical	Feasible	Requires a 150,000-200,000 T/Y integrated pulp and paper mill with investment of $40 million or more.
"	"	
"	"	
	No	
Important	Limited	Production in integrated mill.
Moderate	No	

ISIC	Sector	Value Added	Value of Sales	Amount per year (MT thous.)
		(US$ Millions)		
28	Printing, Publishing, etc.	15	32	
29	Leather Products (Except Furniture)	2	8	
	Tanneries	1	3	
	Shoes, luggage	1	5	
30	Rubber Products	10	34	
	Tires, tubes	5	17	
	Other rubber products	5	17	
31	Manufacture of Chemicals and Chemical Products	63(71)	176(203)	
	Fertilizers (priority project)	16(20)	36(45)	300
	Nitrogen and mixed (N content)	11(15)	21(30)	200
	Phosphate and mixed (P_2O_5 content)	3	9	60
	Potash and mixed (K_2O content)	2	6	40
	Plastic polymers, PVC, PE, PS, etc.	4	10	15
	Explosives, ammonium nitrate, etc.	1	3	5
	Soda Ash	1	3	50
	Caustic soda/chlorine	1	3	30/27
	Sulfuric acid	--	1	30
	Salt (industrial)	1	3	50
	Salt (total)			
	Industrial gases	1	3	

(Con't)

TABLE 9.15 (Con't)

Importance of Economies of Scale	Export Potential	Remarks on Development Strategy
No	No	Newspapers, periodicals, books, etc. Natural forces will develop the sector.
Moderate	Limited	1 million square meters of leather, modern tanneries. (See note under footwear, apparel).
Important	Possible	300,000 tires; 300,000 tubes.
		Based on some exports of urea initially.
Crucial	Feasible	Minimum size plant 140,000 T/Y nitrogen from urea.
Important	Doubtful	Based on imported phosphate, until local material located.
Moderate	None	Based on imported potash, until local material located.
Crucial	None	Based on imported intermediates through 1975.
Important	Doubtful	Based on ammonium nitrate from fertilizer plant.
Crucial	None	Delay-requires large glass markets, cheap salt.
"	Possible	Delay until 1970; basic cheap power and salt.
Important	None	Possibly utilize existing plant from obsolete An Hoa fertilizer complex.
Important	Doubtful	Depends on caustic soda and soda ash projects.
		Total demand 500,000 tons.
Important	Doubtful	Integrated industrial gas plant required.

ISIC	Sector	Value Added	Value of Sales	Amount per year
		(US$ Millions)		(MT thous.)
31	Manufacture of Chemicals (Continued)			
	Synthetic fibers	3	12	5
	Ethyl alcohol, molasses (cattle feed)	1	3	10
	Naval stores, turpentine, gum	(1)	(3)	
	Charcoal	1	2	
	Petrochemicals (ethylene, and propylene based.)			5-10
	Fats and oils	3(6)	9(18)	25(50)
	Paints, varnish, lacquers	2.5	9	
	Pharmaceuticals, medicines	12.5	25	
	Soaps and detergents	4	14	40
	Agricultural chemicals	2	5	
32	Petroleum and Coal Products	25(50)	64(128)	
	Oil refinery products	20(40)	48(96)	2000(4000)
	Coal products	3	12	
33	Nonmetallic Minerals	32(33)	64(66)	
	Cement	13	26	1300
	Glass, flat	1.5	3	

(Con't)

TABLE 9.15 (Con't)

Importance of Economies of Scale	Export Potential	Remarks on Development Strategy
Crucial	None	Based on imported chemicals through 1975.
By-product	Feasible	Sugar by-products, rice by-products.
Moderate	"	Dependent on forestry program.
-	None	Dependent on forestry program.
Crucial	None	Petroleum refinery by-products (delay until 1977).
Important	Feasible	(See food products); modern solvent extract plant and integrated agricultural program required.
Moderate	None	Several flexible competitive producers required.
Moderate	Limited	Special study required for this sector.
Moderate	Doubtful	Synthetic detergents based on imported dodesylbenzene.
Important	Doubtful	Based on imported intermediates; low production costs required.
Crucial	Feasible	Priority postwar project; export markets important.
Moderate	None	Use primarily for thermal power.
Crucial		200,000 T/Y or larger plants, dispersal of clinker grinding.
Crucial	None	Delay until 1975-77; lead bath process desirable.

ISIC	Sector	Value Added (US$ Millions)	Value of Sales (US$ Millions)	Amount per year (MT thous.)
33	Nonmetallic Minerals (Continued)			
	Glass, containers	3	8	
	Bricks, clay, tile	4	7	
	Concrete products	4.5	11	
	Lime (as needed by agriculture)	.5-1.5	1 - 3	30(90)
	Clays, kaolin, etc.	1(2)	2(4)	
34	Base Metal Manufacture	19(20)	65(67)	
	Basic iron and steel mills	8	28	250
	rerolling of imports	(Inc. above)		
	foundries	2	8	10
	Aluminum	1	4	7
	Copper	1	4	2
	Ferroalloys	(1)	(2)	10
35	Manufacture of Metal Products, Except Machinery	18	52	
	Structural products and shapes	3	11	
	Wire nails and other wire products	3	10	30
	Tin cans	1	5	

(Con't)

TABLE 9.15 (Con't)

Importance of Economies of Scale	Export Potential	Remarks on Development Strategy
		Efficient plants located near main markets.
		Geographical location important, modern plants.
		Strategic location of efficient plants.
Moderate	None	Agricultural and construction requirements important.
Moderate	Possible	Depends on exploration activities.
Crucial		Delay until direct reduction process costs decline.
Important		Base industry on imported skelp, etc.
Moderate		Efficient modern plants required.
Crucial	None	Delay until after 1977; import aluminum metal.
Crucial	None	Delay until after 1977; import refined copper metal.
Moderate	Possible	Feasible with cheap power if chrome, nickel, etc. found.
Important		One or two modern efficient producers.
Moderate		" " " " "
		Manufacture products, but not tinplate.

ISIC	Sector	Value Added (US$ Millions)	Value of Sales (US$ Millions)	Amount per year (MT thous.)
35	Manufacture of Metal Products, Except Machinery (Continued)			
	Miscellaneous metal products (incl. agricultural and hand tools)	5	13	
	Cast iron pipe			10
36	Machinery, Except Electrical	11	30	50
	Pumps; water, deep well, etc. motors	2	5	
	Agricultural machinery	2	5	
	Special machinery, textile, food	2	5	
	Office equipment	1	5	
37	Electrical Machinery and Equipment	17	47	
	Radios, TV, receivers	3	9	
	Telephone & communications equip.	1	5	
	Light bulbs	3	7	
	Batteries	2	5	
	Electric wire and cable	1	4	
	Distribution and control equip.	1	3	
	Refrigerator and air conditioners	3	12	

(Con't)

TABLE 9.15 (Con't)

Importance of Economies of Scale	Export Potential	Remarks on Development Strategy
		Flexible product facilities desirable.
		Pipe factory 1975-77.
Important	None	Start with assembly of a few models only of each item and integrate backward, using low tariff policy to prevent premature production; utilize foreign licenses, franchises, or ownership wherever possible.
	"	
	"	
	"	
	"	
	None	Hold entry to limited number of qualified firms.
"	"	Start with assembly of only a few models and integrate backwards, 250,000 radio receivers; 30,000 TV receivers.
"	"	200,000 telephones, standardize, 1 or 2 producers. Start with assembly after 1975.
"	Limited	One efficient major producer, initiate in 1972; 5 million units.
Moderate	Limited	100,000 units, standardize.
Important	"	One efficient major producer.
"	None	" " " "
"	"	Start with assembly of a few models (1975); 10,000 units.

ISIC	Sector	Value Added	Value of Sales	Amount per year (MT thous.)
		(US$ Millions)		
37	Electrical Machinery and Equipment (Continued)			
	Miscellaneous electrical supplies	1	3	
	(Basis: 800,000 kw installed capacity in 1978, 4 billion kwh/year generation).			
38	Transportation Equipment and Vehicles	15	45	
	Motor vehicles, assembly (3-wheeled trucks, etc.)	6	24	
	Motor vehicles, parts and repairs	2	5	
	Bicycles and motor-cycles	3	8	
	Shipbuilding	3	7	
39	Miscellaneous Manufactures	12	30	
	Matches, clocks	1	3	
	Plastic toys and end products	3	12	

(Con't)

TABLE 9.15 (Con't)

Importance of Economies of Scale	Export Potential	Remarks on Development Strategy
Important	None	Flexible production units.
Crucial	None	Initially limit assembly to truck bodies, control models, consider assembly policy in 1973; stock (1978) 200,000 vehicles, production (1978) 30,000 vehicles/year (15,000 cars, 15,000 commercial vehicles); make some parts.
"	None	
Moderate	"	Limit entry to a few qualified firms, 30,000 units/year.
"	"	Primarily for domestic fleet, 5,000 gross tons/year. (Merchant fleet estimated at 300,000 GWT but international fleet would be purchased or leased).
Important	Doubtful	Clock assembly limited number of makes.
Not Impt.	"	Natural forces can develop sector.

TABLE 9.16

Estimated Investment Requirements for Fixed Assets
in Manufacturing, 1970-77
(millions of current US$)

ISIC	Sector	Domestic Markets Only		Domestic Markets plus Exports					
						Approximate Breakdown of Total			
		Foreign Exchange	Total	Foreign Exchange	Total	70-71	72-73	74-75	76-77
	All Sectors	377	641	443	749	108	164	174	303
20	Food prod.	37	77	60	117	13	21	33	50
21	Beverages	7	17	7	17	2	3	5	7
22	Tobacco	9	24	9	24	4	5	7	8
23	Textiles	34	55	34	55	8	15	17	15
24	Apparel, etc.	5	10	5	10	2	3	3	2
25	Wood Prod.	14	25	19	33	8	3	9	13
26	Furniture	1	3	2	6	1	1	1	3
27	Pulp, paper	32	53	45	73	3	30	25	15
28	Printing	4	10	4	10	1	2	3	4
29	Leather	1	2	1	2		1		1
30	Rubber	7	12	7	12	1	3	4	4
31	Chemicals	73	117	82	132	33	39	18	42
32	Petroleum, coal	29	41	44	63		2	15	46
33	Nonmet. min.	28	45	28	45	15	7	7	16
34	Base metals	24	35	24	35	2	3	3	27
35	Metal prod.	20	33	20	33	5	6	11	11
36	Machinery	17	25	17	25	2	4	6	13
37	Electrical	17	25	17	25	2	8	2	13
38	Transport	14	23	14	23	5	6	2	10
39	Miscellaneous	4	9	4	9	1	2	3	3

Mt/day ammonia-urea complex and a larger complex with a capacity of 1,400 Mt/day. A final decision on plant size can be made when security permits and the future market situation is clearer. Work should begin at an early date to assure minimum delay in project implementation. Plans should be carried as far as possible on paper so that construction can begin soon after security is judged to be satisfactory. There seems to be little reason to delay the feasibility assessments.

In planning there must be careful consideration given to rapidly changing fertilizer technology, and an efficient industry cannot be designed without the active participation of foreign fertilizer producers. The project can best be carried out as a joint venture between Vietnamese interests and an experienced overseas firm, with public financial participation required only to the extent that private Vietnamese capital or overseas assistance is not forthcoming. This is not to say that the government should not play an active role in developing the industry, but merely that it should not attempt to control its operation. Decisions on production, pricing, raw material supply, and so on should be left to project management within the confines of explicit guidelines decided upon before construction between the management and the government. This is the only way that an efficient industry can be assured.

Related to this subject is the present structure of fertilizer prices, in which urea is imported at a subsidized rate of exchange. The effective price of urea going into the distribution system therefore is artificially low and domestically produced fertilizer could not compete at this price. If the government wishes to keep retail prices below a certain level, it should do so in the form of a subsidy to domestic producers who should not be made to compete with subsidized imports. Given an efficient industry, with unit costs lower than unsubsidized import prices, a subsidy to domestic producers would represent a lower cost in terms of government of Vietnam resources than the subsidy now granted to importers.

The An Hoa/Nong Son Industrial Complex

A brief account of what the An Hoa/Nong Son project was intended to consist of is given in Chapter 12, and a much fuller account in the 1967 TVA report already referred to.

There could be no more vivid example of the economic consequences of the war than this project, in progress but never achieved, for almost ten years. The security situation in the An Hoa area prevents further construction at this time, but there are other reasons to question the wisdom of continuing the project even when security can be assured. The technology used is out of date. Much of the equipment, in storage for years past in Saigon, has deteriorated, and it is believed that some was actually destroyed in the enemy offensives of Tet and May, 1968. Given the present state of the war and the negotiations, the complex could not possibly be brought into production before 1970, and to do that another US$17 million would have to be spent to supplement US$33 million worth of existing equipment, which is now ten years old and obsolete. If the complex were to go into production, its fertilizer production costs would be extremely high, more than farmers could possibly pay without greatly increased government subsidies. On an impartial review of all the facts, the project simply does not appear to be economically feasible.

On purely economic grounds there is therefore only one possible recommendation:- that a determined effort be made to see what can be salvaged. Although the great part of previous expenditures may have to be written off, an attempt could be made to renegotiate the loans made by French and German interests; and the not inconsiderable number of men who have been trained for the project--engineers, technicians, and managers--will be a valuable asset to a modern fertilizer industry in a more suitable location. Some of the existing plant, to the extent that its condition permits, may have other uses. The steam plant, electrical generating equipment, and transmission lines could still be used to supply power for Da Nang, and the sulfuric acid plant, which is a self-contained unit, if it is intact, can be put into production elsewhere. (If the capital costs of the sulfuric acid plant are to be written off--as they should be--it can probably operate economically.) The most likely use for the Nong Son coal, once it is secure, is as a source of thermal electric power for the northern provinces, though it must be recognized that alternative sources of possibly lower-cost power exist. For the US$17 million of additional investment necessary to bring the An Hoa complex into production, there certainly are several alternative, more profitable (and more beneficial to the people) uses in the I Corps Tactical Zone. Several of them are suggested in Chapter 12.

Some members of the Joint Development Group, though they subscribe to the economic arguments against proceeding with the An Hoa complex as it was originally conceived, properly represent that there are more than economic arguments to be taken into account. They are concerned by the possibility of public disappointment if the principal feature of the An Hoa complex, the fertilizer plant, is discontinued, and by the loss of employment opportunities in a region where postwar unemployment may be serious. Certainly the most strenuous efforts must be made to place in renumerative employment all workers, skilled and unskilled, who have been engaged on this project.

The choice is not an easy one. It lies between recognizing that much money may have been lost on a project initiated by a previous government which was not economically feasible (but saving as much of the investment as can be used in other, economically feasible operations), and spending additional scarce investment capital for uncertain returns on what are substantially political considerations. It is recommended that the government consider the arguments on both sides and decide where the public interest best lies.

The Manufacture and Export of Wood Pulp

In Chapter 8 the potential of Vietnam's forest resources has been identified, and reference has been made to the attractive possibilities for developing prosperous forest-based industries. It is important at this stage to identify the initial steps to be taken in a long-term program for forest exploitation yielding maximum long-term returns to the national economy.

A project which should be given immediate consideration is the development of an export-oriented pulp manufacturing industry to produce long-fiber bleached sulfate wood pulp. The attraction of the project rests on the coniferous timber resources of Vietnam and a market for wood pulp elsewhere in Asia.

Availability of Timber Resources

The timber resources for this project are the hardwood forests of Vietnam and the pine forests found principally in the province of Tuyen Duc. The area of the pine forests has been calculated from aerial photographs as 180,000 hectares (444,600 acres), and the available volume of pine wood has been calculated from ground surveys as at least 5 million cubic meters. The Forestry Administration of the Ministry of Agriculture and the Forestry Branch of U.S. AID have together undertaken to study this forest again for more precise estimates of area, volume, and growth.

Economies of scale are most important in the manufacture of pulp: to be competitive, a mill must produce a minimum of 100,000 tons a year. Using a conversion factor of 4.5 cubic meters of wood to one ton of sulfate pulp, the mill we propose will use 450,000 cubic meters of wood a year for a production target of this order. Three-quarters of this volume, or 337,500 cubic meters, must be coniferous. The other quarter can be mixed tropical hardwoods, which are quite suitable for sulfate pulp and are available in ample volume.

It is important to confirm that adequate volumes of coniferous wood are available for a mill of 100,000 tons capacity. In part, this will depend on the government's policy for the sale of timber from public lands. A pulp industry will require very large capital investment and must operate at almost full capacity continuously. The pine-wood requirements for pulp manufacture therefore must have priority over all other uses, with the possible exception of 60,000 cubic meters a year needed for treated electric transmission poles. If available, additional coniferous timber also could be used for sawmills, but these needs can be considered secondary, particularly since other types of timber can be used for sawn wood.

The inventory now under way will be more accurate and detailed than previous studies; the expectation is that it will confirm the volumes of available coniferous wood assumed above. A period of twenty years is assumed as appropriate for depreciation and debenture retirement, coinciding with the cutting cycle of pine trees. The supplies of pine required by the project for two decades (until a new supply grows) are thus 337,500 per annum, or 6,750,000 cubic meters over twenty years. Of this quantity, 5,000,000 cubic meters are presently standing. The remaining 1,750,000 cubic meters will be derived from half the net annual increment of growth of the existing trees over twenty years. The breakdown is thus:

Hardwood	2,250,000 cubic meters
Standing pine	5,000,000 cubic meters
Increment on pine	1,750,000 cubic meters
Total	9,000,000 cubic meters

The apparent abundance, low cost, and accessibility of this wood are important attractions to investment; it is essential that the government carefully maintain these attractions by offering the wood on realistic terms. This subject will be covered further later in this section.

Export Markets and Investment Strategy

On available information there would appear to be little doubt that the best market for chemical pulp of Vietnamese manufacture will be in Japan, although it may be possible to identify other markets in southeast Asia after further investigation. Because of the large investment involved in a pulp mill and the resulting necessity to provide assured markets for the mill, it will be advantageous to provide a direct link between Vietnamese pulp production and major export markets through equity participation by firms which are part of those markets. Given the present world market for pulp, an obvious link is with Japan.

Japan's deficit of chemical pulp was 14,000 metric tons in 1955 and 299,000 tons in 1965, and it will be 1,344,000 tons in 1975. That nation's 660-odd paper mills have extended themselves beyond the country's capacity to produce basic raw material. The industry therefore is faced with the necessity of developing sources of such materials in other countries.

Natural forests and other sources of pulping material are very common in southeast Asia; but the coniferous component that yields high-value, long-fiber pulp covers only 10 percent of these forests, and often stands in remote and scattered units. Vietnam's coniferous forest is compact and is near the coast. Moreover, the unfilled demand for paper in Malaysia, Singapore, Indonesia, and the Philippines will be 430,000 tons in 1970. These countries are unlikely to become sources of pulp supplies to Japan and other importing nations.

If a pulp project can attract foreign equity capital, it will be assured a portion of the growing world markets; but if these markets are not linked directly to the project through equity participation and shared risk, it will be more difficult to guarantee that the export market will be retained throughout the life of the project.

In this situation, a pulp project provides an important opportunity for foreign assistance to be utilized effectively. The project would most suitably be organized as a joint effort by Vietnamese interests and an experienced foreign company.

Project Specifications

Because of present limitations on coniferous wood supplies, the size of the proposed mill should be limited for the present to 100,000 tons of chemical pulp a year. Its size can be increased if volumes of wood available are found to be greater than those presently estimated. A feasible distribution of production would be 60,000 tons a year for export and the remainder for the needs of the paper manufacturing industry in Vietnam.

The volume suggested for export is considered to be the minimum likely to attract foreign participation in the project. From 60,000 tons of pulp exports, the estimated foreign exchange earnings would be US$8-10 million a year. This level of exports should be retained throughout the life of the project, and none of it diverted to domestic use as Vietnamese markets grow. Pulp consumption in Vietnam can be expected to rise to 60,000 tons per annum by 1978. These requirements can be met by 40,000 tons of sulfate pulp from the proposed mill and 20,000 tons from an increase in pulp production from rice, straw, bagasse, bamboo, or hardwoods. If there are deficits they will have to be made up with importation of pulp materials until forest resources are further developed.

The proposed mill should be designed, however, in accordance with the long-term needs of the Vietnamese market, and it should be the first in a series of pulp industry investments aimed both at exports and domestic needs. An important consideration throughout will be the need to integrate paper production with pulp. This will be considered in a feasibility study which we recommend later in this section.

Estimated capital investment in the proposed mill is US$43 million, of which US$35 million is in foreign exchange and the balance in local currency. Working capital is included in these estimates. Assuming equity participation in capitalization of $20 million, about $12 million might be contributed by an overseas interest and $8 million in local currency by Vietnamese sources. The balance of $23 million in debt (all foreign currency) might be financed by direct assistance from foreign governments, by the International Finance Corporation (IFC) or by other agencies.

Wood Costs for the Project

Stumpage, the sale price of standing timber, should be a market price like any other. Where the timber is government-owned, however, no such competitive free-market price can exist. At what price, then, should the government dispose of this public resource?

As stated above, the foreign exchange earnings of the suggested pulp mill are estimated to be about US$9 million a year on a foreign exchange investment component of $35 millions. Because of the attractiveness of long-term foreign exchange earnings from the export of its timber, the government does not have to realize a direct net piaster income on timber sales. In these circumstances the best measure of stumpage value is the cost of replacing the timber used; that is, the cost of replanting and protecting pine plantations until they are again ready for cutting.

This cost can be taken as 12,400 piasters per hectare, according to Vietnamese foresters who have had experience with pine plantations in Tuyen Duc province, where the mill possibly would be located. About three-quarters of the cost represents planting, the rest protection.

A conservative estimate is that the pine forests will yield 30 cubic meters of wood per hectare, so the area cut over each year will be about 12,000 hectares. For two reasons, such an area need not be replanted in its entirety. First, some land will be suitable and needed for agriculture and should be released from the public domain for that purpose. Secondly, other land will be so rough, steep, remote, or infertile that no expenditure should be made in replanting it, though seed trees would be left. If 2,000 hectares a year should fall into these two classes, the area needing planting each year will be 10,000 hectares and the cost would be VN$125 million. A charge of 280 piasters per cubic meter of wood delivered to the mill is thereby indicated for replacement purposes (VN$125 million/450,000 cubic meters), a figure which, although somewhat high, would be reasonably competitive by international standards.

If this principle of charging for wood replacement cost is accepted, then the amount of usable wood per unit area becomes the main factor in raw material costs. Yield not only influences logging costs, but determines the area exploited and therefore the total cost of replanting. One study has indicated a usable volume of 50 cubic meters per hectare, considerably higher than the yield previously mentioned in this chapter. Presumably the trend will be toward higher yields as artificial plantations are established. Insofar as these higher yields are found to be available, they will result in lower total costs of wood delivered to the mill. This cost is the largest single item influencing the manufacture of pulp, and offers the greatest opportunity for savings.

In exchange for cheap and plentiful wood, the government should insist from the beginning upon standards of reforestation that will insure high survival and rapid growth through careful site selection and preparation and superior planting stock. The mean annual increment of plantations will probably reach 10 cubic meters per hectare, with yields of 200 cubic meters per hectare in twenty years. On an assumed 20 percent increase in production over rated capacity, the industry will need 55,000 hectares upon which to grow wood for the second cycle of cutting. The operating company can reasonably be held responsible for physically replanting only 2,750 hectares each year. As for the remaining 7,250 hectares which will need planting each year, there are several choices. The government might organize and finance a semiautonomous public corporation for the purpose on the analogy of those already operating in various European and African countries, or it might entrust this responsibility to a Central Highlands Development Board, as proposed in Chapter 12. Usually such agencies have their own budgets and their own sources of income.

Increased activity in cutting and replanting so large an area will result in radical changes in land use. Forest land will acquire value; and new opportunities will arise for employment in logging and reforestation. To encourage such activity, the government might transfer forest to private hands under leasehold and give subsidies for growing trees. Steady and profitable outlets for available wood and the product of new plantations will create a new source of rural income and development in the private sector of the economy.

Project Summary

The project described above suggests an excellent opportunity to base an efficient pulp industry on foreign technical expertise and financial assistance. It will lead to more efficient utilization of forest resources, and thereby assure increasing production as volumes of usable wood increase with time. The plan further proposes that the industry will have close links with the local economy. Sales of wood will create a wider base for rural prosperity, will promote higher yields of forest resources and will open possibilities for expanding other forest industries. The project will earn considerable sums of foreign exchange, and transform the presently stagnating and unproductive coniferous forest into a highly productive resource closely tied to a dynamic and efficient industry.

The main characteristics of the proposal are as follows:

1. The project should be a joint venture between a foreign company on one side and the Vietnamese government and industry on the other. The former would supply capital, technical knowledge, and marketing assistance. The latter would supply the timber resource, buildings, operating costs, and certain investment costs.

2. The price paid to the government for timber would be sufficient to replant the forest land after cutting.

3. The local share capital would be about 40 percent.

4. Investment incentives would include free importation of machinery, exemption from income taxes during the first ten years, and guaranteed repatriation of profits to the foreign investors.

5. The product would be available for local or foreign sale in proportion to the equity capital contributed.

6. Well designed and well managed, the mill would reach full production three years after start-up.

The competitive advantages of the proposed mill are low-cost wood, water, and power, from which must be subtracted the costs of transporting imported chemicals and the exported product, neither of which should be excessive. Production costs can be reduced further by reducing the cost of delivered wood. If this can be kept below a maximum of US$4.50 per cubic meter, the rate of return on capital probably will be satisfactory. The usable volume of coniferous wood on a given unit of land area will be of crucial importance.

The best location for a large pulp mill may be at Da Nhim in the province of Tuyen Duc. The advantages of this site are the reservoir and hydroelectric plant nearby, the railway and highway, the surrounding coniferous forests, and the neighboring provincial capital city of Dalat.

It is believed that feasibility studies and detailed engineering design will take about two years. Construction will take another two years and approximately three further years will be needed to reach full operation. Thus, if detailed planning begins in 1970, full operation can be reached around 1977. A full seven years lead time should be used in further consideration of this project.

Implementation Strategy

It is clear that the recommended pulp manufacturing facility cannot be built until the forest areas involved become secure. Nevertheless there is a considerable amount of work that can begin immediately to ensure that actual construction can begin with minimum delay when security is achieved.

As a first step, a feasibility study should be undertaken as soon as possible by an experienced foreign firm, preferably one that is interested in participation in the project. The scope of work for the study should cover:

1. Markets; especially products, size, location, price, competition, and suppliers, both domestic and foreign, present and future.

2. Materials: wood quantity, quality, and costs delivered to the mill; replanting schedules and costs; sources and costs of chemicals and other supplies.

3. Manufacturing facilities: plant size, plant location (taking into account wood supply, transport, labor and supervision, housing, medical facilities, amenities, sources and costs of fuel and power, water supply, effluent disposal, communications, and soil conditions), process flowsheet, equipment list and specifications, labor requirements.

4. Economic analysis, including an estimation of initial project costs (plant start-up expense, working capital, and inventories), and operating costs (materials, labor, supervision and management, utilities, taxes, insurance, interest, and depreciation). The analysis should also include pro forma earnings, project effects on the national economy, means of financing, and a time schedule.

The cost of this study is estimated to be US$50,000 and it would take four months to complete after notification to proceed. The costs might appropriately be provided by the Industrial Development Center, and the Joint Development Group could assist in the preparation of terms of reference and selection of a firm to undertake the study.

The Manufacture of Veneer and Plywood for Domestic Use and Export to the United States

A plan for forest resource development should give primary attention to those industries which have a high gross value of output for each unit of material used and for the products of which profitable and expanding markets exist. For plywood, these output values and markets do exist; they are smaller than those for wood pulp, but are greater than those for sawn wood and other wood-based panels such as fiberboard and particle board. Compared with these other basic forest industries, the manufacture of plywood has the highest rate of capital turnover and the highest employment for each unit of material used. For Vietnam, other important criteria to consider are the investment required for each unit of labor employed and for each unit of material processed. In both cases, the investment in plywood is less than that for other panels or wood pulp.

In comparison with other technically advanced industries, a plywood industry can therefore offer high employment and high value added for a moderate investment cost. Not surprisingly, Asian and African countries have increased their shares of world plywood manufactured from broadleaved species, and they have done so very rapidly. This tropical product has been outstandingly successful in competing for markets in European and North American countries, even where vigorous national industries exist. Examples are the large expanding industries of Gabon, Nigeria, and the Philippines, which use their own timber resources; and those in Korea and Taiwan, which process logs from Sabah and the Philippines for re-export as plywood to America. In 1966 this lucrative trade earned over US$30 million each for Korea and Taiwan. In 1953 neither country made plywood. Now, because of the inherent characteristics of the industry, and because of advantages which these countries either possessed or have been able to create and sustain, they are competing very successfully with Japanese and American products. Vietnam should be able to do the same.

Location

Because of the high unit value of the wood used relative to transportation costs from the forest areas, the plywood industry is not dependent on the presence of nearby timber supplies. The principal requisite is access to port facilities to minimize transportation costs on the finished product. Either Saigon, Nha Trang, or Da Nang would be suitable locations in Vietnam. Since it is desirable to promote industrial development outside the Saigon area, and particularly desirable to foster industry in the I Corps Tactical Zone, Da Nang appears to be the first choice.

The manufacture of plywood is labor-intensive compared with other primary forest industries; an annual processing capacity of 1,000 cubic meters of wood employs 7 persons. The plywood mill we propose will process 40,000 cubic meters of logs per year and should be thoroughly competitive with other producers. The resulting employment of about 280 people, while not spectacular, would represent a highly productive use of labor in the surplus labor situation of the northern provinces. More important, a plywood industry would foster the development of logging and tertiary wood-using industries which would absorb significant numbers of additional workers.

It is as a nucleus from which other industries will develop that plywood manufacture is particularly attractive for Da Nang. The total employment provided should, eventually, amount to at least 1,000 jobs.

The success of Taiwan and Korea rests in part upon the use of veneer log cores for joinery and the making of furniture parts. Da Nang will soon have 300,000 people, and offers a ready market for products that do not enter the export trade. The availability of plywood and residues will stimulate building and other wood-using industries.

The Market for Plywood

Although a Vietnamese plywood industry can be aimed at world-wide markets, the most attractive outlet will be the United States. The U.S. market for plywood has grown very fast in recent years, outstripping the ability of U.S. producers to satisfy growing demand. The result has been a market for imported plywood that has been growing at the rate of 14 percent per annum since 1960. In 1965, the U.S. Forest Service pointed out* that since 1947-48, plywood purchases from abroad have multiplied fortyfold, and that rapidly increasing imports of hardwood plywood can be expected in coming decades. The increase from 1965 to 1966 bore out this prediction: 180,000 cubic meters coming mainly from Asia.**

By 1975 it is expected that net U.S. imports of hardwood, plywood, and sawn wood will amount to about 5.5 million cubic meters, more than twice the average annual imports of 1960-62. At the present time--in sharp contrast to the trade to Europe and Japan--practically all these imports enter as plywood and veneer rather than as logs, despite a substantial tariff (20 percent) on these finished products.***

---

*W. C. Siegel and C. Row, U.S. Forest Service Research Paper SO-17, U.S. Hardwood Imports Grow as World Supplies Expand (New Orleans, 1965).

**Yearbook of Forest Products 1967 (Rome: Food and Agriculture Organization, 1968), Table D-14, p.115.

***Wood: World Trends and Prospects, Basic study No. 16 (Rome; Food and Agriculture Organization, 1967), p. 118.

Most of the recent increase in U.S. plywood imports has come from Asia. The composition of Asian supplies, however, has changed considerably. Japan's share of U.S. plywood imports in 1960 was 49 percent but dropped to 26 percent by 1966. During the same period, the shares of Taiwan and Korea rose from almost nothing to 9.5 percent and 11.3 percent respectively. The share of the Philippines varied between 11 percent and 17 percent during the period, and showed the greatest tendency to follow fluctuations in the U.S. market.

The most difficult competition for Vietnamese plywood exports to the United States will come from Taiwan and Korea, both of which have developed efficient, low-cost industries and aggressive marketing techniques. Nevertheless, there is no reason why Vietnam cannot gain a foothold in this lucrative market (and others) if it concentrates on producing a high quality, low-cost product.

Log Supplies

An obvious reason for developing a plywood industry in Vietnam is, of course, the desirability of putting the nation's forest resources into productive use. From recent photo-interpretation, the five northern provinces are estimated to have the following areas of multicanopied forest:

Quang Tri	201,125 hectares
Thua Thien	311,985 "
Quang Nam	404,050 "
Quang Tin	342,775 "
Quang Ngai	307,725 "
Total	1,567,660 hectares

It has also been estimated, on FAO descriptions of "old growth" forests in Southeast Asia,* that those areas may yield volumes of commercially usable wood as high as 100 to 150 cubic meters per hectare.

If the FAO estimate is even approximately correct and has any pertinence to the forest stands of the I Corps Zone, then there can be no doubt whatever of the capacity of regional forest resources to supply a plywood mill of the size suggested.

*Ibid., p. 46.

Over a depreciation period of fifteen years, the timber used by the proposed mill will amount to 600,000 cubic meters. In all probability the I Corps Zone can eventually support a plywood industry far larger than the one proposed, and this should be given consideration as planning proceeds.

The above comments apply to long-term development of a plywood industry. In the short term it would be hazardous to plan an export-oriented plywood industry based on domestic logs alone; the war has caused disruption in the forest areas resulting in extremely high logging costs, particularly in the northern provinces, where logging costs are further increased by a rugged and difficult terrain. Throughout the country, logging costs are now so high and so uncertain that most Vietnamese sawmills are not operating at all or are doing so at only a fraction of their capacity.

The cost of wood is usually 60 percent of the finished cost of plywood, and a viable industry cannot be built on high-cost timber only sporadically available from domestic sources. Nevertheless, it would be a mistake to postpone development of the industry until security is achieved. It is in the interests of Vietnam to gain an early foothold in the growing U.S. market, and it is desirable to promote early development of industry in the I Corps Zone to alleviate the unemployment which may occur there in the early postwar years.

A short-term solution lies in importing logs to overcome the uncertainties of domestic log supplies. Like Japan, Korea, and Taiwan, Vietnam can import logs from elsewhere in southeast Asia and convert them into plywood for export to the United States and other countries. One of the fastest-growing segments of international trade in forest products follows precisely this pattern. Logs are reported to be available in Vietnam from Sabah for U.S.$55 (VN$6,500) per cubic meter and from Cambodia for even less. This compares with a present delivered cost in Saigon of logs from Tay Ninh province at US$63-68 (VN$7,500-8,000) per cubic meter and with even higher costs in the I Corps Zone. The price advantages of imported logs at this time can be used by Vietnam to stimulate its own industry. Additional advantages of importing logs are those of steady supply at uniform prices and quality, freeing a mill from the uncertainties of procurement at home. These uncertainties may continue for some time after a cease-fire.

Another advantage in the solution suggested is the possibility of commodity exchanges with Malaysia, and especially with Sabah. In 1967, Malaysia imported 390,000 tons of rice for nearly U.S. $50 million. If Vietnam is to export rice, it can do so most conveniently to nearby countries which offer something in exchange. Sabah needs rice and has wood that it cannot process. Both countries would gain from an exchange.

It should be emphasized that the proposal to use imported logs is only a short-term measure and will not prejudice later development of national forest resources. Using imported logs is the only way that an internationally competitive plywood industry can be developed in the early postwar years. After a transition period of (say) five years, as security is restored, roads are built, and logging machinery put to work, a mill at Da Nang should draw its log supplies more and more from the Annamite Range and other parts of Vietnam. Eventually, the industry can be expected to be able to use domestic logs almost exclusively; in the meantime, an important industry will have been established during the critical period of postwar development.

Project Specification and Implementation

Initially, the mill might be designed to process 40,000 cubic meters of logs per year into 20,000 cubic meters of plywood, with room for expansion as and when conditions permit. The required investment should be no more than US$2 million, and the project is entirely suitable to be undertaken by private Vietnamese capital, with assistance from development banking sources.

A study of the timber resources of the I Corps Zone, including information on present logging conditions and the rate at which the delivery of logs can be expanded under peacetime conditions, (will) be started soon (see Chapter 8). The Commissioner for development of the I Corps Zone has been informed of this potential project and is supplying information concerning power supplies, labor, harbor facilities, local equity participation, and other pertinent matters. The Imported Hardwood Plywood Association in San Francisco has been asked to supply data on markets and prices in the United States. Possible markets in other countries (will) be investigated. If the results of these enquiries are favorable, (as they are expected to be), a consulting engineering firm (should be) retained to make a feasibility study. The scope of work for the study will be similar to that suggested in the discussion of the wood pulp industry.

As with the pulp study, it is recommended that the Industrial Development Center should finance this study. The Joint Development Group can assist in defining the scope of work and selecting an appropriate consultant, and will continue to help in other aspects of planning the project.

Action of various kinds by the government will be necessary to attract private investment for the project and ensure its success. Investors obviously should be granted the usual tax advantages, and additional incentives may be desirable to promote industrial development in the northern provinces. In the case of the plywood mill, there are some particular recommendations for consideration. Most important is the duty-free importation of logs and other materials at Da Nang until domestic log supplies and costs become competitive with imports. Second, administrative action should be taken to facilitate the development of the logging industry. Third, an inventory of the forests of the I Corps Zone should be made to confirm the long-term supply prospects. Fourth is the development of the infrastructure to meet industrial needs for power, harbor facilities, and roads.

THE INSTITUTIONAL SETTING FOR INDUSTRIAL DEVELOPMENT

The Role of Government

While it is not proper to base forecasts of future demand for industrial goods on the war-distorted consumption patterns of recent years, it is similarly inappropriate to extrapolate the existing institutional structure into the postwar period. The present structure has evolved through a difficult wartime period and has been forced to adapt to the abnormal economic and political conditions that the war has created. The result of these conditions has been a highly bureaucratic set of government controls and regulations that should diminish in pervasiveness as the conditions that have fostered them disappear. This will not happen without considerable effort on the part of government and industry to reexamine and alter the existing institutional and regulatory environment in terms of the overall development philosophy adopted for the postwar period.

The stated investment policy of the government "focuses its central aim on stimulating the expansion of private enterprises and encouraging the growth of necessity goods and export goods industries."* This desire to stimulate private investment requires the adoption of specific policies which will effectively utilize the particular talents which the private sector can offer to the development process. Not the least of these is the readily apparent entrepreneurial spirit and ability of the present business community.

Two basic elements of future government policy toward industrial development in the private sector are suggested:

1. Promotion of industry, including establishment of investment priorities, creation of a proper physical environment for spreading investment throughout the country (industrial estates, infrastructure investments, and so on), dissemination of information and promotion of feasibility studies for priority industries, creation of a favorable environment for foreign investment, provision of institutional support for exports.

2. Support of industry, including financial support for small and medium industry in which adequate private investment is not forthcoming, stimulation of growth in capital markets, and initial financial support for private development banking institutions.

A third possible element of government policy, the control and regulation of industry, has not been mentioned. This omission has been deliberate, but is not meant to imply that the government should not be the prime mover in guiding the industrial development process. It should; but this can be accomplished through the two elements already mentioned. Control and regulation of industry, as a deliberate government objective, can only result in the reduction of incentives for the private sector and of necessary investment from overseas. It would inevitably grow in relative importance at the

---

* Industrial Development Center, Establishing an Industrial Undertaking in Vietnam (1967).

expense of the other two objectives, and this is exactly what appears to have happened in the last few years.

Today, a private investor is subjected to a complicated series of procedures in order to gain approval and investment privileges for his project. He must seek approval, via innumerable forms, for virtually every detail of the project, including sources of capital, operating and technical procedures (from people who probably know much less about his proposed operation than he does), raw material sources, economic and financial justification, and so on. When and if the project is implemented, he must submit to additional supervision and control from government agencies. Bureaucratic interference of this sort discourages investments and sometimes prevents them from being made, seriously inhibiting the growth of the industrial sector. This is in conflict with the stated goal of government support for private investment, and the system should be changed accordingly.

Within the context of a comprehensive set of national development goals, detailed supervision and control of industry is unwarranted. In addition, such activities absorb a large number of scarce and valuable people who could be used more effectively in industry itself or in development banking institutions.

Institutional Requirements

The IDC can and should serve as the arm of government in promotion and support of industrial development. One basic change in its present makeup would appear to be warranted: at present, IDC serves as the Secretariat for the Investment Commission, the body charged with judging the merits of a particular project for the granting of investment privileges, including tax exemption. In this capacity, the IDC becomes deeply involved in the regulatory and control procedures described above. It is our impression that these activities engage many of the most valuable IDC employees at the expense of their more proper functions, which are industrial promotion and support activities.

It is recommended, therefore, that the Investment Commission be abolished and replaced by a comprehensive and detailed list of priority industries which will receive investment privileges. After preliminary review, if it is judged that a project fits within this list of priorities, then it should automatically be granted these privileges. The IDC should be concerned with the details of only those projects which have applied to it for direct financial assistance. All other projects, in which no IDC or government money will be directly involved, should be allowed to proceed toward implementation without further IDC scrutiny, within the structure of a reasonable set of import regulations. Private investors should be allowed to undertake their own assessments of risk and economic feasibility, without any involvement of the government in these matters.

The responsibilities recommended for IDC, therefore, are as follows:

1. Establishment of the priority areas of industrial development along the lines of the program recommended above under the heading "A Ten-Year Program for Investment in Industry", and continuing review and modification of the priorities to suit changing economic circumstances.

2. Preliminary review of those projects which have applied for investment privileges, and the granting of those privileges to projects judged to fit within the investment priorities. This is a process which should not require the detailed scrutiny carried out at present, and it should demand no more than one man-week of IDC activity for any one project.

3. Direct investment of minority shares (preferably nonvoting) or debt in small or medium industries judged to be important but not sufficiently attractive to secure sufficient levels of private capital. Within the context of reasonable assistance agreements, control of these enterprises should be left in the hands of private management, with technical assistance from IDC as and if required.

4. Undertaking, with overseas technical assistance as required, feasibility studies for priority projects which have not yet been initiated by private industry, and disseminating the results of these studies to private investors.

5. Establishment and operation of industrial estates until such time as the private sector is willing and able to finance this excellent mechanism for fostering industrial development in various parts of the country.

6. Investment of government money in large, strategically important projects which require further capital to supplement private domestic and foreign investment. IDC participation should be in the form of nonvoting equity or debt, and management control should rest in the hands of the private interests (within, of course, mutually agreed guidelines established at the inception of the project).

It is further recommended that IDC serve as the arm of government for administering postwar assistance to the industrial sector from possible consortiums of overseas governments and private investors. Such consortiums would be particularly valuable in the postwar period, and it is important that their efforts on behalf of the reconstruction of Vietnamese industry be carried out with maximum effect on the private sector.

Support to the private sector in the form of capital and technical assistance should be channeled through a viable private development bank, the rudiments of which exist today in the VDB. Such an organization should serve as the primary mechanism for carrying out major capital investment. It should be designed in the form of development banks which have proved successful in other parts of the world. An example is the Pakistan Industrial Credit and Investment Corporation (PICIC), a private organization which has served as the primary means of assisting medium-scale and large-scale industry in Pakistan. As does PICIC, a Vietnamese industrial development bank should serve ultimately as a channel for private foreign investment and assistance from such sources as the International Finance Corporation and the Asian Development Bank. By 1964, seven years after its founding, a full two-thirds (US$50 million) of the net worth of PICIC was in the form of overseas capital, all of which had been put to work in the Pakistan industrial sector. This pattern could be followed with equal success in Vietnam.

The development bank should be responsible for developing markets for private capital, channeling domestic and foreign investment into Vietnamese industry, and providing technical and management assistance to those industries in which it has invested. All of this must be done with a view toward establishing priorities for investment (through investment privileges granted by the government), but the bank management must be reasonably free to pursue those projects which provide an adequate return to itself and private investors. The bank should be entrepreneurial in nature and free to invest in the full range of industrial activities, both large and small.

It is recommended that in its initial stages a full-time advisor be obtained, someone who has managed a successful development bank elsewhere in the world. During the same period, the government should provide the bank with enough funds to get it started, possibly through a low interest loan from overseas. The government should guarantee bonds of the development bank. The bank's goal within a few years should be self-sufficiency, with no further need for direct government assistance.

Both IDC and a private development bank (the VDB or its successors) will require competent and experienced staffs. These can be built up only with significant levels of assistance from overseas. A pool of such assistance exists already in the large AID/Industry staff in Vietnam. It would be highly advantageous if many of these professionals could be assigned to work directly with the two Vietnamese development organizations instead of working in separate offices. Care should be taken, of course, not to saturate the Vietnamese organizations, but, at the same time, close working relationships would maximize the effectiveness of the U.S. industrial assistance effort. The same pattern could be followed with direct management assistance to private industry.

Foreign Investment

For all industrial sectors and products in which economies of scale have been listed as "crucial" or "important" in Table 9.15, and for all sectors with export possibilities, foreign investment (through joint ventures, licensing, and so on) undoubtedly will be required to provide technical, managerial and export marketing know-how. Purely local ownership cannot lead to a high level of world competitiveness. This is apparent from the experience of Korea and Taiwan, where foreign participation has resulted in significant manufacturing gains and increasing competitiveness in world markets.

It probably is not feasible to expect significant new foreign investment until real peace comes to Vietnam. For this reason, special incentives may be needed to induce the entry of foreign know-how in this interim period. This might be handled selectively by management participation without equity, with an option to purchase stock at a later date, but should be limited to projects where economies of scale are favorable.

One potential problem in attracting foreign investment is Article 22 of the Constitution of Vietnam, which states that "workers have the right to choose representatives to participate in the management of business enterprises, especially in matters concerning wages and conditions of work."* As it is commonly interpreted, and from the point of view of potential foreign investors, this provision indicates a highly undesirable relationship between management and labor. Management must have the right and ability to make decisions on production levels, competitive pricing, capital investment, production methods, and so forth, all of which affect labor directly or indirectly. To ensure that this constitutional provision does not frighten off needed foreign (and for that matter domestic) investment, it should be made clear in the required implementing legislation that labor has the right to organize and bargain collectively with management to influence management decisions, but not the right of direct participation in those management decisions.

THE 1969 WORK PROGRAM

The primary requirement of industrial planning in the immediate future will be not for further "studies" as such but for initiation of projects in a few important areas.

It is recommended, therefore, that a working group be established immediately to undertake a review of the recommendations of this report and establish a program for their implementation. The working party (should) consist of representatives of the Joint Development Group, IDC, VDB, AID/ Industry, private industry, and others deemed appropriate. It is recommended that this group choose a limited number of priority projects, set up a program for further work in each, and begin to move into the main stages of implementation. Working support should come from the staffs of each of the

---

*Unofficial English translation; emphasis supplied.

organizations represented. The working group itself should serve as a coordinating body to ensure the parallel efforts of all parties and should conduct discussions on changes to be made to the institutional structure. Specific recommendations for these changes should be made at the end of 1969 or earlier.

CHAPTER 10 DEVELOPMENT OF THE INFRASTRUCTURE

The Joint Development Group has considered in regard to infrastructure, the requirements for development in transportation (highways, railways, ports, inland waterways, and airports), sanitation, telecommunications, power, and housing. When applicable, the emphasis in the formulation of a postwar program in each of these sectors is initially on repair of war damage, followed by longer-term programs over a ten-year period through 1978. The projects proposed in this study incorporate where appropriate the views of the ministries concerned, U.S. AID, and U.S. and GVN armed forces planning agencies.

An effort has been made to consider practicable ways to incorporate in the postwar programs as many elements as possible of the infrastructure already developed by the armed forces. In fact, in some sectors, ports and airports for example, the capacity of the facilities developed by the military, when added to existing civil facilities, probably exceed immediate postwar requirements. The establishment of effective procedures for operation and management is also concerned.

Finally, the Joint Development Group emphasizes that many of the projects listed here are tentative, and much more investigation will be required to demonstrate their feasibility. To this end, recommendations are included for the establishment of continuing planning functions to ensure that postwar programs are fully responsive to the needs of the developing economy.

WAR DAMAGE

Summarized in Table 10.1 are estimates of damage due to enemy activities. These data represent the approximate

TABLE 10.1

Estimated Cost of War Damage
(VN$ Millions)

Facility	Estimated Total Cost
Highways	
Bridges	9,000
Highways	1,000
Ferries, GVN motor vehicles, equipment, etc.	1,000
TOTAL	11,000
Railroads	
Bridges	3,000
Track	2,000
Rolling stock and equipment	1,000
TOTAL	6,000
Inland Waterways[a]	
Little direct war damage; postponed maintenance dredging, nearly 10 million cubic meters required to return all navigable waterways to postwar condition.	
Estimated cost	2,300
Airports	
Minor damage to terminals and navigational aids	
Estimated cost	30
Telecommunications	
Numerous cuts in interprovincial systems, spot damage to radio facilities and buildings	
Estimated cost	500
Electric Power	
Damage to urban transmission facilities, except Saigon	155
EOV and Saigon Power Company	140
Danhim Plant 230 KV lines	285
TOTAL	580
Housing	
Approximately 100,000 housing units	
Estimated cost	10,000

total costs of facilities damaged or destroyed, based on estimates of the ministries concerned in cooperation with technical staff of the Joint Development Group.

The damages summarized in Table 10.1 total about VN$30,410 million. Repair work is already well advanced on some of these facilities, for example, the highways and the railroad. In the sections which follow, specific recommendations are included concerning the extent of war damage repair actually needed in the postwar period.

HIGHWAYS

With a total highway network in excess of 20,000 km, Vietnam has a well-articulated system which is potentially capable of serving all developed areas of the country and all centers of population and production. In cooperation with the Ministry of Public Works, Communications and Transportation (MPWCT), the Joint Development Group has reviewed the present condition of Vietnam's highways, and has suggested in Working Paper No. 35* a policy and program for highway development in the postwar period. The results of these activities are summarized in this section.

Highway Network

The main highways of Vietnam are those of the national system (3,778 km) and the interprovincial system (2,593 km). Provincial and communal roads and city streets, aggregating 13,884 km, constitute the remainder of the system (Table 10.2). The highway network is divided among five highway districts which are administered by the Directorate General of Highways in MPWCT.

The structure of the highway network north of Saigon is characterized by the vital coastal highway QL-1 extending from Dong Ha, near the Demilitarized Zone, 1,343 km south to Saigon (Figure 10.1). Generally parallel to QL-1 are two

---

*<u>Post-War Planning for Highways</u>, Joint Development Group, Working Paper No. 35.

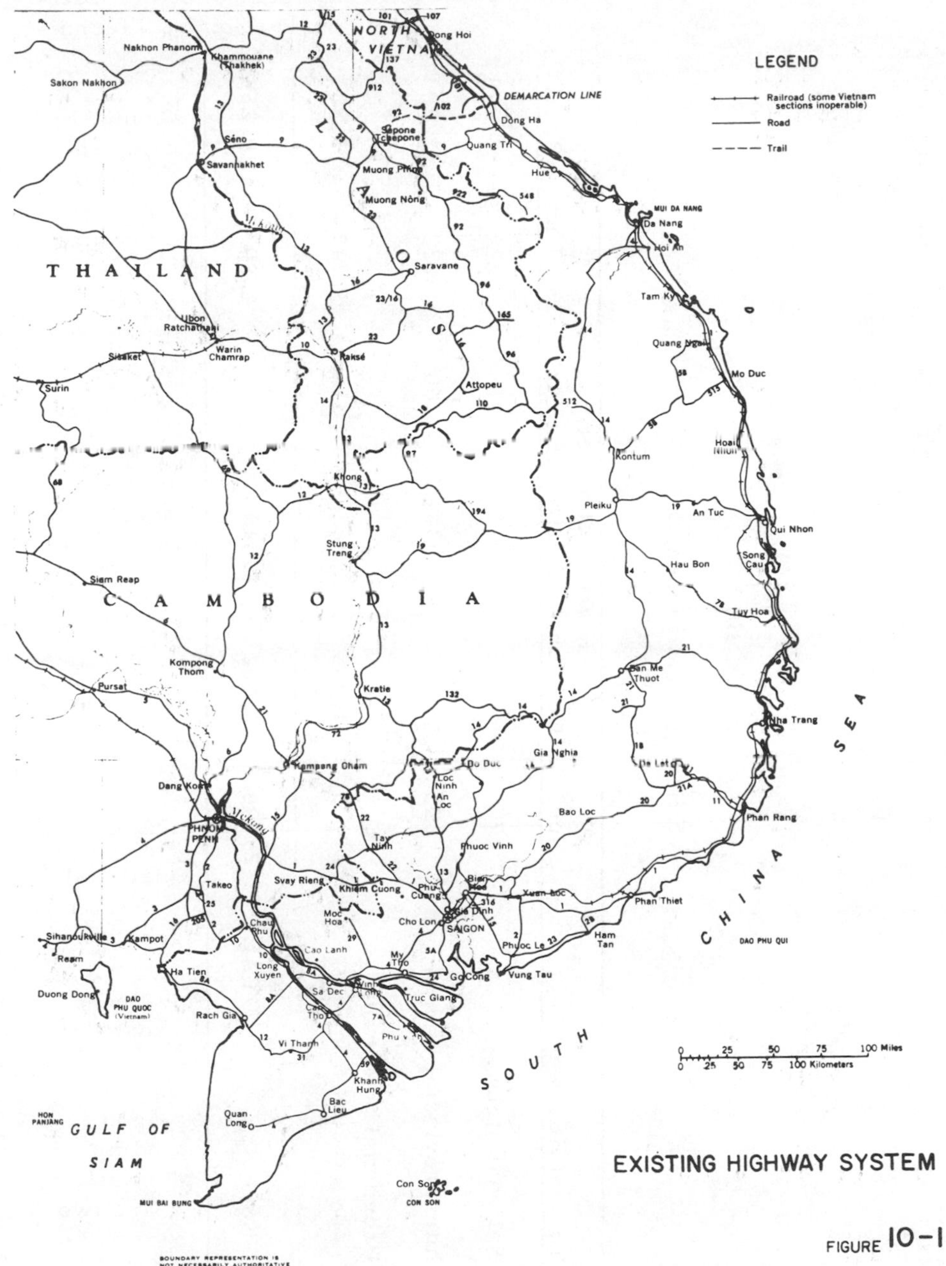

EXISTING HIGHWAY SYSTEM

FIGURE 10-1

TABLE 10.2

Existing Highway Length
(kilometers)

Type of Roadway	Highway District					
	Hue	Nha Trang	Dalat	Saigon	Can Tho	Total
National highway	730	862	1,044	918	224	3,778
Interprovincial highway	143	184	534	900	832	2,593
Provincial roads and city streets	2,025	1,536	2,262	4,314	3,747	13,884
TOTAL	2,898	2,582	3,840	6,132	4,803	20,255

other north-south routes, QL-14 and QL-20, which link Saigon with the main centers of the Central Highlands. At its northern end, Route QL-14 is connected to the coast at Da Nang. These two roads have important implications for the future development of the highland areas. A number of less important routes interconnect these main transportation corridors.

In the general area of Saigon, that is to say the eleven provinces constituting the III Corps Tactical Zone and the Saigon Special Zone, the highway network is radial and nearly all routes converge on the capital.

South of Saigon, National Route QL-4 and connecting highways link Saigon with the principal centers of the Mekong Delta.

The development of highways in the south (in the highway districts of Saigon and Can Tho) reflects the denser population and more concentrated agricultural production of those areas; the density of roads per hectare of cultivated land in southern Vietnam is nearly six times as great as it is in the highland areas.

Present Highway Conditions

While highways are well developed for service to all parts of the country, their geometric and structural standards are inadequate for modern traffic use. The system has evolved over five decades, and most older roads are narrow (4 to 5 meters), with insufficient width of shoulders and inadequate curve radii. The subbase and surface course thicknesses are inadequate for continuous service under modern loads. Insufficient maintenance has compounded these structural defects.

Underlying these deficiencies, however, is the lack of security in some areas, which has prevented proper maintenance, as well as the extensive damage caused by military operations. By 1968, 3,195 bridges and culverts had been sabotaged and many wholly destroyed (Table 10.3). By July, 1968, 2,000 had been repaired either temporarily or permanent, leaving nearly 1,200 to be repaired, or an aggregate of 13,300 meters of bridge construction still to be undertaken. War damage to the highways themselves has also been extensive. In addition to direct destruction by the enemy, the movement of heavy military vehicles, especially tracked units, over existing bridges and highways has contributed substantially to highway deterioration.

TABLE 10.3

War Damage to Highways and Bridges as of 7/1968 (meters)

	Bridges and Culverts		
Status	Number	Length of Facility	Length Damaged
Sabotaged	3,195	80,454 m	34,800 m
Temporarily repaired	1,999	49,860 m	21,500 m
Unrepaired	1,196	30,594 m	13,300 m

Highways	
Length destroyed	70,000 m
Area destroyed	300,000 sq m

Postwar Planning Criteria

When the war ends, the most important activity in the highway sector will be to reestablish communications with areas of Vietnam isolated by road and bridge destruction. All programs for highway development have taken account of this requirement; it will be accomplished by repair or replacement of the war-damaged bridges and highway sections referred to above.

At the same time, a progressive program of highway development should be undertaken. In Working Paper No. 35, the Joint Development Group has proposed a three-year program of highway reconstruction to meet anticipated traffic needs through 1975, followed by a ten-year program of highway development to meet needs through 1985. These are workable plans and are based on a point system of priorities which reflect the rated sufficiency (geometric and structural) of individual highways, economic and social characteristics of the areas served, the proportion of trucks in the traffic flow, and anticipated increases of average daily traffic.

Very little is known, however, of the probable composition and distribution of highway traffic in the postwar years, so that a continuing program of highway planning will be required. This can ensure that highway reconstruction and development afford Vietnam the maximum economic return. In this way, not only may the rate of highway development be modified in accordance with development trends in other sectors and the availability of capital, but changes in highway priorities can be made to provide timely highway service in support of new agricultural or other development activities, as may be required.

Highway planning in Vietnam must also take into account the substantial highway development which has been undertaken for military purposes. Practically all of this construction will serve the purposes of postwar development.

Finally, the highways of Vietnam will need adequate maintenance in the postwar period. The strengthening of the maintenance capabilities of the Directorate General of Highways should be a principal consideration in planning for postwar highway development, and attention should also be directed to ways in which the highway construction capability of the private sector can be enlarged.

First Approximation of a Highway Development Program

A postwar development program in three parts has been suggested in Working Paper No. 35, as follows:

1. Reestablishing communications. To restore communications with areas of Vietnam which have been isolated by the destruction of bridges and segments of highway, a program of emergency construction was proposed. This provides for the temporary repair of 13,300 meters (m) of damaged bridges and 70 km of highway road sections. The total estimated cost,

using temporary construction methods, at approximately 20 percent of the cost of permanent construction, is VN$1,100 million. We estimated that the work could be accomplished within twelve months and would utilize a labor force of at least 5,000 men.

2. Reconstruction phase. Over a three-year period, we proposed the reconstruction of the most heavily used sections of important national and interprovincial highways to improve their geometric and structural standards. Priority would be given to the main access routes in the Saigon area and to portions of QL-1, QL-4, QL-13, QL-15, LT-6, and LT-15 (Figure 10.2). Approximately 374 km of highway, including 6,400 m of bridges, would be rebuilt at an estimated total cost of VN$9,247 million.

3. Development phase. Following the three-year reconstruction phase, the Joint Development Group suggested a longer period of highway development involving some 42 separate projects. On its completion, all major routes in the southern half of Vietnam (Saigon and III Corps and IV Corps zones) would be rebuilt. Relatively less attention was directed to main routes to the north because substantial military construction has already been carried out, especially on QL-1 in the I Corps and II Corps zones. In this development phase, we recommended the rebuilding of 2,300 km of highways and 20,400 m of bridges at an estimated cost of VN$38,380 millions.

The basic standards to which the road system would be reconstructed under this program are based generally on the requirements of the Central Joint Committee on Navigation and Highway Communications (CENCOM), April 20, 1968, which are as follows:

	Two-Lane Pavement	Shoulders
Class A	7.3 m	2.5 m
Class B	6.0 m	2.5 m
Class C	6.0 m	1.5 m

However, the 6-meter (20-foot) paved surfaces of classes B and C are not considered to be adequate for modern vehicles and vehicle flows. As more reliable traffic data become available, it is recommended that the assignment of standards to individual route segments be reexamined. In general, the mixture of traffic in Vietnam, the extensive use of the highways

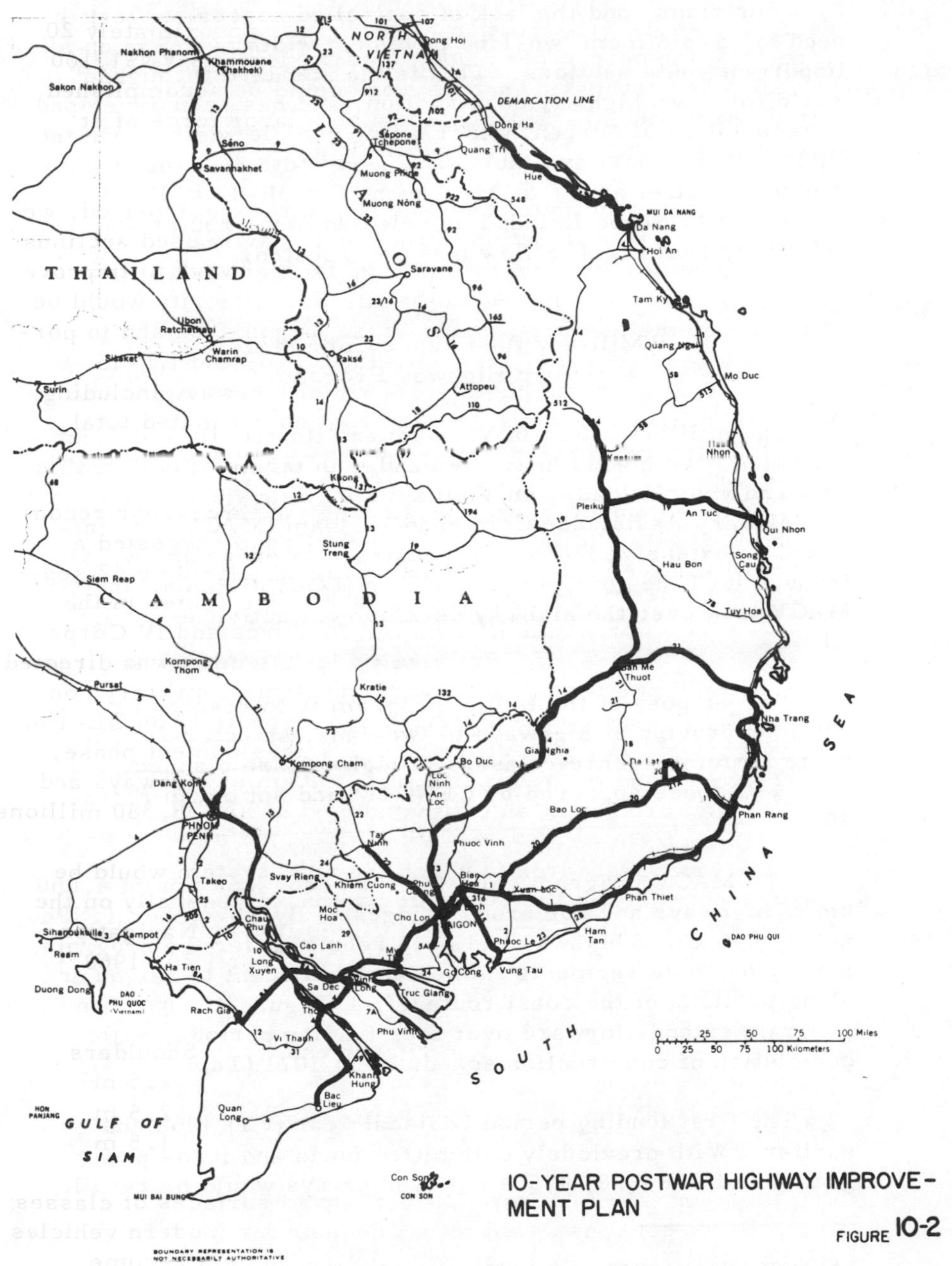

10-YEAR POSTWAR HIGHWAY IMPROVEMENT PLAN

FIGURE 10-2

by pedestrians, and the lack of controlled access suggest the need for a minimum two-lane pavement width of 7.3 m on all-important route sections. This is the standard throughout the world for main highway construction, and has been developed in recognition of currently increasing vehicle widths. On the limited traffic data available, a 7.3-m width is already warranted for QL-4 as far as My Thuan, for QL-13 to Phu Cuong, for QL-15 to Phuoc Le, and on selected other routes where relatively heavy traffic flow may be expected.

Military Assistance Command Vietnam Highway Program

The military effort in Vietnam and its required support facilities have placed heavy demands, in terms of both traffic flow and vehicle loads, on Vietnam's highways. In response, the Military Assistance Command Vietnam (MACV) has initiated an extensive highway reconstruction program, working through its Lines of Communications (LOC) division. In 1968, MACV took over the highway development activities of U.S. AID.

The purpose of the MACV program is to restore national and interprovincial highways to two-lane, structurally adequate systems. Three classes of highway are planned, identical with those approved by CENCOM and set out in Figure 10.3.

The MACV program calls for the reconstruction of 4,060 km of highways and numerous bridges.* By November 1, 1968, nearly 650 km of highway had been rebuilt under the program, mostly on route segments immediately adjacent to Saigon and along portions of the coast route QL-1 (Figure 10.3). The program extends forward over four funding periods, with completion of construction scheduled in 1971 (Table 10.4).

The first funding period is fiscal year (FY) 1968 and earlier. With previously committed funds and funds programmed for FY 68, 1,504 km of highways would be rebuilt,

---

*MACV Highway Program Funding Study, Office of the Director of Construction, Military Assistance Command Vietnam (November 21, 1968).

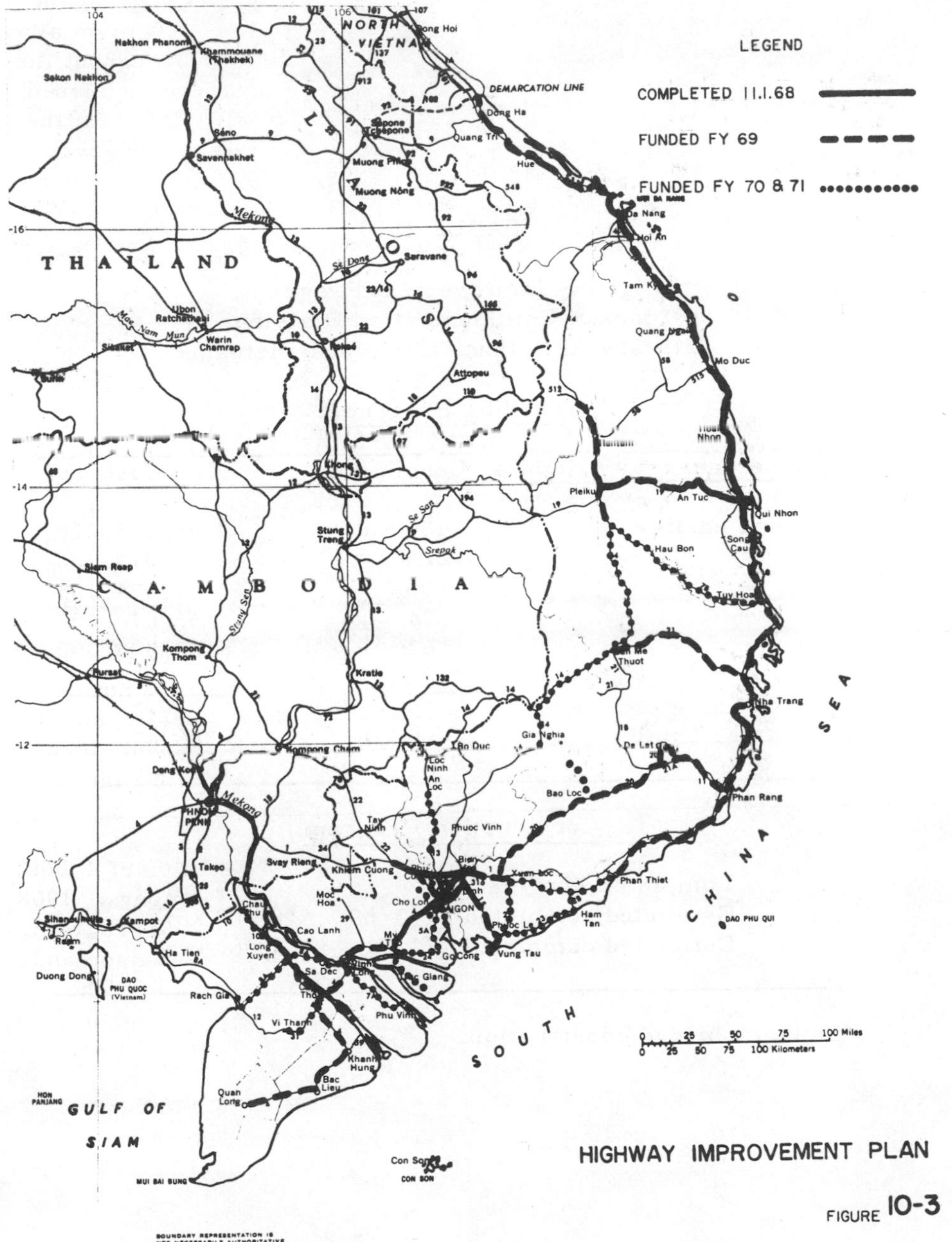

HIGHWAY IMPROVEMENT PLAN

FIGURE 10-3

TABLE 10.4

Highway Improvement Program,
Lines of Communication Division,
Military Assistance Command Vietnam

Funding Program

Fiscal Year	Highway Length (km)	Est. Cost US$[a]
1967 and earlier	480 km	$ 68,015,000
1968	1,024	145,717,000
1969	1,200	97,574,165
1970	1,294	66,070,000
1971	62	9,500,000
Total	4,060 km	$ 386,876,165

Construction Program

Completed 11/1/68	649 km
Estimated completed 11/1/69	1,760 km
Estimated completed 9/1/71	4,060 km

[a]Includes bridge construction.

mainly to Class A standard, comprising the main links adjacent to Saigon (including the Saigon by-pass Bien Hoa/Cu Chi), National Route QL-4 as far as My Thuan, almost all of QL-1 except the segment Phan Thiet/Xuan Loc (scheduled for FY 70) and QL-19, An Nhon/Pleiku. There is also provision in the same period for reconstruction of 65 km of Saigon streets; 20 km of this work was completed by November 1, 1968. Estimated cost is US$214 million.

The second funding period is fiscal year 1969. A further 1,200 km of highway work is programmed for funding in FY 69. This consists mainly of construction to Class B standard. It comprises continuing the reconstruction of QL-4 in the Mekong Delta as far as Ca Mau, the extension of the QL-22 and QL-13 routes further northward from Saigon, and reconstruction of QL-20 to Dalat and QL-21 between Ninh Hoa and Ban Me Thuot in the Central Highlands. Including the FY 68 program, a total of 40 km of the 62-km Saigon by-pass will be funded by FY 69. Estimated cost is US$98 million.

The third period is fiscal year 1970. In this period the program calls for funding construction of 1,294 km consisting of interprovincial routes in the Mekong Delta and the III Corps Zone, most of National Route QL-14 in the Central Highlands, and other highway links not previously rebuilt in the northern section of the country. A substantial additional segment of the Saigon beltway would also be funded. Estimated cost is US$66 million.

The fourth period is fiscal year 1971. The final component of the MACV program is the completion of the Saigon beltway. Estimated cost, US$9 million.

The MACV highway program almost completely duplicates the proposals described earlier in this section. However, we suggest the construction of additional lanes to bring all principal radial routes in the Saigon area up to four-lane standards and in some cases more than this will be warranted. The timing of this additional construction cannot now be precisely established, but the cost estimates shown in Table 10.5 include an allocation for part of it. The only highway link which appears in the previously proposed program and not in the MACV program is the connection between QL-14 at Dao Thong and QL-13 at An Loc. This has been included in the cost estimates presented in Table 10.5.

TABLE 10.5

Postwar Highway Development

Priority	Project	From	To	Class	Length(km)	Est. Const. Cost US$[a]	Remarks
1	Immediate repairs of war damage to restore communications					9,300,000	
2	QL-1	Xuan Loc	Phan Thiet	A	110	13,200,000	Reconstruction
3	QL-13	Lai Khe	QL-14	B	30	3,300,000	Reconstruction
4	LTL-5A	Saigon	Go Cong	B	58	16,240,000	New Construction
5	LT-8A	Vinh Long	Bassac Ferry	B	53	14,840,000	New Construction
6	QL-14	Dragon Mt.	Ban Me Thuot	B	150	16,500,000	Reconstruction
7	QL-14	Ban Me Thuot	QL-13	C	235	23,500,000	Reconstruction
8	LT-8A	Bassac Ferry	Rach Gia	C	79	21,330,000	New Construction
9	LT-10	Long Xuyen	Chau Doc	C	55	14,850,000	New Construction
10	Additional lanes for Saigon Area highways					35,000,000	
					770	168,060,000	
	Design and Supervision of Construction					6,940,000	
	Total					175,000,000	

[a]Estimated construction cost based on MACV-LOC cost factors for CPAF contractor, from "MACV Highway Program Funding Study," dated 11-21-68.
Class A road reconstruction, 120,000/km outside delta
Class B road new construction, 280,000/km in delta, 190,000/km outside delta
Class B road reconstruction, 110,000/km outside delta
Class C road, no cost estimate for MACV CPAF contractor

JDG estimate: Class C road reconstruction, 100,000/km outside delta
Class C road new construction, 270,000/km in delta

Postwar Highway Development

Because of the comprehensive nature of the MACV program and the degree of funding which has already been committed, the Joint Development Group recommends generally that the projects and general priorities established in that program be adopted for postwar planning purposes.

Future funding, of course, is not assured, and the end of the war may produce changes in the fund allocations of the United States. Accordingly, we suggest that the safe assumption is that only the highway reconstruction programmed for funding through FY 69 will in fact be carried out. This comprises 2,704 km of highways and represents an investment of US$312 million. None of these costs are included in the postwar highway development estimates of this report.

Those portions of the MACV program now scheduled for funding after FY 69 might, therefore, form the postwar highway development program for which additional funds are required. It is recommended, however, that only those route segments be included which also appear in the group's program (excluding roads programmed primarily for military purposes) and that the priorities for their construction follow those we have suggested. This construction will be assumed to take place in the period 1971-78, the years following assumed completion of all MACV projects scheduled for funding through FY 69.

In these estimates, it is assumed that the temporary bridge repairs and the highway repairs necessary to restore communications, as recommended in the group's program, will not be included in the MACV program; all this work is included in the postwar development estimates of Table 10.5.

The proposed development program now comprises 770 km of highways projects, exclusive of the addition of lanes on selected routes. It includes the reconstruction of the remaining portion of National Route QL-1, will provide a rebuilt route through the northern section of III Corps into the Central Highlands via QL-14, and will extend an improved route into the Mekong Delta from the vicinity of My Thuan to Rach Gia, via LT-8 (Figure 10.4). This program should be continually reexamined as traffic flow data are accumulated and trends in traffic flow are identified.

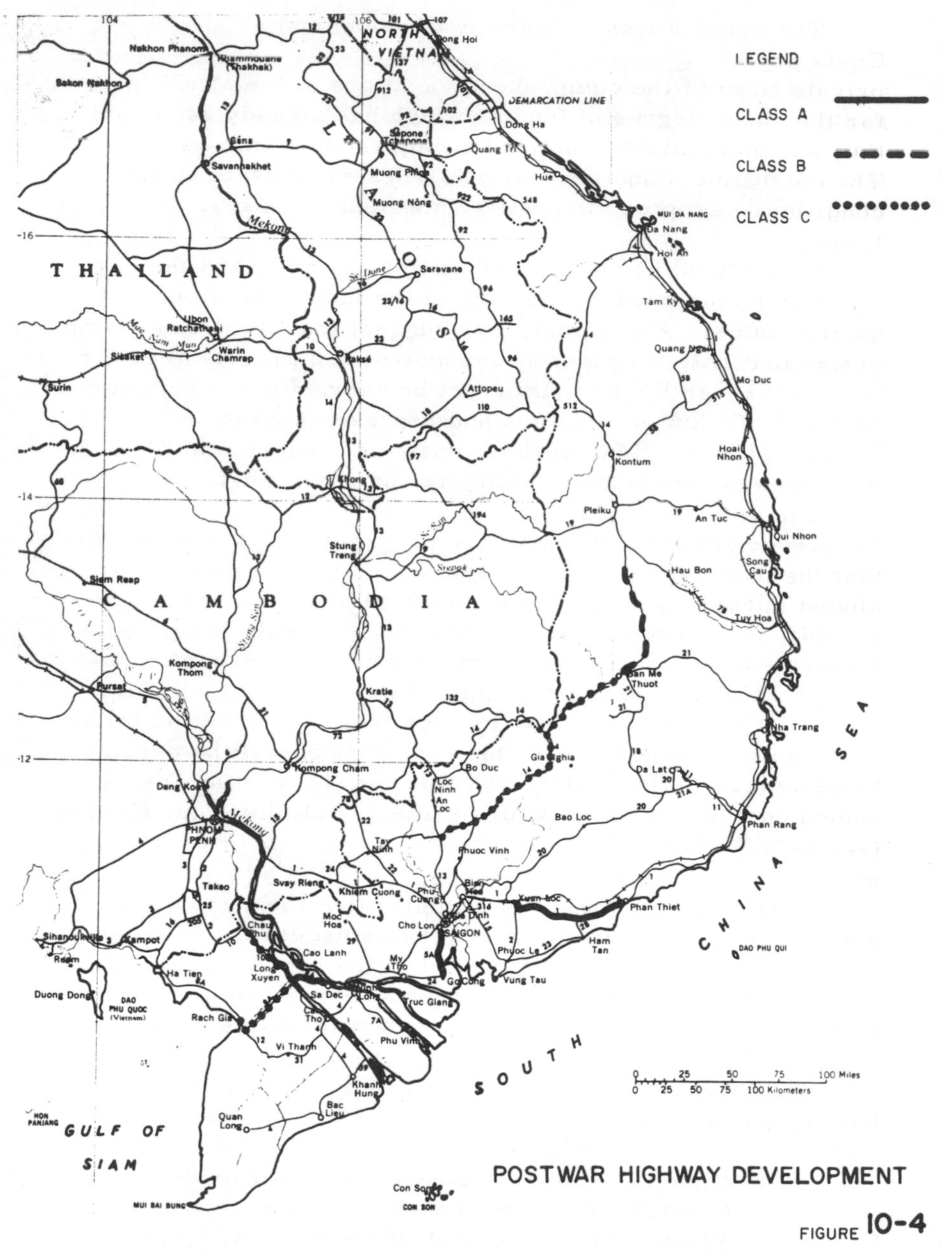

POSTWAR HIGHWAY DEVELOPMENT

FIGURE 10-4

The estimated cost of the program is US$175 million. Costs are based on estimated unit prices for construction by private contractors in Vietnam. MACV's estimated costs for the same route segments are generally lower, because they assume use of troop construction on many highway links. The contract prices used here represent wartime construction conditions and actual postwar construction costs may well be lower.

For these types of construction, foreign exchange requirements are taken to be about 50 percent, so that the program cost in dollars and piasters is as follows:

US$90 million
VN$9,440 million

Capital requirements for the program may be assumed to be evenly distributed over the development period, except that the cost of restoring communications should all be included in the first year after the war.

Maintenance Costs

As yet, the Joint Development Group has not examined highway maintenance operations and costs, but research was undertaken in 1969 on ways to increase maintenance capability (see below). Major elements of the former U.S. AID highway program, and an important element of the MACV program, have been devoted to supplying maintenance equipment and developing appropriate maintenance standards and procedures.

It is assumed that the highway maintenance equipment of U.S. forces and contractors will be left in Vietnam, and that present programs to assist the Directorate General of Highways to activate its existing plant will be completed. On these bases, annual costs of maintenance are taken to be as follows:

Class A road: VN$247,800 per km/yr.
Class B road: VN$212,400 per km/yr.
Class C road: VN$212,400 per km/yr.

Adequate maintenance of the newly built highways of Vietnam is essential to their continued service. It is estimated that annual costs of maintenance, at the unit prices stated, will range from VN$659 million in 1971 to VN$818 million in 1978.

Activities of the Joint Development Group during 1969 were oriented toward assistance in strengthening the highway-planning function and the organization of highway maintenance, assessment of construction capability, and related advisory services.

RAILWAYS

The main line of the Vietnamese National Railway System (VNRS) extends 1,109 km northward along the coast from Saigon to Dong Ha, serving almost all the principal population centers of the country except those of the Mekong Delta. Including branch lines, the total system comprises 1,357 km. Most of it was built in the period 1885-1936, and in the years before the present war it provided the only reliable system for overland haul of commodities. The railway was damaged during World War II and during the Viet Minh wars, but by 1959 it had been repaired and the entire line between Saigon and Dong Ha was operational.

Facilities of the VNRS

The VNRS is an extensive operational system with eleven main workshops, 56 diesel locomotives (provided under Development Loan Fund agreements in 1961-65) and nearly 1,000 freight cars of all types. Track is of one-meter gauge, weighing 27 to 30 kilos per meter, laid on steel ties. Ruling grades on the main line do not exceed 1.5 percent, and 90 percent of the system has grades under 1.0 percent. The Dalat branch line, partly a cog railway, encounters grades of 12 percent. Motive power, grade, and carrying capacities of the cars are reasonably well balanced for efficient operating conditions.

The VNRS has about 3,500 employees; it is an autonomous governmental agency whose management is responsible to a board of directors. The chairman of the board is the minister of public works, communications and transportation.

Conditions of the Railroad in November 1968

Viet Cong attacks on the VNRS began in 1960; in 1964 alone there were 650 separate incidents of sabotage. In total, 620 bridges and nearly 72,000 meters of track have been destroyed or damaged. Locomotives have been damaged nearly 400 times. The VNRS estimates that damage to the system has totalled VN$6,000 million.

In 1968, approximately 460 km of the system was operational.* Owing to insecurity, the 117-km branch north from Saigon to Loc Ninh near the Cambodian border, built in 1960, has been inoperative since 1961.

Railway Operations

For the reasons already stated, traffic on the VNRS has declined sharply in recent years. Between 1957 and 1966, freight carried dropped nearly 50 percent to 229,600 metric tons (Figure 10.5). There was an increase in freight carried in 1967, owing to growing use by the military, especially for relatively short hauls of construction materials.

In terms of both distance and tonnage the ton-kilometers of haul in ten years declined by over 80 percent to 14 million in 1966. In 1967, when traffic was nearly three times that of the previous year, VNRS still accounted for only 27 million ton-kilometers, a decline of 65 percent from 1957 figures.** The decrease in passenger traffic has been even more marked, falling in the same period by more than 90 percent. In the circumstances of severe, recurrent enemy attack and resultant curtailment of operations, this is only to be expected. There have been no less than 1,225 casualties among VNRS employees from enemy action, and the fact that the railway is still operating at all and is even rapidly reconstructing war-damaged segments is a tribute to the strength and dedication of its officers and staff.

---

*Railroad Development, Joint Development Group Working Paper No. 30.

**Resumé on Railroads, U.S. AID, April 1, 1968.

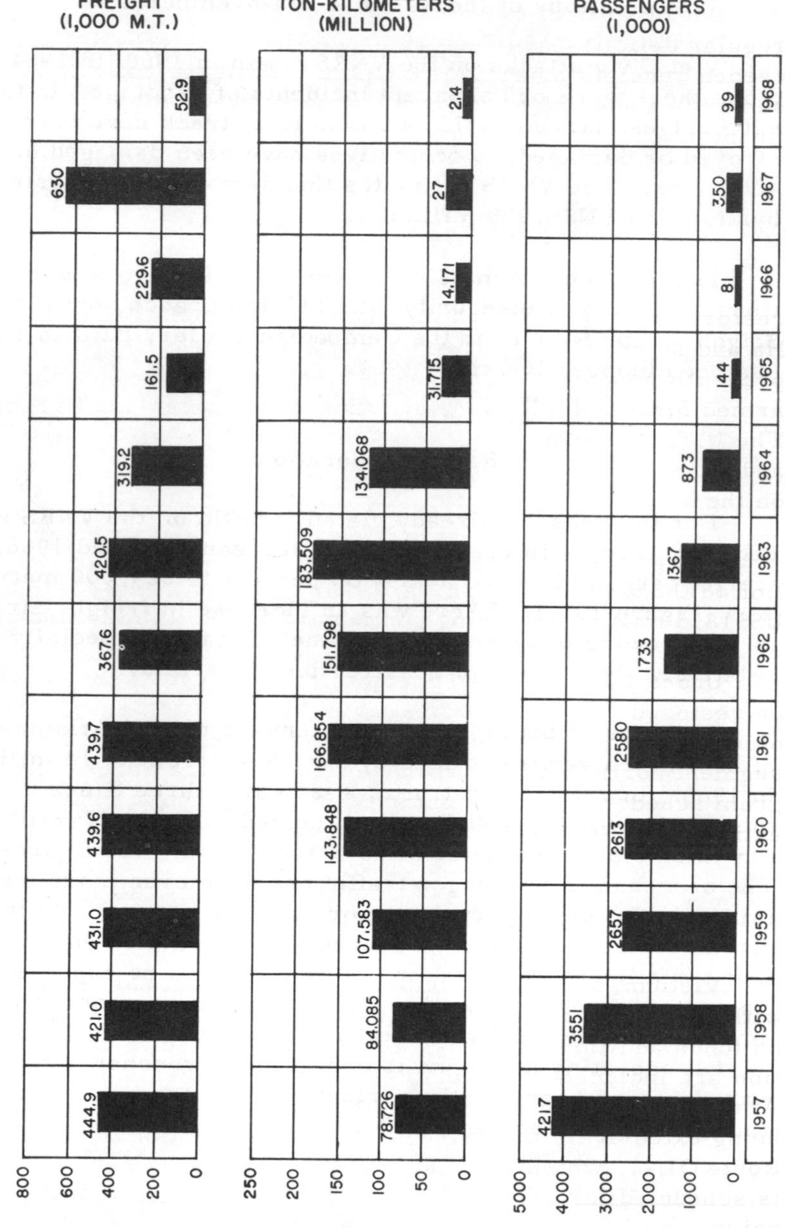
COMPARATIVE FREIGHT AND PASSENGER BUSINESS 1957-1967,
ALSO FIRST (3) MONTHS 1968
FREIGHT
(1,000 M.T.)
TON-KILOMETERS
(MILLION)
PASSENGERS
(1,000)
800
600
400
200
0
444.9
421.0
431.0
439.6
439.7
367.6
420.5
319.2
161.5
229.6
630
52.9
250
200
150
100
50
0
78.726
84.085
107.583
143.848
166.854
151.798
183.509
134.068
31.715
14.171
27
2.4
5000
4000
3000
2000
1000
0
4217
3551
2657
2613
2580
1733
1367
873
144
81
350
99
1957
1958
1959
1960
1961
1962
1963
1964
1965
1966
1967
1968

FIGURE 10-5

But in spite of these magnificent efforts, substantial and regular deficits have been incurred; in 1967 expenditures exceeded receipts by VN$341 million.* Until the railway resumes full operation, it has little prospect of improving its financial operating results.

Present Railway Improvement Program

A railroad rehabilitation project directed at the early restoration of service on the main line from Saigon to Dong Ha and on branch lines (except the spur to Loc Ninh), (is presently in progress.) This is a joint effort by VNRS, the armed forces of Vietnam, and the United States and U.S. AID. The U.S. Army has been active in promoting this undertaking, and (at present) has 200 railroad cars of its own in service on the VNRS for movement of military cargo.

The government of Vietnam has committed VN$970 million to the work, and U.S. AID commodities to the value of US$18.3 million are being contributed by the United States.

Under this program, freight and passenger service will be restored on 762 km of the main line (early in 1969,) leaving only a 279-km gap between Phu Cat and Da Nang and a 68-km segment north of Hue still inoperative (Figure 10.6). Program schedules call for completion of reconstruction on the entire main line (by the end of the year.)

The Railway in the Postwar Period

Vietnam should, therefore, enter the postwar period with a fully reconstructed railway system and consequently no funds additional to those already committed to reconstruction are included in estimates of postwar development costs. At the same time, however, Vietnam's highways are also being extensively improved. The reconstruction of National Route QL-1, which parallels the railway for its entire length, is scheduled for completion at about the same time that the railway will be able to resume full operations.

---

*Comparative Study of Saigon-Da Nang Transportation Modes, Joint Development Group Working Paper No. 33.

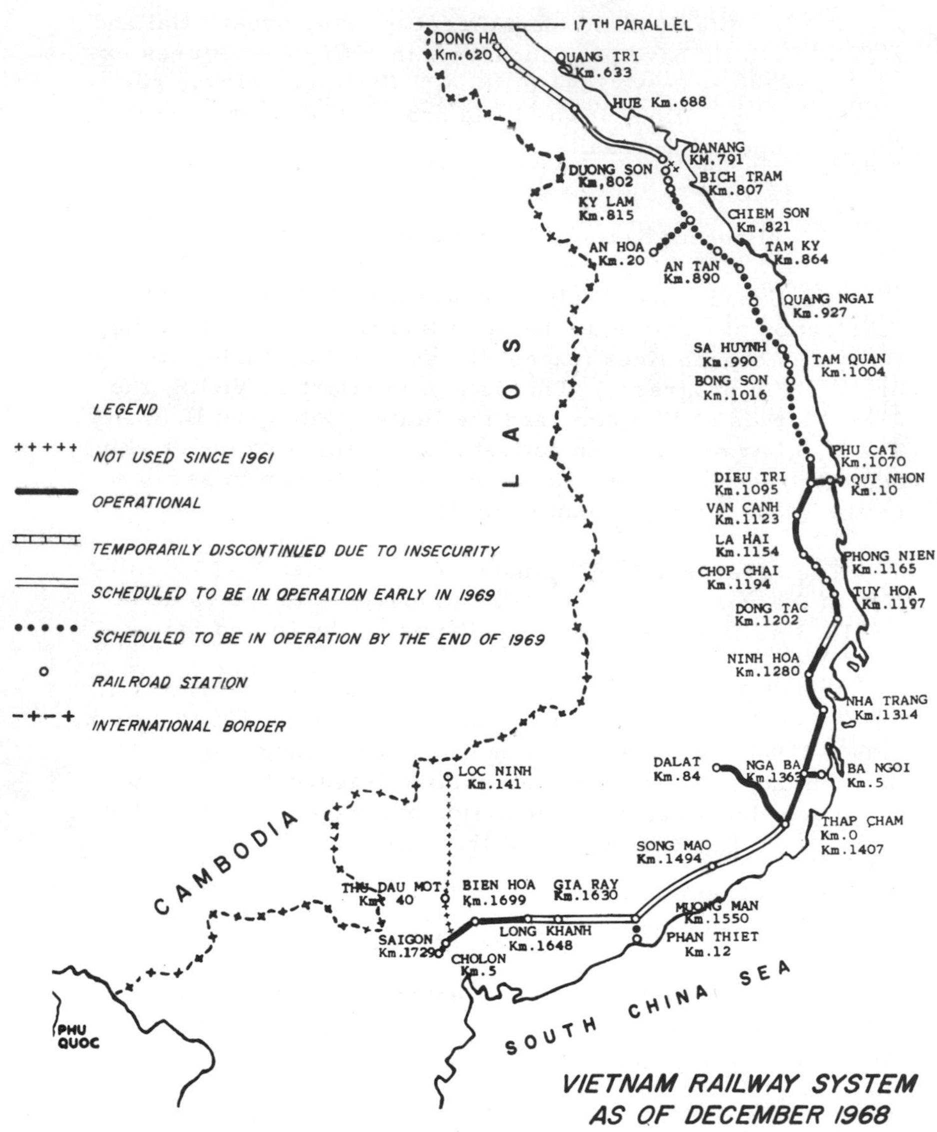
17 TH PARALLEL
DONG HA Km.620
QUANG TRI Km.633
HUE Km.688
DANANG KM.791
DUONG SON Km,802
BICH TRAM Km.807
KY LAM Km.815
CHIEM SON Km.821
TAM KY Km.864
AN HOA Km.20
AN TAN Km.890
QUANG NGAI Km.927
LAOS
SA HUYNH Km.990
TAM QUAN Km.1004
BONG SON Km.1016
LEGEND
NOT USED SINCE 1961
OPERATIONAL
TEMPORARILY DISCONTINUED DUE TO INSECURITY
SCHEDULED TO BE IN OPERATION EARLY IN 1969
SCHEDULED TO BE IN OPERATION BY THE END OF 1969
RAILROAD STATION
INTERNATIONAL BORDER
PHU CAT Km.1070
DIEU TRI Km.1095
QUI NHON Km.10
VAN CANH Km.1123
LA HAI Km.1154
PHONG NIEN Km.1165
CHOP CHAI Km.1194
TUY HOA Km.1197
DONG TAC Km.1202
NINH HOA Km.1280
NHA TRANG Km.1314
LOC NINH Km.141
DALAT Km.84
NGA BA Km.1363
BA NGOI Km.5
CAMBODIA
THAP CHAM Km.0 Km.1407
SONG MAO Km.1494
THU DAU MOT Km 40
BIEN HOA Km.1699
GIA RAY Km.1630
MUONG MAN Km.1550
LONG KHANH Km.1648
SAIGON Km.1729
PHAN THIET Km.12
CHOLON Km.5
SOUTH CHINA SEA
PHU QUOC

VIETNAM RAILWAY SYSTEM AS OF DECEMBER 1968

FIGURE 10-6

This is a newly competitive circumstance. For some years it has been recognized that, except for large volumes over relatively long distances, rail transportation could not compete with truck transportation on a modern highway system in Vietnam. Preliminary studies of rail and truck shipping costs undertaken in 1968 by the Joint Development Group indicated, for example, that the railroad is not competitive with trucking for small shipments (under 4 tons) at distances less than 650 kms; and that it cannot compete with trucking for large shipments (over 15 tons) at distances less than 140 kms.* These are not definitive findings, for the system of truck tariffs in Vietnam is greatly distorted by war and rail tariffs in many cases may be unreasonably low. However, they do illustrate the disadvantages of rail transportation in the face of modern motor truck transportation on reconstructed highways.

Coastal shipping is another potential postwar competitor of the railroad. With railway service interrupted during the war and insecure conditions on many sections of the highway system, coastal shipping has captured a large share of freight traffic, especially military cargoes, northward from Saigon. These conditions are now changing and the role of coastal shipping will diminish; however, it will still compete with the railroad on long-haul movements, especially between Saigon and the coastal ports.

The future of the railway was considered in a 1966 transportation study of Vietnam.** At that time it was recommended that, in the absence of an adequate highway network, the VNRS should be rebuilt in order to provide for heavy hauls over long distances. But it was pointed out that as the highway system developed, the railway would lose most of its passenger traffic and much of its general goods traffic, especially over the shorter distances. Recommendations were made for operating and management improvements, freight solicitation, and reduction of excess labor, with a view to making the VNRS more competitive with the highways in the

---

*Railroad Development, Joint Development Group Working Paper No. 30.

**Vietnam Transportation Study, Transportation Consultants, Inc. (Washington, D.C., 1966).

future, and so enable it to retain a special position as a long-haul carrier of heavy cargo.

The railroad will soon be in a position to assume this role if it can. Its success is not assured. While the railway has an effective physical plant, has established modern operating practices, and has conducted a program of modernization, the inherent disadvantages of its fixed route, combined with a limited demand for haulage of heavy bulk cargoes over long distances and the probable decline in military shipments, may render its continued service impracticable.

The coming years will, in effect, be a trial period in which VNRS operations and financial returns should be closely and continuously observed, so as to develop, if possible, more competitive and specialized services, and at the same time to assess the feasibility of continuing operation.

PORTS

Vietnam's deep-draft port facilities to serve ocean-going vessels have been greatly expanded in recent years, mainly to provide logistic support to the armed forces. In fact, if the facilities now devoted to military use were made available, port facilities in Vietnam would amply satisfy the needs of civil development. This probably will not happen in the immediate postwar period. Even in the longer term, some military use of existing military port facilities should be assumed, although not nearly to the same extent as at present. For these reasons, there will be a need for limited but steady expansion of deep draft marine terminal capacity in the postwar period.

Terminals for coastal vessels at Vietnamese ports have not been improved as part of the military effort; and the severe curtailment of land transportation by enemy action has resulted in unusually heavy traffic on the coastal shipping system in recent years. Most existing coastal shipping terminals are now outmoded, in many cases badly deteriorated, and they have inadequate capacity to meet traffic demands. These circumstances have resulted in excessive congestion and delay to ships; coastal vessels in the Saigon, Nha Trang, Da Nang, Qui Nhon trade, for example, are reported to spend more than two-thirds of their time in port, usually awaiting berthing space.

After the war, with modernization and reconstruction of the highway system and the full restoration of the railway, the demand for coastal shipping will undoubtedly diminish. However, some base traffic for which coastal shipping is the cheapest and most convenient mode will surely continue. This traffic will be generated at Saigon and at those outports having hinterlands of relatively concentrated population and production.

The Joint Development Group has reviewed the recommendations for port improvement made by the director of navigation and by consultants to U.S. AID, and presents in this section for budget purposes summarized estimates of cost of the improvements likely to be justifiable in the first ten years after the war (Figure 10.7).* As postwar trends in waterborne commerce emerge. detailed economic and engineering feasibility studies should be undertaken for each of these projects before steps are taken to finance construction.

Marine terminals for bulk commodities (petroleum oils and lubricants, ores, coal, and so on) are usually associated with private industries or form a functional part of new development undertakings, and are therefore excluded from these estimates. It is assumed that handling capacity in these cases will be built and paid for in accordance with specific industrial needs. It may, however, be necessary to treat the needs of the proposed fertilizer industry as a special case, since location of the industry in the Mekong Delta will require extensive dredging of either the Mekong or the Bassac rivers.

Saigon

Existing Conditions

The port of Saigon, with the equivalent of ten berths for ocean-going general cargo vessels in its commercial section

---

*Port Development, Joint Development Group Working Paper No. 36.

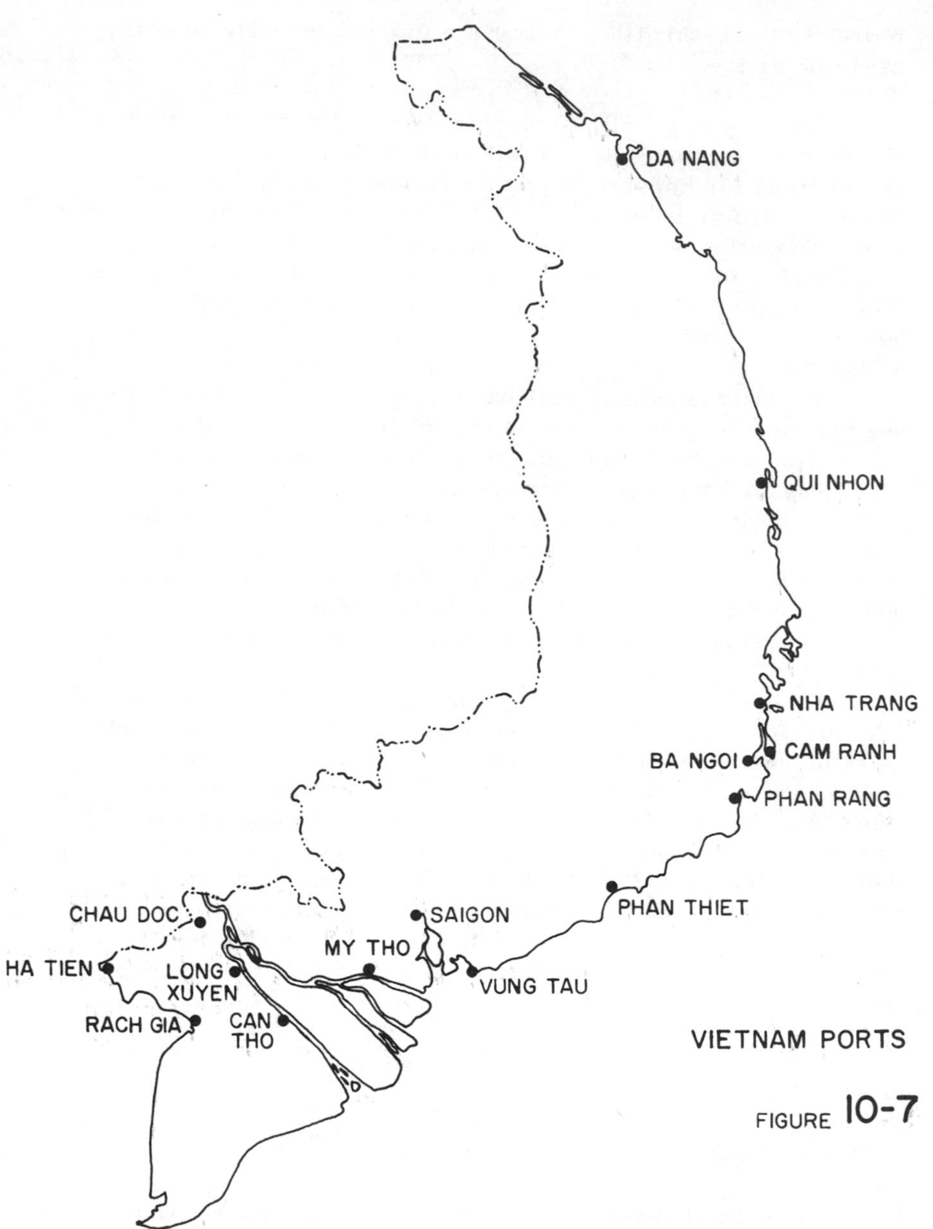

VIETNAM PORTS

FIGURE 10-7

and four modern berths at the Newport military terminal, appears to have adequate capacity to meet present traffic demands. Under the stress of wartime conditions, the port is operating relatively efficiently and, at the commercial port, wharves may be handling up to 250,000 metric tons per year per berth. This is twice the rate normally achieved at modern general cargo marine terminals in the United States. It is accomplished by virtue of a relatively high proportion of bagged or semibulk cargo, which can be handled faster than more diversified general merchandise, by longer working hours than are usually acceptable to stevedore labor, and by a high rate of occupancy of ships at berth.

General Cargo Commerce

Saigon is now reported to be handling over 2,500,000 metric tons a year at its commercial port; forecasts of deep-draft general cargo tonnage in Saigon indicate volumes of 3,200,000 metric tons in 1970, 4,400,000 metric tons in 1975, and 5,500,000 metric tons in 1980.*

Postwar Port Capacity

After the war, the release of the Newport terminal for civil use would probably accommodate deep-draft general cargo demand through 1971 or 1972, and possibly longer. However, it is most unlikely that the Newport terminal will be converted to civilian use by that time, and it is conceivable that the entire terminal will never be released. On this assumption, additional marine terminal construction should probably proceed immediately after the war so that Saigon can handle increasing general cargo demands without undue congestion.

On the other hand, note must be taken of new trends in marine transport, especially the advent of containership services. The use of containers, loaded on specially designed or adapted vessels, is revolutionizing ocean transport. Trends in the industry are still changing, but an expansion of such services is certain; extensive use is already made of containership transport to Vietnam by the U.S. armed forces.

---

*Daniel, Mann, Johnson, and Mendenhall, Development of Harbor Facilities for the Port of Saigon (U.S. AID, 1966).

Berths for container vessels handle over 400,000 metric tons of general cargo per year. They are characterized by broad open working spaces adjacent to the ship for storage and for assembly of containers. Transit sheds are unnecessary. Unless ship-mounted equipment is available, berths are fitted with gantry cranes. The use of one or both of the open berths at the Newport terminal for container services (as at present), and the possible conversion of the present K-10 open berth, at the commercial port, either separately or together, would greatly add to postwar commercial port capacity at little or no capital cost.

Postwar Development

When postwar trends in waterborne commerce can be seen, the question of port capacity for Saigon should be examined in more detail. For budget purposes, however, it is reasonable to assume that some investment in additional port capacity is going to be needed at Saigon during the first ten years after the war, and an estimated construction cost of US$6 million is assumed. This would be adequate for construction of two marginal general cargo berths of 180 to 190 meters in length with transit sheds and related facilities. Alternatively, this sum would be adequate for construction of a single open berth equipped with gantry cranes for container operations.

Other Works

Establishment of a customs-controlled free-trade zone has been suggested on the Saigon River near An Khanh, about 2.5 km below the present commercial port. Free-trade zones are the key to the commercial success of Hong Kong and Singapore; whether Saigon can support the entrepôt activity necessary for a viable customs-free zone of this kind is doubtful at the present time, but the idea is a good one and will bear further study after the war.

Coastal Shipping

All the deep-draft terminal facilities of Saigon's commercial port are available to coastal traffic, and there are literally hundreds of other locations in the port's many waterways where small vessels, especially rice barges and junks from the delta, can be worked. Further development of terminals for coastal traffic at Saigon should not be necessary.

The Directorate of Navigation has represented the need for channel improvements in the Saigon River and for a range of improvements to shore facilities in the commercial port area. An allocation equivalent to US$500,000 per year is made in these estimates for work of this kind.

Over-all, the foreign exchange component of the various works described is taken to be about 40 percent, and the total budgeted development expense for Saigon is as follows:

Foreign exchange: US$4 million
Local currency: VN$775 million

The terminal construction is assumed to take place in the period 1973-75.

Da Nang

Da Nang is the commercial center of the I Corps Tactical Zone and has good connections by road and rail with all the northern provinces of Vietnam. It will clearly be a center for postwar development in this part of the country. Some of the prospects for postwar development in Da Nang's hinterland are reviewed in Chapter 12, and additional development studies of the area are contained in a further report.*

Until very recently, the port of Da Nang provided terminal facilities for coastal vessels only. Deep-draft ships were anchored in the bay and cargo was lightered to and from the shore. The U.S. armed forces recently constructed a deep-draft marine terminal with six deep-water berths on Tien Sha, opposite Da Nang, together with land connections and cargo storage facilities.

The commercial port of Da Nang is on the Song Vinh Dien, near the town center. It consists of a group of concrete and wooden marginal wharves providing berthing space of about 638 meters for coastal vessels. This includes new construction in 1968 which was to have been completed by the end of that year.

---

*D & R Report, "Five Northern Provinces of the Republic of Vietnam" (Urban Development, December, 1969).

Systematic repair, replacement, and possible extension of the coastal vessel berthing area will be required over the first ten years of the postwar period, probably at a rate equivalent to about US$100,000 per year, inclusive of local currency requirements of VN$7 million per year. These funds could also be used for conversion of the U.S. military landing craft terminal located near the commercial port area.

In the long term, Da Nang's ability to attract a substantial share of Vietnam's deep-draft waterborne commerce, in competition with Saigon, is doubtful. Charter vessels will have occasion to call, but steamships are attracted to ports where better opportunities to assemble cargoes are found. Similarly, liner services are not usually scheduled to outports such as Da Nang, preferring surer prospects of larger cargo offerings at major ports.

The deep-draft terminal facilities built by the U.S. armed forces are not conveniently located for efficient civil port operations. However, they represent a substantial investment and their combined cargo-handling capacity, if available for civil use, could easily accommodate deep-draft general cargo traffic at Da Nang for the first ten years after the war. Accordingly, no postwar capital investment in deep-draft terminals at Da Nang is believed to be necessary.

Cam Ranh Bay

Cam Ranh Bay is probably one of the world's great natural harbors. Its protected entrance and the natural deep waters of the bay (5 to 15 meters) afford unusual advantages for development of a marine terminal to serve large ocean-going ships. The U.S. armed forces have taken advantage of this situation and have built on Cam Ranh Peninsula a major port complex comprising several piers and adjacent cargo handling areas.

Because of the natural advantages of the site and the large investment which has already been made, a range of possible postwar uses has been suggested involving forms of industrial and urban development. Regardless of what may eventually happen at Cam Ranh, no further public investment seems to be required for deep-draft general cargo port facilities.

Across the bay from the military port lies the town and port of Ba Ngoi. Here the first construction phase of a new town, Cam Ranh City, intended primarily to house workers in the nearby military facilities, is being completed. At Ba Ngoi there is a small pier for coastal vessels. This has deteriorated badly but is now being reconstructed at a cost of US$500,000. No further investment is deemed likely at Ba Ngoi in the ten-year postwar period.

Other East Coast Ports

The east coast of Vietnam affords a number of other protected locations for port development. Small piers and wharves for coastal vessels have been built at Quang Ngai, Qui Nhon, Nha Trang, Phan Thiet and Vung Tau. Generally, waterborne commerce to most of these ports has been upbound from Saigon and has been dominated by rice shipments. Vung Tau has been recommended as a site for transshipment of cargo from ocean vessels to smaller ships for delivery to points in the Mekong Delta.*

Specific improvement projects for both deepwater and coastal shipping trade have been identified at each of these ports. Each has a definable hinterland area, where rapid postwar agricultural development is likely to occur. While it is unlikely that deep-draft port facilities could be justified at any of these locations, repair and minor expansion of coastal shipping terminals may be appropriate. For budget purposes, the Joint Development Group assumes an expenditure of the equivalent of US$2.5 million for these ports over the ten-year postwar period, divided between local currency and foreign exchange as follows:

Foreign exchange: US$1 million
Local currency: VN$180 million

The Delta Ports

The importance of the delta ports is that they are collection and forwarding points for the delta's agricultural produce

---

*Daniel, Mann, Johnson, and Mendenhall, Development of Harbor Facilities for the Port of Vung Tau (U.S. AID, 1966).

going to Saigon. In 1963, for example, delta river ports accounted for over 1 million metric tons of waterborne commerce; two-thirds of this was rice destined for the capital.

Traffic moves in a variety of small inland waterway barges and self-powered junks, the largest being barges of approximately 200 metric tons dead-weight capacity. These craft wind their way through the intricate canal system of the delta from widely dispersed loading points. While there are limited opportunities for mechanization of cargo-handling to and from the inland waterway craft, the river ports will not require investment in fixed terminal facilities in the ten-year postwar period. Over the long term, of course, there is a prospect for handling rice in bulk form instead of in bags as at present, and in that circumstance, much more elaborate central loading and storage points with mechanical loading and unloading equipment would be required.

In addition to the inland waterway traffic originating in the delta, however, coastal and small ocean-going ships move up the Mekong from the sea. In 1967, from 40 to 60 ships a month made this passage, approximately half of the vessels being destined for My Tho and the rest for Cambodia. The maximum size of a ship is limited to a draft of about 5 meters and a dead-weight tonnage of roughly 2,000 tons. The Bassac is a more direct route into the delta from the sea, but, owing to enemy activities, the channel has been too hazardous for steamship operations in recent years.

After the war, one delta river port, possibly My Tho, on the Mekong, or Can Tho or Long Xuyen on the Bassac, might be developed with terminal facilities for ocean-going ships. The basis for commerce would be the agricultural production of the Mekong Delta, initially rice. In past years, Vietnam exported up to 340,000 metric tons of rice per year. The proposed water-control project for the delta is expected to increase substantially the country's export potential in agricultural commodities.

Can Tho probably affords the best prospects for port development. It is not as close to the open sea as My Tho, but the Bassac channel is less circuitous than that of the Mekong, and dredging requirements to Can Tho would be less than to

My Tho.* While development of another outport directly handling exports from the delta would compete with Saigon and would involve radical changes in the present system of commodity collection, shipment, and distribution from delta areas, the very large potential volume of export trade (possibly 20 percent of the delta's estimated future production of 10 million tons) might afford a valid basis for a new deep-draft port.

A port at Can Tho would require dredging from a point 20 km offshore of the mouth of the Bassac upstream for 110 km. Initial operations could probably take place with a relatively shallow channel of 5 meters at low water (8 meters at high water) permitting access by C-1 and C-2 type dry cargo vessels. Dredging to assure a low water depth of 5 meters would require removal of roughly 3.0 million cubic meters of material.** Later, dredging to a depth of 8 meters at low water would probably be indicated.

The cost of such a development, including first-stage dredging, navigation aids, and terminal and shore access facilities might be in the order of US$8-10 million, of which 40 percent would probably be foreign exchange. The development would probably not take place until the latter part of the ten-year postwar period, though this could be rescheduled to take into account the needs of a fertilizer industry, if, in the event, this is located at Can Tho. The Joint Development Group is including in its estimates an allocation of US$4 million and VN$710 million, distributed equally over the years 1976, 1977, and 1978, for this project.

Summary of Postwar Investment in Ports

Investment in the individual projects discussed in this section will total US$9.8 million and VN$1,735 million over the ten-year postwar period, as shown in Table 10.6.

---

*King and Gavaris-Peril, Mekong River Crossing, (U.S. AID, 1968), Figure VI-19.

**Ibid.

TABLE 10.6

Total Ten-Year Postwar Investment in Ports
(millions)

Port	Investment (US$)	Investment (VN$)	Total (US$)
Saigon	4.4	775.0	11.0
Da Nang	0.4	70.0	1.0
Cam Ranh	-	-	-
East Coast	1.0	180.0	2.5
Can Tho	4.0	710.0	10.0
Total	US$9.8	VN$1,735.0	US$24.5

INLAND WATERWAYS

The natural and man-made waterways of the Mekong Delta total nearly 5,000 km, and water transportation has traditionally been the dominant transport mode of the region (Figure 10.8). In recent years, enemy action has sharply restricted traffic on some canals and a considerable shift to truck transportation has taken place. Because of the war, canal maintenance dredging has been neglected, so a number of waterways are now badly obstructed, though almost all are still navigable to some extent. Estimates by others in recent years indicate that the backlog of maintenance dredging required is about 15 million cubic meters.*

The Directorate of Navigation (DON) maintains a dredge fleet with a rated capacity for dredging of about 10 million cubic meters annually. This represents the approximate volume of maintenance dredging required each year; before the war the fleet was fully utilized in this work.

Through enemy harassment and loss of personnel, the dredge fleet's capability has been severely reduced. Current programs of the DON, U.S. AID, and the Republic of Korea are directed to the training of additional dredge crews and improving dredge maintenance, leading to restoration of the full capabilities of the existing dredge fleet.

*_Ibid_.

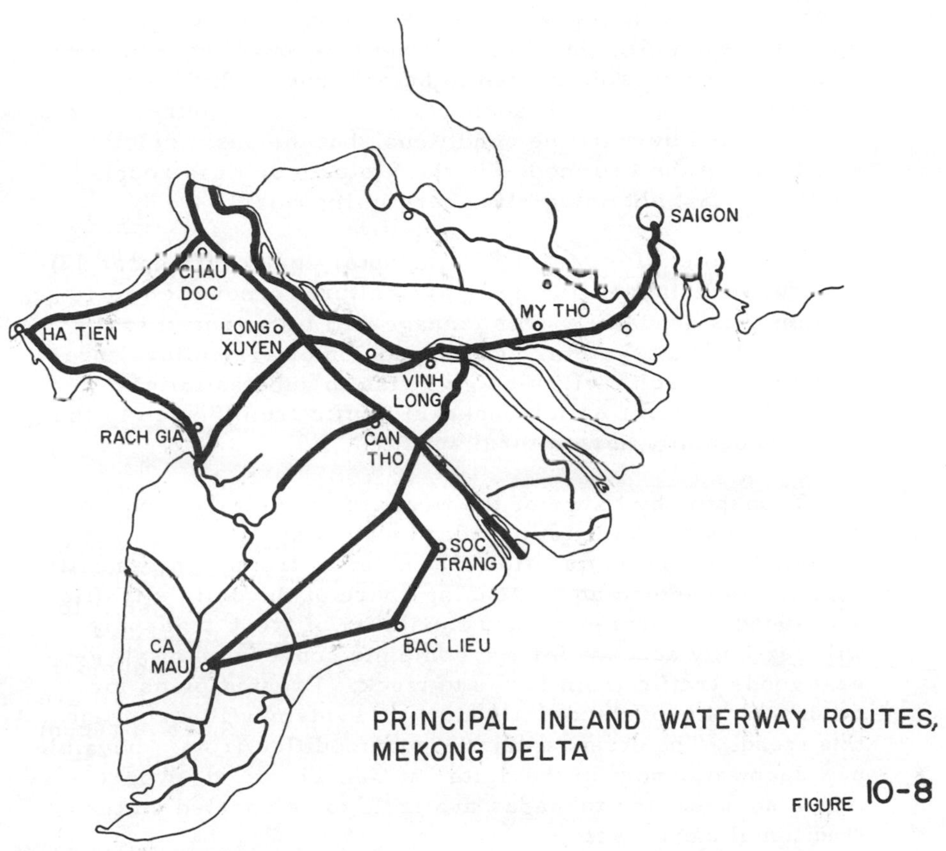

PRINCIPAL INLAND WATERWAY ROUTES, MEKONG DELTA

FIGURE 10-8

Postwar Waterway Development

Where large volumes of bulk commodities are available for regular haul, as is the case for rice between the delta and Saigon, inland waterway transportation is traditionally much cheaper than highway transportation. At the present time, for example, the cost of barge transport between the delta and Saigon is estimated to be only one-fifth the cost of truck transportation. Transportation rates, of course, are now distorted by wartime conditions, but the basic relationship between the two modes in the Vietnam delta is roughly similar to that obtaining elsewhere in the world.

The project for Mekong Delta water control (Chapter 12) may result in increasing delta agricultural production to 10 million tons annually. This tonnage will be potential to the inland waterway system. The expansion of agricultural production in the delta will also give rise to substantially increased opportunities for backhaul traffic from Saigon to the delta, especially agricultural supplies.

Transport by barge of the whole of the delta's produce and supplies by the existing inland waterway system is not likely. There is no question that highway transportation will continue to capture an increasing share of the delta's traffic. The speed, convenience, and flexibility of truck transport will certainly account for the complete conversion of all general goods traffic from barge to truck. Present plans for reconstruction of the delta's highway system will encourage this trend. The direct export of commodities from a possible new deepwater port in the delta, at Can Tho or elsewhere, may also affect the tonnages available to be carried on the traditional canal system.

Ultimately, however, there will remain a substantial movement of freight by barge in the postwar years. To serve this traffic, the inland waterways must be restored to usable depths (at least 2.0 meters on all principal canals). This work can probably be accomplished with the existing dredge fleet of DON, provided steps are taken to ensure dredging operations at full capacity. Some inland waterway improvement is also expected to be undertaken as part of the Mekong Delta water-control project; this would consist of canal deepening for improvement of hydraulic flow characteristics and installation of navigation locks.

For minor realignment of canals, possible construction of new links, and related works, a postwar development budget equivalent to US$5 million is suggested for the ten-year period after the war. Approximately one-half of this amount is assumed to be foreign exchange; the distribution of estimated cost is

Foreign exchange: US$2.5 million
Local currency: VN$295 million

AIRPORTS

Air transportation has been vital to the war effort in Vietnam and at present the country has over 100 operational airports (Figure 10.9). Many of these are now available only for military or military-approved air operations.

Present Programs

Because of the military significance of air transport, most of the current improvements to airports are being accomplished with military funding. Planning for civil aviation requirements is directed primarily to programs for improved operation and maintenance. The Directorate of Civil Aviation (DCA), Air Bases (DAB), and Meteorology (DOM), are active in this effort. The programs funded by U.S. AID and the Department of Defense are directed through a Civil Aviation Advisory Group (CAAG). Primarily advisory programs, they provide for training, air traffic control, navigational aids, and general technical assistance.

Postwar Development of Airports

Having already a very well developed system of airports, Vietnam will probably require no further airport construction for a long time, and certainly none in the ten years immediately following the war. In fact, present yearly passenger air travel (1 million passengers) and civil air freight shipments (10,000 tons) will probably diminish in the postwar period.

As military activities decrease, Vietnam must decide on the ultimate disposition of the airport system. Some airports

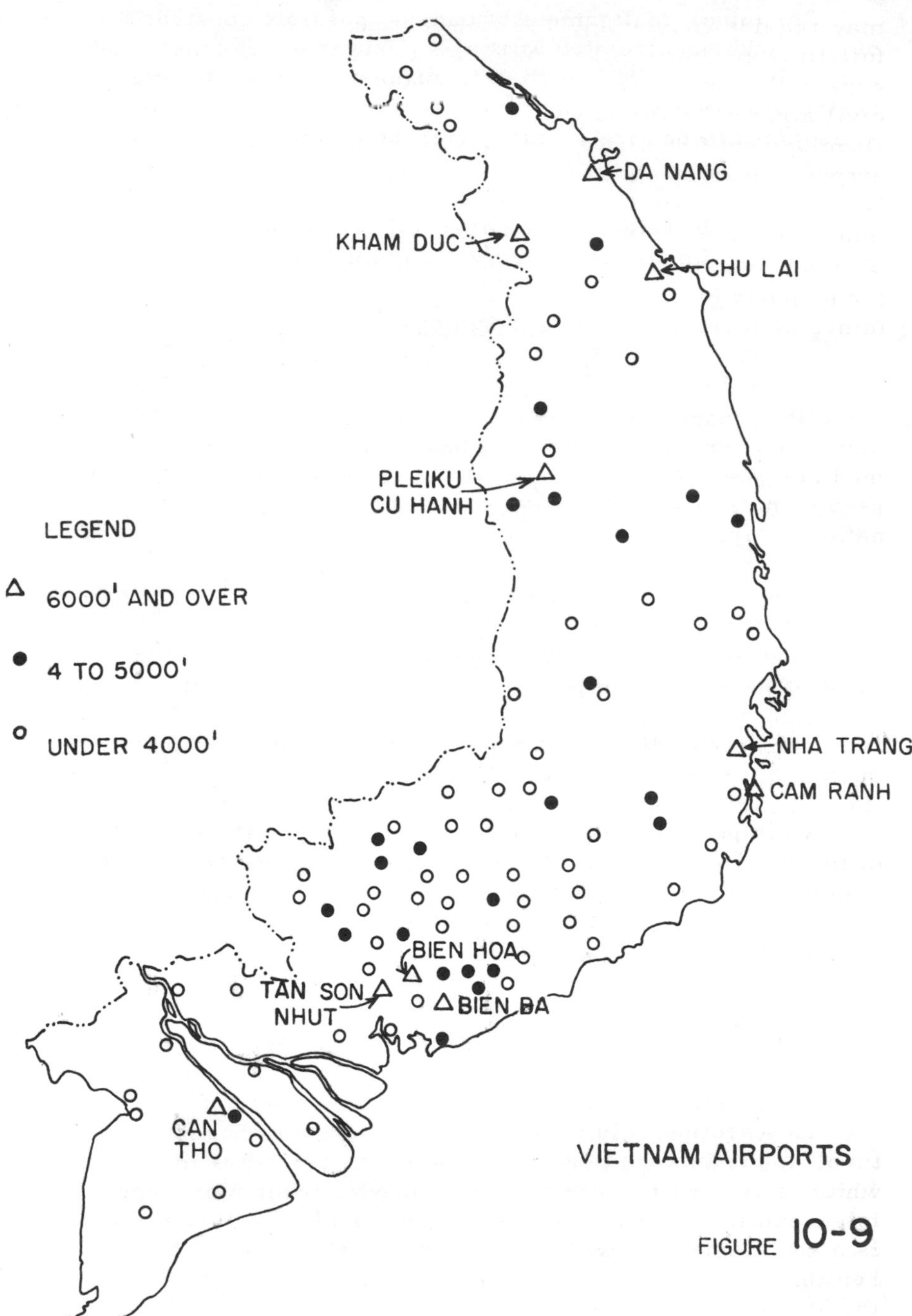

VIETNAM AIRPORTS

FIGURE 10-9

may require substantial modifications for their conversion to full-time civil use; others may need only minor improvements, especially runway lengthening, to meet the needs of modern civil aircraft. Others will not be wanted at all. The Joint Development Group recommends the formation of a postwar airport development group with representatives of DCA, DAB, DOM, Air Vietnam, and the RVN Army to select a manageable system of existing airports for postwar development. The planning of this system will require definition of standards for airports of varying sizes and consideration of expected future patterns of air travel and domestic air freight.

A major question will concern Tan Son Nhut. It is recognized that in the distant future the continued growth of Saigon may conceivably dictate relocation of this facility. In the immediate postwar period, however, it can continue to operate as a joint civil-military airport similar to Don Muang International Airport in Bangkok.

As an airport program is developed, funding requirements can be determined. For budgetary purposes an investment equivalent to US$5 million is assumed. This might comprise 60 percent foreign exchange as follows:

Foreign exchange: US$3 million
Local currency: VN$236 million

A companion study to plan for alternative peacetime uses of those airports which are not needed for air operations is also desirable. While some airports may be abandoned, others may be usable for industrial sites, equipment depots, and similar purposes.

SANITATION

This section concerns programs for sanitation infrastructure, as distinct from the broader subject of public health, which is treated elsewhere (Chapter 11). Adequate sanitation is essential for the prevention and elimination of disease and is a key element in assuring acceptable standards of public health. The Joint Development Group, in cooperation with the Ministry of Health, the Directorate of Water Supply, and other agencies, has begun preliminary consideration of the whole complex of the physical improvements, organization, and personnel requirements for an effective sanitation program in the postwar period.*

Physical Improvements

The principal elements of sanitation infrastructure are the provision of adequate potable water supplies and the construction of sanitary sewerage systems.

Potable Water Supply

The priorities for expansion of potable water supplies in Vietnam are the principal cities and towns. Saigon has a new supply capable of providing 500,000 cubic meters of potable water per day. This is sufficient to provide 125 liters per day for a population of over 4,000,000 persons.

The Directorate of Water Supply has plans and priorities for the improvement of potable water supplies in six provincial towns at an estimated cost of US$36 million. The Joint Development Group is in accord with this program and recommends that this amount be budgeted for postwar development of water supplies in the ten-year period after the war. The estimated foreign exchange component is 60 percent, or about US$22 million. The Joint Development Group also recommends the dissemination of information to rural areas on correct methods for development of rural potable water supplies from rivers, wells, and rain-water catchment.

Not included in this budget estimate are current U.S. AID programs for improvement of the Saigon water distribution system of US$3 million in FY 69, U.S. AID programs for provincial towns of US$1.3 million, and U.S. AID programs for rural water supplies of US$2.2 million.

Longer-range plans for water supply development of the Directorate of Water Supply contemplate the expenditure of the equivalent of US$47 million in ten other provincial towns. Until operating and administrative improvements within the Directorate of Water Supply are effected, and until technical staff now serving with the armed forces are returned or replaced, this program should be deferred.

---

*Sanitation Development, Working Paper No. 37 (Joint Development Group).

Sanitary Sewerage and Storm Drainage

The sanitary disposal of human wastes is critical to the success of a national sanitation program. In Vietnam there are few sanitary sewers and those sewers which exist are old and inadequate to meet modern demands. Standing water is common in residential areas, and during rains storm drains are wholly inadequate to carry the heavy runoff.

There has been no comprehensive consideration of these problems in Vietnam but U.S. AID is about to undertake an examination of the sanitary sewerage and storm drainage requirements of Saigon. The Joint Development Group recommends that similar studies be undertaken for all major towns. These will include inspection of present drainage systems and preparation of plans to carry out urgently needed sewerage and drainage improvements. The estimated cost is US$1.5 million. As part of this effort, simple methods of removing sanitary wastes should be developed. These might include cesspools, large septic tanks, and stabilization ponds.

The large-scale construction of sewage treatment plants is not contemplated during the immediate postwar period. Vietnam's first primary treatment plant is being built at Cam Ranh City, but the country has not yet acquired the expertise to operate major sewage treatment systems.

Sewage treatment requires systems of sanitary sewerage piping, almost nonexistent in Vietnam at the present time. It has been estimated that basic sanitary sewerage for the larger towns and cities might cost around US$500 million. But sanitary pipe systems would be superfluous until waterborne sewage is practical and until urban domestic water supplies are more fully developed. A more modest program, estimated to cost the equivalent of US$40 million, is suggested as appropriate and feasible for the ten-year period after the end of the war.

Other Improvements and Activities

There are a range of other sanitary service improvements and activities needed in Vietnam. These include:

1. The establishment of a revolving fund for purchase of garbage removal trucks by provincial cities, to be recouped by a tax for the service; initial cost, US$3 million.

2. Strict application of Decree No. 10 concerning the sanitary storage and disposal of garbage.

3. Mass education on sanitary garbage handling and disposal.

4. The use of garbage for agricultural manures and animal (hog) food.

5. Construction of simple public latrines in congested areas of cities and towns; estimated cost, US$1 million.

6. Development of standards and dissemination of construction information for family latrines in rural areas.

7. Education on sanitary food-handling at public eating places.

8. Continued programs of pest and insect eradication, especially Anopheles mosquitoes (malaria) and fleas and rats (plague). Widespread public education programs are important in this effort.

9. Slum clearance and refugee resettlement (treated below in the section "Urban Housing").

10. Public health education.

11. Sanitation for emergency (war, flood) conditions.

Legal and Organizational Improvements

The principal legal bases for sanitation are Decree No. 10 (May 16, 1954), which defines regulations for urban sanitation; Decree No. 59 (October 25, 1956), which defines standards for rural health; Decree No. 559YT (April 28, 1954), which establishes the Public Sanitation Service; and Decree No. 560YT (April 28, 1954), which establishes the Provincial Sanitation Services.

There is some duplication between the prescribed activities of the sanitation services as defined in decrees 559YT and 560YT and the Public Health Service. These overlapping functions should be eliminated.

Personnel

None of the sanitation programs suggested can be effective until adequate sanitation personnel become available. Personnel requirements are estimated to be as follows:

14 public health engineers (graduate engineers with one year of training abroad).

320 sanitary technicians (second baccalaureate degree and graduation from the health training course).

500 sanitation cadres (first baccalaureate degree and graduation from sanitation cadre training course).

To provide this staff, the Ministry of Health is planning a National Health Institute to be built at a cost of US$2.5 million. This investment is included in the ten-year postwar development program. The ministry estimates that under its proposed training programs, each year 2 health engineers can be trained abroad and 32 health technicians and 50 sanitation cadres can be trained in the health institute. The estimated annual cost of training is VN$4 million.

Summary of Cost

The components of sanitation infrastructure included in postwar development estimates are as shown in Table 10.7.

TABLE 10.7

Total Postwar Investment in Sanitation

Component	Foreign Exchange (millions)	Local Currency (millions)	Total (millions)
Water supply	US$18.0	VN$212	US$36.0
Sewerage	15.0	295	40.0
Sanitary plans	1.5	-	1.5
Total	US$34.5	VN$507	US$77.5

TELECOMMUNICATIONS

Vietnam's telecommunications network is a complex of diverse systems, some interconnected, some independent. The main components include the national system of the Post Office (PTT), the systems created by the Vietnamese and U.S. armed forces and other agencies, the radio, services of the National Police, the Combined Telecommunications Directorate, and subsidiary networks serving railways, highways, power, civil aviation, and others.

The dominance of military telecommunications is illustrated by the following tabulation of existing telephone connections in Vietnam:

PTT	42,500
ARVN	4,000
U.S. AID	4,000
U.S. forces	55,000
	105,500

It has been estimated that investment in telecommunications by U.S. forces in southeast Asia as a whole approximates to US$2,000 million, the bulk of this being in Vietnam.* Joint studies are being started by ARVN, MACV, and U.S. AID to evaluate the military telecommunications systems, the amounts and types of equipment which may be declared surplus and can remain in Vietnam, the components which may be removed, and the possibilities for conversion of military systems to civil use after the war.

In the military sector, Vietnam has some of the most sophisticated telecommunications equipment in the world. It has a civil system (PTT) which is poorly maintained, understaffed, and physically incapable of installing additional equipment which has already been funded. Most of the difficulties of PTT are results of the war, and especially of the military draft, which has preempted valuable technical personnel; but inadequate salary scales and insufficient training programs also contribute to the organization's technical staff shortages.

---

*"Post-War Telecommunications Planning" (U.S. AID, November 5, 1968).

Through AID, a program for improving the PTT's capabilities is in progress. It includes assistance in installing additional telephones and exchanges, including international circuits. It also includes management reforms directed to the reorganization of the PTT to enable it to function without further foreign support and to produce net earnings for the government. Credits of approximately US$3 million are available for this program.

A concurrent five-year development program to expand the telecommunications services of the PTT has been set up and is to be financed by a loan of VN$1,000 million from the National Bank.

Postwar Development

The PTT's own proposals for telecommunications development after the war call for an investment of about US$74 million in the next ten years. This would cover international, interprovincial, urban, and rural networks and connections. Estimates advanced by AID are approximately the same.

The Joint Development Group, in cooperation with the Ministry of Public Works, Transportation and Telecommunications and officials of the PTT, has reviewed telecommunications needs in Vietnam and generally supports the PTT proposals.* Before investment decisions are made, however, and firm estimates of the probable levels of public expenditures are included in postwar development budgets, more definite information is needed concerning the possible civil applications of the military systems. Firm plans for strengthening the capabilities of PTT to manage an improved national system are also needed before major investments can be considered.

For the ten years after the war, the Joint Development Group believes that a practicable target for public investment in telecommunications should probably not exceed the equivalent of US$30 million, of which about 70 percent would be in foreign exchange. Such a sum is included in the postwar infrastructural development estimates as follows:

---

*Telecommunications Development, Working Paper No. 34 (JDG).

Foreign exchange: US$21 million
Local currency: VN$1,062 million

URBAN HOUSING

The war has had obvious and serious effects on urban housing in Vietnam. In total, possibly 100,000 urban buildings have been destroyed or damaged. Our investigations have taken into account not only the need to repair and replace war damage, but also desirable improvements in housing in the major cities and towns, often quite inadequate for present conditions.*

By almost any standards the urban housing requirements of Vietnam probably run into several hundred thousands of dwellings. The Joint Development Group cannot presently recommend a program for the wholesale rehousing by the government of people living in substandard houses; it does recommend the establishment of appropriate and practicable policies for government participation in this important area of development. We refer in particular to the proposal for a home mortgage bank advanced in Chapter 3.

As a start, the Joint Development Group suggests government financing for the development (including grading, drainage, roads, and utilities) of housing sites, where houses can be built by contractors or private owners. It also suggests budgetary provision for the construction of, say, 100,000 dwelling units over the next ten years. The budget allocation included in the postwar development estimates for these tasks, or possibly others, is the equivalent of US$170 million, of which foreign exchange might be 30 percent, as follows:

Foreign exchange: US$51 million
Local currency: VN$14,200 million

---

* Urban Housing, Working Paper No. 31 (JDG).

POWER

The development plans and projects proposed in this section incorporate where appropriate the views and plans of agencies of the government of Vietnam and of AID. The material presented in the report of the Vietnam Electric Power Management Advisory Team of August 1967* has been considered and used to the extent that it was relevant to the program and projects presented in this section.

The objectives of this section are (1) to review the capability for generation, transmission, and distribution of the existing power system; (2) to present approximations of future electric load and growth requirements for the ten-year period after the war; and (3) to outline briefly a development plan for this period. It is beyond the scope of this study to present detailed project plans; however, general power generating locations are discussed and cost approximations are given. Recommendations for continuing investigations and studies are included at the end of the section.

Present Situation

Generating Capacity

There exists in Vietnam today a serious shortage of power facilities to meet present and projected power needs of the country. The total installed generating capacity, excluding privately owned U.S. military and government diesel generators, is less than 350 megawatts (mw). Excluding the Da Nhim hydroelectric plant (160 mw), which is inoperative because of damage to the penstocks and the transmission line, there remains only 190 mw of installed capacity, most of which (130 mw) is located in the Saigon-Cholon area.

Only about 85 percent of the installed capacity is available on a continuous basis. The installed usable generating capacity is roughly 50 watts per capita in the Saigon metropolitan

---

*"Electric Power Management Advisory Study," Vietnam Electric Power Management Advisory Team (U.S. AID, August, 1967).

area and 4 watts per capita for the rest of the nation; it is a little more than 10 watts per capita for the entire country.

To improve conditions in the rural communities, more than 50 hamlets and districts have been provided with small generating units since 1964. This program was launched under the pacification program of 1964-65 and was continued in 1966 and succeeding years by the Ministry of Revolutionary Development in cooperation with Electricity of Vietnam. In addition, the National Rural Electrification Cooperative Association of the United States is sponsoring three rural electrification projects which are in partial operation.

Transmission and Distribution Systems

Throughout South Vietnam the capacity of the existing distribution systems is inadequate to supply existing and potential consumers.

The Saigon-Cholon area is served by a 66 kilovolt (kv) transmission loop built in 1965 which is in reasonably good condition. As previously mentioned, the 230 kv transmission line from the hydroelectric plant at Da Nhim is inoperative because of damage to towers and insecurity of the area. Distribution substations (66/15 kv) vary in condition from relatively new to old and inadequate. The distribution system is undercapacity in many areas of Saigon and has not been extended to provide service to all new areas. The actual demands are limited to available generating capacity by means of interrupting nonessential loads at peak times.

The distribution systems outside Saigon are generally inadequate and lack capacity to meet present and future requirements.

Operating Agencies

Before 1964, almost all of the electric power industry in Vietnam was in the hands of four French corporations operating under concessions granted by the colonial government before World War II. The exceptions were seven small generating units operated by local and regional administrations.

The Government-owned company, Electricity of Vietnam (EOV), was created in 1964 with broad power to operate the existing government utilities and to promote the electrification of the entire country. During its initial years of operation, most of the plants operated by EOV were derived from Japanese World War II reparations or from AID.

The Saigon Power Company (SPC), with controlling shares held by the government, VN, was formed in mid-1967 to operated all government-owned electric facilities in the Saigon metropolitan area.

At the end of 1967, the most important French concessions expired. With a few minor exceptions where concessions are still in effect, particularly in the five northern provinces, the French generating plants and related facilities have now been surrendered to the Government of Vietnam. Administration of the plants was taken over by SPC in the Saigon metropolitan area and by EOV elsewhere in the country.

While the SPC was formed to operate all electrical facilities in the Saigon metropolitan area, in practice EOV operates a considerable proportion of these, primarily generators provided by AID programs during the period 1964-67. The 1967 decree forming SPC provided that EOV be merged with SPC only in the Saigon-Cholon area; it has been determined, however, that the remaining power facilities in the rest of Vietnam would represent at best marginal operations for EOV. Consequently, plans have been drawn up and negotiations are under way for a complete merger of SPC and EOV into a single independent company, operating on a nationwide basis, to be called Vietnam Power Company (VPC).

Power Requirements

For purposes of these preliminary studies of power requirements in Vietnam, it is convenient to divide the country into three geographical regions: (1) Saigon and vicinity; (2) the area north of Saigon; and (3) the area south of Saigon. Forecasts of power requirements were made for these three areas. These forecasts are the basis for the development of a ten-year expansion and rehabilitation program for the entire country. A discussion of these forecasts follows.

Saigon and Vicinity

The area of Saigon and the surrounding region will, in all probability, continue to be the major electrical load center of South Vietnam. Several forecasts of peak demand in the Saigon-Cholon area have been made over the past several years; the most recent estimate is that of the Vietnam Electric Power Management Advisory Team (MAT) in their report of August 1967, which predicts a maximum peak demand of 559 mw in 1972 and 922 mw in 1975. These load forecasts, according to MAT, are based upon the premise that the distribution systems will be rebuilt, strengthened, and extended, and that generating facilities will be augmented so that pent-up demand for power will be supplied by the end of the period. It is assumed that funds and manpower will be available to carry out the proposed power development program. Under the above-stated conditions, the estimated power requirements were reasonable.

However, the development program suggested by MAT has not been implemented and there appears to be some very serious questions as to when it may be approved and work started. Therefore it does not seem feasible to retain these particular calendar-year estimates as realistic and capable of fulfillment. The JDG considers that a more realistic projected growth rate will require capacity in the Saigon-Cholon area to meet a need of about 500 mw in 1975 and 1,000 mw in 1980. The assumptions that capacity approximating the above figures will be available in 1975 and 1980 must take into account security conditions, the availability of funds, equipment, manpower, and required design and construction lead-time. It is our opinion that a market exists to absorb the above amounts of power and that the above schedule can be met.

Area North of Saigon

Projecting the power needs for the area north of Saigon will be much less precise than for the Saigon metropolitan region. There is currently very little generating capacity and limited distribution of electricity for comparative purposes. The forecasts of power requirements envisage minor industrial development in the large communities and eventually a sizable portion of the power being supplied from multipurpose hydroelectric projects combining irrigation, flood control, and power. Existing installed capacity, excluding the 160 mw at Da Nhim, totals 38 mw. It is our estimate that the power requirements for this area will be 100 mw in 1975 and 200 mw in 1980. The market exists to absorb this power when facilities are built to supply it. The timing for completion of these facilities is dependent on the same criteria as previously mentioned.

Area South of Saigon

The power requirements for the region south of Saigon are estimated to be 40 mw in 1975 and 85 mw in 1980. This projection does not include the large agricultural demand which is discussed in Chapter 12 under the heading "The Mekong Delta" and which will amount to about 300 mw for drainage pumping plus additional power for irrigation pumping over a period of thirty to forty years. Only a fraction of the ultimate demand in the delta will be required in the initial ten years of postwar development.

Development Programs

Current Planning and Development

A number of electrification programs have been planned during the past few years by the government of Vietnam, acting through EOV and by AID, both directly and through consulting firms under contract to it.

The Joint Development Group has considered these programs, described briefly below, in the formulation of its development program for Saigon and vicinity, the area north of Saigon, and the area south of Saigon.

The most recent development plan for the Saigon metropolitan area is the August 1967 plan of MAT. This plan provides for 1,075 mw of generating capacity in 1975 without Da Nhim hydroelectric plant, and 1,031 with this plant. These figures include 132 mw of reserve generating capacity. The estimated capital expenditures for this program, which includes generation, transmission, and distribution facilities, are as follows:

	1972	1975*
Plan without Da Nhim	US$184 million	US$270 million
Plan with Da Nhim	US$162 million	US$250 million

Since the preparation of this plan, there has been little progress toward its physical implementation as proposed. For very practical reasons of financing and technical consideration, it will not be possible to accomplish the program within the time period presented. It is therefore the opinion of the Joint Development Group that the power needs for the Saigon metropolitan area will be met at a slower rate and at a later date than envisioned in the MAT report. Furthermore, the magnitude of capital expenditures for power in the Saigon area would represent an unbalanced allocation of resources when the rest of Vietnam is critically short of power and there are so many other postwar development and reconstruction requirements.

The MAT report is an excellent planning document, however, and it should be used in the execution of the program to meet the power needs of the Saigon-Cholon area; it considers all factors pertinent to good electric utility planning for expansion to meet the power requirements of this area.

An AID grant of US$32 million providing for two 66-mw thermal units, extension of distribution facilities, and management advisory services in the Saigon area has been negotiated; its implementation is contingent upon the merger of EOV and SPC into the Vietnam Power Company referred to previously. The general objective of AID is to develop by 1972 a capability to generate and distribute about 386 mw of power to the Saigon metropolitan area. In view of past delays in effecting this plan, it appears doubtful that the goal of 386 mw installed generating capacity in the Saigon area will be realized by 1972.

AID financing and technical assistance have also been provided for provincial and rural electrification under two separate programs: (1) rural electric cooperatives (up to $5 million); and (2) provincial and rural electrification (approximately $2 million, not including amounts spent under previous programs). Under the first of these, three pilot rural electric

---

*Estimated for transmission and distribution.

cooperatives have been set up with technical guidance from the U.S. National Rural Electrification Cooperative Association (under contract to AID). Good progress is being made and some electric service is being rendered. These three pilot cooperatives are located in different provinces--Tuyen Duc, Bien Hoa, and An Giang--and will supply eventually at least 45,000 customers. It is planned that funds collected from operation of the cooperatives will go into a revolving loan fund for formation of future electric power cooperatives.

The second program for provincial and rural electrification intends to (1) supply diesel-electric units to provincial cities and (2) establish rural service in hamlets by installing smaller units. AID participation in this program is being reduced as Vietnamese financial capacity to continue it increases.

Electricity of Vietnam is presently engaged in planning activities in connection with preparation of a comprehensive program for electrification of provincial towns. In preparing this program, EOV is considering alternative means of generating power on the bases of specific project studies which have been made by its own forces and by others. Since the status of the EOV program is still very tentative, it has not been included in this study.

Joint Development Group Program

The preliminary electric power development program proposed by the JDG for implementation over a ten-year period is described briefly, by area, in the following paragraphs.

Saigon and Vicinity. The minimum objective of the JDG program for Saigon and vicinity is to provide, by 1980 or earlier, the facilities required to generate and distribute approximately 700 mw of power and energy. This amount will not cover all power needs and requirements of the area and, even if it is approved and implemented, efforts should continue to expand the facilities to meet the full prospective demand. We have estimated the projected power market for 1980 to be about 1,000 mw. The continuing AID support program should provide 386 mw of generating capacity by 1972 or 1973, leaving approximately 300 mw to be provided in the seven to eight following years to meet JDG's minimum objective. Generating capacity could be supplied by reactivation of Da Nhim (160 mw), plus installation of additional units at that facility, or thermal generating plants, or by some combination of those means.

The magnitude of capital investment requirements for the facilities required to generate and distribute 300 mw of additional power and energy in the Saigon metropolitan area after 1972 or 1973, over and above the 386 mw scheduled to be available then, is estimated to be about US$100 million.

Area North of Saigon. The ten-year development goal for the area north of Saigon which is recommended by the JDG is to provide facilities for generating and distributing approximately 150 mw of power and related energy by 1980 or earlier. This is about 110 mw more than presently exists. The power needs for this area are projected to be about 200 mw, leaving a deficiency of about 50 mw in 1980. In this section of the country the use of hydroelectric power is one means for reaching this goal. It is recognized that some small thermal or diesel electric plants will have to be installed to meet requirements during the next few years. Over 3,500 mw of hydroelectric power capability have been identified within the Dong Nai, Upper Sre Pok, Upper Se San, Ba, Bo, and Haut Sekong river basins (Chapter 12). Insofar as may be practicable, hydroelectric power should be developed in conjunction with multipurpose river basin projects to achieve lowest cost development. An example is the preliminary proposal for Song Vu Gia dam and reservoir, in the Quang Nam/Quang Tin subregion of the five northern provinces, described in Chapter 12.

Capital investments to provide the additional 110 mw of power and related distribution facilities are expected to approximate US$60 million if the concept of multipurpose projects is followed. Single-purpose hydroelectric projects would result in higher costs in most cases.

Area South of Saigon. For the area south of Saigon, the objective is to provide facilities to generate and distribute a total of 85 mw of power by 1980 or earlier. This is about 70 mw more than presently exists in the area. This additional capacity will meet substantially all of the power requirements for the area except the water control pumping needs described for the Mekong Delta in Chapter 12. Since there are no hydro potentials in this area, generating capacity during the ten-year period will be supplied by thermal plants, diesel-electric generation, or Extra-High Voltage (EHV) interconnections with other sources of supply.

Capital investment requirements for installation of the above 70 mw of power and related facilities are expected to be about US$25 million.

System Planning. The development programs described above are for the most part plans for three separate areas of the country. This will undoubtedly be the manner in which the power systems will expand to meet the needs of each of these areas.

However, during the ten-year period covered by this proposed development program, adequate system planning should be initiated to consider the various alternatives for providing the power needs of the nation. This planning should consider potential as well as existing hydroelectric plants, storage reservoirs to firm hydro capacity, EHV transmission systems, thermal and nuclear plants, and power interchange possibilities.

Future Investigations and Studies

There is a need for additional investigations concerning the future power requirements of the nation and the means by which these requirements can be met. For the Saigon area, the August 1967 MAT report should be used for planning purposes; it should be updated so that the information and recommendations may be more helpful and useful in the future.

For the nation outside Saigon, much remains to be done to project power requirements and to make realistic plans to meet these requirements. It is understood that the group which prepared the MAT report on the Saigon-Cholon area will undertake this work in the near future for the areas outside Saigon. To the extent possible, taking into account security and other factors, these studies should develop plans for generation sites with capacities, transmission networks, and distribution system requirements. The scope and conduct of the studies and investigations should be coordinated with the JDG in order that the findings, recommendations, and proposals are realistically compatible with the over-all plan and concepts now being prepared by the JDG for postwar development in all sectors of the economy.

CHAPTER 11 THE SOCIAL SERVICES: EDUCATION AND PUBLIC HEALTH

The Joint Development Group has not as yet made original studies of education and public health services, but it has become familiar with work done by others. It seems desirable to draw attention to certain characteristics of recent and continuing developments in the social services which have important, but rarely mentioned, implications for the future. While we have no special qualifications to criticize the programs and policies, particularly in education, which have been suggested by a variety of professional authorities and consultants since 1966, those programs and policies do not appear to us to meet the imperative need of planning for the social services not in isolation from the rest of the economy but in the context of it. The suggestions advance, quite understandably, the objectives in particular fields of endeavor which good professional men know to be desirable and believe to be practicable in the short term with resources presently available; they may not necessarily represent what will be feasible in the long term, having regard to future limitations on resources and all the other at least equally exacting demands for priority. There can be little argument that a more balanced and better integrated approach is wanted.

Precisely what the approach should be is a matter of some difficulty. Education especially is a politically sensitive subject in every developing country and the developed ones as well; influential vested professional interests and some deeply rooted traditional attitudes make objective discussion extremely difficult. Inside the Joint Development Group there is no unanimity of opinion concerning the course we might advise the government to take, and this accounts for some difference in treatment in the Vietnamese and this English version of this study. In the Vietnamese version a rather full account is given of educational progress since 1958, of the problems likely to be met in the period immediately following the war, and of the improvements in educational services which might be brought about first in a three-year period of rehabilitation and then in a seven-year period of development assumed to end in 1978. In this chapter the same information is presented in summary form, without disagreement as to what is desirable and what the priorities should be, but with rather more stress on the financial implications, and consequently with some questioning of whether it is realistic to suppose that the objectives can be achieved in so short a time.

In neither version do we advance final solutions to the difficult problems of providing Vietnam with the range and quality of social services most of its people have now come to expect: but in both we raise some fundamental questions for determination by the government in the very early future, not, we suggest, on the advice of teachers and doctors only but also on that of economists and men of state.

THE PRESENT STATE OF THE SOCIAL SERVICES

A first observation is that in the course of the last ten or fifteen years there has been considerable expansion of the nation's educational services and there has also been an improvement in facilities for medical care.

There were nearly two million children in primary schools in 1967, double the enrollment of 1958/59, and there were almost half a million children in secondary schools, as compared to 140,000 in the earlier year. The growth of higher education was even more impressive, with 31,000 undergraduates in the three public and two private universities, as against a mere 9,000 ten years before. In the seven-year period between 1959 and 1966 the number of facilities at which medical treatment could be obtained increased from 979 to 1,710, and the number of hospital beds from 19,000 to almost 27,000. In numerical terms alone, without reference at the moment to the quality of the services provided, this increase in facilities represents a remarkable achievement in time of war. The new facilities have not, of course, by any means satisfied the popular desire for progress. It is estimated that there are still at least a million children of primary school age who do not go to school, but these developments demonstrate an intention to satisfy that desire and they have raised hopes that within a reasonably early future, adequate educational and public health services will be provided throughout the nation. That there should be universal, free, compulsory primary education, for instance, is taken for granted, and this is understandable, since it is predicated in the new constitution.

The quality of the services provided, with one or two exceptions, leaves much to be desired. The number of teachers in primary and secondary schools and in the universities has not increased in the same proportions as the pupils; and in the primary schools, though in 1968 there were 32,000 teachers compared with 19,600 in 1965, properly trained and qualified teachers are in a minority. Most of the nation's primary school teachers are either completely untrained or are people who, having themselves recently completed a five-year elementary course, have then been given only ninety days of instruction to fit them to be teachers in the new hamlet schools. These men and women are paid minimal salaries, VN$3,450 a month: they teach large classes, from 50 to 60 pupils at a time; school hours are short, since in some places two or even three sessions have to be accommodated in the same classroom in a single day. The communities concerned have put considerable effort into the construction of the hamlet schools, and the young teachers bring a great deal of spirit and enthusiasm to their work; but it is questionable whether much more is being provided for the bulk of the country's children than the barest literacy.

A second observation concerns the cost of these improvements in the social services. The capital costs of a primary school are small, VN$110,000 in cash, with construction materials supplied by Civil Operations and Revolutionary Support (CORDS), and labor supplied by the community. The cash costs have been met from the budget of the Ministry of Revolutionary Development, derived in large part from the AID chapter of the national budget. At a cost of VN$110,000 a classroom, an annual program which provides for the construction of 2,500 classrooms and rudimentary training for 2,500 teachers does not, in these conditions, present much of a financial problem. It has in fact been achieved, and there are some who think that if it is maintained at this pace it will make universal free primary education a reality in the early 1970's. Generous overseas assistance has also been forthcoming for the secondary and vocational schools, for certain departments of the universities, for the construction of a few new hospitals and improvements to others, and for other public health services, including training facilities for doctors and nurses. In these circumstances the capital costs of expanding the social services have not been a strain on Vietnamese resources; indeed, if the burden of capital costs were eventually to fall entirely upon Vietnam, the probability is that they would not be so high that they could not be contained within a ten-year development program of the dimensions we presently contemplate, or met, over a reasonable period of time, from Vietnam's own internal resources; but the annually recurrent costs of maintaining and operating these installations are quite another matter.

In fact, very little thought appears to have been given to them. They are, of course, very high, many times higher than the capital investments made in recent years; they already impose severe strains upon the national budget, and they are mounting inexorably. The budget of the Ministry of Education was only VN$409 million in 1955. It rose steadily to VN$1,169 million in 1962 and it was VN$5,721 million in 1968. To a limited extent these increases in cost reflect inflationary pressures and the declining value of the piaster, but what they represent mostly is the cost of running many more schools than there were in the totally inadequate educational system of 1958. The ministry's budget rose by 26 percent in one year alone, between 1967 and 1968, and since three-fifths of the budget is devoted to primary education, it can safely be assumed that this was in large part a direct consequence of the successful prosecution of the hamlet school program.

In 1968 the budget for education did not, on the face of things, represent a very large proportion of the national budget of VN$93 billion; in fact, it was only 6 percent, a very modest allocation by any standards to so important a purpose. However, comparisons are distorted by the fact that so large a share of the national budget, roughly two-thirds, is devoted to defense, and by the probability that defense costs will continue to be very high for at least the first five years after peace returns. If defense costs are excluded, then expenditures on education were almost one-fifth of all government expenditures for civilian purposes in 1968. The budget of the Ministry of Health went from VN$2,000 million in 1967 to VN$2,800 million in 1968, an increase of 40 percent, and a figure of VN$3,467 million has been inserted into the draft budget for 1969, though this includes provision for refugee relief. Again, the ratio in 1968 of public health expenditures to total government expenditures was low, only 3 percent; but if defense expenditures are excluded, then it was 9 percent, significantly higher. Since the budgeted costs of education and public health do not by any means represent the total costs of operating these services (they exclude the contributions from the AID chapter of the budget and the uncosted contributions to hospital services by allied forces and voluntary agencies), the real costs of maintaining existing services in education and public health is probably equivalent to one-third of all governmental expenditures other than defense.

This leads to the next matter for comment, the extent to which Vietnam has now become dependent on external sources for the maintenance of its social services. As mentioned earlier, capital investment costs have been met almost entirely from funds provided by Vietnam's allies; but this is of less concern than the fact that quite a high proportion of the recurrent operating costs have been similarly met. In 1967 the Ministry of Education's budget of VN$4, 235 million was supplemented by VN$2, 000 million allocated by AID. Less than a quarter of this was used for investment; it was applied mostly to salaries and other operating costs. The AID supplement to the Ministry of Health's budget in 1967 was only VN$389 million; but this figure is not by any means representative of the value of the uncosted assistance provided for the staffing of public hospitals by the U. S. and other allied armed forces and by voluntary agencies, including the American Medical Association. With more than twice as many Vietnamese doctors serving in the Army than there are remaining in the ranks of the Ministry of Health, these reinforcements from overseas have been most welcome, and undoubted improvements in the quality of hospital services have resulted. However, the heavy involvement of foreign doctors in what is, after all, a regular function of the Vietnamese government cannot continue indefinitely, and the burden of maintaining these improved services must fall eventually upon the Ministry of Health.

To summarize, these are the characteristics of the existing social services which appear to us to be most relevant to their development in the next ten years: generally in the country as a whole, though obviously not in insecure localities, these services are already developing very rapidly. Development of physical facilities has been achieved largely by generous foreign assistance, which has also been provided for the operation and maintenance of these facilities. In spite of this there are still serious deficiencies in the social services, the most important of which spring from the fact that the development of fully trained and qualified staff has not kept pace with the construction of physical facilities. The budgets of the ministries concerned are insufficient for efficient operation of the physical facilities which Vietnam already possesses, but they have been mounting very rapidly and now represent a very substantial proportion of total government expenditures. In terms of postwar development, the problem is not so much what the country can afford to build but what it can afford to keep up. The general framework of this budgetary problem has been discussed in Chapter 4. This is the context in which planning for the social services should now proceed.

EDUCATION

The Vietnamese version of this discussion of social services and the tables included in it describe in some detail possible objectives for national education in the next ten years. They also describe the organizational and other measures by which these objectives may be achieved.

A population of 22,500,000 is projected for 1978, with 3,360,000 children in the primary school age-group, 4,100,000 of secondary school age, and over 2,000,000 of university age. Although a system of free, universal primary education is postulated in the study, it is not expected to be fully established during this period. Primary school enrollments are thought likely to increase to 3,159,000 (94 percent of the age group) as compared to the 1968 total of 1,969,000 (78 percent of the age group). Secondary school enrollments should increase from the 1968 figure, 471,000 (with only 15,000, or 3 percent of the pupils, in technical secondary schools), to 1,355,000, with a far higher proportion, about 30 percent, in the technical schools; and university enrollments are expected to increase from 32,600 to 95,000, maintaining their 1968 proportion of secondary school enrollments, 7 percent.

To provide for these greatly expanded services, many more trained teachers will be wanted, especially since it is desired to reduce class sizes and improve the quality of instruction. The objective is to reduce class size in the primary schools from 60 to 40, in secondary schools from 41 to 30, in technical secondary schools from 27 to 20, and in the universities from 47 to 30. The resulting requirements for teaching staff will be partially offset if a recommendation in favor of increasing the teaching hours per week is applied; in the secondary schools and the universities these are abnormally short --in the former from 16 to 18 hours a week for the average teacher, and in the latter only 3 hours a week. It is estimated nonetheless that by 1978 the required annual output of new teachers will have to reach 4, 300 for the primary schools (three times as many as in 1968), 1, 600 for the secondary schools, 5, 500 for the technical schools, and about 450 for the universities. Very considerable expansion is needed in training facilities of all types.

By 1978 Vietnam will make substantial progress toward elementary education of improved quality for almost all of its children and toward a system of comprehensive high school education, with adequate emphasis on technical studies, for about one-third of the children in the 11-17 age group. It is not expected, from its own resources, to make great progress in higher education, but arrangements could be made with universities in foreign countries to meet these particular needs until the Vietnamese economy and educational system are strong enough to accommodate them.

These are certainly desirable objectives, and the emphasis on teacher training and technical education will probably find general endorsement. The targets are ambitious ones nevertheless, and some of us question whether the resources likely to be available after the war will permit them to be reached in a period as short as ten years.

It has been assumed, for instance, that Vietnam will be able to devote a steadily increasing proportion of its GNP to education, and that by 1978 this will have reached the figure of 4 percent which UNESCO, at its Karachi conference, suggested as a minimum objective for the Asian countries. Some of us are inclined to question the general applicability of such theoretical standards. How much of the national income can or should be invested in education depends entirely on the circumstances of each individual country, on its changing needs over time, and on its estimate, which can never be a precise one, of what the needs of the economy will be after, say, twenty years, the time required for a new educational policy to take full effect. The salient fact in Vietnam is that the country is still at war, and that even if peace were to come rather soon it is difficult to see any substantial reduction in defense costs for some years, or consequently, any diversion into the social services of the resources now devoted to the maintenance of the armed forces. The proposals summarized in the preceding paragraphs are, therefore, intended to be flexible in their timing; and it could be that the objectives tentatively set for 1978 will not in the event be achievable until five or ten years later.

Four percent of a projected GNP of VN$890 billion in 1978 amounts, as a matter of interest, to VN$35 billion, considerably more than the total public expenditures, after excluding defense costs, made in 1968. Although the budgetary position should improve in the ten years, it does not seem probable that it will improve so much that expenditures of this order of magnitude will be possible.

Moreover the estimated annual recurrent costs assume that the per capita costs per year will remain very much as they are today. Thus it is thought that the annual cost per pupil in the primary school system will rise from a very low VN$2,974 to a still very low VN$3,324; that ordinary secondary school costs will rise from VN$8,190 to VN$9,388; that technical secondary school costs will actually decrease, from VN$32,719 to VN$31,719; and that annual costs of university education will increase from VN$28,680 to VN$30,700. Many doubts will be raised whether it is realistic to apply these figures to a period when a determined attempt is to be made to improve the quality of education by reducing the size of classes and providing more training--and implicitly, higher salaries--for the nation's teachers; and to a period, moreover, in which it is probable that some inflationary pressures will continue to be felt.

Some of us in the Joint Development Group would therefore prefer to treat the recommendations summarized above as a statement of objectives rather than as a plan of action to be carried out in a fixed time span. The objectives are obviously worthy ones; the methods of approach, the framing of a national plan for education by a central committee, followed by a considerable devolution of powers and responsibilities upon regional and provincial boards of education, supported by representative advisory councils, are well worth consideration; but it is extremely difficult to predict at this stage how far circumstances will permit Vietnam to advance toward these objectives in the first ten years after the war. In the first five years, because of continuing defense costs, it may not be able to advance as far as it wishes. Thereafter, it is hoped progress will be faster.

It is certainly desirable that some of the fundamentals of the development of the educational system be examined as early as possible, so that broad national policies can be established. There is no reason why a study of this sort should not be initiated immediately; but if it is going to serve practical purposes it will need to draw upon not only experts in education but also experts in economics, agriculture, industry, and public finance.

There are some important questions to be answered. First, a fundamental one: Is Vietnam satisfied that the present system of conventional education, founded upon French traditions but recently coming under strong American influences, is in fact responsive to the needs and opportunities of a society which is neither French nor American but peculiarly Vietnamese? If fundamental changes are indicated, then the end of the war and the start of an era of development is the appropriate time to make them. Second: What changes ought to be made in the educational system to produce the skills needed for the development of agriculture and industry, for good government, and for the operation of the social services? Finally: How much will these changes cost, how do the costs compare with the kind of budget which the Ministry of Education might realistically expect to be given in the postwar period, and to what extent can any difference between needs and resources be supplied by contributions from the communities served? Both in the Vietnamese version of this chapter and in Chapter 6, strong arguments are presented that Vietnam will not be able to supply itself with the educational services it needs and desires without a realistic sharing of responsibilities between the central government and the country's local authorities.

PUBLIC HEALTH

The last assertion made in regard to education is probably also true, though to a less significant extent, of the public health services. Without expert knowledge of its own of this subject, the Joint Development Group cannot supply more than a few general impressions on the present state of these services and a few observations which may or may not be helpful to the authorities responsible for planning the future course of their development.

A first impression, quite possibly an erroneous and unjust one, is that in recent years curative rather than preventive medicine has dominated the thinking of the Ministry of Health and of its advisors in AID and has absorbed the bulk of the resources and skills allocated to public health as a whole. This has been natural, even inevitable, in a period when the countryside has been too insecure to permit the preventive health services to operate effectively, and the humane instinct to relieve suffering has been able to find expression more easily in the hospitals of the large towns.

Although outbreaks of epidemic diseases have been brought swiftly under control by joint action by the Ministry of Health, AID, and the Vietnamese and allied armed forces, there is no doubt that the effectiveness of the public effort in preventive medicine has declined, while the availability and quality of medical care has improved. Large numbers of trained sanitarians have been lost to the health services, partly to the military draft, partly because of the superior attractions exerted by work opportunities offered by construction contractors and allied military bases; and these men have not been replaced, as Vietnamese physicians and surgeons have been, by reinforcements of qualified men from friendly nations overseas. In contrast, considerable expenditures have been made, on new hospitals not only for the armed forces but also for civilian use in certain province capitals, and on improvements and extensions to other hospitals; training facilities for physicians and nursing staff have been expanded and improved; and a very considerable effort is being made to develop the local manufacture of pharmaceuticals. Obviously this kind of development is entirely desirable; though there is still a shortage of physicians and trained nurses, the training facilities created in recent years should substantially satisfy the requirements of the medical services in years to come.

What is not so desirable is that all these developments in public health have taken place in emergency situations rather than in the context of a long-term program responsive to the country's over-all needs and sensitive to the limitations on its resources. Investments of capital of external origin have been made, and very much larger investments are contemplated, in new installations for medical treatment, without any consideration of the continuing costs of maintenance and operation which will fall upon the national budget. Thus, plans have recently been prepared for the reconstruction of the provincial hospitals at an estimated cost, including staff housing, of US$170 million; but no estimate whatever has been provided of the cost of operating these expensive facilities in, say, ten years' time. Hopefully the operating costs, though they will be high, will be within Vietnam's means; but if they are not they will be found only by transferring resources from other activities, including activities in preventive medicine in the rural areas which might benefit larger numbers of people.

Serious planning for the future is only just beginning, and we have been informed that some preliminary conclusions on the policies to be followed will be available. There are difficult questions to be answered. The principal ones that occur to us in the context of this study are these:

1. How much additional investment in hospital installations should the government of Vietnam be encouraged to make, or to accept, having regard to (a) the extensive military facilities which it should be possible, in a reasonably early future, to convert wholly or partly to civilian use, and (b) the levels of cost of maintaining and operating these installations?

2. What kinds of public health services in the postwar period will procure the greatest benefits to the greatest number at the lowest cost? In putting the question, we do not suggest that the correct mix of curative and preventive medicine can be determined by a simple economic equation. We do suggest that the circumstances of war have emphasized the former at the expense of the latter, that a suitable balance should be restored, and that this is necessary for financial as well as technical reasons.

3. Is Vietnam now ready to establish and implement a program for the control of population growth? The need for this program is discussed in Chapter 5 in relation to manpower and potential unemployment problems, and in Chapter 12 in relation to the future growth of Saigon. These references consist of statements of the adverse effects on the society if population continues to grow at the rate of 2.6 percent per annum, a rate which, though commonly used for population projections in Vietnam, may in fact be considerably lower than the real

figure. This is the place to make a more positive recommendation: this study is aimed at improving the living standards of the Vietnamese people; there are substantial reasons to believe that this can be done within the next ten years, but it is improbable that thereafter living standards will continue to improve if the population continues to increase at this high rate. On the encouraging results obtained from the experimental program now in progress, it seems timely to consider policies of general application and to establish programs for the postwar period.

CHAPTER 12 REGIONAL DEVELOPMENT

National, regional, and local interests in economic progress are not opposed, they are complementary and mutually supporting. Within the context of a development strategy for the Republic of Vietnam, the opportunity can be taken to serve regional and local interests and to satisfy regional and local sentiments, not impairing the essential unity of the nation but, on the contrary, strengthening it.

Successful implementation of the programs suggested in this study will depend on a variety of factors--stable political conditions, adequate resources in money and skills, and good, honest administration, among others; but for some of these programs one particular condition seems to us to be quite indispensable, that of engaging the attention and attracting the participation of the mass of the country's ordinary men and women. The interest of the general public in economic development has to be made apparent if this is to be done; and it is a fact that it can be made apparent more easily in programs directed toward regional problems and opportunities than in those which express only broad national policies and are accordingly fit to be designed and implemented only from the capital.

We believe that in terms of economic development there are substantial advantages to be gained from a policy of decentralization, under which the management of those programs which possess a regional context will be entrusted to representative bodies within the regions particularly concerned. Evidently, it will not be appropriate to apply such a policy to all the programs which we present in this study: fiscal and monetary policies cannot be planned and executed except for the country as a whole; nor can major industrial investments, the feasibility of which depends on national markets or export possibilities; nor can the reconstruction of a national transportation system. But we believe that a policy of decentralization can and should be applied to any programs which deal primarily with regional conditions and problems and which, therefore, are likely to be welcomed and supported in the localities concerned.

We present in this chapter our views on certain programs in which a regional interest is manifest, though a national one is certainly not absent. The problems of water control in the Mekong Delta are perfectly well understood by the people who have their homes and make their livings there; and they, of course, will be the first beneficiaries (though not the only ones) from the kind of improvements we propose to the natural environment which now controls their economic activities. The urgency for a vast program of rural rehabilitation cannot be better understood than it is in the five northern provinces, which have suffered more than any others from the dislocations of war. The Central Highlands have an obvious peculiarity--substantial resources in land and water, and a population consisting mainly of minority peoples who have not yet been brought into the cash economy and who will represent a danger to the stability of the nation until they are provided with opportunities to do so. The problems of Saigon are peculiar too; although every city in Vietnam has grown unnaturally in time of war, in Saigon the changes have been immense and undigestible, so that today, well over two million people are living in a concentrated area whose amenities may be adequate for only a quarter of that number.

In the succeeding parts of the chapter, some ideas are presented on what might be done in the next ten, twenty, or thirty years, or as resources become available, to ameliorate the conditions peculiar to each of these areas. In some cases, these views have been better developed than in others. For instance, a good deal of attention has been given to the development of the Mekong Delta, and project planning is well advanced, simply because it is in this region that the best opportunities for the rapid restoration of the Vietnamese economy after the war occur. Much less attention has been given to the five northern provinces and to the Central Highlands, simply because a full and accurate assessment of the potentials for development in these areas depends upon ground investigations--of soil, subsoil, water, and forest resources--which cannot be undertaken until the war is over.

We recognize, however, that while the potentials of the delta are apparent and will be all-important to the country in the early postwar period, in the long term valuable opportunities for the diversification of the economy may appear in other regions. Some may also appear in the mass of the central lowlands south of Quang Ngai, for which an over-all regional program is not yet suggested; it is difficult to identify, within this long, narrow area, any problems or opportunities common to the whole, which would suggest treating it as a distinct region with a development program of its own; however, there do exist many possibilities for water control and irrigated agriculture projects in the coastal basins, as discussed in this chapter.

Some proposals are also made concerning the organization and management of such regional development programs as may be approved. In no case is it practicable or sensible to advocate the establishment of completely autonomous, independent, regional development authorities to undertake these programs. Although the problems are regional ones, the benefits of economic development will be national as well as regional, and it is impossible to suggest that the central government should divest itself of all responsibility for ensuring that the programs are efficiently carried out. Nor is it to be expected that the legislature, which will be invited to allocate very considerable sums of money to these programs, should not wish to ensure that the money allocated is properly spent. Within each program there will be projects within the responsibilities of the ministries of government, and as long as the ministries have the means to execute these projects--within the general framework of a regional program--there will be no point whatever in asking someone else to do so.

On the other hand, if genuine popular enthusiasm for economic development is to be excited and sustained within the regions, then something more than a purely advisory committee of local notables is required. The precise functions of a development agency within the regions considered in this chapter are bound to vary with the needs and circumstances of each of them; but, as a general pattern, what we recommend is an agency with strong and respected local representation and powers not merely to advise and coordinate, but also, when the need arises, to act. We believe that this is what the ordinary people of the region, whose daily lives stand to gain if these programs are successful and to lose if they are not, will mostly want.

What might be considered a disparity of treatment of the various regions covered is apparent in the following sections. For the five northern provinces, we have endeavored to offer a comparatively comprehensive, although still preliminary, program of development covering all major economic potential; the section on the Central Highlands, on the other hand, provides an analysis which concentrates more, at this stage, on the problems and possibilities of population resettlement and relocation and the institutional framework within which this and related developments can best be accomplished; brief outlines only are presented of the program possibilities in the coastal basins of II Corps and in Saigon and its hinterland (the former focusing on an outline of water resource development, the latter on the relationships of Saigon to its surrounding provinces and its future role as the national capital); and in the delta the primary topic considered is the proposal to achieve very substantial increase in agricultural production through water control. This section, in fact, represents a condensation of a separate report backed by twelve supplementary working papers.

This diversity of approach is due in great part to the manner in which these regional studies have been programmed in our work. The delta, with its richness of agricultural potential, was the obvious place in which to commence investigations and I Corps deserved next priority as the region which has suffered most from the depradations of war. It was the intention of the Joint Development Group in its 1969 work to continue these regional studies and to achieve, if possible, a closer standardization of treatment as well as more definitive statements of the programs appropriate to each area.

THE FIVE NORTHERN PROVINCES (I CORPS)

Later in this chapter attention is given to the problems and potential of the Central Highlands south of Quang Ngai Province. The central plateau and the Annamese Range also make up a substantial part of the land area of the five northern provinces of Quang Tri, Thua Thien, Quang Tin, Quang Nam, and Quang Ngai. Although much that is proposed for the Central Highlands has direct application to the highland areas of the five northern provinces because of topographical and ethnic considerations, and should be recognized as having general validity for the highlands as a whole, it has been decided to treat the politico-military administrative area now known as the I Corps Zone as one region. To do otherwise would, as far as the five northern provinces are concerned, cut across provincial boundaries, inhibit the necessary complementary role which the highlands offer in relation to the coastal areas, and tend toward compartmentalization for the sake of geographical distinction and agricultural similarities, to the detriment of other factors which make up a fully coordinated unit. In the region as it is presently identified, resources should be so harnessed and so integrated that the degree of interdependence between the highlands and the lowlands is enhanced rather than diminished.

In fact, from one point of view the region can be considered as a rough geographical unit. It is bounded on the west by the watershed line of the Annamese Range; on the north by the Demilitarized Zone; on the east by the sea, and on the south by a ridge of high land which separates Quang Ngai province from Binh Dinh. This topographical layout was no doubt one factor leading to the grouping of these five provinces into one region for purposes of military and governmental control. This section of the study is intended to describe the resources, problems, and potential of the region so defined, and at least a first approximation of the course of its future development.

With an estimated population of over 2.9 million, 18 percent of the total population of South Vietnam, the region is characterized by a broad coastal plain, up to 30 kilometers wide, extending from Buc Pho to the 17th parallel. To the west of this plain, the land rises steeply to the mountains of the Annamese Range. Nearly all the region's people live on the plains, where the main concentrations are served by the coastal highway and the railway. The upland areas are thinly populated, and although they have considerable, at present largely inaccessible, forestry resources, they are of little present agricultural significance.

Agricultural production in the region is determined principally by rainfall. The Mekong Delta receives almost daily rains during the period of the southwest monsoon (mid-May to early October), but the movement of cloud is inhibited by the Annamese Range, and the coastal area of the

I Corps Zone receives very little rain in these months. Of an annual rainfall of over 2,500 millimeters, Quang Tri receives only 720 millimeters in the eight-month period January-September, the rest falling during the period of the northeast monsoon, which is concentrated in the months of October and November. Without surface irrigation water or extensive utilization of ground water sources (wherever the water table is near the surface), rainfall for much of the year is inadequate for many crops.

Temperatures during the summer months can be nearly 10°C. above those obtained in the winter, but average high and low temperatures do not deviate from the mean by more than about 5°. Crop varieties are restricted to those adapted to tropical and subtropical climates.

The Prospects For Development

In contrast to the natural wealth and fertility of the south of the country, the development possibilities of I Corps are limited. In terms of input they are likely to be expensive in relation to growth rates achieved, and far less certain in their efficacy.

The base for agriculture is restricted. The sandy soils along the coast appear to be relatively infertile, and a great part of the region consists of terrain where the slopes are too steep for farming. The region is a food-deficit area. The rainfall is largely concentrated in a short season, and there is sometimes severe flooding. Forest resources exist, but security problems have prevented any detailed determination of their extent. Large-scale and imaginative plans for an industrial complex at An Hoa, based on utilization of nearby coal resources at Nong Son, have reached an advanced stage, but implementation of these plans has been held up by lack of security and other factors. Other than a small textile industry, with a cottage industry component for weaving, a sugar mill, and lime manufacture, industrial activity is limited to the small-scale manufacture of construction materials and food processing.

The population is overconcentrated on the line of the main highway through the coastal plain, and is heavily swollen by refugees. Skilled labor tends to migrate either to Da Nang or south to Saigon. Sea fisheries are handicapped by the war, antiquated equipment and lack of knowledge of modern techniques. Access to richer fishing grounds and increased mechanization are prohibited for security reasons.

Economic criteria for the investment of resources usually dictate utilization in an order of priority which will yield the greatest net benefit to the growth of income and employment of the entire country; and if applied to the five northern provinces this principle would argue against a large development effort in the postwar period. Such a policy leads almost inevitably to an unequal partition of development investment among regions, and an inequality of economic growth. It is true that through the mobility of certain resources, and with the spread of accruing income, total benefits may be shared to a certain extent and the degree of inequality of investment partially offset. But there are also noneconomic and political criteria to be applied. Although some regions will inevitably grow faster than others--because of differences in natural resources and population distribution--what is required is a careful compromise between the extremes of maximum over-all cost benefit advantage and optimum regional development for the sake of equality of growth. In the I Corps Zone there should be a sensible effort to exploit such resources as are available in a way which will be complementary to the general national purpose.

In this region, some development potential can be identified. As in the delta, there is an immediate opportunity for improved agricultural production aimed at regional self-sufficiency. In the plains and the principal river valleys substantially increased production is possible by improved control and use of water, permitting more extensive double-cropping of rice and offering opportunities for crop diversification. Increased use of high-yielding rice varieties and improved farming methods, with adequate use of fertilizers and pesticides, would contribute to regional self-sufficiency, and so would improvements in marketing, credit facilities, and feeder roads. Some land can be reclaimed (and further erosion of fertile land prevented) by planting the sand dunes and taking measures to stop saline intrusion from the salt-water lagoons. The sandy soils themselves offer some prospects for more intensive cultivation. The production and processing of tea, silk, and vegetables may provide an incentive for the development of agri-business.

Forest resources may be considerable, and an inventory should be taken as soon as security considerations permit. It is known that extensive stands of valuable hardwoods occur in the forests which cover the greater part of the region, and can be exploited in order to supply an integrated timber products industry, including the manufacture of plywood, at Da Nang. The production and export of cinnamon can be resumed and should be valuable.

Restrictions have been placed on the fishing industry for military reasons. Mechanization is limited for fear that the vessels may be seized by the enemy, and in many coastal areas fishing is actually prohibited. In spite of this, I Corps still produces 16 percent of all marine fish landed in South Vietnam, and can count over 88,000 fishermen, 37 percent of all the fishermen in the country. As these figures indicate, their productivity is low, but the rich fishing grounds of the Gulf of Tonkin offer promising prospects for a substantial industry. Fishing will have to move from in-shore to off-shore, with all the changes in technique, knowledge of navigation, larger, motorized vessels, and improved equipment that this implies. But the manpower is available. Da Nang already has a useful fish landing facility (presently in military use), but ice production and marketing will need improvement, and fish processing, drying, canning, and in particular the manufacture of nuoc nam, fish sauce (of which 1,250,000 liters a year are already being produced), provide further possibilities for industrial growth. Increased use can be made of fresh-water and brackish lagoons and ponds for pond-fish cultivation.

Plans exist for the exploitation of the region's main mineral resource, Nong Son coal, for production of power, fertilizer, and other products in a large industrial complex at An Hoa. The war and other difficulties have prevented the realization of this project, on which very large investments have already been made. Serious doubts have been expressed concerning its economic feasibility. This chapter devotes some attention to this project, which is of fundamental importance to the development of the region; and it has also been discussed in Chapter 9. Whether or not the fertilizer complex is realized, the coal offers a possible source of low-cost energy for the whole region and can be used to serve such industries as cement and lime manufacture, glass, bricks, clay tiles, and ceramics.

The existing route via Khe Sanh and the Se Noi Valley may provide access to the sea for Laos and encourages hope of the potential development of a Laotian-Vietnamese timber trade. The main road network, once it is repaired and maintained, is adequate and the port of Da Nang, as now developed, will provide all the port capacity likely to be required. This deep-water harbor will facilitate water-oriented industrial development as well as sea transportation for the produce of the region. The railroad has been destroyed, but, as described in Chapter 10, it is being restored.

The region has an ample agricultural and industrial labor force. Resettlement of refugees on their abandoned lands should have high priority, and some landless people may have to be relocated in farm settlements in the more suitable highland areas and in the wider river valleys. There may also have to be assisted migration to other regions, but any movement of this kind will have to be voluntary and is unlikely to occur on a large scale.

No developing country can accept, as a deliberate economic policy, the perpetuation of depressed areas by devoting scarce investment resources solely to the more rewarding ones. Priorities will, of course, have to be carefully and wisely established, and if attention is concentrated initially on projects offering the highest yields and quickest returns, as it should be, then the full potential of the I Corps Zone cannot be realized for a good many years. This preliminary account of what that potential may be is followed by a more detailed discussion of those features of it which appear to be most promising.

Agriculture

The problems in agriculture are much more difficult than in other regions. The analysis which follows outlines the more important characteristics of agriculture in the region and suggests some possible courses of action.

As South Vietnam was settled, the northern provinces were the first to be developed, and the lands most suitable for traditional agriculture have been exploited for many years, with a resultant depletion of soil nutrients. Because population density in the coastal plain is extremely heavy, farm units are very small. The principal problem of the northern provinces results from the simple fact that too many people are attempting to practice subsistence farming on the limited area of the coastal plain, so that farm incomes are low. Population pressure has led to some double-cropping and some diversification into animal products, but these desirable developments, though easing the problem, have not yet made any significant impact on it.

Although crops are important in the agriculture of the region, animal products and fish together actually exceed crops in value at the present time. This is because crop production consists mainly of rice, and it is rice production which has felt the most severe effects of the war. The region is a food-deficit area into which large quantities of rice and other cereals, cooking oils, and milk have been shipped regularly. For many years rice imports have exceeded 100,000 tons annually, and a recent estimate of imports has been over 200,000 tons.

Crops were harvested from slightly over 300,000 hectares during 1967, apparently--11 percent of the total land area in the five provinces. However, the actual area cropped was probably considerably less, since some 125,000 hectares are estimated to have been double-cropped. The cultivated area has declined by 15-20 percent since 1964, a direct result of intensification of the war.

Although rice dominates the cropping pattern, just as it does in most other regions of South Vietnam, the preponderance of rice is not as great as it is in the delta. Other crops were harvested from over 20 percent of the cultivated lands. The region produces more than its proportionate share (in relation to population) of corn, sweet potatoes, manioc, and peanuts, but far less of its proportionate share of most other crops, particularly rice, fruit, and vegetables, though vegetable plantings have been increasing quite rapidly since 1963, particularly in Quang Nam, for the Da Nang market. The northern provinces are important producers of sugar cane, tobacco, and tea. The estimated value of production of sixteen principal crops in the region in 1967 was slightly over VN$9 billion.

Yields are generally below the national average. Rice, for example, averaged 1.68 metric tons per hectare, about

80 percent of the yield in the delta. Beans, peanuts, vegetables, tobacco, and sugar cane have yields close of national average, but yields from other crops are much lower; the yields of fruit crops are extremely low.

Fertilizer trials on rice by the Ministry of Agriculture have demonstrated significant responses to chemical fertilizers. For example, in 1965, in fifteen places in Quang Nam province, the application of 60-60-30 fertilizer (60 kg nitrogen and phosphate, 30 kg potash per hectare) gave a 185 percent increase in paddy yield over check plots. This was in unimproved varieties, and better results may be expected from the new improved ones.

Production losses from insects and diseases are difficult to measure. They are certainly large. Future pest and disease control will depend, as do fertilizer programs, on education in the use of pesticides and insecticides and an efficient distribution system. Readily available sources of agricultural credit are essential to the wider use of both fertilizers and insecticides.

The average size of a farm in the region is estimated to be 0.65 hectares. Average farm size in the delta, where population density is about 150 per sq km, is three times this figure, 1.9 hectares. Density in the coastal plain of the I Corps Zone may be as high as 750 persons per m. Less than 30 percent of farmers own all the land they operate: in the great majority of cases, these small farms are of mixed tenure, with the farmer owning a part of his holding and renting the rest. A very large number of very small parcels of land are held under various rental or leasing arrangements of a diversity which makes it almost impossible to consolidate these tiny holdings into economic-sized units.

Farm incomes are therefore very low, probably only half the levels achieved in the Mekong Delta (where they are not high).

With the possible exception of tea and tobacco, essentially all farm and fish production in the I Corps Zone is consumed within the region. Where farms are only 0.65 hectare in size, and concentrate upon rice and other field crops, agriculture is a matter of mere subsistence, and there is little produce to sell. The only cash crop exceptions to this are small-scale vegetable production near Da Nang and Hue and a little tea, tobacco, and sugar cane. Animal products also provide a source of cash income, though a limited one, for many farmers in the region. But generally the average farmer in the northern provinces has little to sell.

Agricultural development in the region will, of course, depend heavily on the potential of the region's soils and the treatment that is applied to them. Most of the arable soil in I Corps are classified as wet alluvials which are waterlogged or even flooded for at least a portion of the year. These soils are ideally suited to rice production and are now usually planted to that crop. But if they were drained they would be well suited to many other crops as well. There are, in the region, some well-drained to moderately well drained alluvials (brown river-level soils) which produce excellent yields of various annual crops and also fruit, peanuts, tobacco, cassava, sweet potatoes, and corn, and citrus, bananas, and jackfruit. They are, unfortunately, limited in area; but the wet alluvials, which are much more extensive, would perform in much the same way if only they were drained.

Much of the land near the coast consists of regosols, reputedly of little economic value because of their poor water-retaining ability and low nutrient status. Land is in such short supply in the northern provinces that even these unpromising soils are exploited, for manioc, peanuts, corn, and coconuts. Yields at the present time are marginal. If full land utilization is to be achieved, these indifferent soils cannot be ignored, but mulching, green manuring, and shelter planting in order to increase organic matter and control erosion will be necessary, and so will fertilizer programs and irrigation.

At the start, the principal efforts should be toward restoring production on lands that have been abandoned during the fighting and increasing yields and production on existing farms. The development of new lands for agriculture may come later, and should be approached with caution, for areas and soils not previously exploited may or may not be suited to present patterns of farm enterprises. Careful organization of new farms will be necessary to encourage production for which domestic or export markets exist, and to avoid uneconomically sized farms which cannot provide satisfactory family incomes.

Within the five provinces the movement of locally produced foods is normally quite restricted, and the existing simple marketing system is satisfactorily serving the purpose of moving to the consumers such produce as farmers have available. It would be a mistake to condemn the present marketing system unless more is known about it and about the specific changes which might improve distribution. Such changes will depend upon future farm sizes, the degree to which farmers specialize, and the types of crops they decide to grow.

An obvious need is to seek crops and other farm produce or combinations of crops that will raise the incomes of farm families. Yields of existing crops can be increased, but even if rice yields were to be doubled on these small holdings, incomes would still be low. Under vegetables the same size of farm would provide better incomes, but this can only be for a limited number of families. Hogs and poultry can be used more extensively to diversify the small farms of the region and to add to farm incomes. All the alternatives, including specialization and diversification, cash and subsistence crops, crops and animals, need careful study.

The consolidation of landholdings to increase the size of farms is another possible approach to the problem. It would imply either conversion of some farmers to other occupations or resettling them in other regions. There are possibilities for the latter course, but in the short term and in present circumstances the consolidation of small holdings is unlikely to make much progress.

Agricultural credit may be a more practical approach. It is not yet readily available to I Corps farmers, although the Agricultural Development Bank now has a representative in each of the five provinces. It made loans totaling VN$133 million to 6,700 farmers in 1967. The average, almost VN$20,000 was higher than the loans made in the delta, and about equal to the average for all of Vietnam. However, loans were obtained by less than 2 percent of the region's farmers, and on this limited scale of distribution credit will not do much to promote growth in the region as a whole.

In summary, and excluding the possibilities of irrigation, which are described later in this section, these seem to be the most promising approaches to agricultural development in the I Corps Tactical Zone:

1. Increased yields of crops already cultivated on existing farms by improved practices and inputs, facilitated by a more generous distribution of supervised credit.

2. An examination of alternative farm enterprises and combinations of enterprises to determine what could be done to raise incomes from holdings now principally devoted to rice.

3. High priority for the reclamation of lands taken out of cultivation because of the war; possibly a lower priority for the development of previously unexploited lands to the extent that suitable areas exist.

Forest Resources

The forests of the region are described briefly in Chapter 8, and so were the disadvantages, in comparison with other regions, which a logging industry in the northern provinces will meet. As suggested later in this section, a plywood industry could create a market for logs sufficiently lucrative in time to overcome the problems of extraction. At this stage an inventory should measure the volume and quality of the timber resources to assess logging capacity. The Forestry Administration could then rationally propose timber reserves and structure a plan for roads and a silvicultural system to regenerate the better species of the forests.

In the meantime, other aspects of the forest have an importance to the economy which may be greater than that of timber. Water is one of them, for the forests are on the watersheds that supply the rice farms of the coastal plain. Logging is highly selective and by itself will probably have little effect upon flow; but forest roads and landings must be well placed to prevent soil erosion. Greater dangers come from shifting cultivation, which affects larger and larger areas as population grows and families experience increasing needs for cash earnings. One solution in the highland areas of the northern provinces may lie in the promotion of permanent crops, such as coffee and cassia, which highlanders could cultivate along with or after their food crops. Thus they would acquire both the cash incomes and a more permanent attachment to the land and, at the same time, the essential forest environment would be maintained.

The region's immediate interest in its timber resources lies in the creation of several forest-based industries for export and domestic use. Two such projects are suggested; the first, dealing with cinnamon bark, has been described in Chapter 8; the second, for the manufacture of plywood, is described subsequently in this chapter under the heading "Industrial Development." The economic importance of these two schemes is that they will provide cash earnings, exports, and employment. In addition, their implementation will automatically foster other forestry activities--inventory, protection, management plans, and reforestation--substantially larger as sources of employment than the projects themselves.

Water Resources Development

The uneconomic size of the region's farm is not the only reason why the region has to import food and why most of its people live at a bare subsistence level. There are other problems: insufficient rainfall during half the year to permit intensive, year-round cultivation; inadequate base flow in the unregulated rivers and streams to allow area-wide irrigation; frequent floods, salinity intrusion into the coastal river reaches, which frequently results in salt-water flooding of lower-lying agricultural lands; and poor drainage conditions on the flatter lands bordering the sea.

The only solution to these problems is control and utilization of the region's water resources to permit intensive, year-round cultivation and crop diversification in the coastal plain. Many studies have been made and plans prepared to improve agricultural conditions during the past thirty or so years--by the former colonial government, by agencies of the government of Vietnam, and by foreign consulting firms. As a result, numerous facilities such as diversion dams, dikes, and canals have been constructed. While these facilities have not been unproductive and have brought benefits to many farmers, they have all been concerned with unrelated specific projects in specific areas, and were not concerned as staged improvements within an over-all regional development plan leading eventually to intensified agriculture throughout the coastal plain of the northern provinces, and major benefits to the region as a whole have not resulted.

Orderly and timely provision of water control facilities, on the basis of a regional development plan aimed at exploitation of the full agricultural potential of the irrigable lands of the coastal plain, will raise the standards of living of farm families and enable the region to meet from its own resources its requirements in food. This report does not present detailed plans for implementing water control facilities; however, general means of doing so will be discussed, and a rough order of magnitude of costs will be given.

Description of the Area

The coastal plain (see Figure 12.1), which is served by seven major rivers and numerous small streams, divides naturally into three continuous reaches: (1) Quang Tri and Thua Thien provinces; (2) Quang Nam and Quang Tin provinces; and (3) Quang Ngai Province. The economic passage of water between the three areas is precluded, and it is necessary to break the region into these three subregional units for study and eventual development of water control facilities. The subregional coastal plain units are similar in that in each, all streams and rivers entering the plain are interconnected before reaching the sea, or can easily be connected, if desirable, for more economic water distribution. The total gross irrigable area in all three coastal subregions together is approximately 410,000 hectares.

Hydrology

Owing to the scarcity or complete absence of streamflow records and the preliminary nature of this study, it has not yet been possible to carry out detailed hydrologic analyses of the major river basins in the region. However, estimates have been made of unit area runoff on the basis of long-term rainfall records. A runoff coefficient of 0.40 was applied to estimated average annual discharge; this was found to be conservative when compared with other areas in Vietnam having similar rainfall patterns and topographic conditions. Average monthly discharges were estimated by applying variable coefficients ranging from 0.30 to 0.50.

Long-term rainfall records (36-year period) at Da Nang which are considered sufficiently typical of coastal plain conditions for the purpose of preliminary study indicate the following average rainfall pattern, expressed in millimeters:

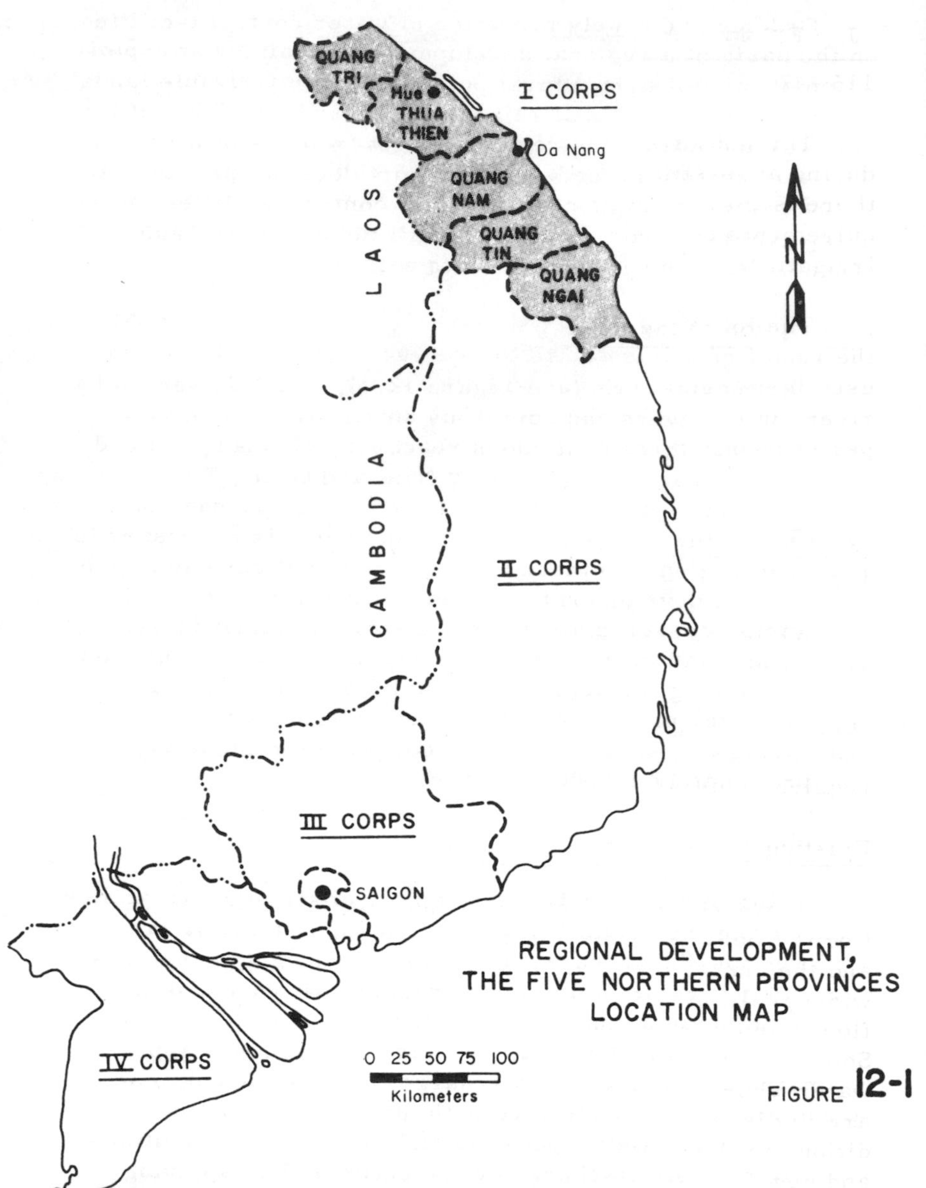

REGIONAL DEVELOPMENT, THE FIVE NORTHERN PROVINCES LOCATION MAP

FIGURE 12-1

J	F	M	A	M	J	J	A	S	O	N	D	Total
115	42	26	31	61	74	76	116	390	568	386	225	·2,110

This average rainfall pattern clearly demonstrates that during at least the six-month period February through July there is insufficient rainfall to meet the consumptive-use requirements of crops. For intensive, year-round cultivation, irrigation is required.

The following unit area discharges, estimated by applying the runoff coefficient 0.40 to average monthly rainfall, were used in determining approximate average monthly flows of the rivers in the region; figures are expressed in cubic meters per second per 100 square kilometers of drainage area:

J	F	M	A	M	J	J	A	S	O	N	D	Average Annual
1.9	0.7	0.4	0.4	0.7	0.8	0.9	1.5	5.3	8.5	6.7	4.2	2.7

While the above unit discharges are only approximate and are not necessarily typical of all drainage areas in the region, they are considered adequate at this early stage of preliminary study to indicate the general order of magnitude of streamflow and to reveal whether storage is required to meet irrigation requirements during low-flow seasons.

Existing Water Control Systems

Water control is not new to the coastal plains of the I Corps Zone. There exist many permanent diversion dams and the annual installation of temporary diversion dams is a widespread practice; dikes have been built to protect against floods and salt water; and there are canal systems and pumps. Some low dams to store water for dry season irrigation in water-short areas are also found. Many of these facilities are in disrepair, largely owing to neglect and insecure conditions in the countryside; however, repairs are being made and new facilities installed in many areas where security permits. The farmers in the region understand the value of water control systems, and are very willing to help in their construction; and to the extent that they have access to water in the dry season and the means to apply it, they practice double cropping as a matter of course.

The government of Vietnam has plans, ready for implementation, which would provide or improve varying degrees of water control for nearly 70,000 hectares at an estimated cost equivalent to US$27.5 million.

Development Program

Because of the large potentially irrigable area (410,000 hectares) and the heavy capital expenditures required to provide effective water control, the construction period to implement these works will need to be spread over a reasonably long period of time. At least a thirty-year period is proposed for construction of the complete facilities, and rather less than a third, about 120,000 hectares, might be developed during the first ten years after peace. In order to achieve this objective, more detailed studies should be initiated at once, so that the over-all development plan can be precisely defined and priorities established for feasibility studies and engineering design. If this is done it will be possible to start action programs within a reasonable period after peace returns.

A general description of the proposed development program for each of the subregions previously defined is presented in the following paragraphs.

Quang Tri/Thua Thien Subregion. The Quang Tri/Thua Thien portion of the coastal plain is continuous from the Demilitarized Zone to Dam Cau Hai above Da Nang. Major features of the subregion, including rivers and their drainage areas, limits of irrigable land, potential storage dam sites, and major population centers, are shown on Figure 12.2. It is estimated that a gross area of 150,000 hectares is suitable for development for irrigated agriculture.

Water reaches the coastal area from eleven readily distinguishable watershed areas. Over 80 percent of the total runoff, however, comes from four rivers, the Song Cam Lo, Rivière de Quang Tri, Song Bo, and Song Huong; the remaining seven have small watersheds and their catchments are almost entirely limited to the plains. Drainage areas, estimated average maximum and minimum monthly discharges and average annual discharges, and the irrigable areas served are all shown in Table 12.1.

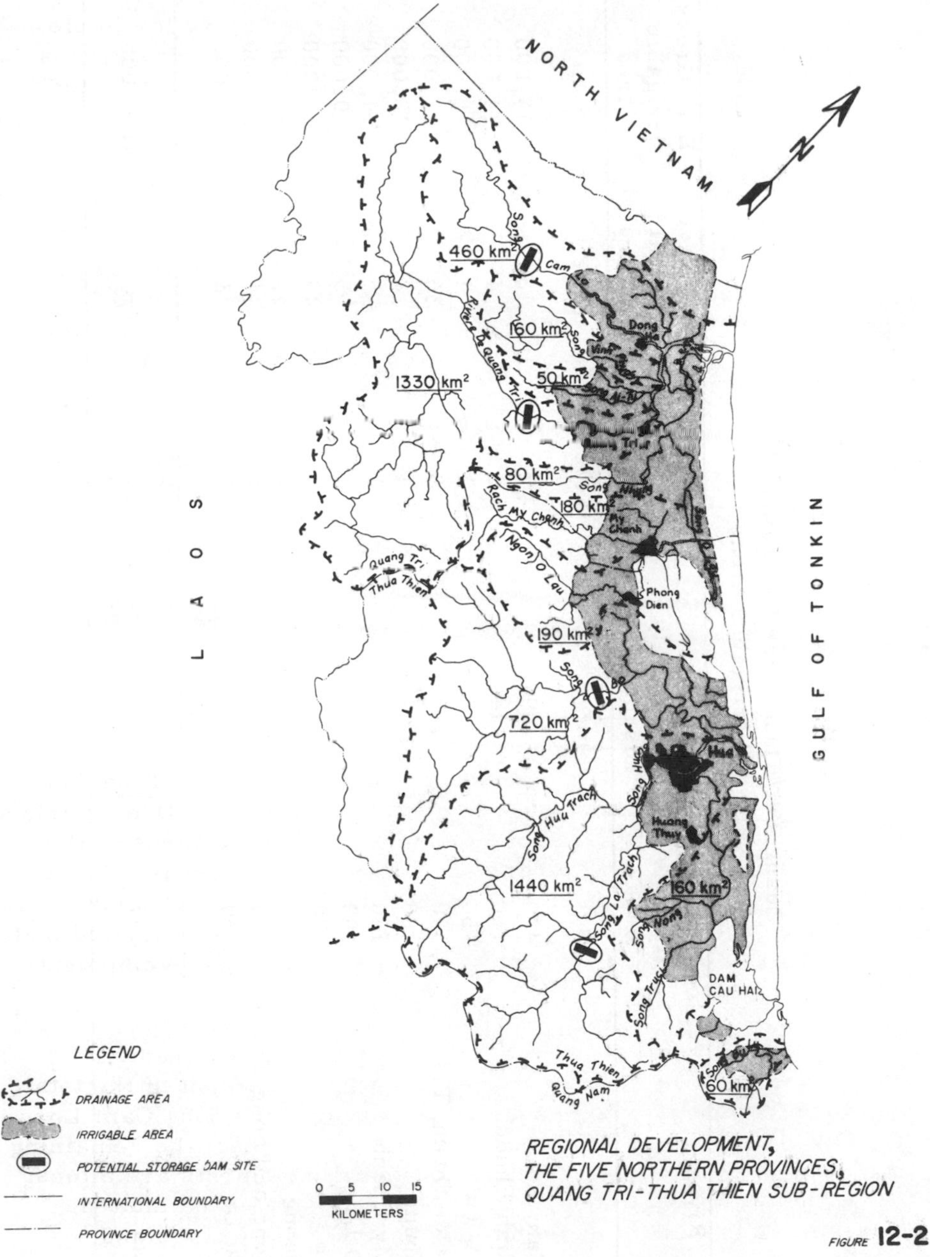

REGIONAL DEVELOPMENT,
THE FIVE NORTHERN PROVINCES,
QUANG TRI-THUA THIEN SUB-REGION

FIGURE 12-2

TABLE 12.1

Quang Tri/Thua Thien Subregion
Rivers and Irrigable Areas

River	Est. Drainage Area	Est. Av. Max. Monthly Discharge	Est. Av. Min. Monthly Discharge	Est. Av. Annual Discharge	Est. Gross Irrigable Area
	km^2	m^3/s	m^3/s	m^3/s	ha
Song Cam Lo	460	39	2	12	19,000
Song Vinh Phuoc	160	14	1	4	4,000
Song Ai-Tu	50	4	<1	1	6,000
Rivière de Quang Tri	1,330	112	5	36	3,000
Song Nhung	80	7	<1	2	18,000
Rach My Chanh	180	15	1	5	14,000
Ngon O Lau	190	16	1	5	10,000
Song Bo	720	61	3	20	22,000
Song Huong	1,440	122	6	39	22,000
Song Nong and Song Truci	160	13	1	4	23,000
Song Bu Lu	60	5	<1	2	4,000
Total	4,830	408	20	130	150,000

The average annual combined discharge of all eleven streams is estimated at 130 cubic meters per second, which suggests that surface runoff is ample to meet crop water requirements over and above rainfall. However, the estimated average minimum monthly discharge totals only 20 cubic meters per second, which is sufficient to irrigate only about 20,000 hectares. In order to provide irrigation water supplies to the entire area, therefore, seasonal storage is required. Four potential storage dam sites have been selected and are shown on Figure 12.2. Of the four, the Rivière de Quang Tri and the Song Bo sites are by far the most favorable, since they have large reservoir and drainage areas. It is expected that dams at at least these two sites will be required to store sufficient irrigation water to meet crop requirements.

With the possible exception of providing power for irrigation and drainage pumping, installation of hydroelectric plants at the above two sites is not considered feasible, owing to lack of surplus water. Conditions for power generation are much more favorable, moreover, in the Quang Nam/Quang Tin subregion, which will be discussed later.

Other major problems in this subregion, in addition to the shortage of irrigation water, are (1) salt water intrusion into the streams and, during floods, onto the lower lying lands; (2) frequent fresh water flooding from the rivers; and (3) inadequate drainage from much of the farm land.

During the dry season, river flows are too low to repel salt water intrusion, with the result that saline waters back up into the lagoons and channels (including the Song Hue); and owing to lack of fresh water, much of the area is thereby rendered unusable for irrigation. During the high-water season, river floods frequently cause the salt water in the lagoons to spill over into extensive areas of low-lying cultivated land destroying the crops; this phenomenon is aggravated by the fact that the passages by which lagoon waters enter the sea are restricted.

Flooding is frequent, widespread, and severe, but of relatively short duration. Flooding to a depth of 1 meter or more occurred in Hue City in 1968 but lasted for less than 48 hours. Property damage due to flooding is generally slight; however, it is reported that every few years a severe flood causes much loss of human life. The most severe floods occur when flood peaks and high tides coincide. The extent to which the restricted passages from the lagoons to the sea (at Thuan An and Dam Cua Hai) and manmade constrictions aggravate the flooding has not yet been determined. The area around Hue and the lagoons is subject to greater and more frequent flooding (including salt water flooding) than any other area in the coastal plain, and detailed studies must be made and steps taken to provide effective flood and salinity control.

To provide adequate irrigation water to meet consumptive use requirements of crops, two storage dams will be required, one on the Rivière de Quang Tri and the other on the Song Bo. These dams will be operated primarily for irrigation storage and releases, but may also serve a flood control purpose; small hydroelectric plants may be installed to provide irrigation and drainage pumping power if found more economical than other means of supplying power.

Complete main and secondary irrigation and drainage systems, with pumping facilities as required, will be provided. Local development associations (described below under the heading "The Mekong Delta") and the farmers themselves should implement tertiary and farm systems. Maximum practicable utilization will be made of existing works, improved and modified as necessary to fit the development scheme. Diversions of water between rivers and streams on the coastal plain will provide no problem, as most are already interconnected.

It is believed that both salinity intrusion control and flood control can best be achieved through the most economical combinations of (1) flood control allocation in the two proposed reservoirs; (2) a series of low-cost flood retention dams on river tributaries; (3) a system of low levees along rivers and lagoons; and (4) a barrage with overflow section (probably gated or provided with stop-log slots) at the Thuan An passage from the lagoons to the sea to control the flow of fresh water and prevent saline intrusion. It is recognized that the Thuan An barrage will preclude the development of a coastal vessel port at Hue, unless a costly lock structure is installed; however, the proximity of the major port at Da Nang raises considerable doubts concerning the feasibility of another port at Hue, especially if the latter were to involve increased costs for flood and salinity intrusion control.

This subregion, under present conditions, has more numerous and more severe difficulties than the other two--less natural streamflow, more frequent flooding, and much more severe salt-water intrusion and saline-water flooding. For these very reasons, it is in this subregion that implementation of water control facilities should start first. The entire development will probably require over thirty years; however, a third of the irrigable, arable area, say 50,000 hectares, could and should be developed during the first ten years after peace.

While cost estimates have not yet been developed, it is believed that their general order of magnitude will be equivalent to US$100 million for the full 150,000 hectares, and to US$60 million for an initial 50,000 hectares

Substantial benefits should result: (1) a firm supply of irrigation water enabling year-round cropping; (2) the provision of drainage facilities; (3) effective control of flooding and salinity intrusion; (4) conditions in which improved cultural practices can be adopted by local development associations with the assistance of the agricultural extension services; (5) the use of higher-yielding rice varieties, thus releasing part of the area now planted to rice to other crops; (6) crop diversification in areas formerly planted mostly to rice as well as in other areas; and (7) the exploitation of some land not now under cultivation. All these will almost certainly result in a favorable benefit-cost ratio.

Quang Nam/Quang Tin Subregion. The Quang Nam/Quang Tin section of the coastal plain forms a continuous gross irrigable area estimated at 140,000 hectares, extending from Da Nang Bay in a southeasterly direction to Dung Quat Bay on the boundary between Quang Tin and Quang Ngai provinces. Major features, including rivers and their drainage areas, limits of irrigable land, and major population centers, are shown on Figure 12.3.

Seven rivers serve the coastal area, and they are interconnected before they reach the sea. Of the seven rivers, two (the Song Vu Gia and Song Thu Bon) contribute nearly 90 percent of total annual runoff. Drainage areas, estimated average maximum monthly discharges, estimated average minimum monthly discharges, average annual discharges, and irrigable areas served are shown in Table 12.2.

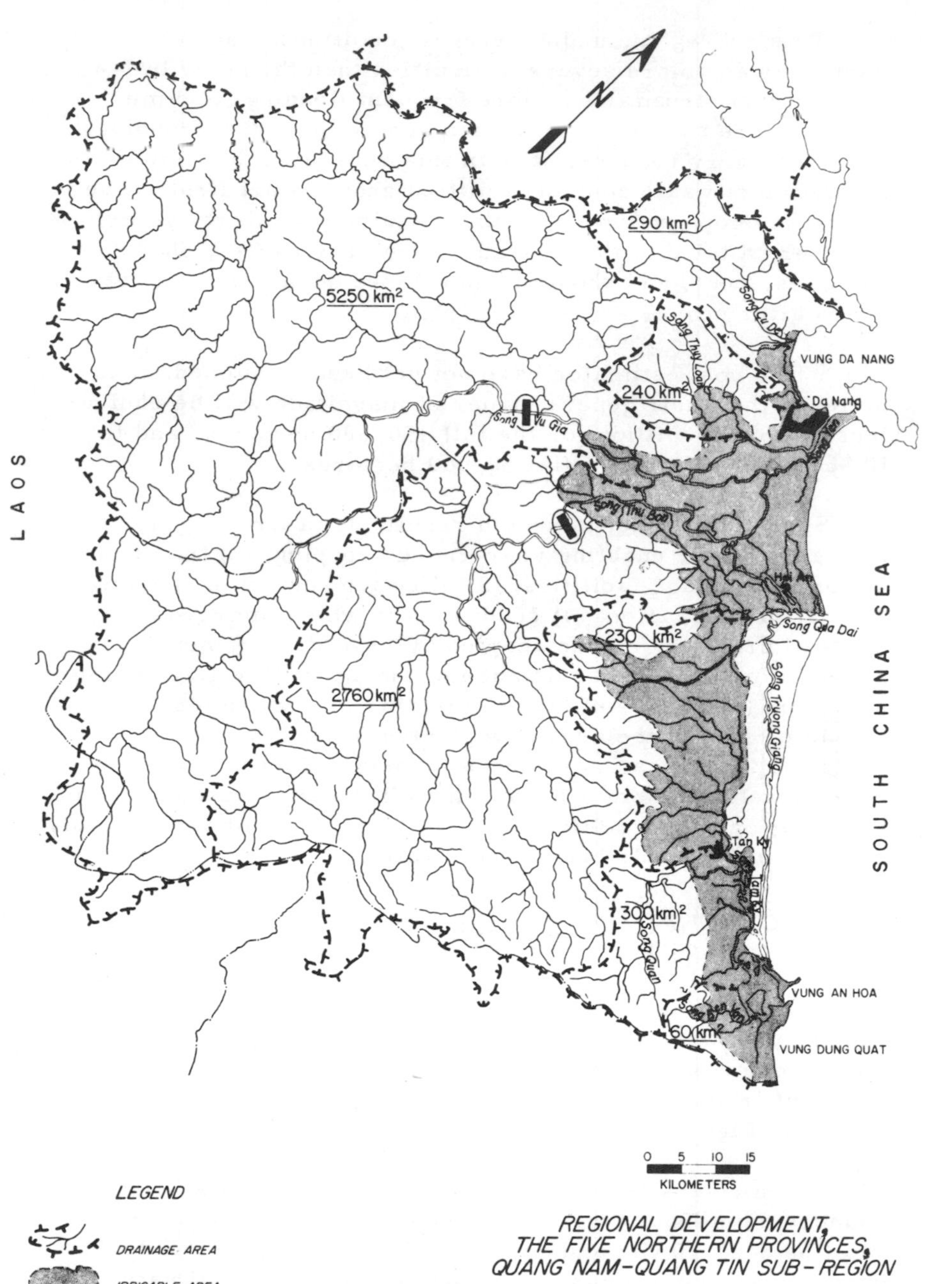

REGIONAL DEVELOPMENT, THE FIVE NORTHERN PROVINCES, QUANG NAM-QUANG TIN SUB-REGION

FIGURE 12-3

TABLE 12.2

Quang Nam/Quang Tin Subregion
Rivers and Irrigable Areas

River	Est. Drainage Area	Est. Av. Max. Monthly Discharge	Est. Av. Min. Monthly Discharge	Est. Av. Annual Discharge	Est. Gross Irrigable Area
	km^2	m^3/s	m^3/s	m^3/s	ha
Song Cu De	290	25	1	8	3,000
Song Thuy Loan	240	20	1	6	8,000
Song Vu Gia	5,250	445	21	142	25,000
Song Thu Bon	2,760	234	11	75	37,000
Song Tam Ky	230	19	1	6	45,000
Song Quan	300	25	1	8	13,000
Song Ben Van	60	5	<1	2	9,000
Total	9,130	773	36	247	140,000

The estimated combined average annual discharge of the seven streams is approximately 250 cubic meters per second, suggesting an ample supply of fresh surface water to meet all crop water requirements not satisfied by rainfall. However, the combined average minimum monthly flow is estimated at 36 cubic meters per second, sufficient to irrigate less than 40,000 hectares, and to meet irrigation requirements for the entire 140,000 hectares under full development storage is required. Two potential storage dam sites have been selected and are shown in Figure 12.3. One or the other of these two dams would provide all the storage needed. At this preliminary stage, the site on the Song Vu Gia is preferred, because of its greater catchment area (the Song Vu Gia contributes nearly 60 percent of the subregion's water supply) and its consequently greater potential as a multipurpose structure.

A dam and reservoir on the Song Vu Gia appear ideally suited for multipurpose development, for irrigation, power generation, and flood control. It is roughly estimated that firm power potential is in the order of at least 35,000 kilowatts (installed capacity around 70,000 kilowatts). This would be enough to relieve existing power shortages throughout the coastal area of the northern provinces and would permit a much more favorable rate structure than presently exists. Installation of a hydroelectric plant at this site would more than compensate for the possible loss of the 25,000-kilowatt thermal plant originally earmarked for installation at An Hoa if, in the event, EOV's proposal is adopted to use this plant to supplement generating capacity in Saigon.

In this subregion, water control problems are generally less severe than in Quang Tri/Thua Thien. First, surface runoff is nearly twice as much, so water shortage during dry seasons is less critical. Secondly, while large flood flows occur nearly every year, widespread areal flooding rarely occurs, thanks to the large carrying capacities of the major streams. Thirdly, though salt water intrudes rather deeply into the channels during the dry season, the area does not experience frequent salt water flooding, as do the lands around Hue. Nevertheless, the subregion has some real problems, and implementation of effective water control facilities is essential to realize its full agricultural potential.

To supply consumptive-use requirements of crops adequately, only one storage dam will be required, preferably on the Song Vu Gia. This dam would serve to generate power, to provide some flood control, and to store irrigation water; the allocation of costs among these three purposes would result in lower water charges on farmers and cheaper power generation.

Complete main and secondary irrigation and drainage systems and required pumping facilities should be provided in the project, and construction of the tertiary and farm systems should be by local development associations and individual farmers. Existing facilities should be incorporated into the project to the maximum extent practicable, with whatever modifications and improvements may be necessary.

Any flood control needed over and above the flood control storage to be provided in the proposed Song Vu Gia reservoir can be achieved by low-cost tributary flood retention dams or levees, or by a combination of both, whichever alternative is shown to be most economic. Irrigation and power releases during the dry season should rectify the existing salinity encroachment into the various channels.

Full development of the above program (140,000 hectares) could be carried out over a period of not less than thirty years, with somewhat more than a quarter of the construction (about 40,000 hectares) being completed during the first ten years after peace. The order of magnitude of capital investment requirements will probably be about the equivalent of US$150 million for the full 140,000 hectare development, and about the equivalent of US$45 million for an initial 40,000 hectares.

The benefits derivable from the project are roughly the same as those arising from the proposals for the Quang Tri/Thua Thien subregion, with the important addition of an electric power generating facility serving the coastal areas of the entire region. Flood and salinity control benefits would be rather less important than in Quang Tri/Thua Thien. Again, economic evaluation should show a most favorable cost-benefit ratio.

<u>Quang Ngai Subregion.</u> Quang Ngai, the southernmost part of the region's coastal plain, comprises a continuous reach of irrigable land with a gross area of approximately 120,000 hectares, between the Quang Tin/Quang Ngai province

boundary on the north, and the limit of I Corps to the south. A map of the area showing major population centers, rivers and their drainage areas, and limits of irrigable lands appears as Figure 12.4.

Four rivers serve the coastal plain, and differ from those in the two northern subregions in that they are not naturally interconnected; however, there should be no difficulty in providing such interconnecting channels as may be required to effect economic distribution of irrigation water. Pertinent river data, including drainage areas, estimated average maximum and minimum monthly flows, and irrigable areas served, are given in Table 12.3.

The estimated combined average annual discharge of these four rivers is around 125 cubic meters per second, so ample surface runoff appears to be available to meet the water requirements of crops during periods of insufficient rainfall. The combined average minimum monthly flow, on the other hand, is estimated at less than 20 cubic meters per second, sufficient for only 20,000 hectares, and storage will be required to meet the requirements of the full 120,000 hectare area judged to be irrigable. Two apparently favorable storage dam sites are shown on Figure 12.4; of these, the Song Tra Khuc site controls three times the drainage area of the site on the Song Ve and is preferred for that reason. It is believed that construction of a dam and reservoir on the Song Tra Khuc will provide adequate storage to meet all irrigation deficits during the dry season.

Except possibly for provision of power to meet irrigation and drainage pumping requirements, installation of a hydroelectric plant at the above dam site is not recommended. This is because of lack of surplus water, and also because the proposed power installation on the Song Vu Gia will sufficiently serve regional needs for the foreseeable future.

The agricultural problems of this area are very similar to those of Quang Nam and Quang Tin.

Adequate irrigation supplies to satisfy consumptive-use requirements of crops during rainfall deficit periods can, it is believed, be provided by a single storage dam on the Song Tra Khuc (though cost comparisons may indicate that two smaller dams will be more economical). If feasible, some

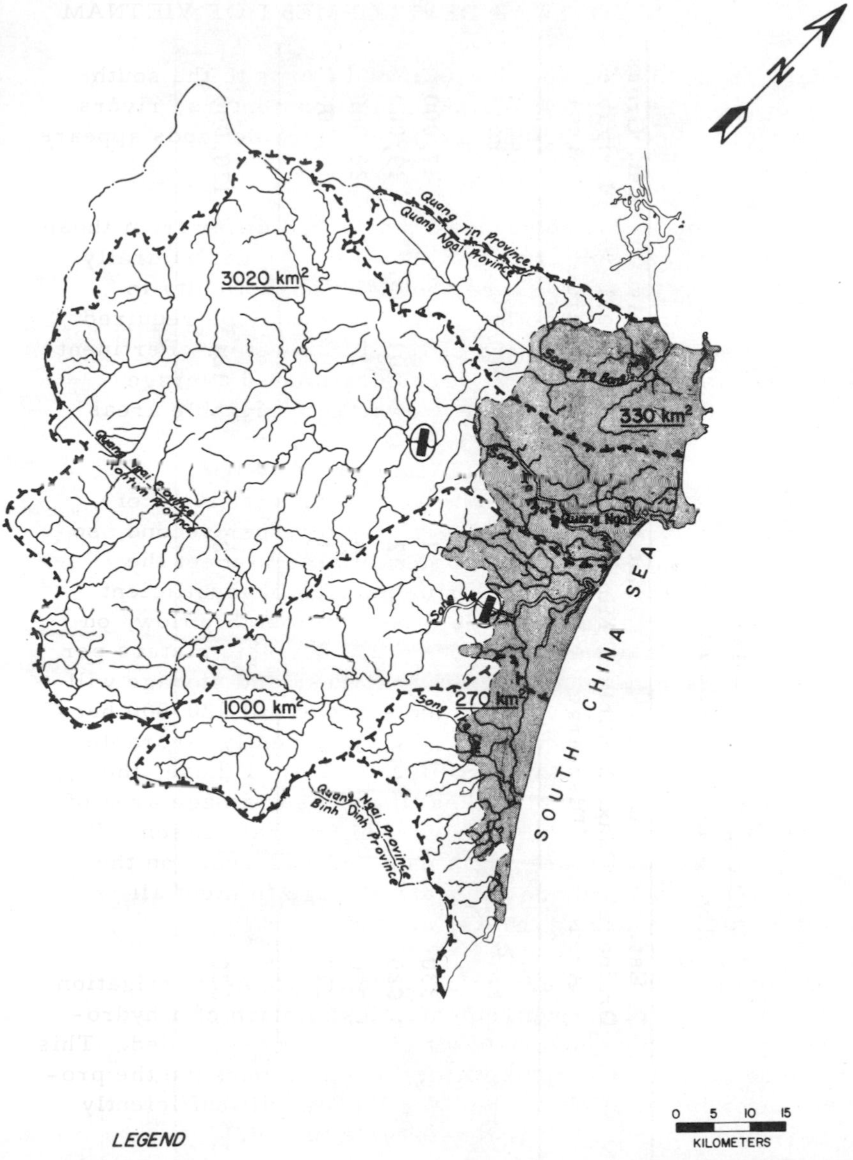

SOUTH CHINA SEA

3020 km^2

330 km^2

270 km^2

1000 km^2

Quang Tin Province
Quang Ngai Province

Quang Ngai Province
Kontum Province

Quang Ngai Province
Binh Dinh Province

Song Tra Bong

Song Ve

Quang Ngai

LEGEND

 DRAINAGE AREA

 IRRIGABLE AREA

POTENTIAL STORAGE DAM SITE

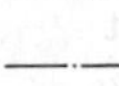 INTERNATIONAL BOUNDARY

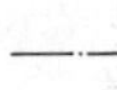 PROVINCE BOUNDARY

REGIONAL DEVELOPMENT,
THE FIVE NORTHERN PROVINCES,
QUANG NGAI SUB-REGION

FIGURE 12-4

TABLE 12.3

Quang Ngai Subregion
Rivers and Irrigable Areas

River	Est. Drainage Area	Est. Av. Max. Monthly Discharge	Est. Av. Min. Monthly Discharge	Est. Av. Annual Discharge	Est. Gross Irrigable Area
	km^2	m^3/s	m^3/s	m^3/s	ha
Song Tra Bong	330	28	1	9	37,000
Song Tra Khuc	3,020	257	12	81	39,000
Song Ve	1,000	85	4	27	26,000
Song Tra Cau	270	23	1	7	18,000
Total	4,620	393	18	124	120,000

additional storage should be provided at the site for purposes of flood control. The project should include complete main and secondary irrigation and drainage facilities, with irrigation and drainage pumping installations as required. As in the other subregions, tertiary and farm distribution and drainage systems should be the responsibility of farmers and local development associations, and existing works should be incorporated into the project to the greatest extent possible, subject to necessary modifications and improvements.

Flood control additional to that provided by the proposed Song Tra Khuc reservoir will be achieved through simple tributary flood retention dams or levees or such a combination of both as may be shown to be most economic. Reservoir releases for irrigation during the dry season are expected to provide effective relief from salt water intrusion into existing channels.

Development of the full 120,000 hectares will be spread over a minimum period of thirty years. Development of 30,000 hectares would be a realistic target for the first ten years. The order of magnitude of capital investment requirements will probably be about the equivalent of US$130 million for full development and about the equivalent of US$35 million for the first 30,000 hectares.

The same substantial benefits are expected to result from this project as those predicted for the neighboring provinces.

Conclusions and Recommendations

From these very preliminary investigations, it is generally concluded that the entire coastal plain of I Corps Zone can be economically developed over a minimum period of twenty years by a program of the type described. The investigations were to be pursued in greater detail in 1969, and they should be taken beyond that date to a point at which feasibility can be appraised with sufficient certainty to warrant full feasibility studies and design. This would afford prospects of starting construction within one year after peace returns.

Table 12.4 provides a recapitulation of the objectives of the program in terms of the land areas to be developed and the capital investment requirements in each case.

TABLE 12.4

Coastal Plain, I Corps Zone;
Land Area and Capital Investment Objectives
for Water Resources

Subregion	Developed Area		Range of Capital Investment	
	10 years	30+ years	10 years	30+ years
	(hectares)		(equivalent million US$)	
Quang Tri/Thua Thien	50,000	150,000	60	180
Quang Nam/Quang Tin	40,000	140,000	45	150
Quang Ngai	30,000	120,000	35	130
Totals	120,000	410,000	140	460

Conclusions. Specific conclusions resulting from this preliminary appraisal are as follows:

The need for effective water control and agricultural development of the entire coastal plain of the northern provinces is clear.

Rainfall and natural streamflow are inadequate to permit intensive year-round cultivation of the total area.

The lands selected, if properly prepared and managed, are productive and capable of yielding economic returns.

There are adequate amounts of surface water to support intensive irrigated agriculture if proposed storage facilities are provided; however, streamflow records are as yet insufficient to determine individual river discharges with enough accuracy to permit design of major control structures.

Drainage facilities, to alleviate conditions in the lower-lying lands, are essential for full agricultural development.

Flood and salinity control measures (particularly in the area around Hue) are also essential for full agricultural development and to prevent further loss of life and property.

Topographic and geologic conditions are favorable for implementing the proposed program.

Implementation of the program will greatly increase agricultural production and farm incomes, and will also, eventually, make the region self-sufficient in food.

Within the proposed water control facilities hydroelectric potential is sufficient to meet regional needs in the early postwar period.

Realization of full benefits will be contingent upon establishment of an organization to ensure development in accordance with the over-all regional program, and upon formation of local development associations to implement distribution and farm water control systems and provide water control and agricultural assistance to the farmers.

Recommendations. The following recommendations are made with a view to more accurate definition of the development program leading into specific staged appraisals, feasibility studies, designs, and construction.

A network of hydrologic and meteorologic stations should be planned and established at the earliest possible date. The stations will be located to provide sufficient basic data to enable more accurate determination of flood magnitudes, salt water intrusion, drainage requirements, surface water availability, and irrigation water requirements.

Land-use maps should be prepared covering the estimated 410,000 hectares of irrigable lands, and showing areas actually cultivated and the major crops planted thereon.

The soils of the coastal plain should be further studied in order to prepare land classification maps indicating suitability for irrigated agriculture and permitting determination of best future land use.

Present yields and production costs should be investigated in sufficient detail for all major crops to permit calculation of regional averages.

Market studies and forecasts should be made to permit determination of the most desirable extent and nature of future crop diversification.

The numerous reports on all water control projects proposed in the last thirty or so years should be reviewed.

Flood and salt water damage investigations should be carried out.

The possibilities of regional power generation in conjunction with regional water control facilities should be appraised.

Preliminary plans should be made for provision of adequate farm-to-market road networks.

General layouts and plans of proposed water control facilities (storage dams, irrigation and drainage systems, and flood and salt water intrusion control structures) should be prepared in sufficient detail to permit preliminary cost determination.

Preliminary benefits based on increased agricultural income under future development should be estimated.

A preliminary economic evaluation of the full development of 410,000 hectares should be made on the basis of preliminary cost and benefit figures.

Immediately there should be discussions with appropriate agencies of the government of Vietnam to secure their participation in the investigative phases of this program (particularly in establishing hydrologic and meteorologic stations, gathering agricultural data, obtaining all available records and reports, preparing an inventory of existing water control facilities, and delineating present government plans for constructing and improving water control facilities).

The Fishing Industry

An important contribution to the economy of the region is made by its many fishermen. The fishing industry, based mainly on Da Nang, produced 58,900 metric tons of sea fish in 1967, or 16 percent of the total production of the country. Thirty-seven percent of all the fishing population of the country, nearly 89,000 men, are to be found in I Corps, as are over 40 percent of the mechanized vessels. In all, the fishing fleet exceeds 23,000 boats. This fleet is almost entirely owner-operated and consists of many types of small vessels capable only of in-shore fishing; very few are equipped to venture out to really profitable waters.

In proportion to the capital investment in and manpower of this fishing fleet its productivity is low even in relation to other regions in Vietnam, and only a fraction of its potential is realized.

To a great extent the industry is controlled by wholesalers, whose interest is to extract what profit can be got from it, so that little or no provision is made for its development from within its own resources. Indeed, fishermen are in debt, their standards of living are low, and their vessels and gear are inadequate and dilapidated. The industry in the I Corps Zone has an important function--to supply the increasing population of the northern provinces, of other regional centers of population, and of the highlands with the fish protein necessary for local diets. In order to do this successfully the industry needs complete overhaul and rehabilitation.

Although this section is concerned solely with the I Corps Zone, the above, and much of what follows as well, may apply equally well to the fishing industry in other regions of Vietnam.

The first logical step is to provide orderly and efficient marketing arrangements and rapid transport facilities to retail outlets to ensure that fishermen get fair returns for their produce and, therefore, some incentive to increase their production. The second is to finance the replacement of craft and gear and the various improvements possible in techniques and equipment.

For both purposes an organization is needed. Its purpose would be to assist the development of the industry by providing marketing facilities and other services so as to reduce the present dependence of fishermen on wholesalers and other middlemen and ensure them a fair share of the proceeds of sale of their catches. A form of cooperative marketing enterprise sounds like an obvious solution, and it has been carefully considered. Fishermen's cooperative societies do exist in the region, but they were not formed for and are not particularly interested in marketing; like most other cooperative societies throughout the country, their performance has been poor. A reformed and strengthened cooperative movement which recently revised legislation may bring about could contribute valuably to the development of the fishing industry, but the movement does not now have the institutional strength or the cohesive membership to undertake marketing functions successfully.

We propose for consideration a new statutory organization, possibly called a Fisheries Development and Marketing Board, in which would be vested control of the landing, movement, and wholesaling of marine fish. The board could eventually be taken over and managed by the fishermen themselves as a cooperative enterprise. Experience elsewhere, particularly in Hong Kong, demonstrates the value of this type of organization in providing incentives for the rapid development of a local fishing industry. The principal function of the board would be the collection and transportation of fish from collecting points in the region to main wholesale fish markets, particularly to Da Nang (where a modern fish landing already exists, although it is presently in military use). In other locations, where wholesale markets do not exist or are insufficient, it would be the function of the board to provide them. In the markets, staff of the board would sort and grade fish into suitably sized lots for sale by public auction, retaining a small commission to cover the cost of its services. Although public financial assistance to the organization would be required at the start, there is no reason why it should not become financially self-supporting and capable (as a nonprofit concern) of returning surplus earnings to the industry in the form of low-interest credit facilities.

Operations of this type would not, of course, result in the accumulation of the very large amounts of capital necessary to promote a thoroughly modern industry. The resources of the board will have to be augmented, perhaps by means of a revolving Fisheries Development Loan Fund, provided by government but operated by the board, which would lend money either against a corporate guarantee of a cooperative society or against collateral offered by individual fishermen, by mortgage of their vessels, for example. Low rates of interest would be charged, and recovery made by deductions from sales proceeds at wholesale fish markets.

There can be little doubt that an organization of the type we recommend is badly needed. Wholesale marketing arrangements at Da Nang at the present time can only be described as chaotic and inefficient. There are no berthing facilities; the boxed catch is discharged into the hands of waiting agents--all women--who either dispose of the fish to other women dealers by negotiated sale, or head-load the boxes to waiting vehicles some considerable distance away for dispatch to retail outlets. There is no discernible sign of a free auction.

Plans are now being made in Da Nang by government Port Authority officials with CORDS Da Nang cooperation for construction of a modern fish market and harbor complex. A site adjacent to the present market has been reserved, and the intention is to provide not only for moorings but also for cold storage, an ice plant, and warehousing. This excellently conceived scheme would do much to improve the situation, and it should be expedited; but a complex of this sort requires careful and authoritative management to ensure that its facilities are properly used and maintained, and management could most appropriately be entrusted to the organization we recommended previously.

All these measures will improve the lot and increase the productivity of workers in the existing industry: what is wanted in the long run is mechanization and modernization of the fleet, and a change from traditional in-shore fishing to middle and distant-water fishing, where the economic opportunities have been shown to be greater. This will necessitate not only large capital investments, but also basic education and vocational training so that fishermen may acquire essential new specialized skills, for example a knowledge of the functioning and maintenance of diesel engines, seamanship, and some concept of navigation by dead reckoning. The next steps in the development of the industry will be by fishing boats of more advanced design to enable fishermen to reach distant fishing grounds expeditiously and to use improved gear, including mechanical gear. There may be possibilities here for growth of the boat-building industry, using local timber resources.

The principal technique in present use is pair trawling. This is wasteful of time and labor, and is being replaced in other countries by single-boat stern otter trawling, and this change in methods is highly desirable in Vietnam too. Moreover, there is now no specialization: small trawls are used to scoop a great variety of fish from the sea areas worked; and such shrimps as are caught are a fortuitous addition to the mixed bag. Specialized vessels using shrimp beam trawls could greatly increase this valuable catch, for which there is a ready export market. Although fair quantities of red snapper are landed, efforts should be made to increase the catch of this species which also has good export potential and may provide a base for a processing industry.

There is no doubt that good possibilities exist for a greatly expanded and improved fishing industry in I Corps (and elsewhere for that matter), contributing valuably to the prosperity of the region and supplying the growing demands for fish protein from a steadily increasing population. Obviously more elaborate studies of the industry, including the detailed structuring of a marketing organization than have yet been made, will be wanted and they should be undertaken as soon as possible.

Without these studies it is not possible to present an exact estimate of the investment and credit likely to be needed to rehabilitate and develop the economic fishing industry. A good marketing facility is already planned for Da Nang, but smaller markets will be required at a number of other fishing centers. A Fisheries Development and Marketing Board will have to be provided at the start with sufficient capital to construct these markets, to employ staff, to engage transport and for other activities. However, the expenditures for the board should not be very large, and will probably not exceed the equivalent of US$500,000; and even on present production a reasonable rate of commission on sales, certainly less than 10 percent, would make the board self-supporting. A greater investment will have to be made for the proposed revolving loan fund; however, in the early years progress will be slow, and a fund of the equivalent of US$1 million should make a significant impact. We envisage both short-term and long-term loans, at low interest rates, for purchase of equipment, construction of boats, and mechanization.

So far this section has been concerned entirely with marine fisheries. The region is not, in fact, particularly well suited to fish culture in ponds: the shortage of agricultural land, and periodic flooding during the rainy season, are deterrents to the extensive construction and operation of fish ponds. However, an important fresh-water fish culture station has been established near Hue, and this is capable of supplying 300,000 fingerlings a year of common carp, gorami, and tilapia to the small fish pond farmers of the region. The opportunities will improve as the water control systems described in the previous section are developed, and there is undoubtedly some scope for more intensive culture in existing ponds and lakes by new methods including the use of artificial foods. A more profitable course in the immediate future, however, appears to lie in more extensive fish cultivation using the brackish and salt-water lagoons which are prominent natural features of the region, especially in Thua Thien and Quang Tin provinces. Much work remains to be done on investigating and surveying the potential of the lagoons, but it is an identifiable regional resource which should not be ignored.

Infrastructure

The development of the infrastructure (transportation, sanitation, telecommunications, power, and housing) and the capital investments it will involve are largely of national importance, and in this chapter they are not considered at any length except insofar as they affect the general development of the region, are of purely regional or local interest, and will enhance or hinder regional resource development. In this respect, the comments which follow are an extension of the views expressed in Chapter 10.

Transportation development requirements discussed in Chapter 10 include highways, railways, ports, inland waterways, and airports. Chapter 10 summarizes plans to reconstruct all main national and interprovincial roads and bridges and to improve their standards, and these plans include the improvement of Route QL-1 from Da Nang to Dong Ha, which is the most important in the region. These major works, together with additional mileage already constructed by the U.S. Army, will adequately serve the region's needs for major arterial highways.

Chapter 10 also outlines a railroad rehabilitation project which will restore the main line from Dong Ha to Saigon, and the spurline to An Hoa, and programs for improving the facilities of the port of Da Nang for coastal shipping. In addition it refers in general to the profusion of airfields which will be left behind by the war. The military airfield at Da Nang is capable of handling the largest commercial jet aircraft; the airfield at Hue is presently being lengthened and resurfaced, and will be suitable for intermediate-size commercial aircraft when completed.

Inland waterways have not previously been and are not likely to be important in the transportation of agricultural or industrial products in the I Corps Tactical Zone. The area has been for many years a food-deficit area, forestry resources remain largely unexploited, and industrial activity is almost nonexistent. Future water resource and irrigation development will involve many dams and pumping stations. To include provision for inland waterway transportation would be prohibitively expensive and would be superfluous in view of the availability of other modes of transportation. The Joint Development Group therefore recommends that emphasis in I Corps be placed on highways and on the railway for major transportation routes, and on feeder roads for local transportation.

Local and feeder roads are required to serve the agricultural population spread widely throughout the coastal plain and those communities located or possibly to be located in remote areas of the highlands, and also for exploitation of forestry resources. The justification for logging roads will depend primarily on the results of a forest inventory intended to reveal the extent and location of timber resources and the prospects for profitable exploitation. In the event, it is possible that most of the region's exploitable timber will be extracted by forest tracks built by the concessionaires to points of connection with major road or rail arterials. As in the rest of Vietnam, there are relatively few areas which are not served by at least a rough unpaved track usable by tri-Lambrettas, a form of transportation which is perfectly well suited to the less accessible rural areas.

The construction of such roads, designed to meet the needs of comparatively small communities, and uneconomical in their utilization of capital in relation to the light traffic loads they carry, might reasonably be regarded as a purely local responsibility. With the evolution of local government, financial assistance from central resources and enhanced local revenues should together provide provincial and village administrations with the resources to discharge this responsibility. If there is a substantial element of self-help, capital costs need not be great; and maintenance costs should certainly be a charge on local resources.

Also of interest both from a national viewpoint and from the viewpoint of local development is the possibility of an extension of international trade via the highway through Khe Sanh to Laos. No definitive assessment has yet been made regarding the political and commercial advantages which might accrue from such a development, but there is no doubt that it would result in the growth of interregional exchanges beneficial to the port of Da Nang. The Joint Development Group recommends that attention be directed to this possibility in 1969.

The sanitation requirements and deficiencies of I Corps are not significantly different from those of the country as a whole (described in Chapter 10). Water supplies are largely from surface water in rural areas and from shallow wells in urban areas like Da Nang and Hue. An AID project to provide a potable water supply in Quang Tri has been completed. An AID-sponsored feasibility study has been completed for a potable water supply in Da Nang and will probably be implemented in the near future, utilizing local surface water.* Da Nang is presently supplied by several shallow artesian wells which yield adequate supplies of fresh water in the wet season but become brackish in the dry season.

Sewage disposal, when implemented, whether the sewage is raw or after primary or secondary treatment, will involve extensive and extremely expensive piping systems and pumping installations for all coastal urban areas. Because of the very high costs involved, the resort in the immediate postwar period should be to simpler means of disposing of sanitary wastes.

---

*"A Feasibility Study--Da Nang Water Supply Facilities" (prepared for Ministry of Public Works, Republic of Vietnam, December 1966, by Ralph M. Parsons Company) (USAID Contract No. 430-1126).

Telecommunications has been discussed entirely on a national basis in Chapter 10.

The problem of reconstructing and improving urban housing on a national scale is also discussed in Chapter 10. The comments made there apply to I Corps as well. The essential is to find viable government policies which will stimulate private participation in both construction and financing of adequate urban housing throughout Vietnam.

Effective staging and utilization of hydropower potential requires that development be on a national scale, and the heavy financing requirements can only be provided by the central government. In Chapter 10, forecasts of demand are presented for three different areas of Vietnam which do not, except in one instance, coincide with the regions defined here. Power development is considered regionally only insofar as it affects the development of local resources; in the case of I Corps, these are the Nong Son coal field and hydroelectric potential described above under "Water Resources Development" and capable of being developed in conjunction with the irrigation project for Quang Nam and Quang Tin. Clearly, a very careful comparative study has to be made of the benefits of both possible developments to the development of the region as a whole before deciding which will be used to provide for the northern provinces. Should the 25 megawatt thermal plant originally intended for An Hoa actually be installed in the region, there would certainly be some advantages--for instance, the employment of a large local labor force in coal mining, and savings in foreign exchange by avoiding the purchase of turbo-machinery and electrical components for hydropower. But until a complete comparative study is made, it cannot be said with certainty that these arguments should prevail.

Industrial Development

With surplus manpower and skilled resources, the possibility of low-cost electric power, a deep-water harbor at Da Nang, some known mineral resources (coal, limestone, and silica sand), the prospects of increased agricultural and fisheries production on which processing enterprises can be built, and timber resources not precisely known but probably valuable, there are promising prospects for substantial industrial development, especially in light manufacturing, in the I Corps Zone. The potential must be explored with method and thoroughness if balanced economic development is to be achieved in a region which is as yet primarily dependent on subsistence agriculture.

One highly promising possibility has already been disclosed--veneer and plywood manufacture for domestic markets and export--and in addition it is appropriate in this section to discuss the case for utilization of the Nong Son coal deposits. A few other industrial possibilities are mentioned briefly, but all will require further examination.

Veneer and Plywood Manufacture

A recommendation for the location of a plywood and veneer mill at Da Nang has been presented in some detail in Chapter 9. Here it is only necessary to repeat the essential features of the proposal, which is one of three industrial projects suggested for immediate consideration.

At the start the industry would depend upon imported logs, until adequate log supplies at competitive costs become available from the hardwood forests of the region. It is proposed to plan for an initial production of 20,000 cubic meters a year (which would call for the employment of 280 people), but the plant would be so designed for substantial expansion as soon as a successful operation on this scale is achieved. The establishment of the industry would, of course, influence the development of the logging and other timber-based industries, and these would provide employment for many more, perhaps up to 1,000 workers. In national terms the importance of the industry lies in its capacity to earn foreign exchange: in regional terms, in its capacity to provide employment and to inspire a variety of ancillary enterprises which in their turn would provide much more employment. Although the industry would at the start, for reasons associated with the war, depend upon imported supplies, once peace returns it would rely upon and exploit a regional resource which is now very little used.

Capital investment in the plywood and veneer mill would be about US$2 million, making it suitable to be undertaken by private Vietnamese entrepreneurs. The industry could be logically located at any deep-water port in Vietnam with reasonably good access to domestic timber supplies. The recommendation in favor of locating the industry at Da Nang is a deliberate one: it responds in part to a need to decentralize Vietnamese industry, still heavily concentrated in the Saigon/Bien Hoa area, and in part to the need to provide diversified employment opportunities in a region in which the agricultural base alone cannot provide acceptable standards of living for the heavy population which relies upon it.

Nong Son Coal and the An Hoa Industrial Complex

There have been several recent studies* of the imaginative An Hoa project, several different views presented of its economic viability, and at least two opinions presented of what should be done with it. However, it appears to be generally accepted that the An Hoa complex cannot produce the principal commodity for which it was intended, chemical fertilizers, at competitive costs, and that if the plant ever goes into production it can only be sustained by heavy and continuing government subsidies. Whether political considerations should prevail over the economic arguments is not for the Joint Development Group to say.

Understandably the An Hoa project has created as much hope and expectation inside the I Corps Zone as it has inspired doubt outside it. The future of the project now has to be resolved in one way or another, if only to clear the way for the establishment of a definitive industrial development strategy for the northern provinces. Superficially, at least, the production of fertilizer from Nong Son coal appears to offer a substantial base for industrial development, higher levels of local employment, and the provision in the region of a commodity which will be needed in increasing quantities as agricultural development proceeds. Such a project, if it were economically viable, might have large and beneficial effects on the regional economy as a whole. If the project is not viable, on the other hand, it may have very harmful ones.

The assessment of the fertilizer complex made by TVA in 1967 was that this feature of the complex would not be profitable, but might break even if something like US$20 million

*Feasibility Studies by TVA and by Paul Weir and Company.

of previous investment were written off. This was not encouraging, but two new factors incline us to be even more pessimistic. In the first place there appears to have been further substantial damage, deterioration to the complex, its buildings, foundations, and plant already erected since the TVA report was written. In the second place, recent technological advances in fertilizer manufacture have put it beyond doubt that the rate of accruing obsolescence of the plant as it was designed will be even more rapid than was formerly appreciated. We can expect further improvements in this dynamic and progressive technology, and it would be unrealistic not to accept the fact that a plant which was designed about a decade ago cannot remain competitive in what is virtually a new era of fertilizer production technology. A good part of Vietnamese industry, as mentioned in Chapter 9, is modern and has up-to-date equipment and technology, and what could be a most important branch of it should not be handicapped by built-in obsolescence.

At this stage, on what are purely economic grounds, and on such evidence as has been made available to us, we cannot recommend the production of chemical fertilizers at An Hoa.

It may be helpful, in making a decision, to have a statement of what the resource in question consists of and what use the project is intended to make of it. The following information is drawn from the reports cited.

Briefly, it has been estimated that at 60 percent recovery, the known minable reserves at Nong Son amount to 2.7 million metric tons of strippable and 4.5 million metric tons of underground coal. There are unproven possibilities in adjacent areas. The presently planned output is 300,000 metric tons per year and the known reserves are therefore sufficient for the normal life of a power plant and chemical complex amortized over 24 years.

The quality of the Nong Son coal, as far as is known, is inferior, and does not compare with the anthracite found in North Vietnam and formerly imported into South Vietnam. If it had not been for the cessation of trade between the two Vietnams, the low-grade Nong Son coal would not have been thought worth exploiting. The concessionary rights to the deposits were originally held by the Bank of Indochina, and were made over to the Republic at independence for a token payment of one piaster. Transportation costs make it impossible to envisage the use of coal of this quality outside of the I Corps Zone, and in fact in Saigon electricity-generating plants are rapidly being converted to oil fuel.

The power plant and chemical fertilizer complex at An Hoa was based on the use of the Nong Son coal. The power plant was to have a generating capacity of 25,000 kw. The chemical complex was to have taken the output of 16,000 kw, leaving the balance for transmission to Da Nang and elsewhere. The complex itself, including the power plant, was planned to consume 250,000 tons of coal annually, leaving 50,000 tons of the Nong Son production to be consumed in other local markets. If the chemical complex were not realized, then 160,000 tons would be required by the power plant, leaving the balance of planned production (140,000 tons) to be consumed in a variety of ways possible--an addition to generating capacity, cement manufacture based on the lime deposits of Van Xa in the lime kilns (which already use some Nong Son coal in their primitive ovens), and other industries such as brick, clay, tile, and ceramics manufacture and glass-making.

The basic equipment for the complex, including the power plant and high tension transmission to Da Nang and Hue, 170 miles of lines, with insulators and six transformers, has already been purchased with French and German loans, and the equivalent of US$7.9 million has already been spent on the electric power aspects of the project, the total estimated cost of which is reckoned at US$9.6 million. Much more, of course, has been invested in plant for fertilizer production.

Whether or not the chemical complex proceeds, it is clear that some profitable and economic use should be found for the Nong Son coal, the region's principal known mineral resource. There is, unfortunately, no realistic use presently in sight other than for thermal power generation, and at that only inside the I Corps Zone. The high sulfur content of the coal makes it unsuitable for iron or steel manufacture and its phosphorous content makes it unsuitable for manufacture of calcium carbide. But the cost of electric power delivered at Da Nang from the power plant at An Hoa has been estimated at about VN$2.5-3.5 per kwh. This is considerably less than power based on fuel oil is likely to cost; and it is only half of the present unit cost in Da Nang (VN$6), where existing capacity is inadequate to meet demands. On the other hand, it may not be less than the cost of power delivered from hydroelectric generation, for which there are also possibilities, described in an earlier section of this chapter, within the region. The demand for power in the northern provinces, however it is met, will certainly rise rapidly. Some forecasts are given in Chapter 10, and they exceed the projected capacity of the An Hoa/Nong Son plant.

There may eventually be other industrial uses for coal, but they have not yet been investigated in any detail; the manufacture of briquettes from anthracite mines and cement production based on lime deposits at Van Xa are two examples. Vietnam now imports more than 350,000 tons of cement and uses over 600,000 tons. There is only one substantial plant in the country, at Ha Tien, which has a capacity of 250,000 tons. An additional plant in the I Corps Zone with a 100,000 ton capacity would use up to to 10,000 tons of Nong Son coal, useful, if not sufficient on its own to support a mining industry.

What we suggest--on only economic grounds--for the An Hoa/Nong Son complex is essentially a salvage operation. It will consist of the possible use of the coal for thermal electric power generation and other rather limited uses within the region, and of the possible use of the sulfuric acid plant, in or near Saigon, to produce sulfuric acid, a necessary industrial commodity, from imported sulfur. The conclusions concerning the complex are based, necessarily, on what is now known of the qualities of the coal resources. It must be mentioned that there is a possibility that quality will improve with depth, and after the war an exploration program of drillings to bedrock should be undertaken. Whatever the results, they are unlikely to change the conclusions reached concerning the use of the resource for the production of chemical fertilizers.

Tourism

A profitable secondary industry, tourism, may arise in the I Corps Zone. The scenic and zoological attractions of the Bac Mah Range, hunting, and the architectural and historical interests of the ancient capital and citadel of Hue are assets capable of development. No other developing country has received as much international attention as

Vietnam, or such publicity. With a good network of main highways and an airport at Da Nang capable of receiving large commercial jet aircraft, the region lacks only modern hotels of international standard to be able to compete with other areas of the country for a steady flow of foreign tourists once peace is restored. And it should not be forgotten that Hue is of at least equal interest to Vietnamese nationals as well. The place can be made as attractive as Dalat, which, whatever its charm, has no historical associations whatever.

Saigon has a reputation in prewar times that can probably be restored rather easily. Most tourists will land in Saigon; but few people will make the long trip up country unless a conscious coordinated effort is made to attract them. This can be done, and if it is, a valuable invisible export will be added to the region's economy; tourist-based industries--handicrafts (including the deservedly famous lacquerware and silk), floating restaurants and hotels on the Perfume River, automobile tours--will expand to meet the demand. There are very substantial possibilities.

The governmental agency for tourism is fully conscious of this potential, and plans are being made for the attraction of visitors. At the start, these will be mostly Vietnamese citizens, very many of whom are attracted by the associations of Hue and the contrast between the northern provinces and the rest of the country. The traffic will commence as soon as reasonable security is assured, and we recommend that steps be taken now to reconstruct and reopen the main hotel in Hue (built originally for use by the International Control Commission) so that some additional first-class hotel capacity can be available to meet the need when it arises; but other good hotels will be needed as well, and the attention of private enterprise should be drawn to this potential.

Refugees and Other Social Problems

The coastal plains of the northern provinces are already densely populated in comparison with other areas of Vietnam, and large numbers of refugees have crowded into the towns and resettlement hamlets in search of protection. The refugee problem is more acute in I Corps than in any other region. Numbers fluctuate greatly as military activities in the hinterland shift in location and intensity, but a typical twelve-month pattern in the past few years shows a generation of approximately 1 million refugees each year, of which some 700,000 find places in resettlement hamlets or return to their villages, and 300,000 do not. By July 31, 1968, there were 650,000 unsettled refugees in the I Corps Zone, the greatest concentrations being in Quang Nam and Quang Ngai provinces. There is little interregional migration of refugees. The I Corps refugees are almost all from within the region, but they create serious social and infrastructural problems in the already overpopulated areas which they enter.

What problems will the refugees present in the long run? Informed opinion is that about 75 percent of them will return to their homes as soon as it is safe to do so, though they will need assistance in rebuilding their homes and farms. Most of the others may be expected to stay where they are, and a good many will find employment in development projects and in industry. Population density will continue to strain regional resources, but not as much as the present numbers of refugees suggest. Some relocation will be desirable, and settlement schemes in the foothills of the highlands inside the region and in the Central Highlands areas of the II Corps Zone may be advisable, though large-scale voluntary movements of people are improbable.

Inside the I Corps Zone there may be as many as 100,000 families who will need financial assistance if they are to return to their former farms or relocate themselves on new land provided by the irrigation and water control schemes recommended in a previous section. To enable them to reconstruct their homes, purchase seed and stock, and restore the productivity of their fields, substantial cash grants supplemented by credit facilities will be required. Cash grants for house construction and for subsistence expenses until the first harvest will be necessary in very many cases; but other assistance can appropriately be given by loan, with generous repayment terms and at low or no interest rates. At this stage estimates of cost are difficult, but cash grants may average VN$30,000 per family and if the average loan is approximately the same, total requirements will be about VN$6 billion or US$50 million. This is not an extravagant sum for putting so many of the war's principal sufferers back into business, especially if wise administration of loans succeeds in giving them better lives than they had before.

This task is formidable but essential to political stability and the future of the economy. The refugees represent at least 60,000 hectares of formerly productive land which must be brought back into production with a minimum of delay.

Unemployment is possible in the urban areas of the I Corps Zone as the stimulus to the economy from large numbers of troops and many military bases is reduced. This danger may be exaggerated. There will surely be a substantial military presence in the region many years after any military accommodation or political settlement has been achieved, and though present levels of civilian employment by the military may be reduced a little, they are not likely to fall to a level at which serious unemployment would result. Reconstruction programs to repair the damages inflicted by war on almost every part of the infrastructure will usually be labor-intensive in character and will provide work for many thousands of people for at least three and probably five years. By that time the developments proposed in this study in agriculture, forestry, and industry will hopefully provide new opportunities for gainful employment. One fact is sure--that the concentration of population in the urban areas which is one result of the war has some degree of permanency, and to that extent has altered the economic and political character of the region. It emphasizes the need to pursue industrial and manufacturing development based on forest, mineral, and other resources.

Account must also be taken of the small groups of highlanders who are racially and linguistically distinct from other Vietnamese even if they share a common nationality. Their numbers in the five northern provinces are estimated by the Special Commission for Highland Affairs at 109,000. Agriculture is their only means of livelihood, and economic progress implies a change from a subsistence to a cash economy by the improved agricultural practices and employment in forestry enterprises. For a small number of them, as described previously, there are very good opportunities in the production of cinnamon bark.

It should not be forgotten that many of the highlanders too are numbered among the refugees. They will need assistance in restoring their lives to at least the same degree as others. They may need more if they are to be brought fully into the economic life of the region.

The Organization of Regional Development

The Office of Commissioner for Development of I Corps Zone has been established by decree, and an appointment has been made. The commissioner, who has a deputy commissioner to assist him, operates from within the Ministry of National Economy, and intends to establish offices both in Saigon and Da Nang. A fund of VN$100 million was established some time ago for unspecified development purposes in the region, and very little, if any of it, has been spent. The ideas presented in this chapter have been discussed with the commissioner and, indeed, to some extent, draw upon his own.

The functions and powers of the commissioner have still to be determined, but they will obviously include the identification and study of development opportunities and the coordination of the work of governmental agencies concerned with the exploitation of these opportunities. The commissioner will also be called upon to prescribe priorities. As controller of a special development fund for the area, he should influence project selection and can expedite realization of plans. His position inside the Ministry of National Economy should ensure that the development needs of the region are well represented in the central government.

In regard to other regions, the Mekong Delta and the Central Highlands for a start, an argument has been presented for statutory regional development authorities with a good deal of freedom to pursue their purposes in the regions for which they are created. The argument does not necessarily apply to I Corps Zone. After all the presently visible development opportunities have been discussed, no central unifying central theme for development emerges, though the scope of the works proposed for the exploitation of water resources comes close to one. But the program we recommend for the northern provinces consists essentially of unrelated projects which are not interdependent.

The need for coordination of the efforts of all governmental agencies concerned with the economic development of the northern provinces is clear, but it can probably be met by the Office of the Commissioner for Development. This does not preclude the establishment of special agencies for specific purposes, such as a Fisheries Development and Marketing Board or a Northern Provinces Water Resources Authority. The commissioner for development, or his deputy, might appropriately preside over both. For another major project in the development of the region, the rehabilitation of the refugees returning to their own villages, we do not think it necessary to establish a specialized agency.

Local participation by the people principally affected, those being resettled, is of course a most desirable ingredient. The task, however, is mainly an administrative one: most people will be eager to return to their lands as soon as security is assured, and the essential thing is to provide sufficient, honestly administered financial assistance to make sure that the refugees enjoy at least their former standards of living and perhaps better them. The processing of grants and loans will certainly be an onerous task, and so, where loans are given, will be the supervision of the borrowers to ensure that loans are used to the good effect for which they were intended. The Agricultural Development Bank might be a suitable agency to undertake this responsibility, but to do so efficiently will require more staff than the bank presently commands. We are persuaded, therefore, to recommend that this important feature of the regional development program be entrusted to the Ministry of Social Welfare and Refugees which is already active in this area and has a substantial and experienced staff.

In the ministry there is now a capacity for handling large numbers of refugees, including the processing and making of regular payments to them. As the refugees return to their own lands these responsibilities will diminish, and the capacity acquired by the agency could be diverted to the new task of supervising the loans made to refugee families for economic purposes. The formation of local committees acting in an advisory capacity to the ministry would certainly be desirable, and the commissioner for the development of I Corps Zone should be closely associated with the work.

Summary Conclusions

The general objectives of the program for the northern provinces are summarized as follows:

1. Intensified agricultural production on the coastal plain by water control and irrigation with related industrial development and agri-business in the towns.

2. Exploitation of highland forestry resources, from the development of wood-based industries and the restoration of the trade in cinnamon.

3. Transportation improvements including highway access to Laos to further international trade exchanges and greater utilization of the port capacity of Da Nang.

4. The modernization of commercial fisheries.

5. Electric power development--either by utilizing the Nong Son coal and the An Hoa generating plant, or by alternative hydroelectric development, whichever is determined to be most beneficial.

6. Industrial development, in particular a plywood and veneer factory at Da Nang, wood-based industries related to this, cement manufacture, the manufacture of other construction materials such as bricks and tile, and possibly the exploitation of silica sand for flat glass making.

7. Promotion of the tourist industry.

8. The resettlement of refugees and other war-displaced persons to bring back into production large areas of arable land abandoned during the war.

None of these programs can be implemented until security returns. A good deal can be done, in every case, to have projects ready for financing and implementation whenever that may happen. This is the principal task in the region composed of the five northern provinces.

THE CENTRAL HIGHLANDS OF II CORPS

With, at present, very little known about the agricultural potential of the soils of the Central Highlands, and only a little more known about the potential of its rivers and forests, it is not so easy to define the substance of a development program for this distinctive geographical area of Vietnam. The Central Highlands region is distinctive not merely by the peculiarity and range of its topography and other environmental conditions, but also because it presents special problems. These are concerned with the following facts: generally, apart from such concentrations of population as Dalat and Ban Me Thuot, the region remains recognizably inferior to the rest of Vietnam in social and economic advancement; allowing for large areas of difficult terrain, it is sparsely inhabited in comparison with the neighboring central lowlands; finally, its population is composed substantially, though not entirely, of people whose racial origins are different from those of the majority of the nation, who are removed from the main currents of national life, and who, remaining outside the cash economy, can contribute little to the national income except the maintenance of their own existences.

A principal assumption for a development program for the Central Highlands is that its people do not live outside the cash economy from preference, but because they have not had opportunities and inducements to enter it. A principal objective for the program is to provide them with the same opportunities for economic and social advancement as other Vietnamese, so that they can compete with them on terms of mutual respect. In Vietnam (as in many other countries), the problems of racial discord are unlikely to be disposed of until this is done.

In the whole of Vietnam the highlander communities have been variously estimated to number anything from 600,000 to 1,000,000 people. Probably they represent about 5 percent of the total population of the Republic. Although there are communities of non-Vietnamese origin in some 23 provinces in all (and although purely ethnic considerations are clearly not the only ones to be taken into account), it is suggested that a development program for the Highlands should provide primarily for those provinces in which the highlanders are most numerous. These are Kontum, Pleiku, Thu Bon, Darlac, Quang Duc, Tuyen Duc, and Lam Dong, comprising an area of just under 50,000 square kilometers, about 30 percent of the total area of Vietnam (see Figure 12.5). The area coincides largely, though not completely, with the basins of the Se San and Sre Pok rivers; and it is the traditional home of five of the largest of the highland communities, the Jarai, Bahnar, Rhade, Koho, and Mnong. It may be appropriate for

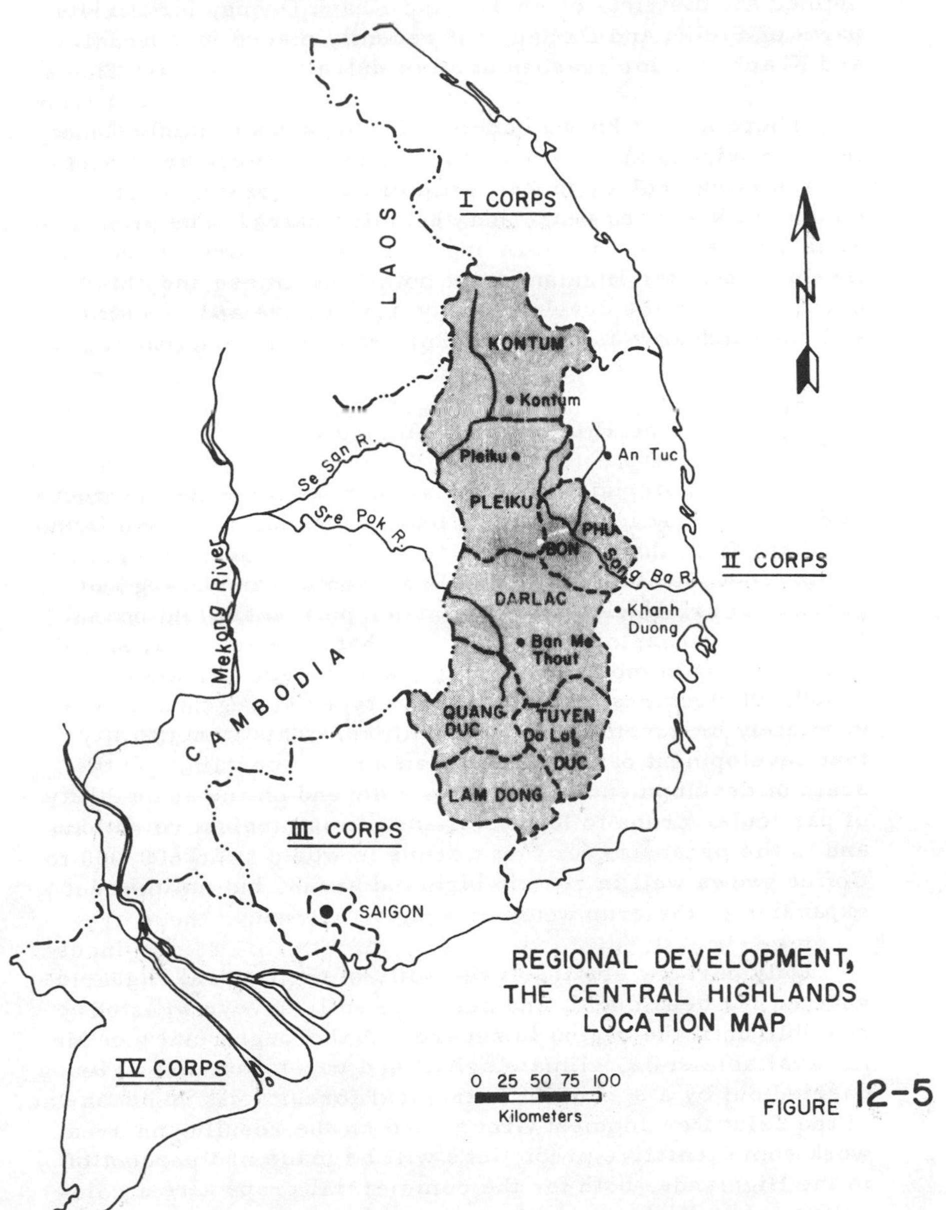

REGIONAL DEVELOPMENT, THE CENTRAL HIGHLANDS LOCATION MAP

FIGURE 12-5

purposes of development to include in the region as above defined the districts of An Tuc and Khanh Duong, formerly parts of Pleiku and Darlac, but recently placed in Binh Dinh and Khanh Hoa for reasons of administrative convenience.

There are no known commercial deposits of minerals in these provinces at the present time, though there are areas of promising geology in which minerals exploration ought to be undertaken when peace and security return. The presently visible prospects for improving the lives and fortunes of the inhabitants of the Highlands--of both Vietnamese and other origins--lie in the development of agriculture and forestry and such industry as should spring from these activities.

The Prospects for Agriculture

Studies of aerial photographs, to be checked and corrected in due course by investigations on the ground, provide a first approximation that, because of the steepness of the terrain, about 1,800,000 hectares (mostly in Kontum and Quang Duc provinces) are likely to remain under permanent (but not all necessarily unexploited) forest; but that as much as 1,500,000 hectares now in more open forest, and possibly another 1,000,000 hectares now under other types of vegetation, can ultimately be developed for agriculture. This is not to say that development of so extensive an area is certain, for the scale of development will obviously depend on the adaptability of particular crops to local soil and climatological conditions, and to the prospects for these crops in world markets. Coffee grows well in certain highland areas, but unlimited expansion of the crop would clearly be unwise.

Only cursory studies of the soils of the Central Highlands have so far been made, and adequate soil surveys will not be possible until the region is secure. A thorough review of all the available soils, climatological and vegetation data is being carried out by a specialist in tropical forest soils on behalf of the Joint Development Group, and on the results of his work some tentative predictions will be made of the potential in the Highlands, both for the commercial crops already cultivated in Vietnam (such as tea and coffee) and for other crops with good prospects in world markets. But in most cases, extensive field investigations and trials will be necessary to develop firm recommendations concerning the expansion of one crop or another.

Nevertheless, there are promising indications that considerable increases in production are possible. Even at the present time, highlands agriculture does not consist exclusively (as is sometimes erroneously supposed) of shifting cultivation of low-yielding rice varieties; nor, where shifting cultivation occurs, is it practiced recklessly without regard to the regeneration of the forest fallows. A good deal of evidence is available that change is occurring and can be accelerated, and there is more than one indication of a more promising future for the region's agriculture.

The outstanding example of progress in agriculture in the Highlands is, of course, the profitable production and highly skilled cultivation of a great variety of fruits and vegetables in Tuyen Duc Province. It is true that in this area the industry depends largely upon the enterprise and energy of refugees from North Vietnam who installed themselves at Dalat after 1954, and the participation of the original inhabitants of the area has been quite limited. However, the favorable conditions found at Dalat are certainly not unique in the Highlands, and, subject to the capacity of internal and foreign markets to absorb production, similar developments can be promoted in a number of other places.

The export possibilities for certain of the fruit and vegetable crops should not be discounted. In the years 1958 to 1960 there was, for instance, an encouraging increase in exports to Singapore. This commerce can probably be resumed and expanded, though it will require an efficient packaging and marketing organization and rigorous insistence on quality.

While it may be true that shifting cultivation is the general system of agriculture in the Highlands, with anything from 4 to 20 hectares of land per family either under crop or in fallow at any one time, this is not always true. Wherever conditions are right and suitable land is available, permanent agriculture is practised by the highlanders, and a rather remarkable variety of crops is cultivated in addition to rice. Many farmers have permanent rice fields, and most, it is said, have gardens and orchards at their homesteads. In a recent report* mention is made, among other crops, of the

*Gerald C. Hickey, The Highland People of South Vietnam: Social and Economic Development.

occurrence of manioc and corn, of a complete range of garden vegetables, of tea, coffee, rubber, peanuts, sesame, and pepper, of many varieties of tropical fruits, tobacco and areca, coconut, kapok, cotton, indigo, and cinnamon. This does not suggest that the crop possibilities are limited; on the contrary, it suggests excellent opportunities for diversification.

At present, nearly all farming in the Central Highlands is limited to the wet season, generally during the period of May through October, when 85-90 percent of the total annual rainfall occurs; in most years insufficient rain falls in any of the remaining months to meet the consumptive-use requirements of crops or pasture (though sufficient rains occasionally occur in April and November). Irrigation is virtually nonexistent, even though perennial flows are available in most streams throughout the area. As a result, double cropping is impossible in the present farming system, except for minor areas planted to fast-growing cash crops and to IR-5 and IR-8 rice varieties which have recently been introduced.

Major agricultural improvements can be realized through the implementation of a series of small to medium sized water control projects, which would supply irrigation water (permitting year-round cultivation) and also provide flood control and drainage facilities where needed. Over 21,000 hectares in the Upper Se San Basin and nearly 80,000 hectares in the Upper Sre Pok Basin have already been identified as potentially suitable for irrigated agriculture; aerial reconnaissance and map studies of these two basins have indicated that even greater areas might ultimately be developed, possibly up to an additional 50,000 hectares. General locations of irrigable areas are presented on Figures 12.6 and 12.7.

The Upper Sre Pok Basin

Generally centered upon Ban Me Thuot, the Upper Sre Pok Basin offers by far the greatest agricultural potential in the region owing to the presence of relatively large land areas which lie well for irrigation. Rainfall in the basin averages about 1,700 millimeters, of which roughly 85 percent falls during the period from May through October, and irrigation during the November through April dry season and occasional supplemental irrigation during the wet season, to meet deficits which may occur from time to time, will be necessary.

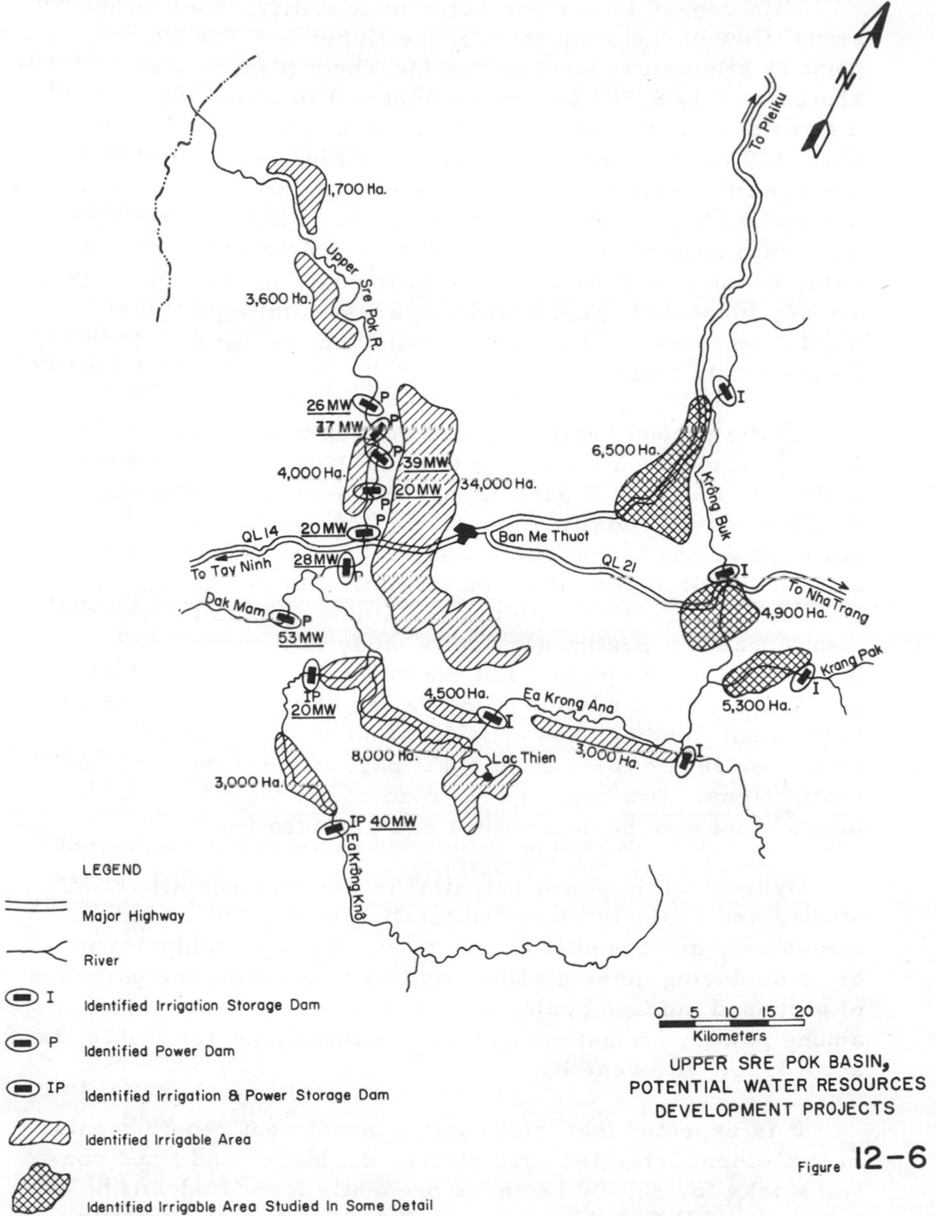

UPPER SRE POK BASIN, POTENTIAL WATER RESOURCES DEVELOPMENT PROJECTS

Figure 12-6

With regard to surface water availability, the average annual flow of the main stem of the Upper Sre Pok River at a point 15 kilometers west of Ban Me Thuot (drainage area, approximately 8,700 square kilometers) is about 160 cubic meters per second; the average maximum monthly flow is about 460 cubic meters per second (in November); and the average minimum monthly flow is roughly 35 cubic meters per second (in April). These approximate flow figures suggest that, with regulation by means of seasonal storage, ample water supplies will be available to irrigate the 80,000 hectares already identified, plus additional areas totaling at least 50,000 hectares should the necessity and the opportunity to do so ultimately arise.

Of the 80,000 hectares noted above, three areas totaling 16,700 hectares on the Krong Buk and Krong Pach tributaries of the Sre Pok (see Figure 12.6) have been studied in some detail; however, additional hydrological, soils, agricultural and engineering investigations are required to permit reasonably confident appraisal of the feasibility of developing these three areas, together with the remaining potential development areas. A preliminary soils study is presently in process. Certain portions of the basin, particularly the flat Lac Thien area and some of the valley bottoms, are subject to frequent flooding, and consideration of flood control measures should form an integral part of more detailed investigations. Drainage and farm-to-market road requirements must also be determined and provided for.

Hydroelectric power potential in the area has also been studied and projects identified totaling nearly 300 megawatts (previously discussed in Chapter 10). Every attempt must be made during more detailed studies to combine the purposes of proposed storage projects to enable allocation of costs among power, irrigation, and flood control, as applicable, in accordance with benefits.

It is expected that total capital investment requirements to implement irrigated agriculture, drainage, and flood control works for 80,000 hectares presently identified will be of the order of US$80-100 million. It is likely that once full production is reached this development would more than treble present farm incomes, with a resulting very favorable benefit-cost ratio. At least 35,000 farm families, a sizable proportion of the indigenous peoples of the Highlands, could thus be provided with a much higher standard of living than they now enjoy.

Clearly, for both practical and economic reasons, the development of the entire basin should not be undertaken too rapidly. Perhaps a construction period of twenty to thirty years would be practicable. However, in the interests of economy, a general development plan and implementation schedule should be prepared before any one specific project is started. Early plans for institutional and organizational development must also be made to ensure the successful operation of projects; this should include farmer training in use of irrigation water and improved cultural practices, and encouragement of crop diversification.

As an initial area of development during the first ten years after peace, 30,000 hectares, at a capital cost of the equivalent of US$30-35 million, does not seem unreasonable. Such an area would benefit some 12,000 farm families.

The Upper Se San Basin

The Upper Se San Basin, which includes two of the principal towns in the region, Pleiku and Kontum, is not nearly as well suited to irrigated agriculture as the Upper Sre Pok Basin because of its more rugged terrain. However, it appears that areas totaling from 10,000 to 20,000 hectares are potentially suitable for development in addition to the 21,000 hectares identified in previous studies.

Annual rainfall averages approximately 2,000 millimeters (somewhat greater than in the Sre Pok Basin), with roughly 90 percent falling during the May through October wet season. Irrigation water is necessary for year-round cultivation.

The average annual flow of the Upper Se San River at the Cambodian border (drainage area about 9,700 square kilometers) is approximately 270 cubic meters per second; average maximum monthly flow is about 550 cubic meters per second in October; and average minimum monthly flow approximates 65 cubic meters per second in April. More than sufficient surface runoff is available to supply water to all potentially irrigable land, though storage will be required in small tributary basin projects to carry over the dry season.

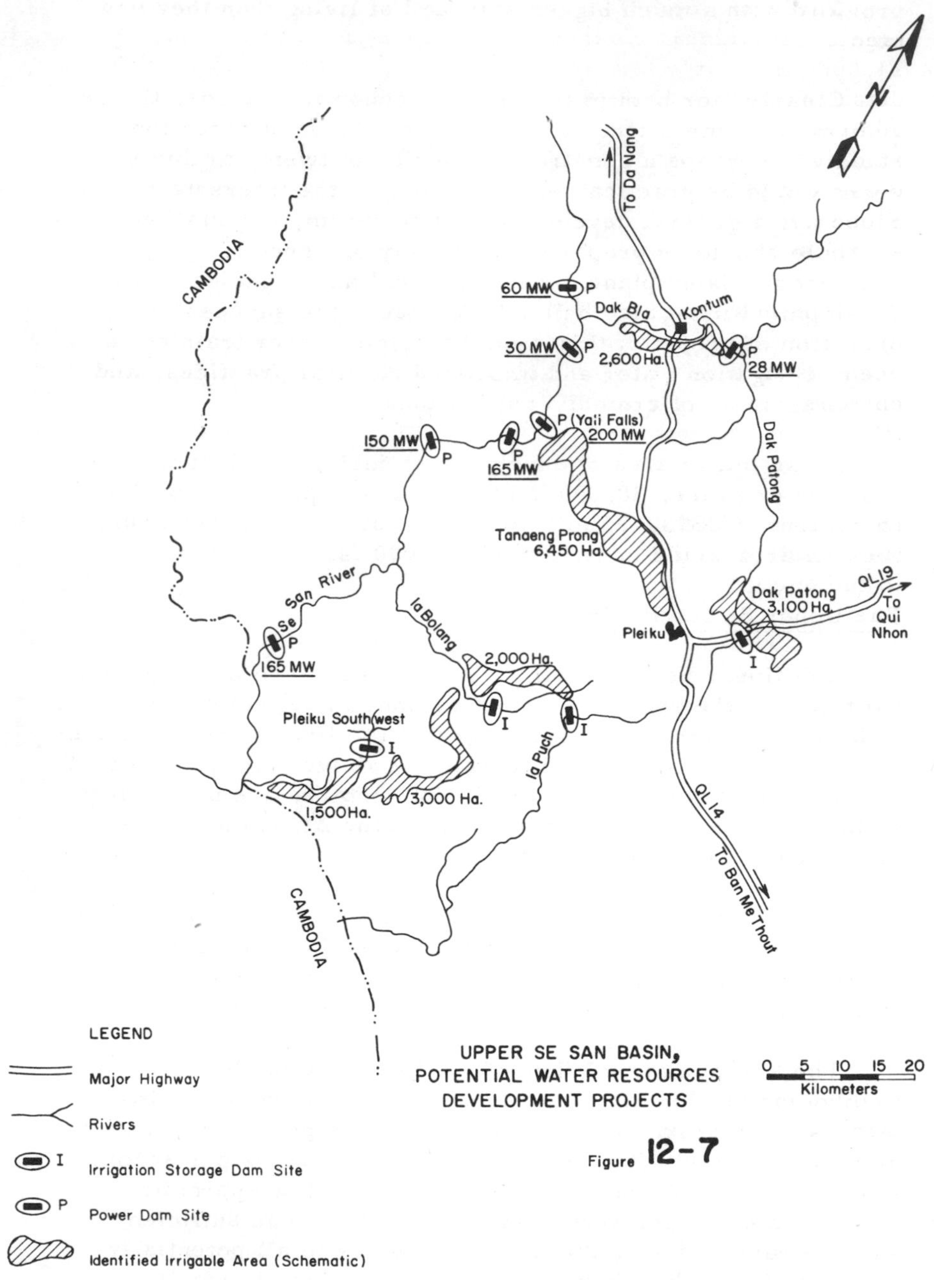

UPPER SE SAN BASIN, POTENTIAL WATER RESOURCES DEVELOPMENT PROJECTS

Figure 12-7

Three projects (Kontum, Tanaeng Prong, and Dak Potong (see Figure 12.7), comprising 6,900 hectares of the total of 21,000 previously identified, have been investigated in some detail; however, as in the case of the Sre Pok projects, additional agricultural, soils, hydrological, and engineering studies will be required before the feasibility of developing these and other project areas can be appraised with assurance. Flood control, drainage, and farm-to-market road requirements should be determined and provided for.

Hydroelectric power projects totaling approximately 800 megawatts have been identified in the basin, and these have been discussed in Chapter 10. Insofar as possible, and for obvious economic reasons, multipurpose project development (for power, irrigation, and flood control) is desirable.

The order of magnitude of capital investment requirements to develop irrigation, drainage, and flood control works for the 21,000 hectares previously identified will probably amount to the equivalent of US$20-25 million. As in the Sre Pok Basin, year-round cultivation and crop diversification should more than treble present farm earnings, and result in a highly favorable benefit-cost ratio. This area would enable over 8,000 farm families to enjoy a much improved standard of living.

Development of the projects should be undertaken in an orderly manner over a period of, say, twenty years on the basis of priorities established within an over-all basin plan and implementation schedule. In the first ten years after peace, development of some 10,000 hectares (benefiting about 4,000 farm families) is considered reasonable. The order of magnitude of capital costs would probably be the equivalent of US$10-12 million.

Possibilities for irrigated agriculture also occur in the valleys of the Song Ba (in Phu Bon province) and the Upper Dahnim River. With the exception of an investigation of the soils of the Song Ba,* these possibilities have not yet been studied.

---

*Thai Cong Tung, Study of the Soils of the Middle Song Ba Valley.

Some useful comparisons are possible with the northeast provinces of Thailand, which have peoples and an environment not dissimilar from those of the Central Highlands. In recent years kenaf, corn, and manioc have all been successfully introduced as commercial crops in Thailand. Corn and manioc are already grown in the Vietnamese Highlands, and kenaf was grown until a few years ago, mostly in the new settlements for lowland Vietnamese established during the regime of President Diem. Production of kenaf has now disappeared, partly because of the failure of these settlements to maintain themselves against insurgency, partly because of the sheer lack of any marketing organization to transfer the crop from farm to factory.

As they are grown in northeast Thailand, corn and kenaf do not support high standards of rural living. At present prices, net earnings to farmers might approximate to US$65 and $85 per hectare respectively, and it is questionable whether an average highland family will be capable of cultivating more than 1.0 or 1.5 hectares of either crop in addition to producing its own food--which, for many years to come, will continue to be its prime consideration. It must be admitted that at least some of the enthusiasm for kenaf and corn in Thailand is probably due to the unnaturally low rice prices decreed by the government of that country: in Vietnam (where there is a need to produce animal feeding stuffs and raw materials for the sack factories), it may be necessary to subsidize farm prices in the early years.

Nevertheless, even without subsidies, at present prices crops such as corn and kenaf can provide a highland family with its cash requirements (and with more cash than it presently earns), and would provide it with at least an introduction to the cash economy. This would be a useful start, not a final objective, for highland farming may reasonably aspire to greater prosperity in the long run than these particular crops are likely to afford.

The undulating natural grasslands of the Darlac Plateau, about 100,000 hectares in extent, have suggested to many people a potential for a substantial cattle industry in this area, and similar conditions are found in other parts of the Highlands as well. The prospect is worth investigating. At the present time, cattle contribute to the economy only as draft animals, little is known of the nutritive qualities of natural grasses, and only modest experiments have been made to test the adaptability of better grasses. In the present state of knowledge, we are not inclined to assert that a valuable beef-cattle industry will establish itself rapidly after the war on these uplands; we are perfectly ready to believe that there may be a long-term potential which will warrant careful investigation and experimentation and may also warrant some investment when the results of these are available.

The Prospects for Forestry

The prospects for forestry are good. They were defined in general terms in a preliminary report by the Joint Development Group* and have been described in Chapters 8 and 9, though not in the particular context of the seven provinces for which a regional development program is recommended. Only a cursory account of the resources available will be given here, with a rather fuller account of what their exploitation may do for the regional economy.

Unquestionably, the most valuable asset of the Central Highlands in resources available for immediate exploitation is an area of 180,000 hectares of natural pine forest covering parts of Tuyen Duc Province (and also parts of two neighboring provinces not included in the region). The pine forests can produce lumber and poles and are already doing so, the latter having some potential for export to other southeast Asian countries. They can also provide the raw material for large-scale production of high-grade paper pulp, both for manufacture of paper in Vietnam and for export. There are some useful by-products (two-needle pine, for instance, is a source of resin and turpentine) so that the region's pine forests may provide a base for some secondary as well as one major industry.

In their natural state, the pine forests will support this kind of industrial development for a period of from ten to twelve years, and, of course, as exploitation proceeds, a program of reforestation will need to be undertaken along with it. Reforestation has already been started on a small

---

*Preliminary Report on Forestry in Vietnam, Working Paper No. 17 (Joint Development Group, January, 1968).

scale, at Angkoret near Dalat. It has cost something like US$110 a hectare, a cost which can probably be reduced substantially by improved techniques, some mechanization, and a larger scale of operation. Per hectare, the artificial pine forests will be much more productive than the natural forests supplying industry at the start.

Besides the pine forests, there are in the Highlands far greater areas of mixed hardwood forest, containing some valuable species which already enter into world trade and many others for which profitable uses may eventually appear. Some of the best hardwood forest, 1,800,000 hectares in Kontum and Quang Duc provinces, is on difficult terrain which is unlikely to attract logging enterprises while easier opportunities are available further south and east; but 1,500,000 hectares of more open forest in Pleiku, Darlac, and Phu Bon, ultimately intended for development in agriculture, offer easier access and are likely to be attractive to timber companies as soon as peace returns. Because of existing insecurity, all the hardwood forest is now inaccessible (as at least some of the coniferous forest is not) and neither the exact area of this forest nor its condition (taking into account defoliation and the other destructive incidents of war) is known. The hardwood forests of the Highlands have not been previously exploited on a large scale, partly because of the occurrence of similar stands of good timber trees closer to the centers of population, and partly because of the roughness of the terrain on which they grow and the extra extraction and transportation costs which a logging operation would therefore incur. None of these factors will prove an insuperable bar to profitable exploitation when peace returns. On the contrary, such is the demand for high-quality hardwoods that we expect to see keen and spontaneous interest in these resources by both Vietnamese and foreign timber companies.

In terms of a development program for the Central Highlands, the significance of the existence of such resources has three aspects.

First, the resources will provide employment. Whatever degree of mechanization can be introduced into the reforestation program for the pine forests and into logging operations in both pine and hardwood forests, there will also be a demand for professionally and technically qualified men and for large numbers of semiskilled and unskilled workers.

The reforestation program alone, which might eventually extend to 10,000 hectares a year, will call for an especially large labor force, though not necessarily a full-time one. We have estimated that the program will offer 80 days work a year to some 15,000 men.

A principal objective of the regional program is to attract into the cash economy some of the inhabitants of the Highlands who now live outside it. This can be done, as suggested by the introduction of commercial crops into the subsistence farming system. But it can be done equally well by offering paid employment. To many of the indigenous peoples of the Highlands, work on a reforestation project or a logging site may prove to be more congenial and more rewarding than life on the farm; and reforestation, logging, and other timber operations are in fact trades at which, because of their familiarity with the environment, the highlanders may well prove to be more adept than the lowland Vietnamese. Wages paid on the reforestation projects will amount to about 320 million piasters a year, representing cash earnings of at least 20,000 piasters to each of the families engaged, a valuable supplement to their scanty farm incomes.

One or two specialized training institutions should be set up under the program, so that people can be equipped to develop any natural aptitudes for work in the forest industries. However, though we think it possible that work of this sort may especially appeal to young men from the highland communities, we do not recommend that training in and the exercise of these trades should be reserved exclusively for them. There will be other people in Vietnam looking for work when the war is over; and we doubt whether the highlanders themselves would benefit from such specially favorable treatment. What they will benefit most from, and what we suppose they mostly seek, is an opportunity to compete with other Vietnamese on equal terms. To enable them to do this, whatever forestry training schools are set up in the Highlands should be equipped to fit men for skilled technical positions as well as for the semiskilled tasks--for the people of these uplands will not be content to be hewers of wood for others forever.

Second, the suitability of Tuyen Duc (and perhaps other provinces) to cultivate the raw material for paper pulp, a resource for which the demand in world markets is good, will enable highland farmers, of both Vietnamese and non-Vietnamese origin, to grow a commercial tree crop in addition to supplying their own needs in food. In Working Paper No. 17, a tentative estimate was offered that a five-hectare plot of pine will produce family incomes of VN$20,000 a year, and five hectares may, in the event, be less than a family can maintain after providing its own subsistence and a limited volume of marketable crops.

Although the costs of a reforestation program will have to be met in the first instance from public funds, it should not be too difficult to provide arrangements which will enable five-hectare or larger plots to pass subsequently into private or family ownership, and for the government to recover its investment by stumpage fees. Private ownership of commercial forests should not be considered revolutionary; there are some private forests, of admittedly limited area, already in Vietnam, and it is understood that until all forests were taken into the public domain in the regime of President Diem, it was customary for communities to be compensated for timber removed from the lands they considered to be their own. If this policy is accepted for at least part of the reforested area, it will at once redress an old grievance and reduce maintenance costs. The successful land development and settlement projects of Malaysia, though based almost entirely on rubber or oil palm, might be useful examples to follow or adapt.

The third and last point is relevant to the institutional recommendations made later in this chapter. The forests of the Highlands can also provide a source of local revenue--by way of royalties and other taxes--for a regional agency charged with the implementation of the development program. The costs of the program will be high, involving not merely direct investment in agriculture and forestry but also substantial expenditures on transportation, resettlement, public health facilities, and education, and for the most part these costs can only be met by generous provision of funds on the part of the central government and the legislature. However, a regional source of financing for at least a proportion of the regional development program is surely desirable. In the Mekong Delta, the appropriate regional source of revenue may be charges imposed by a regional development authority on farming communities for the water with which it serves them; in the Central Highlands, one appropriate source could be royalties charged (it is hoped at reasonable rates) to those enterprises who exploit the forests for private profit. The forests are the Highlands' obvious and most rapidly exploitable natural resource and can supply at least some of the means to promote development in other sectors of the economy.

Land Development and Resettlement

While the first objective of the regional development program is the improvement of the lives of the people, Vietnamese and non-Vietnamese, of the Central Highlands, it is no less a concern that this extensive area, almost one-third of the entire country, should be made to contribute to economic growth and national wealth to the fullest extent of its resources. A recommendation in favor of a regional program is not to be taken as implying that the Central Highlands should be maintained in economic isolation from any of the neighboring regions of Vietnam, or from the country as a whole. The development of the Highlands cannot be considered except in the context of the total national interest; this lies principally in removing, as far as resources permit it to be done, the existing disparities between one region and another, and permitting the entire nation to move toward prosperity together.

The question is raised whether the present population of the Central Highlands is capable of full exploitation, in the national interest, of the region's resources in soil, water, and forests. Knowledge of the extent of those resources is still insufficient, but all the available evidence suggests to us that the present population is not.

A program of assisted resettlement from other regions of Vietnam will simultaneously promote the beneficial exploitation of highland resources and relieve the economic situation of other regions (the five northern provinces are a prime example), where the pressure of population on land is heavy, the problem of the refugees is serious, and living standards stand still or decline. We recommend that a program of this type be included in the plans for the future of the Central Highlands. We add that the program does not have to be limited to the assisted resettlement of citizens of purely Vietnamese origin. Among the refugees, there are tens of thousands of families ethnically similar to the indigenous peoples of the highland provinces, and as fully in need of assistance in reestablishing their lives as the refugees of Vietnamese stock. The program should cater to all alike.

The difficulties inherent in relocating lowland Vietnamese, or any other people, in a strange environment are obvious, and the country's previous experience of resettlement is discouraging. The record is clearly described in the report by Gerald Hickey* and the facts are well known in any case. Briefly, under legislation enacted by the government of President Diem in 1957 and 1968, over 50,000 families of lowlanders were moved into the Highlands and other underdeveloped areas of Vietnam. Of these, about 20,000 lowland families were moved into the Highlands, and in addition about 7,000 highland families were moved from their traditional homes to new locations in the same region. The movement of the indigenous families was carried out partly to make way for the immigrants, and partly with better intensions, to persuade them to adopted settled agriculture. Although some of the projects were well organized and administered, generally both types of movement have ended in failure. Partly because the element of compulsion was removed with the fall of President Diem, and partly because of growing insecurity, people began to abandon the new settlements, and today it appears that only a fraction of the settlers still remain where they were put. It must on the other hand be mentioned that the settlers have not necessarily left the Highlands and returned to their native villages on the coast. Considerable numbers of them are now concentrated in and around towns like Ban Me Thuot and Pleiku, and there is a possibility that some at least will return to the settlements when the war is over.

Insecure conditions in the countryside contributed largely to this failure, but there were other reasons, which, we believe, would have prevented success even in times of peace:

1. Most important, and most clearly to be avoided in the future, was the complete disregard of the feelings of the highland peoples and of their interest in lands which they regarded as theirs, even where they did not always effectively occupy them.

2. Many of the lowland settlers were compelled to abandon their original homes; not having chosen the move, they had no heart in the movement from the start and no determination to make settlement a success; these, of course, were the first to leave in 1963 and 1964.

---

*Hickey, op. cit.

3. There were some ill-chosen sites, and some faulty judgments concerning the commercial crops to be grown. Rubber, for instance, was not a good choice in all conditions of soil and climate. Kenaf was often a better one, but arrangements for processing and marketing were inadequate.

4. The government of the day simply attempted too much in relation to the limited resources at its command. If settlers are to be given better opportunities for making a living than they had at home, and at least as good social services, then settlement becomes an expensive business. It cannot be done cheaply.

These are the principal errors to be avoided in any successful resettlement program in Vietnam. In a report by the Joint Development Group, the following observations were made:

> The fact of regional and communal antipathies has to be recognized. However, we believe it would be wrong to assume that the people of the Central Highlands would necessarily oppose resettlement and land development programs irrespective of the conditions under which these are undertaken. Properly organized, these programs should benefit the indigenous communities every bit as much as they do the settlers, and they may be influential in attracting these communities into the cash economy and helping them to achieve the standards of living which, as citizens of Vietnam, they are entitled to share with other Vietnamese. The Joint Development Group would not advocate resettlement programs in disregard to the natural reactions of people already living in the areas selected for resettlement. It does advocate: negotiation with the communities concerned . . . . straightforward recognition of any traditional interests they may sustain in the area . . . (compensation) to the extent that rightful interests are impaired by resettlement, and an undertaking to assist the indigenous communities within the area at least as generously as any newcomers, so that they too may enjoy the benefits of a stable and progressive agriculture.*

---

*Proposal for a Resettlement Program, Working Paper No. 10 (JDG, October, 1967).

Those are still our views, and there are two implications in the resettlement program we now propose. First, that the cost estimates must include compensation in cash or in kind for those people who will be hurt or inconvenienced by resettlement; second, that the minorities must be accommodated within the program--not within two different and discriminatory ones, as in the time of the Diem government. This means that they must receive some of the best land, including the irrigable lands available in the Sre Pok and Se San valleys, and that highland families must be given ownership of as much of these lands as they need to make a decent living. This will not be less than the area needed by a lowland family; and as regards choice of site, the highland communities might reasonably be given the preference.

Any movement from the lowlands should be voluntary. In the last few years there have been signs of willingness on the part of a few refugee villages in Quang Tri province to move into the Highlands, but this interest may disappear when the war ends and they are presented with what will seem to many a more attractive alternative--returning to the villages familiar to them, ruined as the condition of some of these places may be. It is recognized that in the early years of the program there are unlikely to be large numbers of lowland families volunteering to move into the Highlands, but this may be all to the good. We can rely on the numbers to increase if success is first demonstrated by a few successful settlements, cultivating the crops best adapted to the soil and climatic conditions of a particular site, and selling them for reasonable prices.

In any event, it is eminently desirable in, say, the first five years of the program, to demonstrate to the highlanders that the program is designed in their interests as much as or perhaps more than it is in the interests of the immigrants. In the early years of the resettlement program, before organizational efficiency had been developed, a large spontaneous movement of people from the coastal plains into the Central Highlands might be a positive embarrassment. Some of us are inclined to believe that in the early years of the program there will be no voluntary movement whatever of farm families from the plains to the Highlands. There might, on the other hand, be a sizable movement of lowland families engaged in commerce or artisanal pursuits into the little towns of the region, and, later, some profitable agricultural development by lowland families in the vicinity of the towns, as has happened at Dalat.

This, and other reasons, including the important one of the financial resources likely to be available, argue in favor of keeping the resettlement program down to manageable size. What sort of size does this mean?

In a period of less than five years the government of President Diem, with some compulsion, succeeded in moving almost 60,000 families into new settlements throughout Vietnam, but did not succeed in keeping them there. This kind of figure, if the work is done properly, would be an ambitious target for twice that length of time, and it may be sensible to aim at a more modest one. It will take some years for a land settlement agency to acquire the capability to cater to large numbers of people efficiently, and even when organizational efficiency is achieved it will physically be extremely difficult to move more than 10,000 families a year and provide properly for their needs in their new locations. A convincing demonstration, on however small a scale, is essential at the start, and quite clearly the resettlement program must be carefully phased so that one can be given. We envisage a modest beginning, 1,000 or 2,000 families a year, with these coming entirely from highland communities already living in the seven provinces or in neighboring areas in the Highlands.

The costs will be large nevertheless. A site for a project investigated in Tuyen Duc province offered some bottom land for rice and other subsistence crops, lower slopes suitable, after terracing, for the production of vegetables, and enough other land to provide each family with about 4 hectares of pine plantation. The costs per family were roughly estimated at US$2,000, the largest single element of cost being the terracing of the lower slopes. This alone came to US$1,765 per hectare, or about US$900 per family. Naturally, the costs will vary from site to site. At some places the heavy costs of terracing will be unnecessary, but instead the capital costs of small irrigation systems may amount to as much as US$1,000 per hectare, and at least US$2,000 a family. At sites adapted to other tree crops than pine, the costs of establishing and maintaining the crop to maturity will greatly exceed the US$100 a hectare which the pine will cost: the successful settlement schemes in Malaysia are based mainly on rubber and oil palm, and cost the government of that country an initial outlay of from US$4,000 to US$6,000 per family, though, at least in principle, part of this is subsequently recovered from the settlers.

Without examination of each selected site a precise estimate of costs cannot be given, but inclusive of compensation, US$3,500 per family seems a reasonable figure to adopt for present purposes. On that basis, a resettlement program serving the needs of 40,000 families, about one-third of the indigenous population of these seven provinces, will call for a capital investment of US$140 million. Part of this would be offset by the costs of irrigation, previously discussed in this chapter, but an investment of this order would be an ambitious undertaking in the first ten years, a firm step toward the economic development of the human and natural resources of the Central Highlands. At the start we would not recommend the government to aspire to more.

Organization and Finance

In a period of ten years, expenditures on the projects previously recommended in this program will be of the order of magnitude of US$150 million, distributed as shown in Table 12.5. The total shown there does not represent the complete cost of all desirable economic and social development to be undertaken in the Central Highlands in the decade immediately following the war. It omits (1) private investments; (2) essential social capital investments; (3) infrastructure investments; and (4) expenditure to improve traditional agriculture and animal husbandry.

TABLE 12.5

Recommended Ten-Year Postwar Expenditures, Central Highlands

Project	Expenditure (US$ Millions)
Irrigation	45.0
Resettlement (excluding irrigation)	95.0
Reforestation	10.0
Total	$150.0

1. The private investments expected, which in the case of the pulp mill alone might be of the order of US$50-60 million, are omitted. The mill will not, of course, necessarily be sited in the Central Highlands region (either Phan Ranh or even Cam Ranh, if water supplies can be assured, might be a more suitable location). It is not unreasonable to hope for additional private investments, totaling US$10-15 million in logging, sawmilling, and other wood-based enterprises, food processing and packaging, and the service industries.

2. Also omitted are essential investments of social capital, notably for education and public health: In Chapter 11 the view is expressed that Vietnam would not, in the decade immediately following the war, command the resources to provide for security, move toward economic independence, and also equip itself with the full range of social services that it seeks. We suggested that if resources are directed in this decade toward the development of the economy, then fully adequate services of this kind might be within reach in the next one.

However sound this argument for Vietnam as a whole, there are good reasons for making a special case of the Central Highlands, where the social services, noticeably less developed than in the rest of the country, should not be allowed to fall further behind. In this region we recommend consideration for the following:

2a. A steady expansion of the primary school system, adding new classrooms to existing schools and constructing as many new schools a year as are necessary to bring the region up to national standards within the next ten years.

2b. At least a commensurate, perhaps a greater, effort to promote secondary education, especially for the indigenous communities, so that more young men and women from the region can qualify for entry to the universities, and therefore for professional employment, in the 1980's.

2c. A considerable increase in teacher training facilities, in order to improve the quality of primary education in existing schools and to provide a base for later expansion of the educational system as a whole.

2d. Facilities for technical training in agriculture, forestry, and the engineering trades (including the training centers referred to in the chapter on forestry) directed deliberately to supplying those skills which the growing economy will demand.

2e. Generous assistance to the regional university at Dalat.

There has been no attempt at this time to estimate what a program of this kind would cost in the next ten years; and similarly no estimate has yet been made of the essential requirements in preventive and curative medicine. In both cases, these appear to us to be matters of national concern, and, as such, more fitly provided for in national development plans than in the context of a regional program to be administered (as we recommend) by a regional agency whose primary purpose will be to promote economic development. Education and public health are both proper concerns of ministries of the central government, and we do not envisage that any purely regional agency will be competent or equipped to provide for them.

However, the expenditures suggested as appropriate for a ten-year resettlement program do include some provision--which might best be put at the disposal of the ministries concerned--for the establishment of primary schools and simple public health facilities at each project site.

3. Any investment in the infrastructure is omitted. This is clearly a matter of local as well as national concern, but the heaviest expenditures will be directed to projects of national significance--the construction or reconstruction of national and interprovincial roads (including, for example, routes 20 and 21, between Dalat and Ban Me Thuot; Route 14, between Ban Me Thuot and Kontum; Route 7b, between Phu Bon and Tuy Hoa; and the extension of Route 14 from Kontum toward Da Nang), the national telecommunications system, and, possibly, large-scale development of hydroelectricity sites on the Dong Nai, Se San, and Sre Pok rivers. None of these is suitable to be treated as a project of purely regional significance. However, limited hydroelectric development at certain sites on the Se San and Sre Pok--a few thousand kw at one or more places--might well be considered in conjunction with irrigation development and in the context of a regional program.

Local roads are another matter. They will be necessary to provide access to new settlement projects and areas of exploitable forest, and for marketing the produce of these areas. Within the settlement areas, the estimates previously suggested include some provision for simple road construction, and within forest concessions, road construction should be the responsibility of the concessionaires (though their works will serve the purpose of agricultural development when the timber is extracted). However, some public expenditures on local road construction will certainly be necessary.

Until sites are selected, it is impossible to do more than guess at what this will amount to. In the topographic conditions of the Central Highlands, a simple earth road with a gravel surface will probably cost about US$1,000 a kilometer. It is reasonable to envisage a construction program of about 1,000 kilometers in the seven provinces in the next ten years, and the equivalent of US$1 million might suitably be added to the regional program to meet this requirement.

Similarly, the regional program might also appropriately provide for amenities and services in the small highland towns which have developed rapidly during the war and will continue to grow steadily after it. In Ban Me Thuot and the rural area immediately around it there are now said to be 100,000 people, practically half the total population of Darlac province. An Khe (27,000), Khanh Duong (15,000), and Hau Bon (10,000) are no longer insignificant villages but little towns. They have a purpose to serve in their provinces and districts--as centers for the timber-based, food-processing, and service industries, for commerce, banking, and administration, and for educational and public health facilities. As the development of agriculture proceeds and wealth grows, their importance will increase; and in all the places mentioned, and in Pleiku and Kontum and possibly some others as well, there will be a need and a demand for the amenities associated with life in the cities--efficient electric power supplies, markets, water and sanitation, and recreational facilities.

Not to satisfy such a demand would only encourage the drift to the principal, already overcrowded, centers of population, Saigon and Da Nang, something which, as we recommend elsewhere in this study, should certainly be avoided if it is possible to do so. Moreover, it will be the towns and their amenities, not the forests and the mountains, which at least at the start will attract lowland families from the overpopulated plains; and many of the highland families too will gradually turn to the towns for the diverse employment opportunities they offer. During the war many highland farm families have resorted to places like Pleiku and Kontum, are now engaged in commerce and the service industries in them, and are unlikely to leave when the war ends. This is an entirely natural and healthy development. The towns will provide markets for surplus foodstuffs, perhaps inspiring substantial agricultural development in the rural areas surrounding them.

An estimate of the costs of providing the amenities mentioned to towns in the Highlands is not yet possible. We assume an order of magnitude of the equivalent of US$10-20 million in the next ten years.

4. The program also omits such expenditures as will be necessary to improve the agriculture and animal husbandry of that large proportion of highland farmers who will continue for the time being, no matter what superior alternatives are offered to them, to pursue their traditional activities and modes of life. On the dimensions which we believe practicable in the first ten years after the war, the resettlement and irrigation developments we recommend will not accommodate more than a third of the indigenous population of the Highlands, and inevitably most, if left to their own devices, will continue to do precisely what they are doing now. What they are doing now may not be as bad as is commonly supposed, but it does not provide them with anything like the standard of living they ought to enjoy.

We make the assumption that within the existing agricultural system considerable improvements may be possible in crop varieties, cultural practices, fertilizer applications, and so on; and we believe that it is by starting with improvements within the present system that it will be possible, ultimately, to persuade people to change the system itself. Nothing can be as educational in its effect as a program of assistance which will increase yields and production inside the agricultural pattern which farmers presently prefer: This will not perpetuate inefficiencies; it will, on the contrary, supply the confidence necessary for change.

Exactly what can be done in this way needs more investigation, though the experiments and demonstrations in the

Agricultural Experimental Station at Eak Mat have provided some highly promising indications. Very tentatively, the costs of education and assistance in a ten-year period might amount to the equivalent of US$4-5 million, and an allocation of this order might appropriately be included in the regional program.

Including expenditures for local roads and amenities and agricultural education, (3) and (4), the total requirements for specifically regional projects might amount to approximately US$170 million. If the irrigation developments on the Se San and Sre Pok can be carried further in the first ten postwar years than the 40,000 hectares presently proposed, then the requirements might rise to as much as US$200 million.

Institutional Framework

At the start of this chapter, a belief was expressed that, in some cases, the effective management of programs of regional interest might best be assured by the establishment of agencies with strong regional representation and whatever powers and functions the regional circumstances may dictate. The recommendation seems particularly appropriate to the Central Highlands, where the reserved and presently disadvantaged highland communities have somehow to be persuaded to play a fuller part and get for themselves a better share in the progress of the nation.

What a Central Highlands Development Board might do is, among other things, (1) manage the public forests of the region within the conditions prescribed by the Forest Law (and by such changes in the law as may occur if the recommendations made in Chapter 8 are applied). This would include management of a reforestation project presently estimated to cost US$10 million. It could (2) manage all the land development programs envisaged for the Central Highlands, including local irrigation systems such as those planned for the Se San and Sre Pok basins. And it could (3) carry out or assist local authorities to carry out works of local significance, including agricultural education and assistance, the construction of farm-to-market roads, and the provision of other desirable town and village amenities.

In addition, the regional development agency could assume another function of special significance to the future of the Highlands and its peoples: on behalf of the latter it could act as trustee of the extensive areas of unoccupied land in the seven provinces, titles to which are unclear or in dispute.

This could be most important. Undoubtedly, a major cause of dissatisfaction in the Highlands has been the forfeiture by a previous regime and conversion to public ownership of communal interests in land which were strongly maintained in local traditions even though unsupported by documented titles. Succeeding governments have corrected this situation in principle, but in practice, at least in numerous cases, land in the Highlands is still disposed of and used as if it were in the gift of the government's local representatives and as if no other interests in it existed. Where individual titles are few and unrecorded, and effective occupation of land is difficult to prove, we recognize the temptation to do this; and, indeed, it is possible that there is no legally effective way of awarding titles to families and individuals except by the government's taking possession of all unoccupied lands first. However, if that was the motive, very few of the indigenous inhabitants of the Highlands have so far benefitted from it.

The agricultural development of the Highlands may depend more than upon any other factor in providing security of tenure for a family or village on the land it farms. A visible demonstration by the government of its intentions might profoundly affect the response of the minorities to the programs suggested for the Central Highlands, including importantly any settlement programs which are intended to benefit not only the minorities but, at a later time, immigrants from the lowlands as well. Such a demonstration might come most easily from the existence of a regional agency, composed largely of men of regional origins, administering and disposing of the extensive areas of land in the Highlands to which titles are presently in doubt. This would include important areas of permanent forest from which, as it is opened to exploitation, royalties and other taxes could be derived to defray the costs of regional development; and it would include other extensive areas presently under forest, but eventually likely to be put under agriculture, within which individual and family titles will have to be awarded. As a start, the agency might register, record, and acknowledge all communal interests in land; negotiate with communities possessing interests in land required for resettlement and development; compensate them in cash at realistic values, or by grants of other land of equivalent area and quality where loss of rights occurs; and continue the process, recently begun by the present government, of awarding documented individual titles where ownership can be clearly demonstrated.

Wherever highland families are persuaded, by the programs suggested in this report or by any others, to adopt settled agriculture, individual titles should be awarded without delay, and with a minimum of conditions and formality. While this is not the kind of function to be prescribed for most regional development authorities, the expeditious handling of land matters is important to the economic and social development of the Highlands. We believe it to be in the public interest to see that it is achieved by a responsible body properly representative of regional opinion.

The question remains how a responsible body representative of public opinion can best be assured. The answer may be found in the provisions of the Constitution which relate to the Council for Ethnic Minorities. One-third of the members of the council are to be appointed by the president, presumably from among Vietnamese specialists in highland affairs, and two-thirds, a clear majority, are to be elected by the minority communities. The functions of the council are consultative, and the composition of a Central Highlands Development Board is an obvious matter on which it ought to be consulted.

COASTAL BASINS OF II CORPS

The twelve provinces comprising the II Corps area have a population of about 2.5 million. Of this total population, roughly 700,000 live in the seven highland provinces (subject of the preceding section of this chapter), and the remaining 1.8 million live in the five coastal provinces--Binh Dinh, Phu Yen, Khanh Hoa, Ninh Thuan, and Binh Thuan. This section is confined to a general discussion of the coastal provinces followed by a more specific, but still preliminary, program for development of water and land resources.

In the context of regional development as presented in the other sections of this chapter it is difficult to identify problems and opportunities common to the whole within the five coastal provinces. The five northern provinces form a recognizable geographical unit characterized by a broad, nearly continuous coastal plain which will lend itself well to a coordinated regional program for developing water resources and improving agriculture. The Central Highlands is distinctive as a region in that it is less advanced than the rest of Vietnam, has difficult environmental conditions, presents numerous special problems, is sparsely inhabited, and has a population with racial origins different from the rest of the country. The five coastal provinces, unlike the two regions just mentioned, do not lend themselves well to an over-all regional development plan since, physically, the coast does not form a near-continuous plain; rather, it is comprised of a series of relatively small deltaic areas at the mouths of the rivers which suggest independent project development. It is important, however, that in program planning, consideration be given to the possible advantages of interdependence both among the coastal basins and between the highlands and the lowlands.

All the coastal basins in II Corps are connected both by the national railroad and National Highway No. 1. The center of activity of each province is usually located within the largest coastal basin in the province. Major towns are Qui Nhon, Tuy Hoa, Nha Trang, Phan Rang, and Phan Thiet.

Areas presently under cultivation total roughly 200,000 hectares, of which about 150,000 hectares are planted to rice. It is reported that about one-half of the rice area is double cropped and yields are less than 2 tons per hectare per crop. Over half of the rice production is from the Qui Nhon area of Binh Dinh Province.

Fishing, too, is an important occupation in the coastal areas of II Corps, producing about one-third of the total national catch. Yields per fisherman and boat are well above the national average in Binh Thuan, equal to it in Ninh Thuan and Khanh Hoa, and substantially below it in Phu Yen and Binh Dinh. Phan Thiet in Binh Thuan province is a large fish-processing center accounting for almost half the national nuoc nam production and a sizable portion of the total production of cured and dried fish.

Each coastal center also represents a center of trade, although port facilities are adequate only at Qui Nhon and Nha Trang. Cam Ranh is a special case in that it is an excellent natural harbor of far greater size than can apparently be supported by its hinterland. Development of Cam Ranh will probably occur as a result of special circumstances not necessarily related to the region.

Water Resources Development

The problems of the coastal basins of the central lowlands are similar to those of the coastal plain of the five northern provinces as described above. Average farm size (about 0.7 hectare) is uneconomical, resulting in a majority of the people living at subsistence level; rice yields are low; many areas are subject to frequent flooding; some areas are subject to salt water intrusion and insufficient rainfalls to permit year-round cultivation (especially in the south); most rivers have inadequate base flow to enable area-wide irrigation; and drainage conditions are poor, particularly on the flatter portions bordering the sea.

To ameliorate these conditions it is proposed that a development program be established with full control and utilization of the water and land resources of the five provinces as its eventual objective. This program should provide for comprehensive detailed studies of the several potential coastal basin projects in the area; establishment of development priorities; and consideration of interdependence, particularly regarding crop diversification; i.e., each basin does not necessarily have to be entirely self-sufficient in its agricultural production. This report presents a general, tentative outline of such a program together with a rough order of magnitude of costs; however, detailed implementation plans and specific development priorities cannot be presented until much more detailed appraisal studies are made.

Many studies have been carried out, and various facilities, such as diversion dams, dikes, and canals, have been constructed over about the past thirty years. These facilities have been both productive and beneficial, especially in the Qui Nhon, Tuy Hoa, and Phan Rang areas; however, they can only be considered partial solutions to the problems of the coastal basins; more land (much presently unused) can be brought into intensive, year-round cultivation through provision of storage, flood and salinity control and drainage works by orderly and timely development of each basin.

There are ten major rivers serving the coastal areas of the five provinces. The estimated gross irrigable area within the coastal basins is 400,000 hectares; assuming there are at least 320,000 net cultivable hectares within this figure, eventual full development would bring at least an additional 120,000 hectares under cultivation. Irrigable areas and river basin drainage areas are presented in Figure 12.8; Table 12.6 lists the major rivers and drainage areas with rough estimates of average annual and minimum monthly discharges and gross irrigable areas served.

Of the ten basins only one, the Song Ba, serving the Tuy Hoa area, has sufficient runoff to meet irrigation water requirements without seasonal storage. There are several apparently suitable storage dam sites within the five provinces, including the Song Ba; alternative schemes should be studied for providing storage including the possibility of diversion from the Song Ba to neighboring basins. It is also noted that the natural runoff of the Song Cai (serving the Phan Rang area) is supplemented by tail water from the Da Nhim hydroelectric plant which, with re-regulation, will enable year-round irrigation of nearly half of the irrigable area in the basin.

The incidence of flooding and saline intrusion varies considerably in the ten coastal basins. Generally, the most serious floods occur north of Tuy Hoa and they are most severe in the Qui Nhon area; the same general statement also applies to saline intrusion in the dry season. Some areas around Qui Nhon are subjected to frequent salt water flooding also. Flood and salinity control should form an integral part of project development through means of storage allocations, flood retention dams, dikes, and tide gates in various combinations to be determined by economic comparisons.

With the possible exception of providing power for irrigation and drainage pumping, installation of hydroelectric plants at storage dams is not considered feasible owing to relatively low streamflow and low available head. The Song Ba is an exception to this general statement; however, power developments on this river would probably be single purpose, unless implemented in conjunction with potential irrigation projects in the upper reaches in the Central Highlands.

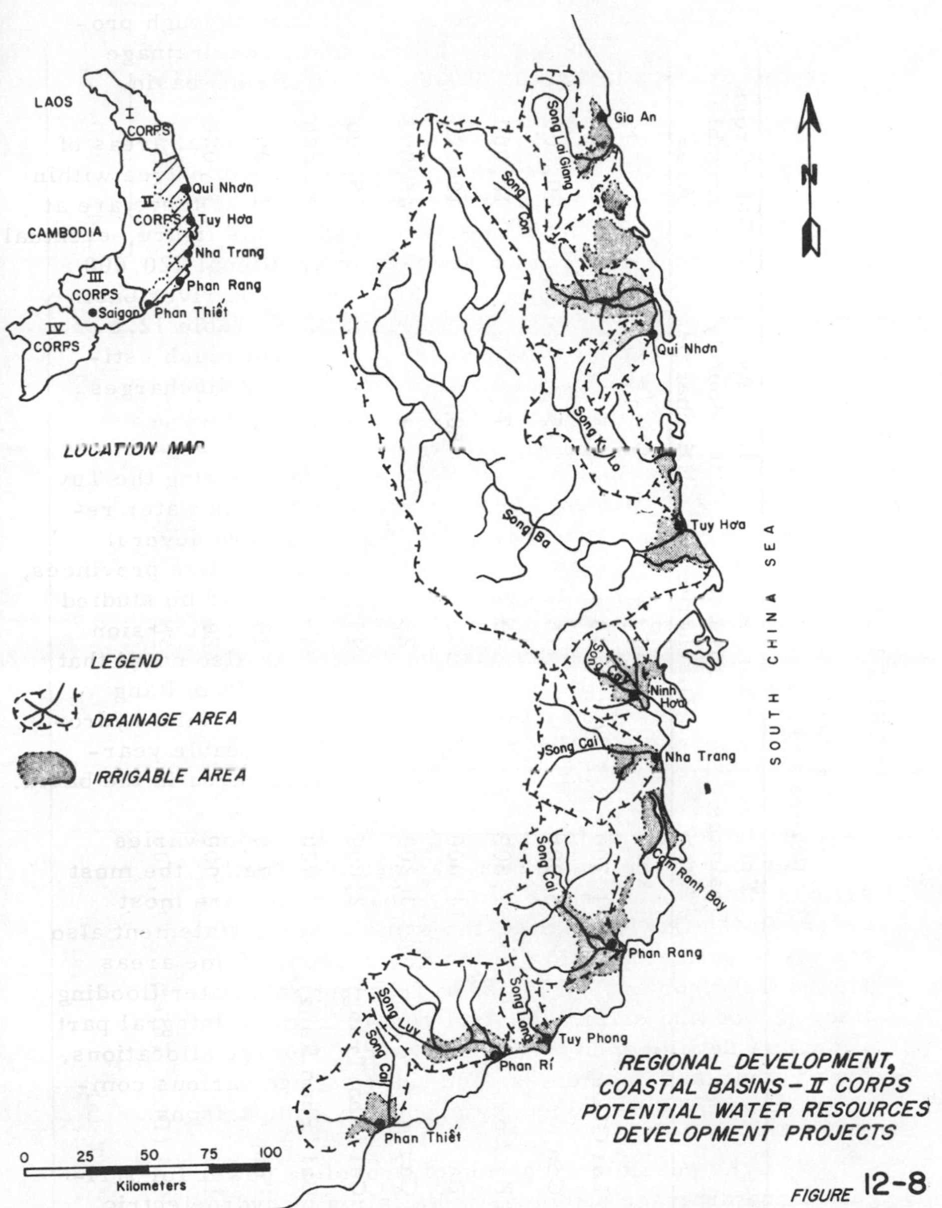

REGIONAL DEVELOPMENT, COASTAL BASINS — II CORPS POTENTIAL WATER RESOURCES DEVELOPMENT PROJECTS

FIGURE 12-8

TABLE 12.6

Coastal Basins, II Corps,
Rivers and Irrigable Areas

River	Est. Drainage Area	Est. Av. Annual Discharge	Est. Av. Min. Monthly Discharge	Est. Gross Irrigable Area
	km^2	m^3/s	m^3/s	ha
Song Lai Giang	1,300	30	5	30,000
Song Con	3,000	75	15	100,000
Song Ky Lo	1,800	40	7	10,000
Song Ba	14,000	300	50	40,000
Song Cay	1,200	25	4	45,000
Song Cai (Nha Trang)	2,000	40	6	15,000
Song Cai (Phan Rang)	3,700	40	7	70,000
Song Long	700	10	2	10,000
Song Luy	2,000	20	3	35,000
Song Cai (Phan Thiet)	1,900	20	3	45,000
Total				400,000

To permit crop diversification, drainage facilities must be provided, particularly in the flatter areas adjacent to the sea; it is envisaged that some drainage pumping plants will be required to effect this.

In designing and implementing the coastal basin projects, fullest practicable utilization should be made of the many existing facilities; for example, at least 20,000 hectares are presently commanded by canals in the Phan Rang area. Some areas, such as Phan Rang, Tuy Hoa, and Qui Nhon, will require less capital expenditure than others to develop because of considerable existing works in these particular localities. However, no attempt is made in this study to estimate costs by project. Rather, an over-all, average rough order of magnitude cost of equivalent US$1,300 per hectare is assumed as adequate to cover capital cost requirements to implement water control works. On this basis, capital costs for a total estimated 400,000 hectares would be in the order of the equivalent of US$520 million.

Total development of the coastal basins will probably require at least thirty years to accomplish; a quarter of the total irrigable area, say 100,000 hectares, might be brought under development during the first ten years after peace, at a rough capital cost equivalent to about US$130 million.

Construction of project works is only a beginning. To ensure success, (1) crop diversification on the basis of land capability and markets must be encouraged; (2) agricultural extension services, including instruction in irrigation methods, and farm credit must be provided; (3) improved seed varieties and fertilizers must be developed and made available; and (4) local associations must be organized to facilitate proper water use, distribution of seed and fertilizers, crop storage facilities, marketing, collection of water and drainage charges for loan repayments, and other such services. In connection with this last purpose, attempts are presently under way to establish associations in the Phan Rang area; to date results have been mixed, with some confusion and disagreements between villages.

If the projects are properly designed and organized, substantial benefits should result, including (1) firm supplies of irrigation water for year-round cropping; (2) proper drainage; (3) effective flood and salinity intrusion control as applicable; (4) conditions in which improved cultural practices can be adopted by local development associations with the assistance of the agricultural extension services; (5) use of higher-yielding rice varieties, thus releasing large areas now planted to rice to other higher value crops; (6) crop diversification; and (7) exploitation of considerable areas of land not now under cultivation. These will almost certainly result in favorable cost-benefit ratios.

More detailed project appraisal studies will lead to the establishment of priorities among the ten basin projects. At this time it is proposed that, in general, development should start in the two southernmost provinces of Ninh Thuan and Binh Thuan, since these comprise the areas of greatest need, having the lowest annual rainfall (only 600 to 1,000 millimeters). Orderly development could then proceed toward the north.

Over-All Development Possibilities

The above discussion covers only a tentative program for developing the land and water resources of the coastal basins. Considerably more research and investigation are required before a more definite over-all development plan can be drawn up. Also, there are other potentials besides water resource development which should be studied with a view to evolving a regional plan for postwar economic development of the five provinces; such a plan might comprise the following elements, in addition to water control and agricultural improvement:

1. Improvement of the fishing industry and establishment of fish-processing facilities.

2. Establishment of a forestry and wood products industry.

3. Improvement and diversification of agriculture in the river valleys.

4. Reconstruction of ports, railroads, and highways as needed for commerce and transportation throughout the region.

5. Development of Cam Ranh Bay.

SAIGON AND THE SURROUNDING PROVINCES

This section sets forth preliminary proposals on basic policies and objectives for the long-range development of Saigon and the surrounding provinces. The area concerned comprises Saigon, the special capital zone of Gia Dinh Province in which it is located, and the ten surrounding rural provinces. The whole coincides with the III Corps Tactical Zone.

The population of this area approaches 5,000,000 people (nearly one-third of the nation), 40 percent of whom live in the city of Saigon, which with nearby centers accounts for nearly all of the nation's manufactured goods. The rural provinces themselves produce two-thirds of Vietnam's sugar, nearly all of its plantation-grown rubber, and 15 percent of its rice crop.

Saigon and the surrounding provinces occupy land of geographical transition between the Mekong Delta to the south and the Central Lowlands and Highlands to the north. The southwestern provinces are flat delta lands and contain the area's two largest cities (Saigon and Tay Ninh), as well as a large mangrove swamp which penetrates some 30 kilometers inland (Figure 12.9). The northern provinces include the Mekong Terrace and contain areas of rougher terrain which fall away in the southeast to the Dong Nai Valley and the coastal plain.

A variety of land uses occur. The coastal plain and uplands in the north support dense forest stands which contain many of Vietnam's most valuable trees. The delta lands and the Dong Nai valley are generally rich rice lands which also produce tea and sugar cane. In a 30-kilometer-wide belt west and north of Saigon is found most of the country's plantation rubber.

The center of the Cao Dai faith is in the city of Tay Ninh, and the Brahmanist Chams are also active in Tay Ninh Province. The Stieng and other Montagnard peoples are found along the Cambodian border and in the rising hills to the northeast.

SAIGON AND SURROUNDING PROVINCES

FIGURE 12-9

The city of Saigon presents a complex cultural picture and contrasts greatly with its rural hinterlands. Because of the considerable topographic and socio-economic diversity, Saigon and the surrounding provinces do not now constitute a unified region. The grouping of provinces surrounding one of the great cities of southeast Asia lacks internal identification and meaningful interrelationships. The disparities of the area were emphaszied with the breakup of French Indochina and have been intensified by the present war. They have been accentuated by the military infrastructure that has been built largely in the vicinity of Saigon, which has altered the pattern of urban-rural relationships. Differences have also been accentuated by extensive migration to Saigon, not only of refugees but also of rural people seeking the broader economic opportunities of the city.

For the area as a whole, the principal issues of further development planning are twofold: (1) a determination of the opportunities for production in the rural provinces and a definition of the relationships of those provinces to Saigon; and (2) an identification of the ways to satisfy the immediate and urgent requirements for support of the fast growing city of Saigon, and a definition of its longer-term role with respect to the surrounding provinces and to Vietnam.

The Rural Provinces

The rural provinces present a variety of opportunities and challenges for future development. Generally, the provinces nearest Saigon are active agricultural areas with well-established practices and land-uses. There are potentials for agricultural improvement, however, in terms of the stimulation of higher production and new crops, the rehabilitation of the existing rubber plantations (or their renewal with high-yielding clones), and the introduction of livestock, to name typical opportunities. Fairly broad studies of land capability and crop adaptation to the various ecological subdivisions within the area are required. Fish industries may be important and the possibility of establishing brackish-water fish ponds along the fringes of the mangrove swamp should be investigated.

Settlement of presently unused land may afford exceptionally favorable development opportunities; attention should be focussed initially on two sections; the northern provinces, and the Dong Nai Basin, which affords irrigation possibilities in its lower reaches and hydroelectric possibilities in the highlands.

Land needed for other uses will no doubt ultimately decrease the total area under forest. The spread of urbanization implies intensive agriculture for market crops and the value of land for timber will become relatively less important in areas nearer Saigon. But the outermost rural provinces include at least 1.5 million hectares of high dense forest and smaller areas of forest which man's activities have modified to some extent. This area presents the best opportunity for exploiting and growing tropical hardwoods.

The large block of mangrove southeast of Saigon has been severely damaged by defoliation activities, but the mangrove tideland is important. Here the age-old process of land building is taking place. Mangroves, the forerunners of tomorrow's dried land, are the retainers of today's tidelands. Vietnam will need the land they are building some day and studies should be made to identify the real potential for preservation of this area.

Apart from Saigon, Tay Ninh and Vung Tau are the main possibilities for programs of urban amplification within the area. Their role in the possible future decentralization of Saigon, as discussed later, should be studied. Related studies are required to assess the possible postwar uses of such military infrastructure as airfields, bases, and hospitals.

Saigon

Saigon functions today as the seat of government, principal port, business and commercial center, transport hub, and military headquarters for all of Vietnam. It is, in fact, Vietnam's only viable urban concentration.

Over the past twenty years, its dominant position over the rest of the nation has been growing at an increasing rate. Its population has nearly tripled since 1950, and it is continuing to absorb people from rural and less-developed areas throughout Vietnam. It has been estimated that the population of Saigon and Gia Dinh could approach 5,000,000 by 1980, and over 9,000,000 by the end of this century.

Present-day Saigon dates from 1867 and is a French establishment. (The ancient citadel is in Gia Dinh.) In 1954 Saigon was united with the Cholon, and in 1966 was further enlarged by the acquisition of the low-lying area east of the Saigon river. Saigon's French roots are evidenced in its wide tree-lined boulevards, squares, arcades, and axes. Its downtown or core area is perhaps the best example of Western-influenced urban design in southeast Asia. Cholon, on the other hand, reproduces in spirit and form its Chinese-oriented urban counterparts elsewhere in Asia. It is a rich mixture of intermingling uses; small shop-houses, hotels, restaurants, and industries, all close together in one totally urban complex.

In 1943, at what was probably the end of effective French rule in Vietnam, the population of the former independent city of Saigon stood at 500,000. Today, the consolidated city of Saigon/Cholon has over 1,640,000 inhabitants, and another 1,000,000 live in Gia Dinh Province. Together they contain some 2,700,000 persons, or slightly over 16 percent of Vietnam's total population, and 85 percent of the country's urban population.

Except for specialized military installations, virtually no new public works facilities and commercial buildings have been built in Saigon since 1950, and the increased population has continued to be served by the prewar municipal infrastructure.

The architecture and general form of Saigon reflects the inherent physical deficiencies of its site. The delta soils on which it is built are deep, clay types, with bed rock well below the surface. Thus the construction of high-rise structures is especially expensive and difficult.

In recent years, a limited expansion of Saigon has occurred along two axes. One extends toward Tay Ninh on the north, and the other extends easterly along the highway to Bien Hoa. The northern expansion consists chiefly of indigenous houses arranged in clusters that approximate rural settlements. The expansion to the east and Bien Hoa is more sophisticated, and consists of more permanent houses, industrial buildings, and various kinds of military facilities. This new growth has been taking place in the areas that are best suited for urbanization, since the terrain to the south and west of Saigon is technically and economically less fitted for this purpose.

Important today, and especially for tomorrow, are the military support facilities that have been built in and near Saigon. These installations, chiefly the ports and camps, are of permanent value and they will undoubtedly influence future growth patterns and land usage. The wharfs that have been built along the Saigon River, the New Port and Long Binh Camp and the airfield at Bien Hoa, will likely become important features of Saigon's landscape.

The Dominance of Saigon

In most developed countries there is a hierarchy of cities of population size and economic activity: although the largest city may occupy the leading role in the economic life of the country, as in the case of New York, London, Paris, and Rome, there are other cities that challenge the largest one in size and may surpass it in certain kinds of economic functions, as is true of Chicago, Los Angeles, Manchester, Lyon, and Milan. In most underdeveloped countries the capital city is dominant in every respect and the city second in size is only a fraction of the size of the largest. Bangkok, Manila, Phnom Penh, and Rangoon, all neighboring capital cities, are at least five times as large as the next biggest city in their respective countries. Saigon is six times larger than Da Nang, the next largest city in Vietnam.

The secondary cities of southeast Asia, as in Vietnam, exist as extensions of the primary ones; they are immature and have little self-determination. In Vietnam there are only six autonomous cities (Cam Ranh, Da Lat, Da Nang, Hue, Saigon, and Vang Tau). Other important urban centers, such as My Tho and Tay Ninh, are formed as collections of villages grouped together.

In most cases, the rates of growth of the primary cities of southeast Asia are almost one-third faster than those of the secondary centers. The attractions of Saigon are of many kinds, only one of which is traceable to the greater security of life in the city. The other attractions, a more varied life and wider economic opportunities, will persist and perhaps grow stronger in the postwar period.

The forecast of a Saigon population of 9,000,000 in the year 2000 (Saigon and Gia Dinh) is closely paralleled by current projections of 8,000,000 for Bangkok by the same year. Calcutta, with an estimated current population of 7,500,000, has already attained this range. These huge urban concentrations are hard to comprehend in the circumstances of Saigon, which is struggling to provide the bare essentials of urban services based on an infrastructure built for a population of only 500,000.

The implications of the possible future growth of Saigon are significant. City building will drain natural resources; based on accepted costs per capits for urban infrastructure, it is estimated that as much as US$10 billion might be required in additional investment in Saigon to support a population of 9,000,000.

Policies for Development

A long-run problem is to make sensible adjustment to the attractions of Saigon while, at the same time, to supply incentives and specific programs to encourage growth outside the city. It is impossible, and probably undesirable, to stop the growth of Saigon, but it is reasonable to have as a target a rate of growth which is less than the rate for other cities in the country; that is, it is reasonable to adapt urban policies to encourage the more rapid growth of secondary cities.

We believe that there are two main criteria or objectives for policies affecting Saigon. The short-run objective is to move or alleviate the worst of the pressures now bearing on the city, so that it can function more effectively and secure some breathing space in which to initiate longer-run programs. Second, we believe that the long-run development strategy for Saigon will be most economically attractive and politically feasible if it aims at decentralizing economic activities, building outward rather than completely rebuilding the core city or the central business district, and that steps to encourage the growth of other cities and of new satellite cities close by are some of the ways to move outward.

The Vietnamese text of this section presents a comprehensive assessment of Saigon's existing and probable immediate postwar needs for public work facilities and essential social services. In the short run, Saigon is faced with a rescue operation for, in some essential respects, the city is breaking down in the performance of the functions of a major city, and the situation seems likely to continue to deteriorate in the immediate future. This deterioration is caused primarily by the unbelievable inflow of people into the city, with a consequent overburdening of municipal facilities and infrastructure built for a city of only one-third the size. The problem is most starkly seen in traffic conditions and in housing. It is also apparent in all other municipal services but not to the same extent.

It is fruitless to speak of deliberate planning for the future development of the metropolitan area while these immediate problems threaten to break down the functions of the city. The Joint Development Group has suggested immediate measures to correct or at least to mitigate the worst of the problems in transportation, housing, and utility supply. The time when palliatives or half-hearted measures could suffice has long passed. Nothing short of very strong, even draconic, measures will suffice. If at least some improvement in present conditions can be achieved, there are intermediate measures that may be taken to further improve the situation in the city. And if these in turn can be undertaken, it will then be time to turn to long-run planning on a considered basis.

We have not recommended comprehensive planning for Saigon now primarily because the need to be comprehensive frequently leads to paralysis of action. If a few vigorous programs are undertaken, much of the remaining planning can follow in due course without any loss of time or efficiency. But we believe an immediate task of national planners is to consider the extraordinary problems facing Saigon in the future with a view to devising policies for diverting, checking, or transferring some part of the anticipated growth. The future development of Saigon must be considered in relationship to the nation as a whole and not only to the city alone.

Saigon as the capital of the Republic has already established for itself what seems to be an appropriate national role. But this function as the nation's capital requires a highly specialized city--one of dignity and formality, with broad landscaped streets and malls and buildings of high architectural quality, a city that reflects the image and aspirations of the nation. This is the primary role that should be emphasized for Saigon. A secondary, national role as financial center is already in being and will probably, and logically, continue.

Saigon's regional role, its relationship to the adjacent provinces, has been that of a port city large enough to supply adequate higher-echelon urban services. The proper role for the port should be regional. The urban services required by the region, such as higher-order medical and educational facilities, should not be developed in the area if these services or facilities could be placed elsewhere.

Saigon's real future lies with programs that are instituted now. At present there are no proven techniques to cope with growth on the scale that is occurring here. In the interest of the nation and the future of the city, a beginning must be made to deemphasize its attraction and to decentralize some of its present functions. There are a number of techniques that might be investigated.

In the long term, programs of family planning may have impact on Saigon's growth; more direct results could flow from budget programming that reoriented priorities for investment to other urban centers. Industrial development, expansion of government services, and provision of new educational and health services are example of the kinds of growth that might be directed toward outlying urban centers. Encouragement and planning of new satellite towns near the primary city is a technique used successfully elsewhere. At Saigon's present stage of development this may be premature, but it should not be ruled out for the future.

To consider these questions, we believe a high-level group of citizens, possibly one composed of responsible local citizens, government officials from pertinent ministries, and perhaps interested persons from agencies of other governments or world organizations, should be formed. This group may take the form of an ad hoc body or one with semigovernmental status. It may be formed to create on the part of the citizens, government officials, and others an awareness of the scope of national urban problems. This group, if provided with a professional staff, could also be the coordinating and recommending agency for all urban proposals.

THE MEKONG DELTA

Early in the JDG studies in 1967, it became apparent that increasing agricultural production in the Mekong Delta represents a major opportunity for the economic development of Vietnam. In October 1967, the JDG issued its Working Paper No. 3, A Program for Mekong Delta Development, which describes the potential of the delta and outlines a long-term program of water control and agricultural improvements required to attain this potential. The paper recommends a continuing program of study, which has been carried out by the JDG.

A preliminary appraisal of a proposed Mekong Delta development program has been prepared. The delta as herein defined is that portion of the Mekong Delta lying within Vietnam comprising the sixteen southern provinces, lying south of the West Vaico River. The proposed program envisons a massive increase in agricultural production in the delta through the application of water control and other inputs.

This section describes the region, analyzes existing and potential agricultural conditions, describes present water control problems and proposes solutions, examines the organizations proposed for delta development, discusses a proposed development program, and presents a preliminary appraisal of the program.

Description of the Region

The Mekong Delta is a vast, flat alluvial plain located in the lower reaches of the Mekong River in Cambodia and Vietnam. The area in Vietnam is slightly over 3.7 million hectares. The delta is very flat, with elevations above 5 meters occurring only in a few places.

The population of the delta is about 6 million people. Most of the population lives in towns, villages, and hamlets located at intersections of or along the banks of the rivers and canals. Virtually all of the population is engaged in agriculture and related activities, with principal emphasis on rice. The major towns, which are usually provincial capitals, serve as commercial centers for the surrounding agricultural areas.

Waterways are the dominant mode of transportation in the delta. Highways are few and in poor condition, becoming more so as the distance from Saigon increases. The transport system is oriented toward connecting the hinterlands to the major river towns and connecting these towns to the Saigon region.

Climatic conditions in the delta are dominated by the monsoons. Annual rainfall averages about 1,800 millimeters over the entire Delta, ranging from 1,000 millimeters in some interior areas to over 2,400 millimeters in the southern part. Much of the rain occurs in intense local showers and there is considerable year-to-year variation in rainfall. The rainy season extends from May to November, with only occasional rains during the rest of the year.

The annual flood of the Mekong is a major hydrological feature of the delta. As the river rises during June and July, extensive overbank spill occurs from both the Mekong and Bassac, covering large land areas with up to 3 meters of water. The second major hydrological feature is the influence of tides during the low flow season. Tidal ranges of 3 meters in the South China Sea and over 1.5 meters in the Gulf of Thailand cause flow reversals in the rivers and many other small channels interlacing the delta, causing salinity intrusion in these channels throughout about one-third of the delta. Due to the extreme flatness of the delta, drainage is a problem during the rainy season when river stages are high. Tidal action also inhibits proper surface water drainage in the lower delta.

The Mekong Delta is alluvial, formed from deposition of sediments from the Mekong. These deltaic materials are generally fine-textured sediments, with coarser grades found along the river banks and finer materials together with peat and muck formations found in more poorly drained areas away from the river. In the lower delta and along the coast, soils have been subject to a marine environment.

The predominant economic activity in the delta is the production of rice and related processing and commerce.

FIGURE 12.10

Mekong Delta

N
W
E
S
Phnom Penh
CAMBODIA
AN LOC
TAY NINH
PHUOC VINH
PHU CUONG
BIEN HOA
GIA DINH
SAIGON
MOC HOA
TAN AN
CAO LANH
MY THO
Mekong R.
LONG XUYEN
Bassac R.
VINH LONG
BEN TRE
CAN THO
RACH GIA
PHU VINH
KHANH HUNG
CA MAU
GULF OF THAILAND
SOUTH CHINA SEA
MEKONG DELTA
0
20
40
60
80
100
SCALE IN KILOMETERS

Other agricultural crops are grown on a small scale and usually for local consumption. Livestock, principally chickens, ducks, and hogs, is also raised, and marine and river fishing are practiced throughout the delta.

Agriculture

Existing Conditions

Of a total land area in the delta of slightly over 3.7 million hectares, about 2.1 million hectares, or 57 percent, is readily suitable for agricultural production from the standpoint of fertility. In 1967 just under 1.7 million hectares were under cultivation, 1.56 million hectares in rice and the balance in other crops.

Generally, rice cultivation consists of a single crop each year planted in May or June and harvested at the end of the rainy period in October or November. Three distinct systems of rice culture are used, each adapted to the natural conditions prevailing in different parts of the delta. These are single-transplant, double-transplant, and direct-sown floating rice. The introduction of new high-yielding varieties such as IR-8 is very recent and not yet extensive.

The three basic systems have been developed over the years to adapt to water conditions encountered in the delta. In the upper part of the delta annual flooding of vast areas requires the use of floating rice, which is capable of growing at a rate and to a height such that the heads remain above water as the flood rises. In the middle part of the delta, where flooding is not a serious problem but drainage of local rainfall is poor, double-transplanted rice is grown in an effort to develop plants which are tall enough to survive under high water levels in the fields in which the final transplant is made. Single-transplanted rice is grown in the lower delta, where flooding and poor drainage are a less serious problem.

Single-transplanted rice is the most common in the delta, being grown on 760,000 hectares. Maximum yields range between 2 and 3 tons of paddy per hectare. Floating rice is grown on 500,000 hectares of the upper delta, where the land is subject to heavy annual flooding over a period of several months. Floating rice is a wonderfully adapted crop but yields are low, usually only about 1 ton of paddy per hectare.

Delta rice production in 1967 was about 3.3 million tons, with average yields slightly over 2 tons of paddy per hectare cultivated. This was about 70 percent of the total Vietnam production.

About 31 percent, or 1 million tons, moved into the channels of trade. Half of this amount was sold in the delta and the other half, or 500,000 tons, was exported to Saigon for consumption or redistribution to other parts of the country. The price of paddy at rice mills in the delta averaged about US$114 per ton during 1967.

Other crops grown include manioc, mungo beans, peanuts, soy beans, sweet potatoes, corn, bananas, coconuts, tree fruits, pineapple, sugar cane, tobacco, and vegetables. Except for areas located around the major towns, other crops are grown as a part of the rice farming operation, on river and canal bank lands close to the farmer's home. Livestock raising is also usually an adjunct to the basic farm operation. Fishing is often a commercial activity encompassing offshore and river-boat fishing, fish trapping, and fish raising in ponds.

In terms of value, the five most important crops, other than rice, grown in the delta are mungo beans, bananas, coconuts, tree fruits, and vegetables. The delta produces 70 percent of Vietnam's ducks and duck eggs, almost 60 percent of the chickens and chicken eggs, and about one-half of the hogs and buffaloes. The fish catch in the delta is 37 percent of Vietnam's total, over half being river fish.

Soils and Land Capability

Soil types in the Mekong Delta are based upon five different environments: coastal soils, highly acid estuarine soils, river alluvium, Mekong Terrace soils, and mountain soils in the western end of the delta. The coastal soils and river alluvium comprise about 94 percent of the total, and only a very small portion of the remaining soils has any agricultural significance.

The coastal soils are of marine origin and occur as sand bars, tidal flats, and mangrove swamps. The sand bars cover 26,000 hectares in long strips parallel to rivers and shorelines and are presently moderately productive. The tidal-flat soils encompass just over 900,000 hectares in the lower delta representing former tidal flats, depressions, and tidal creeks. They are moderately to highly productive. The soils of the mangrove swamps (225,000 hectares) are saline, poorly drained, silty clay mudflats.

The river alluvium soils are found in the so-called backswamp areas, along river banks, and in alluvial plains. The backswamps are low-lying, poorly drained areas where acid and very acid alluvial soils exist. Acid soils are moderately productive after leaching, but highly acid soils are generally unproductive. Highly acid soils comprise some 1,170,000 hectares in the Plain of Reeds and in scattered areas of the Ca Mau Peninsula. Their cultivation is limited and production is either low or impossible under present conditions. Among the less acid backswamp soils are 655,000 hectares which are only moderately acid and when adequately drained are highly productive. River-bank soils cover some 102,000 hectares along the banks of the Mekong and Bassac in the upper delta. Rice yields are fair but other crops grow well. Alluvial plain soils include 248,000 hectares and are moderately productive.

Hydrology and rainfall are the major factors affecting the exploitation of soils in the delta. Soil fertility will become a significant factor only after water control is achieved, and then mostly as related to crops other than rice. Under strict water control conditions, rice is adaptable to a wide variety of soil characteristics and, aside from those soils where toxicity is a problem, rice will be a highly productive crop in the delta. With water control, 2,135,300 hectares of delta soils will support high-yield double cropping in rice. In this same category, some soils are also particularly adaptable to other crops. Of the remaining low productivity soils, opportunities for improvement in the highly acid series are limited, but the peat soils, given special treatment, can be highly productive in vegetables and other high-value crops.

Market Projections

The future of crop production in the delta can be viewed in terms of projections of domestic and export requirements for crops, livestock, and fish for the 1970-90 period. The estimated demand for agricultural products from the delta during this period are shown in Table 12.7. Domestic requirements are based upon population projections and the highest levels of per capita consumption for the 1962-67 period. No changes in the consumption pattern are reflected. Export projections are tenuous due to rapid changes in production in various countries, particularly as related to rice, and only 20 percent of the total 1990 rice demand was forecasted for export. The determination of the proportion of country requirements to be met from the delta was established on the basis of historical trends and the best judgments available of future patterns. The delta is the largest and most economical source of most of the products listed.

TABLE 12.7

Estimated Demand for Delta Agricultural Products, 1970 and 1990

(tons)

Commodity	1967 Production	1970 Demand	1990 Demand
Rice (paddy)	3,287,000	4,350,000	9,963,800
Manioc	39,370	94,450	363,200
Mungo beans	13,715	15,850	29,400
Peanuts	1,735	2,200	4,450
Soy beans	3,550	5,900	10,750
Sweet potatoes	79,230	105,600	188,200
Corn	8,655	16,500	36,750
Bananas	131,360	220,000	390,550
Coconuts	117,235	160,100	267,500
Tree fruits	126,900	220,750	289,800
Pineapples	20,900	42,100	75,350
Sugar cane	148,180	505,250	844,200
Tobacco	3,155	4,600	5,450
Vegetables	54,005	72,500	173,100
Buffaloes	-	58,000	97,200
Cattle	-	21,100	35,250
Hogs	-	187,550	313,350
Poultry	-	71,600	119,650
Eggs	-	778,000	1,245,000
Fish	103,695	162,200	271,600

Production Potential

The basic requirements for realizing the full crop production potential of the delta are water control (protection from flooding, improved drainage, salinity control, and wet and dry season irrigation), improvement in agricultural practices, utilization of high-yielding rice varieties, and use of improved strains of crops other than rice.

Water control is basic. Under existing conditions, the only possibilities for major expansion in rice production lie in the extension of cultivation into areas of suitable soils where rice is presently not grown. The resulting production increase would be about 1.25 million tons, which, although a major amount, is insufficient to meet more than short term needs.

Improvements in agricultural practices under existing water conditions can also be undertaken. Delta-wide application of better seed, new fertilizers, and improved cultural practices might increase yields by as much as 0.5 tons per hectare, a total production increment of 1.0 million tons. This would require a massive program of research and extension with only limited promise for increased production.

The introduction of the new, high-yielding rice varieties into the delta must be handled with caution if provision for water control is excluded. While it is possible to provide proper water control at the farm level in scattered locations, the widespread cultivation of these new varieties will require water control.

Proper water control in the delta will permit changes in the present system of rice production, extension of the growing season, a more intensive type of crop production, and use of new and improved varieties.

Important changes in rice production systems will result from flood control and improved drainage. Protection against flooding in the upper delta, together with partial improvement in drainage, would permit the growing of single-transplant rice on the 500,000 hectares where floating rice is now grown. Improved drainage would also permit a change from double to single transplant on 300,000 hectares in the middle delta. Introduction of improved agricultural practices at this stage would raise single-transplant yields to 3.0 tons per hectare in these areas.

In the lower delta, salinity control will permit a longer rice-growing season with higher yields and higher returns over present single-transplant practices and provide the opportunity to grow a second short-season crop.

The provision of irrigation in both wet and dry seasons will permit much more intensive use of delta lands than the present one rice crop per year. The controlled, year-round application of water will allow not only the growing of two rice crops per year, but other cropping combinations involving rice and other crops of higher value. For example, it would be possible for a farmer to grow five rice crops in two years, or two rice crops and a secondary crop per year, or one rice crop and three vegetable crops per year. Grain or vegetable crops could be included, depending upon soil characteristics and markets. The potential is enormous.

All elements of water control (flood control, drainage, salinity control, and irrigation) are required for the widespread utilization of new high-yielding rice varieties in the delta. However, yields of 4 to 6 tons per hectare per crop can be reasonably expected.

Delta production of rice is expected to grow from the present 3.3 million tons to almost 10 million tons in 1990 in order to meet projected demands. During this period, several transitions will occur: from floating rice to double or single transplant, from double to single transplant, and ultimately to new high-yielding varieties.

The production of about 8 million tons to meet estimated domestic requirements in 1990 could be accomplished by increasing yields to 4 tons per hectare on the 1.5 million hectares presently under cultivation through the use of improved varieties (6 million tons) <u>and</u> either increasing the area under cultivation by 500,000 hectares or double cropping 500,000 hectares (2 million tons). To supply the additional production of 2 million tons required for export by 1990, an additional 500,000 hectares could be double cropped.

Among other crops presently grown successfully in the delta and for which experimental work indicates high yields from improved varieties are peanuts, soy beans, mungo beans, corn sorghum, sweet potatoes, cassava, pineapples, sugar cane, tobacco, kenaf, vegetables, mangoes, oranges, coconuts, and bananas. Analysis of farm income indicates that many of these, alone or in combination with rice, will provide a higher return to delta farmers. Production of many of these crops will increase greatly while others may be more adaptable to other areas in Vietnam. Projections of demand indicate an increase of about 350 percent in production in the delta. Although part of this increase can be accomplished through increased yields, at least 300,000 hectares would be devoted to these other crops. This could be accomplished by several means. Some of these crops could be grown in rotation with rice. Some could be grown on lands now planted to rice but more suited to other crops, with rice production requirements maintained through further double cropping of rice. Some could be grown very well on the less productive soils not considered suitable for rice.

In any event, land does not represent a limiting factor in attaining estimated production targets for 1990. The theoretical potential of the delta for rice production might be roughly defined as the production of two crops of high-yielding varieties per year, yielding 4 tons per hectare per crop, or 16 million tons.

Livestock raising, principally hogs and poultry, and the production of livestock feed show great promise in the delta. Success will require improvement in the local breeds, greater attention to disease control, and improvement in marketing facilities. High-yielding varieties of sorghum appear particularly well suited for growth in the delta as livestock feed.

Fishing conditions will need to be closely observed during the change in water conditions resulting from construction of the water control system. However, there is no reason to expect adverse effects on fishing if proper measures are taken. Production of fish should continue to be more than adequate to meet local needs and increases in river fish production for export from the delta may also be anticipated.

Agricultural Program

An agricultural development program directed at realizing indicated production goals must reach directly the millions of delta farmers who are hard-working and clever individuals who can and will adapt to new practices and new crops. Large and far-reaching programs will be required, however, to provide the delta farmers with the opportunities to benefit from the proposed water control improvements and to obtain thereby the productivity and increased incomes which are potential to the region.

The device we recommend to bring the agricultural, economic, and social advantages of the delta's proposed development program to the farmers is the local development association. These associations are conceived as organizations of farmers, possibly grouped by village, and ranging in size from 2,000 to 5,000 hectares, with farm populations from 5,000 to 15,000 people. The local development associations would provide a vehicle for accomplishing agricultural research and extension, provision of physical inputs, provision of agricultural credit, improvements in the marketing process, and resolution of land tenure questions.

In order to take full advantage of water control in the delta, many agricultural innovations and changes must be instituted. The best means of field preparation and water application to various crops, the best new rice varieties and new crops, the fertilizers and insecticides, the best means of improving livestock and fish culture, the best controls of plant and livestock diseases, will all have to be anticipated and allowed for in the projection of new agricultural practices. These determinations will require a great research effort in the delta. But more importantly, once these optimum solutions are arrived at, several million farmers will have to be educated in their use. A program of research and extension is therefore central to the delta program.

Six large pilot areas in the delta have been identified and recommended for early intensified development. These pilot areas are designed to be the forerunners of some 770 local development associations which will provide the organizational framework for intensive agricultural development throughout the delta. The six pilot areas are so located in various parts of the delta as to be representative of the various conditions encountered. They are designed to provide fairly large-scale areas for testing and demonstrating the best technical and organizational ways to achieve the agricultural goals of the program for later widespread application throughout the delta. They will be focal points for intensive agricultural investigation and study, not only in the context of research and trial, but also in the determination of the best ways of transferring the results of research to large groups of farmers.

A variety of scientific and technical talents will need to be applied intensively to these pilot areas. Research will be performed by a number of research teams which will service the six pilot areas. An extension team will be assigned to each pilot area, to assist the farmers in upgrading their production methods, utilizing the results of the concurrent adaptive research being conducted by the research teams.

The manpower needs for staffing the delta agricultural program are very great. Ultimate development of some 770 local development associations, each encompassing an average of 2,700 hectares devoted to intensified agriculture, will require large numbers of highly trained and experienced research specialists, farm managers and operators, marketing experts, extension agents, and engineers. Current estimates of the availability of such manpower indicate a serious shortfall. Heavy emphasis must therefore be placed upon improving education in agriculture at all levels.

Physical inputs include seed, fertilizer, insecticides, and equipment, and their ready availability at fair prices is an essential element in improved agriculture. Projecting requirements to over 2 million hectares under multiple cropping indicates the scale of the ultimately required supply and distribution system. At the present time, the distribution of these inputs in the delta is primarily a function of private dealers, and there is no conclusive evidence of unfair pricing. It appears that the simplest and most direct means of handling the increased demand for these products is to encourage the continued participation and expansion of private entrepreneurs in this field. Supply of equipment from commercial sources or by custom operation is projected with the local development associations acting as agents for the farmers.

Credit in greatly increased amounts will need to be available to farmers, farmers' associations, dealers, and others engaged in the marketing and supply of agricultural goods. Aside from widespread informal credit arrangements among families, friends, and neighbors, the three principal sources of credit in the delta at this time are the commercial banks, dealers and merchants, and the government-sponsored Agricultural Development Bank.

It is estimated that by 1990 the total loan funds needed in support of the delta agricultural program will total VN$25 billion. A reasonable share which might be contributed by the public sector through the Agricultural Development Bank might be one-half, or VN$12.5 billion.

Care must be exercised in establishing credit procedures so that they may remain simple while providing some degree of control over the use of loan funds.

The local development associations will require large sources of credit, presumably governmental, in order to construct their water control facilities and perform land leveling operations. Within this credit structure it might be possible to devise a channel of loan funds to the farmers.

The local development associations, in cooperation with governmental and private channels, will provide an organizational framework within which to achieve the required improvements in the marketing process. Improvements in rice drying, warehousing, and milling will be required to handle increased tonnages efficiently at minimal loss. The provision or improvement in these facilities can be accomplished on a large scale, either communally through the local development associations or by arrangement with private commercial interests.

The transportation system in the delta consists primarily of waterways. Such highways as do exist are in need of substantial rehabilitation. The government has plans for rehabilitating both modes of transport to an extent that transportation will not be a limiting factor in handling delta production for many years.

As the delta moves into a more complex modern agriculture, there will be need for various marketing services and regulations will need to be established for quality control and grading, for warehousing, and for the sale of agricultural products. Reliable marketing information should be quickly disseminated. Cooperative marketing will have a distinct advantage to the farmer in obtaining a fair return from his crop and this will be a major function of the local development associations.

The establishment of land tenure is basic to agricultural development. Unless a farmer is secure in the possession or use of his land, he will not make the efforts required to increase his production and improve his livelihood. The question of economic farm size must be accounted for. If land reform results in the continuation and intensification of farm poverty through the establishment of farms too small to provide a living, it will be a tragic failure. In the delta, indications are that a farm family can derive a satisfactory income under improved conditions from two hectares of rice double-cropped. The same results can be obtained on lesser areas if part or all of the land is devoted to vegetables or other high-value crops or if a supplemental livestock operation is included. Average delta land holdings are now just under 2 hectares. This average is close to an uneconomic farm unit and considerable attention will have to be devoted to farm size in the context of land productivity under various crops, family income levels, off-farm employment, and other factors.

Water Control

Present Conditions

The basic problem inhibiting the growth of agricultural production in the delta may be stated in very simple terms: the delta farmer is unable to control the application of water to his crop. It is a tribute to his resourcefulness that he is able to wrest a livelihood from his land under the wide variations in water conditions which exist.

In the upper delta over 500,000 hectares are flooded annually with depths up to 3 meters. In the middle delta the intense rainfall during the growing season does not drain from the land because of its flatness and tidal action in drainage channels. In the lower delta salinity intrusion during the low flow season seriously shortens the period in which crops can be grown. Virtually all rice is grown throughout the delta during the rainy season and the farmer is at the mercy of too much or too little rainfall during critical periods of growth. There is insufficient flow in the river during the dry season to provide a fresh-water supply for irrigation. Beyond these immediate factors, the effect of uncontrolled standing water on the land during much of the time results in soil toxicity in wide areas.

Water Control Schemes

The four needs for water control in the delta are protection against floods, improved drainage, control of salinity intrusion, and supply of irrigation water during both wet and dry seasons. To accomplish all of these purposes, some combination of water control systems in the delta and upstream storage reservoirs will be needed. The function of the delta water control system, simply put, would be to seal off the agricultural lands of the delta from floods, from high river stage, from the tides, and from the encroachment of salinity; and to control the ingress and egress of water to and from these sealed areas as required to provide for the four basic water control needs. The design of this system must take account of the extent to which it is technically and economically feasible to partially meet these basic needs through the multipurpose operation of large reservoirs proposed for construction in the upstream riparian countries.

A study program was undertaken during the summer of 1968 to analyze the hydraulic response of the Mekong Delta to various schemes of water control. Two principal questions were addressed. The first dealt with the effectiveness of large upstream storage reservoirs in reducing floods to the extent required to prevent heavy and widespread overbank flooding in the delta. The second dealt with the ability to construct levee and bypass systems in the delta which would protect large areas against floods, but which would not adversely affect historical flooding conditions in unprotected areas.

The analytical tool used for these studies was the Mathematical model of the Mekong Delta which had been prepared by SOGREAH for the Mekong Committee. This model, installed on a computer in Bangkok, simulates hydraulic behavior in the delta as it responds to various flow conditions in the river as it enters the delta, and to rainfall conditions in the delta itself.

In the analysis, the delta (both the Cambodian and Vietnamese portions) was divided into thirteen large areas for which levee systems could be simulated singly and in various combinations. Representations of three possible flood bypass channels were also incorporated. The 1961 flood was used as the basic hydrologic input to the model, and the effect of delta rainfall and evaporation was simulated. Studies were performed to determine the extent and depth of flooding in the delta under natural conditions and with the flood control operation of the proposed Pa Mong and Stung Treng projects. Other studies determined the effect of levee protection of various individual areas and various combinations of areas in the delta. The leveeing of all of the proposed development units in Vietnam was one of these combinations, as was the leveeing of the entire delta, including Cambodia.

The analyses revealed that none of the assumed upstream reservoir capacities will result in full control of flooding in the delta, although the larger amounts would theoretically permit a reduction in the magnitude of delta flood protection works. These larger amounts, however, are probably at the upper limits of possible development at the two mainstream sites. A rough comparison of the relevant alternative costs indicates that flood protection works in the delta are far less expensive than any reasonable allocation of the cost of upstream projects for this purpose. Furthermore, the construction of reservoirs in the capacities needed to effect flood control to an extent permitting a significant reduction in magnitude of delta flood protection works cannot be expected to take place for decades.

The analyses also demonstrated that the construction of levee systems for flood protection in the delta is feasible without undue adverse effect in unprotected areas provided that proper attention is given to upstream levee alignments and flood bypasses are constructed. It has been concluded, therefore, that provision for full protection against natural floods should be incorporated in the delta water control system.

The need for improved drainage is primarily due to the extreme flatness of the delta. The problem becomes particularly acute during the wet season when river stages are high. This high stage also occurs in the numerous waterways which interlace the delta and is further affected by high tidal fluctuations. It is not realistic to expect river stages to be significantly reduced by upstream flood control storage. Therefore, alleviation of drainage problems needs to be dealt with locally by provision of adequate conveyance channels and pumping facilities.

Salinity intrusion becomes serious during the dry season, when the delta river and waterways stages are low. In these circumstances, tidal action forces salt water into the various rivers and channels for various distances and at high tides causes substantial overbank spill in large areas. Again, it does not appear that upstream storage can significantly alleviate this problem, and dikes and channel barriers will be required to protect the areas now subject to salinity intrusion.

Irrigation requires the construction of facilities in the delta for conveyance of fresh water from the river to the lands to be irrigated. There are serious limitations on the source of fresh water for irrigation in the delta during the dry season. Under natural low river flow conditions, salinity intrudes up the main river for about 40 kilometers to the vicinity of Can Tho. Further reductions in low flow could have serious consequences in allowing saline waters to intrude further upstream. Therefore, widespread dry-season irrigation in the delta will require augmentation of natural low flows from upstream storage reservoirs. Indications are that the amounts required will be within the capacities of multipurpose operations of either of the two major mainstream storage projects under consideration by the Mekong Committee.

Proposed Water Control System

Provision of water control for the agricultural lands of the delta requires facilities for the performance of four functions. A fifth, transportation, must also be accommodated. These facilities must be combined in various sequences into a scheme of water control that is multipurpose in nature and adapted to the various conditions encountered in different parts of the delta. The four basic functions are flood protection, drainage, salinity control, and irrigation. The facilities comprising a full water control system should be designed in the most effective and economical manner such that each function would be combined with and fully compatible with the other functions required at each stage of development. Water control implies that the beginning, duration, depth, and quality of water on the farmers' fields will be controlled within certain limits. Some areas of the delta may require two or more functions before a substantial increase in agricultural production may be realized; in others, some functions do not apply.

Water control facilities have been further subdivided into principal and local works. The principal works, such as levees, dikes, main transportation canals, drainage canals, irrigation canals, principal pumping plants, and navigation locks, will be developed as project facilities by a central organization called the Mekong Delta Development Authority. The local facilities, such as secondary and tertiary irrigation and drainage canals, farm or village dikes (bunds), small pumping stations, and land preparation, will be developed under the auspices of farmers' organizations called Local Development Associations.

Flood protection in the delta will be provided by a levee and flood bypass system. The system will consist of levees placed adjacent to the major rivers, the Mekong and the Bassac, their distributaries and connecting links to the downstream limit of overbank flooding. The levees will also extent laterally from the right bank of the Bassac near the Cambodian border to the Gulf of Thailand to form the southern boundary of a flood bypass from the Bassac to the gulf. A primary levee will also be constructed from the left bank of the Mekong near the Cambodian border along the southern boundary of the Plain of Reeds to form the southern boundary of a flood bypass into the Plain of Reeds and the Vaico River.

Drainage of excess rainfall from the delta lands will be provided through a system of collector laterals and major conveyance canals. The latter will dispose of the drainage either to the sea or the major river courses. The existing navigation canals will be used to the maximum extent possible. At locations where conveyance capacity of existing canals is insufficient, the canal will be enlarged or a new parallel canal will be constructed. Collector laterals will be provided so as to receive water by gravity from the local development association lands and discharge by gravity to the major conveyance canals. The major conveyance canals will have low-lift pumping plants spaced at intervals to develop the necessary gradient for flow at the desired capacity. Terminal pumping plants will lift drainage water into the sea and river channels.

It is contemplated that drainage improvements be made in two stages, an initial stage sufficient to create conditions suitable for single-transplant rice culture and a final stage to improve drainage to the extent required for the cultivation of improved varieties under closely controlled water conditions at any time of the year.

Control of intruding surface salt waters will be provided by control structures or earth barriers in canals and sloughs, rehabilitation of existing dikes along the seacoast and rivers, and construction of new dikes where required. The works required for salinity control will in part be provided by the drainage system.

The facilities to be provided for irrigation are those necessary to divert water from the main river channels and distribute it to the local development association lands. Water will be diverted upstream from the intruding salt water in the river and conveyed in the major conveyance canals and laterals previously installed for the drainage system with modifications where required.

The pumping plants provided for drainage will be used with additional capacity provided where needed for irrigation. Pumping plants will be provided where necessary at the river diversion points. Small pumping plants will lift water from the major conveyance canals into the local collector laterals previously provided for drainage.

The existing primary water transportation network in the delta will be incorporated into the water control system, and transportation will be maintained through the provision of navigation lock structures in those canals which will continue to serve as major transportation arteries as follows: (1) at intersections with primary levees; (2) to bypass pumping plants and control structures; and (3) at intersections with salinity dikes. Surface transport will be facilitated through construction and extension of bridges and causeways, incorporating roads on canal embankments and salinity dikes, and common use of rights of way.

Local development associations will consist of individual units composed of one or more villages encompassing an area of between 2,000 and 5,000 hectares. These organizations will serve individual farms and the facilities to be constructed, operated, and maintained by the associations will include any works needed to drain excess rainfall from or transport irrigation water to individual farms. These facilities will connect to the principal canal system of the authority.

Organization

Mekong Delta Development Authority

An interagency seminar was organized jointly by the National Committee for the Mekong and the Joint Development Group in November, 1967. At these proceedings, delta development was discussed by representatives of the ministries and the departments within them. The proceedings concluded with the unanimous passage of the following resolution:

> For the full exploitation of the potential of the Mekong Delta, the proper coordination of departmental and extra-governmental agencies must be assured.
>
> For this purpose the best solution, if it is possible, is to set up a separate Authority, provide it with the requisite duties, functions and powers, grant it financial independence, and place it above political influence. Such an Authority would both undertake projects in cooperation with other governmental agencies responsible for development planning in Vietnam, and support the Ministries and their departments in their investigational and project activities.

A proposal for establishment of a Mekong Delta Development Authority was made by the Joint Development Group to the Offices of the President and Prime Minister in March 1968. This has not yet been approved for two reasons. First, it was considered premature to establish such an authority before the dimensions of the delta development program had become clear. It is believed that the present study removes this obstacle. Second, it was decided that creation of the authority should be subject to debate and approval by the legislature. Scrutiny and full discussion by this body is highly desirable, since the authority's ability to perform its functions will depend upon full public understanding of its program. It is recommended that a decree establishing the Mekong Delta

Development Authority be submitted to the legislature for action as soon as possible.

The authority, as proposed, will be concerned with the management of the waters of the Mekong River in the delta. It will be responsible for investigating, planning, promoting, designing, constructing, and implementing projects and programs for the control and utilization of the water resources of the region for agriculture, transportation, and other purposes. It will establish and enforce standards for the beneficial use of water. It will promote and assist the establishment of farmers' organizations for the local control and utilization of water and the development of agriculture.

The foregoing functions are limited in two respects. First, the authority is concerned with water, and beyond encouraging and assisting in programs for its beneficial use, the authority will not engage directly in broad programs of economic and infrastructural development which are unrelated to the water resource and are properly the functions of other agencies. Second, the authority is not considered a master agency which will deal directly with millions of delta farmers. Instead, it will deal with the broad aspects of water control and will promote the organization of separate farmers' organizations responsible for development on the local level. These organizations, numbering in the hundreds, are termed here Local Development Associations.

To the extent feasible in the context of achieving program goals, the authority may assign certain elements of the program by agreement with other agencies. Program control, however, must rest firmly with the authority.

Initially, the authority's operations will need to be financed through appropriations from the national budget and by loans from domestic and external sources. The authority should also be empowered to levy and collect charges for water control services from the local development associations and other customers, and to issue bonds.

It is not contemplated that the scale of water charges levied by the authority be adequate to recover all costs of the water control program. They should certainly be sufficient to cover the costs of operating and maintaining the authority's water control facilities and to recover some part of the interest and capital charges. The whole complex subject of authority charges for water control in all its aspects merits careful investigation.

Local Development Associations

The principal responsibility of the proposed Mekong Delta Development Authority is to design, construct, and operate major facilities for the regional control of water. It would be unrealistic to imagine that the authority can reach directly the millions of farmers who make their living in the delta.

A new approach should be put forward and local development associations, organizations of farmers, committed entirely to the farmer's interest, are recommended. Their formation is likely to start with the authority carefully explaining to the farmers in selected villages the over-all delta program and by specific offers of assistance to farmers in organizing to undertake development activities in their locality. A regular pattern should be applied throughout the delta. The authority should explain fully and honestly what a local development association is expected to do, and what the authority is prepared to do for it in return--and, having done this, to assist the farmers in organizing themselves. Local development associations will operate best if organized within the areas of existing villages and their component hamlets.

A local development association must provide for the construction and maintenance of local water control works, provide its members with agricultural technical instruction and assistance, assist its members in securing adequate quantities of the most important supplies, provide storage and marketing facilities where private enterprise is not forthcoming, offer its guarantee for loans extended to its members, ensure that laws and regulations concerning water use are observed, and secure for each of its members rights of way, the right to use water, and the facilities for water control as are necessary for the proper development of its members' farms.

The relationship between the local development associations and the authority will be a contractual one. The contract will define the functions and activities which the particular association undertakes to perform, the assistance and services which the authority undertakes to supply to the association, and the regulations concerning the beneficial use of land and water which the association agrees to observe.

The concept of the local development association requires a great deal of further study and planning and, most important, testing under field conditions in the delta. Immediate steps should be taken to select a few typical villages within the delta in which studies in depth can be carried out. These villages will serve as pilots to the organizing of all villages in the delta.

The most important objectives of the pilot associations will be to test:

1. Social and political practices to determine the practicality of introducing local development associations within the village structure.

2. Water control and agricultural production techniques to achieve maximum agricultural production.

3. Methods of educating farmers to change their agricultural practices as required to upgrade production.

Six areas have been selected as representative of the many conditions found in the delta. Within each of these, an existing village should be chosen for detailed investigation and planning of a local development association. Villages should be selected in the vicinity of My Tho, Can Tho, Long Xuyen, Soc Trang, Quan Long, and Rach Gia to serve as the initial pilot associations.

Program Schedule

Factors Affecting Schedule

It has not been possible to establish a specific schedule for implementation of the delta program at this time, although a general time frame can be foreseen from the projections of demand for the various crops. A number of important factors affecting program schedule are discussed below.

The market for delta crops over the years will be a basic factor controlling the pace of development. The projections of demand for delta products indicate the need for rapid improvements, particularly in rice production. A conservative indication of the delta potential for rice production assumes that 2 million hectares could be double-cropped with improved varieties yielding 4 tons per hectare per crop. Total production would be 16 million tons. Current market projections estimate a demand for delta rice of 10 million tons by 1990. This indicates the need for substantial progress toward full development of the entire delta in the next twenty years.

The delta is an outstanding rice production area, and will continue to be so, but it also presents great opportunities for the production of other crops, many of which offer a better economic opportunity than rice to the farmer. On the other hand, the delta is a vast area, and substantial areal expansion into other crops will necessarily be a gradual process due to market limitations and due to the need to introduce new cropping systems on a large scale. In the very long term, diversification is undoubtedly the major potential of the delta. However, the prediction of the course and rate of diversification is extremely uncertain. It is largely due to this uncertainty that the economic analysis of the program presented in this report was based upon the production of rice alone. For this same reason, flexibility in land use must be a major factor in shaping the delta development program.

Extension of the area under cultivation and improvements in agricultural practices under existing water conditions would produce fairly substantial short-term increases in total rice production. However, these factors alone will not be adequate to increase production to the extent required to meet the projected increases in demand. It is therefore proposed that these improvements not precede, but coincide with, the implementation of the first step in water control development in each part of the delta.

There will be certain requirements which will control the sequence of the various development steps in the delta. In the large areas presently inundated by overbank flow, protection against floods must precede all other improvements. In areas now subject to salinity intrusion, control measures must be taken to permit the introduction of irrigation and double cropping. Initial drainage provisions must be made in present floating and double-transplant rice areas before changing over to single-transplant culture. Full drainage provisions are a prerequisite to the widespread introduction of improved varieties.

Rice is a crop which is very adaptable to water conditions. This factor permits flexibility in determining the various development steps in a particular area. As water control improves, it is possible to increase productivity by shifting to the higher-yielding types of rice. It is therefore not necessary, as it often is with other crops, to change the physical conditions affecting agriculture from the existing to the ultimate stage in a single discrete step. A more gradual shift is possible assuring reasonable continuity in the improvement process.

Delta farmers have been growing rice for decades, and with remarkable results considering the very adverse water conditions under which they are forced to operate. With this basic expertise, it is unlikely that the shifts in rice culture proposed in this study will result in a serious lag in increasing production. The shift from floating rice to double or single transplant in presently flooded areas will be the most difficult due to the major change in cultural practices and the increased labor requirements. Expansion into other crops, particularly those not grown extensively in the delta, will have to be more gradual.

The delta is a very large area and the physical facilities proposed for water control are large and extensive. Their financing and construction must be scheduled over a reasonable period of time. Similarly, organizations must be created to implement delta development. Besides a central Mekong Delta Development Authority, this study contemplates the creation of some 770 local development associations throughout the delta. The formation of these organizations will be a long process. Finally, a program of this magnitude requires very large numbers of skilled manpower. It is estimated that the agricultural program alone will need several thousand highly trained professionals and technicians. A massive training effort will be required over a long period to meet these needs.

The need for upstream reservoir projects is of less importance to the delta than was anticipated in earlier studies.

Flood protection will be provided in the delta itself and the principal need for upstream storage will be to provide supplemental water supply for dry-season irrigation. With the many other water control improvements possible, the need for dry-season irrigation is not of great importance in the early stages of the program. However, the 1990 demand projections indicate the need for a major upstream reservoir project in the 1980's.

Improvement Steps

In order to evaluate the economy of the delta program in the absence of a specific program schedule, a series of improvement steps were postulated, each dealing with a particular improvement in water control and the resulting change in cultural practices leading to increases in rice production. These steps relate only to rice cultivation, although other crops will play an important part in the future of the delta. Four consecutive water control improvement steps were defined and were applied to twenty four different zones in the delta to determine the effect of each step upon development in each zone. The development of each zone is likely to follow such a sequential course, but application of such an analysis to the entire delta will not be possible since the over-all development process will represent some combination of individual steps taken in each zone or group of zones. The steps are as follows.

Step 1. In those zones presently subject to inundation by the annual flood of the Mekong, flood protection facilities will be constructed and initial drainage provisions will be effected in sufficient degree to permit the cultivation of single-transplant varieties of rice. Completion of this step will permit the growing of one crop of single-transplant rice instead of floating rice throughout the areas now flooded each year. Expansion of single-transplant cultivation into areas of suitable soils not presently cultivated in these zones was included in this step and the introduction of improved agricultural practices was also assured. Annual yields as a result of this step are estimated to be 3.0 tons per hectare.

Step 2. Step 2 encompasses the provision of salinity control and initial drainage improvements in the zones not covered under Step 1 and the initiation of irrigation throughout all parts of the delta. These improvements will provide the capability for double cropping of single-transplant rice by careful scheduling of seedbed planting during the dry season to avoid excessive diversion from the dry season river flow. Improved agricultural practices will be introduced in zones not covered in Step 1. Firm agricultural management and a strong delta authority are necessary in combination at this point to assure close control of water use during the dry season. Annual yields as a result of this step are estimated to be 5.5 tons per hectare (3.0 tons from the first crop and 2.5 tons from the second).

Step 3. When upstream storage facilities are completed and the dry season river flow is augmented, irrigation water can be provided to cultivate one crop of a high-yielding rice variety during the dry season. It will be necessary to accomplish extensive land leveling so that water depths on the field can be strictly controlled, but the full drainage improvements required for wet season cultivation of improved varieties will not be needed. This step will permit the cultivation of one crop of an improved high-yielding rice variety during the dry season and one crop of a single-transplant rice during the wet season. Annual yields as a result of this step are estimated to be 7.0 tons per hectare (4.0 tons from improved varieties and 3.0 tons from single transplant).

Step 4. The last stage of development provides for complete drainage and irrigation capability. Under these conditions, it will be possible to cultivate at least two crops annually of the improved high-yielding rice varieties. The primary canal system will need to be extended and additional project pumping facilities will have to be constructed. Local development associations must increase the capacity of their internal conveyance systems above that provided for irrigation to handle increased drainage. Annual yields as a result of this step are estimated to be at least 8.0 tons per hectare. It should be emphasized strongly that at this stage, the delta water control system is capable of supporting a highly intensive, multicropped agriculture to provide benefits far in excess of those justified by a continuing rice monoculture.

Economic Analysis

The preliminary economic analysis of the delta program completed at this time was not structured to produce an overall benefit-cost ratio. Instead, it was designed to determine the economic viability of implementing the four sequential water control improvements steps in each of the twenty four separate zones in the delta. The reason for this approach was to evaluate the effect of each element of water control upon different parts of the delta which exhibit widely varying water conditions and agricultural practices and which require different types and degrees of water control.

Recommendations

It is recommended that the first stage of the delta water control system consist of flood protection, initial drainage facilities, and agricultural improvement (Step 1 development) in the northern part of the Nam Phan unit. This area comprises a total of 425,000 hectares and represents an area currently subject to heavy flood and the least productive in terms of yields per hectare. The area is relatively secure. It is believed that starting the delta program here will directly attack the worst physical problem in the delta, that of flooding, and thereby will have a relatively greater initial impact on delta development at reasonable cost. The costs of the levee system needed to protect this area from flood and the initial project drainage facilities required to permit the growing of single transplant rice are estimated to be US$70 million.

A second area which involves different water control elements and which merits early attention is the eastern portion of the Cao Lanh unit. Except for the upstream portion of the area, there are no flooding problems, and it would be possible to go directly to Step 2 development. It is recommended that this area be accorded second priority for early development. The area comprises about 189,000 hectares, some of which is presently being double cropped (rice with other crops). The provision of flood protection in the upstream portion, salinity control in the downstream portion, and initial drainage improvements throughout would permit irrigation and a move toward crop diversification. This is particularly important since the area is close to the Saigon market. Project costs are estimated at US$68 million.

CHAPTER 13 SUMMARY

The following is a brief, chapter-by-chapter summary of the policies and programs recommended throughout this study.

FRAMEWORK AND GROWTH PATTERN OF THE POSTWAR ECONOMY

Long-run economic objectives over the first ten postwar years are an increase in per capita income by one-third and in GNP by 50 percent. Initially, a reconstruction period lasting from two to three years will be required in which many of the distortions caused by the war must be corrected or ameliorated. Resettlement programs must be consolidated to strengthen rural society and to bring abandoned land back into production, as must educational programs to improve the productive capability of the young labor force. Transportation and telecommunications must be restored, and self-sufficiency in rice should be rapidly achieved, followed by the resumption of agricultural exports. The damaged production facilities of industry must be reconstructed, the production rate of declining industries restored, and new industries established. To achieve these objectives, domestic and foreign capital must be mobilized and inflationary pressures moderated.

A minimum expansion plan for the economy would require a 1 percent annual increase in the per capita income and 4 percent in the GNP. The maximum growth path has been estimated at 6 percent in the first three years and 7 percent in the subsequent seven.

Expansion of exports is the key to independence from concessionary foreign aid, and a substantial increase is called for, accompanied by a gradual relative decrease in imports.

Although the deficit in the balance of payments may not be eliminated in the tenth year, it should be at a level which could be financed by capital inflows, supply loans, and other revenues.

Public expenditures other than those concerned with defense will have to be reduced from over 20 percent in 1968 to 15 percent in 1978 and shift from consumption toward public investment. However, the maintenance of a defense and security budget equal to 15 percent of GNP is postulated. Tax revenues will have to increase from 9 to 15 percent of GNP over the decade. To achieve the rate of growth envisaged, over-all investment should reach at least VN$600 billion, of which the government will probably have to bear half. Heavy emphasis on the role of private enterprise envisages that the private sector will undertake all industrial investment and the major share of housing investment.

During the decade the amount of foreign aid required will be in the order of US$2.5 billion.

ECONOMIC POLICIES FOR GROWTH

The choice between public action or private initiative in the channeling of resources is of overriding importance. Although the energies of both the public and private sectors are needed to complement each other, an open economy leading to rapid and efficient development of resources and equitable distribution of the benefits of growth is to be preferred to central direction. Divestment by government of some of its industrial investments is endorsed, and the need to free the private sector from controls and bureaucratic procedures is emphasized.

A deliberate program to stimulate agricultural growth is a necessity, and the granting of priority to industry as a recipient of investment would be an error. Caution is needed in the planning of an import substitution policy. Considerable opportunities exist but there should be no overprotection of local industry.

The highest priority should be given to the development of export markets if economic growth is not to be stunted or depend unduly on foreign aid. It is estimated that the ratio of foreign trade to GNP for satisfactory development should be 15 to 20 percent. A trade gap over a ten-year period of some US$3 billion is projected, but opportunities for earning foreign exchange through services and for private capital inflows are assessed; it is concluded that some US$2.5 billion in concessionary foreign aid over the next decade will be needed. Development with price stability is unlikely and it is suggested that price increases should be kept within a range of 5 to 10 percent.

The benefits of expanding development regionally throughout southeast Asia should not be overlooked during the concentration on national development.

MONETARY POLICIES

After the war there will be an immediate need to replace direct regulation of economic activity (necessary in wartime for the control of inflation) by more normal fiscal and monetary measures. A strengthened financial sector will be essential for mobilizing savings and capital, and incentives will be required for the expansion of commercial banking, although the four special financial institutions now providing credit and financial services will have to continue to take the lead in meeting the credit needs of industry and agriculture.

The level of loanable funds or bank credit which will be required to finance investment and increasing economic activity may need to rise to approximately five to fifteen times the amounts now available, and it will be essential to encourage the growth of savings. To this end, interest rates should be increased immediately to encourage the transfer of cash holdings to deposits and to decrease the liquidity of the monetary system. Expanded facilities for a money and capital market will be needed, as will a secondary market involving stock issues and home mortgages and accommodating the growth of insurance.

The overvaluation of the piaster should be remedied by a once-and-for-all adjustment that can be maintained and that will contribute effectively to equilibrium in the foreign exchange market. A stable rate contributing to confidence and to incentives for development investment is essential for economic growth.

FISCAL POLICY

Fiscal policy in wartime is not concerned with directing resources to secure growth or with attaining revenues in a way that will not disturb incentives. Normal peacetime expenditures are postponed, fixed capital is allowed to depreciate, and military expenditures are directed to certain civilian programs. But military priorities do not equate with civilian requirements and some excess capacity is created. A special problem of adjusting from a wartime to a peacetime economy will be the decision to let some of this capacity be written off.

At present, public investment is only 5 percent of total expenditures, and private investment is equally low. The net investment rate must be doubled or trebled, and this can best be achieved by the transfer of funds from military expenditures to development programs.

Investment resources will have to be acquired from the private sector through an efficient tax system. The present system is ill prepared for peace and is basically unproductive, inequitable, and inefficient. Consolidation and simplification are required: The system should be based on income and wealth, contain a broad-based tax on consumption, and include a selected excise tax system. It is suggested that the patente should be converted to a base of gross income for many taxpayers, which could eventually be changed into a value-added tax, and that fuller exploitation of certain excise taxes should be achieved. A different structure is recommended for taxes on foreign trade. They should provide not only a major part of government revenues, but also the appropriate incentives and protection to promote exports and assist in import substitution, and to establish vigorous local industries.

Suggestions are made for ways to improve expenditure decisions through a better use of the budget. The basic shortcomings of the traditional "line-item" presentation--the lack of forward planning, program selection, establishment of priorities, and assessment of cost effectiveness--are noted. It is recommended that progression to a program-budgeting process should be initiated at first in one selected area of activity and then be expanded when experience has been gained and trained staff become available. Proposals are made for greater flexibility, for the control and limitation of subsidization of local authorities, and for further delegation of central government developmental activities to provincial and village governments.

EMPLOYMENT, MANPOWER, AND SKILLS

Redeployment policies will be required to meet possible reductions in the numbers of military personnel and in employment opportunities in war-related industries, and for the rehabilitation of refugees. There will be problems created by natural population growth. Although no sizable demobilization within five years is forecast, limited releases of Army personnel possessing particular skills will be necessary. However, it will be important to ensure that the armed forces are used for economically productive purposes when not engaged in security operations and that they do not compete with or reduce the demand for labor in the civilian sector. The interruption of the industrial and service activities that support the war effort will lead to some redundancy, but the problem is not considered serious: Some residual employment will be perpetuated and alternative opportunities in growing service industries and in reconstruction activities will be created. Proposals to streamline the civil service may not be a practical possibility in view of postwar expanded governmental activities, but surplus civil servants should readily find alternative employment in the regional development authorities and in expanding provincial and local governments.

Numerically, the refugees pose the most serious problem but the probability is that 75 percent of them will return to their lands if sufficient financial assistance is given to them. The balance will need to find work in reconstruction and in the industrial sector generally or in government-sponsored public works activities.

The greatest demand for labor will be in agriculture. If the opportunities are fully utilized, all refugees wishing to return to an agricultural way of life should be absorbed. Forest resources may also provide up to 60,000 jobs exclusive of the timber processing industries. Industry will not be a significant employment source in the immediate postwar period.

Although serious unemployment is unlikely, with labor availability growing at a probable rate of 300,000 a year, the conclusion is inescapable that Vietnam must take effective measures to limit population growth or accept reduced standards of living in the long run.

INSTITUTIONAL DEVELOPMENT

Effective implementation of development plans will require a strengthened and broadened institutional framework. The Directorate General of Planning has been ineffectual and the National Planning Council has denied the executive support necessary to discharge its functions. The establishment of a permanent and a political Institute of Planning and Development is accordingly recommended. Its primary concern would be with internal development problems, but it should have authority to contract with external agencies and negotiate for grants and other forms of assistance. A Board of Trustees that would consider the merits and content of its research program is proposed.

Although most recommendations in this book concern the functions of ministries and can be planned and executed on a national level only, a policy of decentralization should be applied to many development activities. For this purpose, regional organizational arrangements, varying in accordance with the requirements of the regions treated, are suggested.

For full local development, local resources should be mobilized by representatives of local institutions, and here the elected village councils will have a substantial contribution to make. Some legislative and administrative reform is recommended to increase the capacity of these local authorities.

AGRICULTURAL DEVELOPMENT

The increased production necessary to improve standards of farm living will be achieved partly by the better use of lands under cultivation and partly by opening new lands for development and settlement. Extensive opportunities for programs of the latter type exist.

Rice production should be aimed initially at equaling domestic requirements. Although marketing prospects are uncertain, the likelihood is that potential markets exist and exports may be resumed by the 1980's. In view of the importance of rubber to the economy, it is recommended that all possibilities of revival and expansion be examined thoroughly. Tea will continue to be an important export item, and there may be opportunities to increase significantly exports of peanuts, copra, and processed cassava during the next twenty years.

The priorities should be increasing the outputs first of those commodities already produced primarily for domestic consumption but which are in short supply; then of commodities that have been and still are being exported in some volume; and finally of products currently imported in bulk but which may have a production potential in Vietnam.

There are prospects for intensified, diversified, and expanded crop production, and a potential for important animal protein and fish production.

Applied rather than basic research is required, and soil surveys must be completed if future land development is to proceed satisfactorily.

Effective extension work and the "improved village" concept should be expanded. Training programs need to be implemented at several levels to meet the shortage of adequately trained personnel.

Substantial amounts of agricultural credit will be required for the production effort. An estimate is offered that by 1980 requirements will reach VN$30 billion, of which the public sector should probably provide as much as 50 percent.

Larger-scale integrated units may have an important part to play. It is recommended that a limited number of such units, particularly in livestock and fisheries, should be established to determine their potential contribution.

Encouragement of the private sector to continue expansion in the provision of inputs and services to the agricultural sector is advocated, and government involvement is considered unnecessary.

The fragmentation of large holdings, irrespective of the consequences on production and farm income, is undesirable. Many crops cannot be grown economically and competitively other than on a large scale, and land reforms should not be carried so far as to make such profitable enterprises and potential employers of labor impossible. The solution to rural poverty in some areas may be found in an efficient farm labor force rather than in small tenant holdings.

The market structure is well attuned to the prevailing patterns of agricultural production and presumably will adjust to rapid changes in production provided restricting action is not present and credit becomes more readily available.

Future work will comprise the continuation of basic land capability studies, the planning of specific package programs for representative areas from which pre-feasibility studies can be derived, an intensive examination of marketing, a comprehensive study of agricultural credit, and a more definitive study of the livestock industry and postwar fishery development.

FORESTRY

The principle interest of Vietnam in its timber resources lies in the promotion of wood-based industries, recommendations for which are presented in Chapter 9. The importance of forest assets to the regions is described in Chapter 12.

Three specific subjects are discussed in Chapter 8: (1) a recommendation is made that traffic in cinnamon bark, prohibited at present, should be permitted and a profitable potential market exploited; (2) a policy of admitting greatly increased log imports from Cambodia to improve the supply of timber for the delta is advocated; (3) a reorganization of the sawmilling industry is considered necessary to increase output and lower costs.

Procedures for licensing and taxing log production are cumbersome, subject to abuse, and require overhaul. Required credit should be supplied by the Agricultural Development Bank. Forest policy and forest taxation generally require revision.

The work program for 1969 included an evaluation of the capability of the forests of the northern region to supply a plywood factory, a plan to rehabilitate the nation's forests, the definition of the policies and strategies of postwar forestry work, and programs for the establishment of forest reserves and national parks and for the reforestration of the pine areas of Tuyen Duc and the plain of Than Rang.

INDUSTRIAL DEVELOPMENT

The main effort in the postwar period of recovery needs to be directed to the reconstruction and repair of industrial installations, bringing into production half-completed projects, and to the revival of depressed industries.

The highest priority should be placed on the production of inputs to the agricultural sector at the lowest possible price, although production should be delayed--in rare cases subsidized--until markets are sufficiently extensive for production costs to be attained at or below the c.i.f. price without duty. Production of most major basic commodities should be permitted only when production costs can approach world competitive prices without duties. In the manufacturing sector, priorities should be placed on the categories in which costs can be reduced to the point where exports can be expanded rapidly. The choices are between high protection leading to high costs and inefficient use of resources, or development in the key sectors of efficient, capital-intensive industries based on high labor productivity and low input costs. The adoption of the second alternative is urged.

There is a tendency toward proliferation of small plants that could not survive if faced with the free entry of competing imports. The small-plants philosophy based on profitability and high protection levels will lead to greater long-run foreign exchange costs and will be at variance with the primary objective of growth in foreign exchange earnings through efficient import substitution and enhanced exports.

The shape and size of the manufacturing sector in 1978 is predicted, and value added in manufacturing is estimated to reach twice its present level. The projected capital investment requirements range from US$108 million in 1970 to

US$304 million in 1977, with a total investment requirement in the eight-year period of US$759 million.

An analysis of opportunities in a wide range of manufacturing activities is offered and three projects are selected for immediate consideration: the production of nitrogen fertilizer, a project for the manfacture and export of long-fiber, bleached sulfate pulp, and a project to manufacture veneer and plywood for domestic use and export.

The role of government toward industrial development should exclude control and regulation as deliberate policy. Control and regulation can only result in the reduction of incentives for the private sector and of necessary investment from abroad.

DEVELOPMENT OF THE INFRASTRUCTURE

The emphasis in the formulation of a postwar program in each of the infrastructural sectors is initially on repair of war damage followed by longer-term programs over a ten-year period. Practical methods of incorporating much of the infrastructure already developed by the armed forces is given special attention, as is the establishment of effective procedures for operation and management. In highways, the suggested work falls into three phases: the re-establishment of communications within twelve months, a reconstruction phase lasting for two years, and finally a development phase lasting from 1971 to 1980, involving some 42 separate projects for rebuilding all major routes in the southern half of Vietnam. On the assumption that foreign maintenance equipment will remain in Vietnam, the estimated annual costs of maintenance will range from VN$659 million in 1971 to VN$818 million in 1978.

Although reconstruction of the railroad has already been scheduled, some doubt is cast on its future viability.

Adequate deep-draft port facilities already exist; however some investment in additional port capacity at Saigon, with channel improvements to the Saigon River, and some repair, replacement, and extension of the berthing area at Da Nang are proposed. There is a requirement of the development of a Delta River port and for the restoration of delta inland waterways to usable depths for barge traffic.

Decisions on the ultimate disposition of the airport system and alternative peacetime uses of airports not needed for military operations are required and should be entrusted to a Postwar Airport Development committee.

Government plans for the improvement of potable water supplies are endorsed; it is recommended that studies be made of sewage and storm drainage requirements for all major towns.

The PTT proposals for telecommunications development are also endorsed with the recommendation that more detailed information is needed on the possible civil applications of the military systems.

Appropriate and practical policies for government participation in the reprovisioning and improvement of urban housing are necessary.

Existing power generating capacity is summarized, a preliminary power demand forecast presented, and a general ten-year development plan outlined.

THE SOCIAL SERVICES: EDUCATION AND PUBLIC HEALTH

Planning in education and public health must be related to the feasible and integrated with over-all development policies. The capital costs of expansion are not unduly burdensome, but the recurrent cost of maintaining and operating such installations already imposes a severe strain upon the national budget and is steadily increasing.

The objectives of national education over the next decade appear desirable, but the targets are ambitious and there is some doubt whether resources will be available during so short a period. Some fundamental questions need examination: is the conventional system responsive to the needs and opportunities of the society; to what extent can it provide skills needed for the scheduled development programs; and to what degree can the communities contribute?

In the field of medicine, recent development has been in curative rather than preventive facilities. A suitable balance must be restored for financial as well as technical reasons. Serious consideration must be given to the levels of recurrent costs, and additional investment should be modified with regard to the extent to which military facilities would be converted to civilian use. A program of population control must be implemented if living standards are to continue to improve.

REGIONAL DEVELOPMENT

National and regional interests in economic progress are complementary; substantial advantages can be gained from a policy of decentralization applied to all programs concerned primarily with regional conditions and problems that need not necessarily be planned and executed at a national level.

The Five Northern Provinces

The development possibilities of the five northern provinces are limited by the restricted base for agriculture, the relative inaccessibility of much of its timber resources, and the extent to which military activities have caused the abandonment of large areas of land and swollen the refugee population to over 50 percent of the total of the whole country. Because the population is overconcentrated in the coastal plain, land holdings are uneconomically small. But some not inconsiderable postwar development potential can be identified. In particular there is an immediate opportunity for improved agricultural production; high priority must be given to the reclamation of lands taken out of cultivation because of the war. The most important of the improved inputs to agriculture will be irrigation; over 440,000 hectares of irrigable land that would benefit from irrigation from storage dams, from salinity intrusion control, and from flood control have been identified.

Since great potential is seen in the fishing industry, proposals are made for improvements in marketing and for rehabilitation of the industry through improved credit arrangements.

There are reasonably promising prospects for some industrial development. One immediate opportunity, a veneer and plywood factory, is suggested. The possible use of Nong Son coal for thermal electric power generation and other limited industrial uses in the region is considered.

A profitable secondary industry in tourism has considerable prospects.

Proposals are made for the rehabilitation of many of the refugees either on their former lands or relocated on new lands provided by the irrigation and water control schemes recommended.

Although in other regions an argument is presented for a statutory Regional Development Authority, it is probable that in this region, where no central unifying theme for development emerges, the coordination of development efforts by the Commissioner for Development will be sufficient.

The Central Highlands of II Corps

Considerable increases in agricultural production and excellent opportunities for crop diversification seem possible in the Central Highlands. Irrigation is virtually nonexistent and major agriculture improvements can be realized through the implementation of a series of small- to medium-sized water control projects, which are identified. Desirable opportunities for multipurpose development and hydroelectric projects totaling over 1,000 megawatts have been noted. The natural grasslands suggest a potential for a substantial cattle industry and the prospects for forestry are good, particularly in providing the raw material for large-scale production of pulp.

A program of assessed resettlement from other regions is recommended and an initial program serving the needs of 40,000 families is called for. Proposals are also made for improvements to the amenities and services in the small highland towns.

The establishment of a Central Highlands Development Board is recommended to manage the forests, all land development programs, the construction of farm and market roads, and the provision of town and village amenities. It is suggested that such a board could act as trustee of the extensive areas of unoccupied land in the central provinces.

Coastal Basins of II Corps

The tentative program for the development of the ten relatively small, separated deltaic areas of the II Corps region is offered; it concentrates on the control and utilization of the land and water resources. Some 400,000 hectares of potentially irrigable, cultivable land are identified, and suggestions are made for storage, flood and salinity control, and drainage works in order to bring this land into intensive, year-round cultivation. Fullest practicable utilization of many existing facilities in the design of these projects is advocated; an over-all, average rough order of magnitude of costs equivalent to US$1,300 per hectare is assumed to be the capital cost requirement for implementation. A quarter of the total irrigable area might be brought into development in ten years at a cost of about US$130 million, the entire scheme taking some thirty years.

Saigon and the Surrounding Provinces

Preliminary proposals for structuring the long-range development of the Saigon urban area and its ten surrounding provinces are put forward. It is concluded that although Saigon must retain its appropriate national role as the capital city of Vietnam and a secondary role as financial center, its growth must be slowed if the optimum relationship between it and the rest of the country is to be created. Some of its functions must be dispersed and its role deemphasized. The development of competitive outlying areas, artificial satellite cities, and dormitory towns is advocated.

Briefly discussed is the variety of opportunities and challenges for future development in the rural provinces.

The Mekong Delta

A preliminary appraisal is presented of a proposed Mekong Delta development program aimed at a massive increase in agricultural production through the application of water control and other inputs. Six large pilot areas are identified and recommended for early intensified development. Protection against floods, improved drainage, control of salinity intrusion, and supply of irrigation water during both wet and dry seasons are required. It is demonstrated that construction of upstream reservoirs in the capacities needed to affect flood control significantly in the delta will take many decades and that flood protection works proposed would be far less expensive than any reasonable allocation of the cost of upstream projects. A system of by-passes and levees placed adjacent to the major rivers is proposed with a flood by-pass. Drainage of excess rainfall will be provided by a system of collector laterals and conveyance canals; salt intrusion will be controlled by structures in canals and the rehabilitation and provision of dikes along the sea coast and rivers.

To provide the necessary inputs, local groupings of farmers primarily at the village level and to be called Local Development Associations are proposed. An Authority is also recommended to manage the waters of the river and to promote the design, construction, and implementation of project programs for the control and utilization of its water resources.

Four development phases are identified: (1) flood protection facilities and initial drainage in areas presently subject to inundation to permit cultivation of single-transplant varieties of rice; (2) salinity control, initial drainage, and irrigation in the rest of the delta to provide the capability for double cropping of single-transplant rice; (3) when upstream storage facilities are completed and the dry season river flow is augmented, the provision of irrigation water to cultivate one crop of high-yielding variety rice during the dry season, and one crop of single transplant rice during the wet season; and (4) complete drainage and irrigation capability.

It is recommended that the first stage be implemented in the northern part of the Nan Phan area. It is also suggested that early implementation should be considered in the eastern portion of Cao Lanh where it would be possible to proceed directly to the second phase.

ABOUT THE

DEVELOPMENT AND RESOURCES CORPORATION

Development and Resources Corporation (D&R) is in the private business of planning, executing, and managing programs and projects for the development of human, natural, and physical resources, and in attracting the public and private investment capital necessary for such development. Established as an employee-owned enterprise in 1955 by David E. Lilienthal, D&R has engaged in development programs and projects in the United States, Latin America, Europe, Africa, the Middle East, Asia, and Australia.

David E. Lilienthal, President and Chairman of D&R, was a founding director and chairman of the Tennessee Valley Authority, the first chairman of the U.S. Atomic Energy Commission, and has had broad executive experience in private enterprise.

D&R maintains corporate headquarters in New York, but also has offices in Washington, D. C., and Sacramento, California, and project staffs on assignment around the world.